The regional novel has been remarkably neglected as a subject, despite the enormous number of authors who can be classified as having written regional fiction. This interdisciplinary collection of essays from leading literary critics, historians and cultural geographers, addresses the regional novel in Ireland, Scotland, Wales and England. It establishes the broader social and political contexts in which these novels emerged, and by combining historical and literary approaches to the subject explores contemporary manifestations of regionalism and nationalism in Britain and Ireland. *The Regional Novel in Britain and Ireland, 1800–1990*, covers novels from the eighteenth century to the present day, and will be of interest to literary and social historians as well as cultural critics.

THE REGIONAL NOVEL IN
BRITAIN AND IRELAND,
1800–1990

THE REGIONAL NOVEL IN BRITAIN AND IRELAND, 1800–1990

Edited by K. D. M. SNELL

Department of English Local History, University of Leicester

CAMBRIDGE
UNIVERSITY PRESS

PUBLISHED BY THE PRESS SYNDICATE OF THE UNIVERSITY OF CAMBRIDGE
The Pitt Building, Trumpington Street, Cambridge CB2 IRP, United Kingdom

CAMBRIDGE UNIVERSITY PRESS
The Edinburgh Building, Cambridge CB2 2RU, United Kingdom
40 West 20th Street, New York, NY 10011–4211, USA
10 Stamford Road, Oakleigh, Melbourne 3166, Australia

First published 1998

Printed and bound in Great Britain by Biddles Ltd, Guildford and King's Lynn

Typeset in 11/12½pt Baskerville [GC]

A catalogue record for this book is available from the British Library

Library of Congress cataloguing in publication data

The Regional Novel in Britain and Ireland, 1800–1990 / edited by K. D. M. Snell.
p.   cm.
Includes index.
ISBN 0 521 38197 5 (hardback)
1. English fiction – History and criticism.   2. Regionalism in
literature.   3. English fiction – Irish authors – History and
criticism.   4. English fiction – 19th century – History and criticism.
5. English fiction – 20th century – History and criticism.
6. Literature and society – Great Britain – History.   7. Literature
and society – Ireland – History.   8. Great Britain – In literature.
9. Ireland – In literature.   I. Snell, K. D. M.
PR868.R45R44   1998
823.009′32 – dc21   98–30152   CIP

ISBN 0 521 38197 5 hardback

Contents

vii

Preface and acknowledgements

This project began in the mid 1980s, as part of an investigation into cultural regions in the British Isles. It grew out of a widely shared concern over political and cultural centralisation during the last two decades of the twentieth century, and the effects of this on regional cultures. Such issues have taken many forms in political debate, and their prominence has been growing for many years. In this book on the regional novel, we hope to encourage interdisciplinary study of a literary subject that has received very little attention in the relevant academic fields, despite its obvious importance and popularity among so many local readers in Britain and Ireland.

It was originally planned to include county-by-county and city bibliographies of regional fiction in this book, covering all four countries of the British Isles. Work for these was funded by the British Academy, and very large bibliographies resulted. These bore testimony to the extraordinary array of (sometimes forgotten) regional fiction that has been written over the past two centuries. Limitations of space and production costs inhibited the publication of these bibliographies here, and this bibliographical work will now be published as a separate volume. The two books – one scholarly and interpretative, the other bibliographical – should serve as a welcome aid to interdisciplinary study and appreciation of regional fiction in the future.

This book's scholarly chapters have been written by some of the leading literary critics, cultural historians and geographers working today in Ireland and Britain. I have been most fortunate in their participation, and for their tolerance of this editor, an historian prone to cross disciplinary boundaries. Some contributors also waited a long time for their chapters to appear, and Wynn Thomas and Liz Bellamy abided the delay with considerable patience and courtesy. Another chapter was planned on East End London fiction, by Raphael Samuel, but the illness and sadly premature death of this fine scholar and friend has meant that London regional fiction goes uncovered here. I am indebted also to W. J. Keith, John Lucas, Linda McKenna, Ray Ryan, Joanne Shattock and Tony Wrigley for many helpful comments, and to Simon Ditchfield, Ian Dyck, Andreas Gestrich, Ralph Gibson, Franco D'Intino, Barry Reay, Tom Sokoll, Steve Taylor, David Thomson, Hiroko Tomida and Michael Yoshida for advice on regional fiction outside the British Isles. The assistance in particular of my colleagues Charles Phythian-Adams, Harold Fox, David Postles, Margery Tranter and Alasdair Crockett has been a constant pleasure. The University of Leicester, in sustaining the Department of English Local History, created excellent facilities that were indispensable for the project. To these colleagues, and this institution, I extend my warmest gratitude.

John Barrell's chapter, and the chapter by Stephen Daniels and Simon Rycroft, were published respectively in the *Journal of Historical Geography*, 8:4 (1982), pp. 347–61, and in the *Transactions of the Institute of British Geographers*, 18:4 (1993), pp. 460–80.

Department of English Local History,   K. D. M. SNELL
University of Leicester.

CHAPTER I

The regional novel: themes for interdisciplinary research
K. D. M. Snell

DEFINITION

'Novels of character and environment' – that was how Hardy described his 'Wessex novels'.[1] What is meant by 'the regional novel'? Inevitably, there are problems of definition, even definitions that rival each other in scope. Yet most readers agree about who the quintessential 'regional' writers are. The definitions on offer have much in common, although there will always be a large number of novels that fall into borderline categories. By 'regional novel' I mean fiction that is set in a recognisable region, and which describes features distinguishing the life, social relations, customs, language, dialect, or other aspects of the culture of that area and its people. Fiction with a strong sense of local geography, topography or landscape is also covered by this definition. In such writing a particular place or regional culture may perhaps be used to illustrate an aspect of life in general, or the effects of a particular environment upon the people living in it. And one usually expects to find certain characteristics in a regional novel: detailed description of a place, setting or region, whether urban or rural, which bears an approximation to a real place;[2] characters usually of working- or middle-class origin (although in some regional novels people of these classes may be absent, and in a few the focus may be on a family or lineage and its connection with local landscape or history); dialogue represented with some striving for realism; and attempted verisimilitude.[3]

---

[1] Thomas Hardy, 'General preface to the Novels and Poems', Wessex Edition, vol. 1 (1912), J. Moynahan (ed.), *The Portable Thomas Hardy* (1977; Harmondsworth, 1979), p. 694. (Place of publication is London unless otherwise indicated.)

[2] Hence for example one would not include Tolkien's *Lord of the Rings* as a regional novel: the place names and terrain may occasionally be based on recognisable fragments of a known landscape, yet this is clearly an imagined landscape. Hardy's 'Wessex', however, far more tightly located in English geography, provides a setting one would certainly class as regional.

[3] See P. Bentley, *The English Regional Novel* (1941), pp. 45–6.

I

'Regional' thus conceived is not the same as 'national', but it does not exclude that: the term includes regional writing within the four countries of the British Isles. A 'nationalist' novel, say of Wales, lacking clear regional specificity within Wales would not be included here; but a Welsh regional novel might in some cases be open to interpretation as a 'national' novel. We should note that such an understanding of the subject allows it to overlap with other literary genres, like regional romances, regional historical novels, novels dependent upon local folklore, industrial novels, or novels dealing with the life and times of people associated with a certain place, exploring their relation to that place.[4]

It is worth considering how the regional novel has been defined by the few literary critics who have approached it as such. The Yorkshire regional novelist Phyllis Bentley, author of the short book that is one of the few available discussions, argued that the regional novel may be seen as 'the national novel carried to one degree further of subdivision; it is a novel which, concentrating on a particular part, a particular region, of a nation, depicts the life of that region in such a way that the reader is conscious of the characteristics which are unique to that region and differentiate it from others in the common motherland'.[5] She was writing during the Second World War, and the language of those years is prominent in her definition. More recently, the important (and virtually the only) discussions have come from W. J. Keith, R. P. Draper and Ian Bell.[6] These justify their careful usages, but I

---

[4] Extensive county-by-county and city bibliographies of regional novels set in Ireland, Wales, Scotland and England will be published as a separate volume by K. D. M. Snell in due course. These should aid local readers, librarians and academics. The two main works currently available are Stephen J. Brown, *Ireland in Fiction: A Guide to Irish Novels, Tales, Romances and Folklore* (New York, 1969), and L. LeClaire, *A General Analytical Bibliography of the Regional Novelists of the British Isles, 1800–1950* (Paris, 1954). Both these include items that are not fiction, and Brown includes works on the Irish abroad. LeClaire is still valuable, but is very incomplete, dated and most inaccessible.

[5] P. Bentley, *English Regional Novel*, p. 7. She wrote that 'locality, reality and democracy are the watchwords of the English regional novelist'; and as the main merits of regional novels she stressed verisimilitude, representations of landscape, and her view that 'the regional novel is essentially democratic. It expresses a belief that the ordinary man and the ordinary woman are interesting and worth depicting', pp. 45–6.

[6] W. J. Keith, *Regions of the Imagination: the Development of British Rural Fiction* (Toronto, 1988), see especially his valuable discussion on pp. 3–20; R. P. Draper (ed.), *The Literature of Region and Nation* (1989); I. A. Bell (ed.), *Peripheral Visions: Images of Nationhood in Contemporary British Fiction* (Cardiff, 1995), which in addition to some valuable essays on regional fiction also contains essays by novelists; R. Williams, 'Region and class in the novel', in his *Writing in Society* (1983). See also M. Drabble (ed.), *The Oxford Companion to English Literature* (1932; Oxford, 1985), p. 816, who refers to the regional novel as 'a novel set in a real and well-defined locality, which is in some degree strange to the reader'. She added that from about 1839 'the localities described in regional novels were often smaller and more exact . . . Later novelists became ever more

depart here from Keith's focus only on rural fiction. The urban regional novel is such a crucial part of the genre that one cannot omit it. Nor does one want to regard cities as any less 'regional' than other areas: without making any value judgements, London and its districts in this regard are as 'regional' as parts of County Kerry, and the regional fiction of such cities should be treated accordingly. For our purposes, a sense and description of region may be wholly urban, as in the start of *Alton Locke*: 'I am a Cockney among Cockneys. Italy and the Tropics, the Highlands and Devonshire, I know only in dreams. Even the Surrey hills, of whose loveliness I have heard so much, are to me a distant fairy-land, whose gleaming ridges I am worthy only to behold afar . . . my knowledge of England is bounded by the horizon which encircles Richmond Hill'.[7] Alternatively, the idea of region may be as rural as Hardy's account of the Blackmoor Vale, which to Tess was 'the world, and its inhabitants the races thereof . . . Every contour of the surrounding hills was as personal to her as that of her relatives' faces; but for what lay beyond her judgement was dependent on the teaching of the village school'.[8]

Any definition must also stress the way in which such novels seek to conceive a regional or local world and its people. In such fiction the apparently real is mixed with the imaginary, the known with the unknown. W. J. Keith's book was rightly entitled *Regions of the Imagination*. The relation between fact and fiction varies considerably in regional fiction, between authors, and between the different literary movements which informed the artistic and social purposes behind many of the novels. The variety of such relationships has been especially marked during the twentieth century. If one compares regional fiction with documentary or historical writing, it is clear that work from the latter forms differ from much regional fiction in laying claim to deal with 'facts', with truth as perceived by the author. However, in conceptual schemes, choice of detail, and manners of evocation, historical or documentary writing can be as much an art form as regional

interested in precise regional attachment and description'. One should also draw attention to the definition in F. W. Morgan, 'Three aspects of regional consciousness', *Sociological Review*, 31, no. 1 (1939), pp. 84–6. He stressed the novel's 'absorption in a particular locality: absorption and not merely interest . . . The area, too, must not be too small', and, he continued, 'The true regional novel has people at work as an essential material: it has become almost the epic of the labourer'; the regional novel 'produces a synthesis, a living picture of the unity of place and people, through work'; and with regard to landscape, it provides 'an atmosphere which is not transferable'.

[7] C. Kingsley, *Alton Locke* (1850; Oxford, 1983), p. 5.
[8] T. Hardy, *Tess of the D'Urbervilles* (1891; Harmondsworth, 1982), ch. 5, p. 75.

fiction, where the latter deals with a perceived reality.[9] Referential claims
by historians are similar to those often made by novelists – think for
example of Hardy's assertion that

At the dates represented in the various narrations things were like that in
Wessex: the inhabitants lived in certain ways, engaged in certain occupations,
kept alive certain customs, just as they are shown doing in these pages . . . I
have instituted inquiries to correct tricks of memory, and striven against temp-
tations to exaggerate, in order to preserve for my own satisfaction a fairly true
record of a vanishing life.[10]

There are many differences between regional fiction and other forms
of writing, but in this context I would not assert them in too rigid a
way. For regional fiction may often supplement other descriptions as
a further way of imagining, realising or knowing life, character and
social relations, with unique imaginative and evocative potential.

We shall turn shortly to interdisciplinary possibilities for study. But
it is important here to point to the variety of the regional novel, which
is one reason why it has usually been subsumed within other literary
genres. Beyond its most predictable forms, and retaining strong elements of the above definition, this genre may on occasion encompass
romance, historical novels, mystery or detective novels, novels dependent upon regional folklore (even turning folk tales into fictional form),
and in a few cases – like Colin Wilson's account of a future Nottingham
– may even stretch to science fiction. One could take any region of the
British Isles to illustrate this point. Let me do this for the neglected
literature of the Channel Islands. These islands have certainly provided
a setting for regional fiction that comes close to the usual associations of
the genre, like Ethel Mannin's *Children of the Earth* (1930), comparable
to rural regional novels by Kaye-Smith or Mary Webb. Yet besides
this, one finds historical novels like Edward Gavey, *In Peirson's Days: a
Story of the Great Invasion of Jersey in 1781* (1902), J. E. Corbiere, *Mont
Orgueil Castle: a Tale of Jersey During the Wars of the Roses* (1890), Philip
Billot, *Rozel: an Historical Novel* (1945), or William Ferrar, *The Fall of the
Grand Sarrasin* (1905). A further historical subject concerns the German
occupation of the Islands, which has been the theme for novels such

---

[9] I think here also of E. Leach's defence of social anthropology as a form of art, and his view of
social anthropologists 'as bad novelists rather than bad scientists', in his *Social Anthropology*
(Glasgow, 1982), pp. 52–4.

[10] Hardy, 'General Preface', pp. 695–6. The role of 'oral history' in regional novels by Scott,
C. Bronte, George Moore, Dickens, Bennett, Hardy and others, is discussed in P. Thompson,
The Voice of the Past: Oral History (1978; Oxford, 1984), pp. 28–9.

as Sheila Parker, *An Occupational Hazard* (1985), Michael Marshall, *The Small Army* (1957), Peggy Woodford, *Backwater War* (1974), John Ferguson, *Terror on the Island* (1941), Sheila Edwards, *The Beloved Islands* (1989), and Jack Higgins, *Night of the Fox* (1986). There are also detective novels with a strong local setting, such as the Bergerac series, that are derived from other media;[11] novels that make use of certain financial connotations of the islands, like Nicholas Thorne, *Money Chain* (1987); and those which take issues of local and national politics as their subject matter, like Desmond Walker's *Bedlam in the Bailiwicks* (1987) or *Task Force Channel Islands* (1989). Here, as elsewhere, one also finds novels heavily dependent upon the actual or assumed folklore of the islands, best known among them being Victor Hugo, *Travailleurs de la Mer*,[12] but also including such works as Sonia Hillsdon, *Strange Stories from Jersey* (1987). The islands have also provided the setting for much children's fiction, which is less my concern here,[13] as well as novels that might be termed science fiction, like Hugh Walters, *The Blue Aura* (1979); fiction dealing with the lives of well-known figures connected with the islands, such as David Butler, *Lillie* (1978), or Pierre Sichel, *The Jersey Lilly* (1958); as well as romances like Anabella Seymour, *Dangerous Deceptions* (1988), and other forms of regional writing that fall outside the above classifications, or which combine elements of them. The regional novel can encompass many such works, beyond the usual equation of the genre with essentially rural and 'provincial' works like *Adam Bede* or *The Return of the Native*.

EARLY ORIGINS AND GROWTH OF REGIONAL FICTION

The circumstances from which the earliest regional novelists emerged deserve special attention. Sir Walter Scott, drawing in part upon Maria Edgeworth, interpreted character and speech within a Scottish historical setting, using vernacular surroundings which were often lowly and imbued with local narratives and folkloric traditions. His 'anthropological' work did not recognise distinctions between biography, fiction and history, so that one reads him as if 'in a suspension between

---

[11] Michael Hardwick, *Bergerac: The Jersey Cop* (1981).
[12] Translated as *The Toilers of the Sea* (1888). Compare the view that Hugo's book cannot 'in any way be relied upon as giving anything like a correct view of the popular superstitions of Jersey', in J. S. Cox (ed.), *Guernsey Folklore, Recorded in the Summer of 1882* (1971, 1986), p. 5, as reprinted from an article by 'A. P. A.' in *The Antiquary* (November 1882).
[13] For example Viola Bayley, *Jersey Adventure* (1969).

creative writing and historiography'.[14] In particular, the social range of his characters was to be a common feature of subsequent regional fiction.[15] Before him, one may take Maria Edgeworth's *Castle Rackrent* (1800), written it seems in 1797–9, as probably the first regional novel. Prior to this regionality in fiction had frequently been presented in terms of regional stereotypes, epitomised by supposed traits of people from different areas. Thus John Barrell, in discussing *Roderick Random*, draws attention to the range of provincial character and dialectal 'types' in Smollett's work, to characters who have become isolated from their regional settings, losing some of their identity as they are abandoned to the mobile plots and loose form of the picaresque novel.[16] In contrast to such use of regionality – involving much regional stereotype in characterisation and a stress on an elite overview that alone could coordinate such great diversity – the regional novel came to establish much firmer regional settings, developing characterisation within such contexts, showing awareness of regional influences on people and social relationships, and, in a great variety of ways, interpreting these relationships or using them to develop more complex and explanatory depths of character.

Walter Allen, in *The English Novel*, made a considerable claim for Maria Edgeworth's *Castle Rackrent*. He commented that its date of publication, 1800, marks 'a date of the first importance in the history of English fiction, indeed of world fiction'. Edgeworth, he argued,

occupied new territory for the novel. Before her, except when London was the scene, the locale of our fiction had been generalized, conventionalized. Outside London and Bath, the eighteenth-century novelist rarely had a sense of place . . . Maria Edgeworth gave fiction a local habitation and a name. And she did more than this: she perceived the relation between the local habitation and the people who dwell in it. She invented, in other words, the regional novel, in which the very nature of the novelist's characters is conditioned, receives its bias and expression, from the fact that they live in a countryside differentiated by a traditional way of life from other countrysides.[17]

[14] R. Crawford, *Devolving English Literature* (Oxford, 1992), p. 126, and see his ch. 3, on 'Anthropology and Dialect'.

[15] See for example K. Tillotson, *Novels of the Eighteen-Forties* (Oxford, 1954), pp. 86–91, 142; H. Auster, *Local Habitations: Regionalism in the Early Novels of George Eliot* (Cambridge, Mass., 1970), pp. 24–6.

[16] J. Barrell, *English Literature in History, 1730–1780: An Equal Wide Survey* (1983), ch. 3. And see J. M. S. Tompkins, *The Popular Novel in England, 1770–1800* (1932, 1969), pp. 187–8, on national and regional character 'types' in fiction in the late eighteenth century.

[17] W. Allen, *The English Novel: a Short Critical History* (1954; Harmondsworth, 1986), p. 103.

We can note here the acknowledgement of London and Bath settings in earlier fiction, a point (following our genre definition) that others may wish to pursue. However, Allen's emphasis has since been adopted by others. George Watson for example, in his introduction to *Castle Rackrent*, saw this book as 'the first regional novel in English, and perhaps in all Europe'.[18] It was, he suggested, documentary in purpose, concerned with that branch of human knowledge later termed sociology, and as such Edgeworth's regional writing – together with Scott, Burns and Crabbe (and Rousseau in France)[19] – may represent a 'vast literary revolution', that was continued by Turgenev. *Castle Rackrent* promoted 'an aspect of human knowledge which novelists and poets, not historians, inaugurated . . . the novels of Maria Edgeworth and of her first pupil [Scott] are decades in advance of the historians in their social concern'.[20]

In many ways, *Castle Rackrent* is a generic description or caricature of the life and manners of a 'certain class of the gentry of Ireland some years ago', as Edgeworth put it, a class of Irish squires that could have existed in virtually any part of Ireland. It is sometimes thought that her subject is Ireland rather than any region within it. She wrote of how 'Nations as well as individuals gradually lose their identity', as will occur, she felt, in the union with Great Britain – a misjudgement of interest today.[21] Her preface contained no hint that her concern lay with the characteristics of specific regions of Ireland. Yet one senses elements of this in her details of dialect, local agricultural terms (for example, a *loy*),[22] tenurial arrangements, characteristics of middlemen or 'journeymen gentlemen'; popular superstitions and folklore like the fairy mount,[23] or the right to be buried in certain churchyards;[24] mention of the regionality of Caoinans (funeral songs),[25] and the burning of death-bed straw and of funerary practices. Such detail places the novel in a broad region of the Irish midlands, and the main setting appears to be County Longford.[26] Her novel is also regional in having a certain gentry family as its subject. Other novels subsequently appeared that one might think of as 'regional' in a similar sense, especially with regard to a tight association of such families with particular areas, and

---

[18] G. Watson, Introduction to *Castle Rackrent* (1800; Oxford, 1980), p. vii. Or see H. Zimmern, *Maria Edgeworth* (1883), p. 108, and particularly the essay by Liz Bellamy in this volume.

[19] J.-J. Rousseau, *La Nouvelle Héloise* (1761), presented a view of country life in the Vaud, set in romantically landscaped gardens at Ermenonville, thirty miles north-east of Paris.

[20] Watson, Introduction to *Castle Rackrent*, p. viii.

[21] M. Edgeworth, *Castle Rackrent* (1800; Oxford, 1980), pp. 4–5.

[22] *Ibid.*, p. 16. [23] *Ibid.* [24] *Ibid.*, p. 106. [25] *Ibid.*, p. 101. [26] *Ibid.*, p. 116.

the often unquestioned assumption that the history and identifying features of an area may be entwined with its gentry family, so closely were
they identified. It might be argued that the regional novel could only
develop in a fuller social sense when such neo-feudal signification was
relinquished, that the gentry themselves had become the least regional
of classes. One certainly finds a move away from such gentrified focus
in Scott and most succeeding authors. Yet the narrator of *Castle Rackrent*,
Old Thady, is himself a lowly gentry servant, and the issues of land,
tenure and lineage (so important in Edgeworth's account) themselves
tie the novel to lowland Irish land issues in a way that justifies the label
'regional'. The national question is always present however, justifying
LeClaire's view that the regional novel in its early years, until about
1830, and notably in Edgeworth and Scott, was a genre above all concerned with this issue – one, we should add, to which it has repeatedly
returned.[27] The point is reinforced in Edgeworth's presentation of her
work, which she laid

before the English reader as a specimen of manners and characters, which
are perhaps unknown in England. Indeed the domestic habits of no nation
in Europe were less known to the English than those of their sister country,
till within these few years. Mr Young's picture of Ireland,[28] in his tour
through that country, was the first faithful portrait of its inhabitants. All the
features in the foregoing sketch were taken from the life, and they are characteristic of that mixture of quickness, simplicity, cunning, carelessness, dis-
sipation, disinterestedness, shrewdness and blunder, which in different forms,
and with various success, has been brought upon the stage or delineated in
novels.[29]

The role of the regional novel in regional stereotyping, and further
issues of regionalism and nationalism, will occupy us later.

An important feature accompanying this emergence of the regional
novel was an interest in the more realistic portrayal of regional topographical, economic and cultural traits. Representations of barely recognisable British landscape elements heavily overlaid with classical
imagery increasingly gave way to ways of depicting people in their

---

[27] L. Leclaire, *Le Roman regionaliste dans les Iles Britanniques* (Paris, 1954).
[28] Arthur Young, *A Tour in Ireland* (1780), an account by the agricultural commentator and
improver of Ireland in 1776–9.
[29] Edgeworth, *Castle Rackrent*, p. 97.

regional settings.[30] A taste for fidelity in imitations of nature, for close attention to detail, as in the Dutch painters, became more manifest after about 1770. This was especially so from the early 1780s 'in a good measure, in consequence of the direction of the public taste to the subject of painting', as Hazlitt wrote in his essay on Crabbe; a poet who, like Goldsmith, Clare or Elliott, was strongly associated with such realist preference.[31] In addition to this poetry of the anti-pastoral – and growing out of the picturesque writing of the period from the late 1760s – a very large topographical literature of exploration developed, notably of the Lake District and north Wales, but also of many other regions.[32] The popular guides of the last quarter of the eighteenth century, and in particular the tours of Arthur Young or Gilpin[33] – blending as they did practical agrarian instruction with the fading ethic of melancholy ruin, and, in the case of some of Young's tours, information about landlord artistic taste – were important aspects of the changing nature of internal tourism and instructive travel. There was certainly a tradition of topographical writing, such as that by Fiennes, Kilburne or Defoe, but the scale of the late eighteenth-century developments was unprecedented. Between 1770 and 1815, for example, at least eighty books describing trips through Wales were published; and among the imaginative writers 'discovering' this principality were Wordsworth, Coleridge, Southey, Shelley, Scott, Peacock, Landor and De Quincey.

[30] See in particular J. Barrell, *The Dark Side of the Landscape: The Rural Poor in English Painting, 1730– 1840* (Cambridge, 1980); D. Solkin, *Richard Wilson: the Landscape of Reaction* (1982).

[31] W. Hazlitt, *The Spirit of the Age, or Contemporary Portraits* (1825, 1969), p. 267. See also J. Barrell, *The Idea of Landscape and the Sense of Place, 1730–1840: An Approach to the Poetry of John Clare* (Cambridge, 1972).

[32] See T. Gray, *Journal in the Lakes* (1769); J. Clarke, *Survey of the Lakes of Cumberland, Westmorland, and Lancashire* (1787); W. Hutchinson, *Excursion to the Lakes in Westmoreland and Cumberland, in the Years 1773 and 1774* (1776); W. Gell, *Tour of the Lakes made in 1797* (1968); J. Housman, *Descriptive Tour and Guide to the Lakes, Caves, Mountains and other National Curiosities in Cumberland, Westmoreland, Lancashire* (Carlisle, 1800); T. West, *Guide to the Lakes, Dedicated to the Lovers of Landscape Studies* (1778); W. Wilberforce, *Journey to the Lake District from Cambridge, 1779* (1983); N. Nicholson, *The Lakers: Adventures of the First Tourists* (1955); M. Andrews, *The Search for the Picturesque: Landscape Aesthetics and Tourism in Britain, 1760–1800* (Aldershot, 1989). On north Wales, see T. Pennant, *A Tour in Wales* (1784); W. Bingley, *North Wales; Including its Scenery, Antiquities, Customs and some Sketches of its Natural History* (1804); and on Scotland, the very saleable work by T. Pennant, *A Tour in Scotland* (1771, 1772), one of the aims of which was to 'conciliate the affections' of England and Scotland.

[33] A. Young, *A Six Weeks Tour Through the Southern Counties of England and Wales* (1769), *A Six Months Tour Through the North of England* (1770), *The Farmer's Tour Through the East of England* (1771); W. Gilpin, *Observations Relative Chiefly to Picturesque Beauty, made in the Year 1772 on Several Parts of England, Particularly the Mountains and Lakes of Cumberland and Westmorland*, 2 volumes (1786).

Such internal tourism appears in its early days to have been associated with a largely visual and sometimes quaint interest in 'scenery',
that term of the mid- and late eighteenth century: a feeling for a
picturesque landscape that was often depersonalised or unpeopled, tied
to certain artistic genres and influenced by ideas in landscape garden-
ing.[34] By the mid-nineteenth century however, at the same time as a
proliferation of 'hand books for travellers', regional fiction was becoming one of the most important means by which regional landscapes
were distinguished from a generalised countryside. The genre was taking over some functions of the visual arts, particularly of oil painting,
and was now independently contributing to more diverse, literary and
symbolic aesthetics of landscape. It was now to be crucial as a way in
which particular landscapes ('countries') became structured and known,
going well beyond a largely pictorial form of knowledge.

Superimposed on this more variegated sense of landscape was an
interest in the working lives and technologies of industrial and rural
workers: an eagerness to view, or represent, other people in 'commu-
nion' with their places of work, even if this relationship was often infused (by middling-class observers) with romantic and pastoral colour at
some remove from local working consciousness. This tendency survived
long after the period of Wordsworth's 'Michael'. It was manifested in
many changing ways, and for our purposes it is worth observing that
the subjective associational motives underlying it were important in the
popularity of regional fiction. The examples come to mind randomly.
There were to be many in the history of Victorian photography, including key figures like Henry Fox Talbot, Octavius Hill (in particular his
studies of sailors and fisher-girls), Frank Meadow Sutcliffe, P. H. Emerson
or Henry Peach Robinson. Emerson, well known for his studies of East
Anglian life and landscape, repudiated 'composition pictures' and other
studio contrivances, advising photographers to take their cameras out-
doors and photograph real people in their native environments, aiming
for 'as true an impression . . . as possible'.[35] As with much of the photography, empathetic interest could also have strongly gendered aspects:
I think of middle-class women from Liverpool decked out as female

[34] On internal tourism, see I. Ousby, *The Englishman's England: Taste, Travel and the Rise of Tourism*
(Cambridge, 1990); J. Buzard, *The Beaten Track: European Tourism, Literature, and the Ways to
'Culture', 1800–1918* (Oxford, 1993); M. Andrews, *The Search for the Picturesque: Landscape Aesthetics
and Tourism, 1760–1800* (Aldershot, 1989).
[35] P. H. Emerson, 'Photography, A Pictorial Art', *The Amateur Photographer*, 3 (19 March 1886),
p. 139.

'Welsh peasants' in the Llandudno photographic studios for their *cartes de visites*, of Arthur Munby and his preoccupations,[36] or the itinerant 'Walter' stalking regional variety in his feminine prey.[37] More generally, one could mention Mayhew, Engels, Angus Bethune Reach and many other social investigators; Alexander Somerville,[38] the Welsh writing of George Borrow,[39] and later the Victorian folklorists; the English folk dance and song revival,[40] and its Celtic counterparts, or the 'back to the land' movement. There have been many similarly inspired developments in the twentieth century. For example, the motivations behind the modern 'real-life' working museums of farming, vernacular architecture or industry, like those of the Rhondda, St Fagans, Ruddington, or Cultra, are surely in the same tradition. So much in museum culture caters to morally driven curiosity and empathetic habits of mind. The moral, almost fraternal and self-identifying, qualities of internal tourism and historical interest became visible in a great variety of regional, ideological, class, and sexual guises, and these were particularly strongly manifested in the writing and buying of regional fiction.

The emerging style of antiquarian British historiography was a further shift in taste that expanded demand for *historical* fiction set more firmly in identifiable locales. In the crucial early nineteenth century one thinks particularly of Grose, Carter, Hall, Gough, Britton, and Southey, coupled with ballad collections, Scott's own *Minstrelsy of the Scottish Border* (1802–3), and the *Gentleman's Magazine*, itself one example of a frenetic interest in the archaeology of the medieval period at the turn of the century. This repeated, some decades late, the demand for ascertainable, non-classical imagery in British landscape painting, of a sort that might appeal to genteel middling classes. It also had a strong political dimension in its faith in 'time-hallowed' feudal institutions, upheld as a last bulwark of stability against the influence of American and French democratic politics. Hazlitt wrote of Scott as 'a mind brooding over

[36] D. Hudson, *Munby: Man of Two Worlds* (1972); L. Stanley (ed.), *The Diaries of Hannah Cullwick, Victorian Maidservant* (1984).

[37] 'Walter', *My Secret Life* (1972). This preoccupation with working women seems to have been widespread. Walter or Munby were extreme examples, but such traits are manifest in many regional novelists, like Hardy or Gissing.

[38] A. Somerville, *The Whistler at the Plough* (1852; Manchester, 1989); and see his *Letters from Ireland during the Famine of 1847* (Dublin, 1994).

[39] G. Borrow, *Wild Wales: Its People, Language and Scenery* (1862). He began his tour of Wales in 1854. Both Borrow and Somerville reported in great detail, and with an attempt at dialectal realism, the conversations they had with poor people encountered during their travels.

[40] For recent discussion, see G. Boyes, *The Imagined Village: Culture, Ideology and the English Folk Revival* (Manchester, 1993).

antiquity – scorning "the present ignorant time" . . . The old world is to him a crowded map; the new one a dull, hateful blank.'[41] Scott's work, with its close topographical references and connection to historical legend, was itself subsequently used in county directories throughout the nineteenth century, to give further appeal to the localities whose distinctiveness and historical attributes were being described alongside their general and family histories, and their physical and current economic characteristics.[42] Locally-based antiquarian historical writing was a remarkable feature of this time, which also saw the growth of many county antiquarian and archaeological societies. There were many who, like Southey, hoped to preserve 'local history . . . everything about a parish that can be made interesting – all of its history, traditions and manners that can be saved from oblivion'.[43] In Wales, rather earlier, this tendency was apparent in Edmund Jones, *An Historical Account of the Parish of Aberystruth* (1779), and Thomas Pennant, *The History of the Parishes of Whiteford and Holywell* (1796). There were many other examples, varying between the semi-fictionalised account, as in the case of John Galt's *The Annals of the Parish* (1821), and what might today be termed as historical writing.

In the developments affecting the genre of print-making, there was also an increasingly popular demand for picturesque and topographical illustration. Turner's *Liber Studiorum* series between 1805 and 1819 was planned as a hundred engravings, divided into categories under the headings Historical, Mountainous, Pastoral, Marine and Architectural. His designs for topographical works, published by W. B. Cooke, included the copper-plate and early steel-plate engravings entitled *Picturesque Delineation of the Southern Coast of England* (1814–26), and the *Views in Sussex* (1816–20), as well as his illustrations for the series *The Rivers of England*. Copper-plate was being replaced by steel around 1820, and this had major implications for the productivity, circulation and cost of such engravings, making them more widely available. Further prints by Turner, *The Ports of England*, appeared between 1826 and 1828. Between 1825 and 1838 he engraved ninety-six *Picturesque Views in England and Wales*. He was also commissioned to produce illustrations for literary

[41] W. Hazlitt, *The Spirit of the Age, or Contemporary Portraits* (1825; 1969 edn.), p. 96.
[42] For an example of this, see the frequent use of myths and legends as described by Scott in T. F. Bulmer, *History, Topography and Directory of Northumberland (Hexham Division)* (Manchester, 1886).
[43] See Southey's letter to the (regional) novelist Anna Eliza Bray, cited in R. M. Dorson, *The British Folklorists: a History* (1968), p. 95.

works, including those of Sir Walter Scott.[44] Many other artists par-
ticipated in these developments, including David Cox,[45] Thomas Girtin,[46]
Richard Earlom, George Cuitt, Andrew Geddes, Hugh Williams,
Samuel Prout,[47] Julius Ibbetson, or John and Cornelius Varley. Finden
and Batty's *Welsh Scenery* appeared in 1823, and thousands more prints
of Welsh scenery were to appear subsequently, drawing upon the work
of artists like Henry Gastineau. Nor should one forget David Lucas'
mezzotint engravings for Constable's *English Landscape Scenery*, with their
illustrations of such places as Weymouth Bay, Yarmouth, or Old Sarum.
These aimed, as Constable stressed, to promote the study of all features of landscape scenery in England, from simple localities to places
of exceptional grandeur.

It is certain also that the continental wars had directed travellers'
attention in an unprecedented way to the resources offered by Britain.
At this time the combination of extended wartime mobilisation, state
intervention, improved transport, enormously significant socio-economic
changes, and the growth of popular radicalism underlined the regional
cultures that comprised the British Isles. The impetus to agrarian
improvement, driven by the food shortages and high prices of the
Napoleonic Wars, the heightened fervour for enclosure, the evident profit to be made from agricultural investment, and the transition towards
short one-year leases and greater tenant-farmer (and other occupational)
inter-regional mobility stimulated an interest both in farming and
related practices in different regions. The writings of commentators
like Young's great rival William Marshall, the General Views of the
Agriculture of different counties, or the eclectic letters and reports to
the *Annals of Agriculture* were part of this growing interest in the regional
viability of investment in an increasingly divergent and specialised
agricultural and industrial economy. A more regionally nuanced
knowledge of landscape, local manners, customary behaviour, locally
different market measures, levels of poor relief, and economic conditions in general was needed for informed investment. These were all

---

[44] Turner toured Scotland in 1818, producing the illustrations for Scott's two-volume *Provincial Antiquities and Picturesque Scenery of Scotland* (1819, 1826).
[45] D. Cox, *The Young Artist's Companion; or, Drawing-book of Studies and Landscape Embellishments* (London, 1825).
[46] See J. M. W. Turner, *River Scenery* (London, 1827), or T. Miller (ed.), *Turner and Girtin's Picturesque Views* (London, 1873); S. M. Morris, *Thomas Girtin, 1775–1802* (New Haven, 1986).
[47] See his *Studies of Cottages and Rural Scenery* (London, 1816).

considerations which became even more material during the railway age and the regional specialisations associated with it.[48]

The regional novel, therefore, emerged at a time of complex change and national reassessment, and some of the major elements – cultural, aesthetic, social and economic – of this early nineteenth-century context have been sketched above. Our priority now must shift to rather different concerns: the question of why the genre and its various forms have been so neglected in disciplinary and critical study; or, to give this question more precision – for there has certainly been abundant study of individual authors – why has the regional novel, *as regional*, been ignored? Why, in so many thousands of critical studies of the novel, is there usually no mention whatever of the regional novel? Auster commented in 1970 on how 'the regional novel in England appeared still to be a relatively obscure and neglected topic.'[49] Only rarely, he continued, 'have modern critics of any stature concerned themselves, even briefly, with the subject of regionalism; when they have done so their attitude has generally been one of condescension, if not outright scorn'.[50] 'Regionalism in English fiction, as distinct from American, when regarded at all, is normally regarded as something of a curiosity, and a curiosity of no significance. Enduring literature, it is said, is universal: only second-rate writers are regional'.[51] Auster was writing on George Eliot. The view that he describes was earlier epitomised by Q. D. Leavis, when she wrote that 'there are excuses for a scepticism that refuses to consider that subject [regional novels] as more serious than a future academic classification'. It has rarely achieved even that. 'We register a suspicion', she wrote of authors like Phillpotts, Kaye-Smith, or Mary Webb, 'that the esteemed regional novel is some commonplace work of fiction made interesting to the Boots Library public by a painstaking application of rural local colour'.[52] The idea that scrutiny of regional

---

[48] J. Langton, 'The Industrial Revolution and the regional geography of England', *Transactions of the Institute of British Geographers*, no. 9 (1984), 164; W. J. Keith, 'The land in Victorian literature', in G. E. Mingay (ed.), *The Victorian Countryside* (1981), p. 139.

[49] Auster, *Local Habitations*, p. vii.   [50] *Ibid.*, p. 19.

[51] Auster, *Local Habitations*, pp. 14–15. Or see P. Keating, *The Haunted Study: a Social History of the English Novel, 1875–1914* (1989), p. 332, on how regional realism 'is still usually ignored by academic and metropolitan critics'.

[52] Q. D. Leavis, 'Regional novels', *Scrutiny* 4, no. 4 (March 1936), p. 440.

fiction could shed light on questions of 'organic community' was far from her mind. Such novelists epitomised that disintegration of tradition, authority and civilised standards of taste that Leavis complained about elsewhere.[53] Apparently its American forms were, as in England, 'a cashing in by a professional fiction-monger on a knowledge of an attractive locality, or 'an excuse for left-wing propaganda'.[54]

This critical tone was associated with the development of literary studies over this period as a centralised academic discipline, a formulation that left it stranded for too long from history and other areas of study, although one that has recently been much questioned both within and without the discipline. Interpretation of the regional novel stood to gain from cross-disciplinary association, and lost much from the way in which literary study was devised. Relevant here is a matter that has lurked behind much antipathy towards study of the 'regional novel' as such. Few would deny that defining the 'regional novel' for study can imply an extrinsic agenda, a socio-cultural approach to texts concerned with matters other than earlier Leavisite judgements about literary value, and one that is *ipso facto* still likely to be received with lukewarm enthusiasm in some quarters. The formal emergence of a new discipline, let alone its more recent convolutions and antagonisms, has often delimited the repertoire of questions tolerated within it. Leavis' dismissiveness occurred at a time of expanding output of the regional novel, when writers like Walter Greenwood or George Orwell were supplying new political agenda for the representation of working-class life, sensitively handling social and human dimensions of the great slump and the problems of the depressed areas.[55] The prior realist and naturalist traditions of the regional novel bespoke a relevance of novels to social context that should have been obvious, and should have implied a critical agenda to match, one that would also have incorporated regionalism in debates about 'realism'. Attacks on the entire genre for ostensible political reasons – and we have just seen an example from Leavis – could easily have been rebutted. Certainly a foregrounding of locality, region and cultural distinctiveness frequently constitutes a kind of political statement, for example a reaction against centralised government. Realism and naturalism often carried certain political presumptions. And many regional novels had a nationalist purpose at the

---

[53] Q. D. Leavis, *Fiction and the Reading Public* (1932; London, 1965), ch. 4.
[54] Leavis, 'Regional novels', p. 440.
[55] See A. Croft, *Red Letter Days: British Fiction in the 1930s* (1990), on regional novels in the 1930s.

root of their loyalties, a pre-emptive 'nationalism' tied to particular regional cultures, and a defence of language. In these senses literary regionalism is undeniably political. Yet there is no predisposing *conventional* political bias in regional fiction, in the ideological terms Leavis had in mind: this fiction ranges from Henry Williamson to Lewis Jones.

The way in which literary criticism ordered itself as an autonomous discipline contributed to the neglect of the regional, contextual and historical aspects of fiction. The ahistorical bent of much literary theory (with the exception of Marxist and much feminist theory) has often resulted in little regard being paid to regional history, to writers' contexts, to the creation of methods by which to study literary milieux, to the local connections between writers and the extent to which they saw themselves as writing within certain regional traditions, and to their dependency upon a sense of place, whether their own or that of their readers. As an exception to such criticism put it: 'the study of literature in the present century has been, in effect, de-historicised'.[56] Literary criticism established itself as an exercise in a certain type of critical appreciation of salient texts, a training in refined judgement. In the 'new criticism' of the 1940s and 50s in particular, an extreme form of emphasis only on the texts (and few at that) discountenanced any study of author, circumstances, or social context. And this feature, at least, has been shared by structuralist and post-structuralist theory; the latter has been described as 'a wholesale retreat from geography and history into a domain of pure "textuality" in which the principle of indeterminacy smothers the possibility of social or political "significance" for literature'.[57] Academic critics are without doubt the most 'centralist' and displaced of all readers, and much of their work has had limited appeal to the reading public. A literary sociology too, that might also have extended strong historical strands, has been slow to develop, especially in Britain, even though the *communicative* role of any novel – its messages to intended or actual readerships – has always invited such an approach. The suspicion persisted in academic literary circles that the purpose of literary sociology was ambiguous and untrustworthy, that it was perhaps above all concerned not with studying selected

---

[56] Keating, *The Haunted Study*, pp. vii–viii.
[57] S. Slemon and H. Tiffin (eds.), *After Europe: Critical Theory and Post-Colonial Writing* (1989), pp. x–xi. They comment rather strongly on 'the production of an institutionalised army of ridiculously credulous readers – "critics" who systematically shut out the world in order to practice . . . a textual form of interior decoration'.

great novels, but with using the novel to study the world external to it.[58] The result may well have been damaging to the endowment and credibility of literary criticism. As Escarpit wrote: 'Literary history has held – and still holds fast – to the study only of particular writers and their works, to a biographical and textual commentary. It has considered the aggregate context as a sort of decoration best left to the inquisitive mind of the political historian.'[59]

Yet it would be wholly tendentious to suggest that the problem lies mainly with literary criticism. Historians themselves have traditionally been dependent upon various forms of literary 'evidence', including novels, but have made virtually no attempts to set the bounds to what a writer may know and be able to express of his or her society and its social relations: to understand in what areas authorial knowledge is likely to be limited, occluded, or distorted, and for what artistic and social reasons. On the contrary, too often they have tried to prove the 'accuracy' of the novel in question, or the credentials of its author, just as they try to buttress the credibility of their other sources. An unimaginatively straitened view of 'literary value' can follow easily from such preoccupations. The use of fiction as 'evidence', assumed to be commensurate with more traditional standards of historical 'evidence', has not eased interdisciplinary communication. Many historians have not appreciated that literary texts cannot be forced to yield information or 'evidence' that they do not intend, and are unable through context or intention to give.[60] Through the absence of an effective literary sociology, and in the dearth of precautionary schemas treating such issues, the potential links from history to literary criticism remain undeveloped, and are shunned by many literary critics partly in response to the crudity of those forms of social history that they commonly encounter. That

---

[58] I do not wish to deny the justification of such suspicion. See e.g. L. Goldmann, 'The sociology of literature: status and problems of method', in P. Davison, R. Meyersohn & E. Shils (eds.), *The Sociology of Literature, vol. 6: Literary Taste, Culture and Mass Communication* (Cambridge, 1978), p. 171: 'this sociology proves to be all the more fertile the more the works studied are mediocre. Moreover, what it seeks in these works is more documentary than literary in character'. Goldmann stressed, however, that literary sociology was concerned 'with the mental structures, with what might be called the categories which shape both the empirical consciousness of a certain social group and the imaginary universe created by the writer'. (*Ibid.*, p. 171). It is clear that such preoccupation is relevant to *all* regional novelists, but that consideration of this also has significant bearing on more traditional literary-critical questions of originality and authorial distinctiveness.

[59] R. Escarpit, 'Why a sociology of literature?', in P. Davison, *Sociology of Literature*, p. 137.

[60] There are a few notable exceptions to this criticism, like D. Cannadine, *This Little World: The Value of the Novels of Francis Brett Young as a Guide to the State of Midland Society, 1870–1925* (Worcester, 1982).

history has itself very often been indifferent to regional differences.[61] Historical methods reliant upon literary sources have too frequently lacked appropriate caution, independent confirmation from other sources, and a defined and delimited social and regional focus. In addition, historians have rarely appreciated the specific questions and genre traditions to which a literary work was addressed, the senses in which such a work formed a dialogue with its own artistic history. Nor have they often defined or comprehended those shifts or moments in history which suggest new potential or meanings in a text, new intepretations of an author in altered situations, and the contextual links from present to past that underlie their own options, choices and interpretations.

It is clear then that regional fiction is not an historical 'resource' in the same form as conventional historical 'evidence', that it does not have a simple mimetic function, representing the structures of a pre-existent reality. Its role in representing 'things as they are', for example, is often complicated through a juxtaposition with the rather different function of representing a didactic model of how things ought to be. Such precautions cannot be emphasised too strongly, especially to historians. And yet few historians can afford to bypass fiction, especially in the British Isles, where regionally nuanced cultural description is so weak compared to many continental countries. The novel itself, in its earliest days, developed from non-fictional forms, from letters, journals, biographies or historical chronicles, all preoccupied with the details of social living, and after Scott these influences widened in fictional traditions. Fine social, occupational and regional distinctions were persistently and subtly articulated in many regional novels, dealing with ambiguities and discernments that most scholarly disciplines rarely approach. The literary critic John Lucas wrote of how 'the provincial novel in the nineteenth century is not only concerned with the nature of social change but uniquely well placed to record and explore how it happened, note its effects on individual lives, on patterns of living, on communities', and he added that it is 'supremely well equipped' to handle questions of class and human separation.[62]

---

[61] It has been rightly observed by J. Langton that much recent historical writing 'has been marked by a further relegation of regional differences to the very lowest level of concern. Modern approaches, like modern societies, have no place for regions . . . All of significance is conceived of in terms of national sectors, trends and interest groups'. See his 'The Industrial Revolution and the regional geography of England', *Transactions of the Institute of British Geographers*, 9 (1984), 146. One could write an extensive critique of social history, highlighting its neglect of region.

[62] J. Lucas, *The Literature of Change: Studies in the Nineteenth-Century Provincial Novel* (1977; Brighton, 1980), pp. xi, 119.

In addition, literary consideration of social and political questions has been prominent. To neglect this point, and the questions that arise from it, is to miss key elements, political themes and reformist intentions in works like *North and South, Yeast, Sybil, Alton Locke,* or, rather later, novels like *Love on the Dole* or *The Ragged Trousered Philanthropists.* The 'artistic' merit of such books, like the artistic, evidential or rhetorical merit of the regional reports in the parliamentary blue books (as read and used extensively by Kingsley or Disraeli), requires assessment partly with an eye to the way these novels addressed regional subjects, working experiences, traditions or histories. Their authors certainly felt themselves to be interpreting local issues and grievances for national political purposes, appealing in part to regional readerships, while also drawing the attention of metropolitan readers to them.[63] Such literary use of distinctly regional documentation was a new phenomenon in the 1840s, of crucial importance in the emergence of the regional novel; it was quite different to the fiction of earlier writers like William Godwin. This carefully focalised writing also increasingly eclipsed local poetry as the medium of moral concern or warning, important though much of the Chartist poetry was. It was a new departure too from the didactic fiction of Hannah More,[64] or from the non-regional moralism and noetic perspective of writers like Harriet Martineau, whose policy-oriented fiction had popularised certain general and theorised expedients in poor-law reform and taxation.[65] The developments of the regional novel in the 1830s and 1840s were clearly influenced by changes in governmental investigative procedures, select-committee collection of tabulated information and statistics, the verbatim question-answer format of government reports, and by a new respect for small factual and almost photographically precise visual details, rather than by the sweeping moral, political or economic ideals of the previous decades. Interesting scholarly

---

[63] On novelists' use of blue-book evidence, see S. M. Smith, 'Willenhall and Wodgate: Disraeli's use of blue book evidence', *Review of English Studies*, 13 (1962); S. M. Smith, 'Blue Books and Victorian Novelists', *Review of British Studies*, 21 (1970), and in particular her *The Other Nation: the Poor in English Novels of the 1840s and 1850s* (Oxford, 1980). See also W. O. Aydelotte, 'The England of Marx and Mill as reflected in fiction', in *Journal of Economic History*, supplement 8 (1948); I. Kovacevic, *Fact into Fiction: English Literature and the Industrial Scene, 1750–1859* (Leicester, 1975); A. Kettle, 'The early Victorian social-problem novel', in B. Ford (ed.), *The Pelican Guide to English Literature*, vol. 6: *From Dickens to Hardy* (London, 1958); P. J. Keating, *The Working Classes in Victorian Fiction* (1971); G. Beer, 'Charles Kingsley and the literary image of the countryside', *Victorian Studies*, 8, no. 3 (1965), pp. 243–54.
[64] H. More, *Coelebs in Search of a Wife* (1808).
[65] H. Martineau, *Illustrations of Political Economy* (1832–4); *Poor Law and Paupers Illustrated* (1833); *Illustrations of Taxation* (1834).

work has begun on the relation between empirically ascertained working experiences and fictional re-creations; but there has been little attention paid by historians to the effective fictional ways in which post-1834 issues were popularised, and to the changes that made the 'social-problem' novel and its characteristics such a viable medium at that time.[66]

When one views at a general level the efforts to bridge the disciplines of history and literary criticism, in connection with regional fiction, one finds them limited, and commonly biographical. This is true whatever the period discussed. They frequently amount to a recognition that many regional novelists have used a 'real' landscape; and discussion has followed to connect or relocate the historical landscape of the novel to its geographical equivalent, with the encouragement, bemusement or annoyance of the novelists concerned. Some of this work has been substantial and creditable. Hardy's bird's-eye topography has been explored by many scholars, like H. C. Darby.[67] Similar exercises have been undertaken for Mrs. Gaskell, R. L. Stevenson, Charles Kingsley, the Brontës, Dickens, George Eliot, D. H. Lawrence, Mary Webb, James Joyce, Virginia Woolf, Neil Gunn, Alan Sillitoe, Catherine Cookson and others, often with strong biographical purpose, occasionally by the novelists themselves.[68] Sometimes the emphasis here has been

---

[66] On the later nineteenth century, these issues have been covered in the fine work by P. Keating, *The Haunted Study: a Social History of the English Novel, 1875–1914* (1989).

[67] H. C. Darby, 'The Regional Geography of Thomas Hardy's Wessex', *Geographical Review*, 38 (1948), pp. 426–43. See also D. Maxwell, *The Landscape of Thomas Hardy* (1928); O. D. Harvey, *Puddletown, the Weatherbury of 'Far from the Madding Crowd'* (Dorchester, 1968); J. Stevens Cox, *Hardy's Wessex: Identification of Fictitious Place Names in Hardy's Works* (Guernsey, 1970); D. Kay-Robinson, *Hardy's Wessex Re-Appraised* (Newton Abbot, 1972); D. Kay-Robinson, *The Landscape of Thomas Hardy* (Exeter, 1984); A. Enstice, *Thomas Hardy: Landscapes of the Mind* (1979); D. Hawkins, *Hardy's Wessex* (1983); H. Lea, *The Hardy Guides: Touring Companion of Thomas Hardy* (Harmondsworth, 1986); D. Hawkins, *Hardy at Home: the People and Place of his Wessex* (1986); G. Beningfield, *Hardy Landscapes* (1990). For a rather different focus, see W. J. Keith, 'Thomas Hardy and the literary pilgrims', *Nineteenth-Century Fiction*, 24 (1969), pp. 80–92.

[68] P. Ackroyd, *Dickens' London: an Imaginative Vision* (1987); G. Prettejohns, *Charles Dickens and Southwark* (1974); H. E. Wroot, *The Persons and Places of the Brontë Novels* (New York, 1906); A. Pollard, *The Landscape of the Brontës* (1988); S. Chitty, *Charles Kingsley's Landscape* (1976); L. Stott, *Robert Louis Stevenson and the Highlands and Islands of Scotland* (Stirling, 1992); W. Reid Chappell, *The Shropshire of Mary Webb* (1981); L. Spolton, 'The spirit of place: D. H. Lawrence and the East Midlands', *East Midlands Geographer*, 5 (1970), pp. 88–96; H. T. Moore & W. Roberts, *D. H. Lawrence and his World* (1966); G. Hardy & N. Harris, *A D. H. Lawrence Album* (1985); R. Spencer, *D. H. Lawrence Country* (1980); M. Bennett, *A Visitors Guide to Eastwood and the Countryside of D. H. Lawrence* (Nottingham, 1992); K. Sagar (ed.), *A D. H. Lawrence Handbook* (Manchester, 1982); B. Pugh, *The Country of My Heart: a Local Guide to D. H. Lawrence* (Nottingham, 1972); D. Norris, *Joyce's Dublin* (Dublin, 1982); J. McCarthy, *Joyce's Dublin: a Walking Guide to Ulysses* (Dublin, 1988); R. Nicholson, *The Ulysses Guide: Tours Through Joyce's Dublin* (1988); B. Bidwell,

on the region, illustrated or analysed in more complex fusions and personal understandings through literary fiction. In other work the novels discussed have been contained within clear regional boundaries.[69] These boundaries have also sometimes been those of class.[70] A large guidebook literature, for 'literary pilgrims', has developed, representing an approach that deserves analysis in its own right.[71] A rather different and ambitious programme has been initiated by geographers like Gilbert, Langton or Butlin, who have promoted agendas of another kind, for example in connection with the effects of industrialisation upon the sense of region.[72] It has also been clear to some that human geography must involve study of regional novelists.[73] Recent analysis, once again largely by cultural geographers, has focused upon the symbolic and iconographical representation of past regional environments.[74] These various approaches informed by the discipline of geography are still few in number, but they promise well in their supply of more diverse agenda for study.

The Joycean Way: a Topographical Guide to Dubliners and A Portrait of the Artist as a Young Man (Dublin, 1981); V. Igoe, *James Joyce's Dublin Houses* (1990); J. M. Wilson, *Virginia Woolf, Life and London: a Biography of Place* (1987); A. Sillitoe, *Alan Sillitoe's Nottinghamshire* (1987); A. Sillitoe, 'A Sense of Place', *Geographical Magazine* (August, 1975), also in his *Mountains and Caverns* (1975); Daphne du Maurier, *Enchanted Cornwall: Her Pictorial Memoir* (Harmondsworth, 1989); Winston Graham, *Poldark's Cornwall* (1983); Catherine Cookson, *Catherine Cookson Country* (1986); R. Talbot, *Cadfael Country: Shropshire and the Welsh Borders* (1992).

[69] For example, F. J. Snell, *The Blackmore Country* (1906), with its discussion of Baring-Gould and Phillpotts. More recently, see for example the very different approaches of C. W. Sizemore, *A Female Vision of the City: London in the Novels of Five British Women* (Knoxville, 1989), on Margaret Drabble, Maureen Duffy, P. D. James, Doris Lessing and Iris Murdoch; J. W. Foster, *Forces and Themes in Ulster Fiction* (Dublin, 1974); A. MacRobert, *The Novels of Dumfries and Galloway* (Dumfries, 1992).

[70] R. Williams, *The Welsh Industrial Novel* (Cardiff, 1979).

[71] See many of the above references, and also J. Freeman, *Literature and Locality: the Literary Topography of Britain and Ireland* (1963); D. Eagle and H. Carnell (eds.), *The Oxford Literary Guide to the British Isles* (Oxford, 1977); M. Drabble, *A Writer's Britain: Landscape in Literature* (1979); D. Daiches & J. Flower, *Literary Landscapes of the British Isles: a Narrative Atlas* (1979); F. Morley, *Literary Britain: a Reader's Guide to Writers and Landmarks* (1980).

[72] E. W. Gilbert, 'British Regional Novelists and Geography', in his *British Pioneers in Geography* (Newton Abbot, 1972); J. Langton, 'The Industrial Revolution and the regional geography of England', *Transactions of the Institute of British Geographers*, 9 (1984), pp. 145–67; D. Pocock (ed.), *Humanistic Geography and Literature: Essays on the Experience of Place* (1981), and his *The Novelist and the North* (Dept. of Geography, University of Durham, Occasional Publications, no. 12, Durham, 1978).

[73] L. Spolton, 'A "Novel" Geography', *The Nottinghamshire Countryside*, vol. 11, no. 8 (April, 1949), pp. 1–2. More recently, see J. R. Short, *Imagined Country: Environment, Culture and Society* (1991).

[74] D. Cosgrove & S. Daniels (eds.), *The Iconography of Landscape: Essays on the Symbolic Representation, Design and Use of Past Environments* (Cambridge, 1988). The question of what is symbolic, and why, requires local knowledge to explain the meaning and association of local features, and here extra-textual approaches seem especially valuable in their bearing on the regional novel.

THE RURAL REGIONAL NOVEL

Certain key novelists aside, the frequent identification of the regional novel with rural areas has also been a factor that has inhibited discussion of the genre. We can remind ourselves of how fiction on rural society, and the development of more varied forms of the rural novel – invaluable as one complex opening to understanding rural life – were lampooned in a clever, caricatured fashion by Stella Gibbons. Her book is still a force to be reckoned with when considering the faults and strengths of rural regional fiction.[75] This is also a book that reminds us of the problem of an over-historical approach to regional fiction, in that it highlights the importance of literary form and convention in determining the content of the genre. *Cold Comfort Farm* had its justification. It was written in response to an outpouring of overly dramatised rural novels, which often seemed to impose social Darwinist sentiments onto the perennial tensions between town and country. For example, John Lindsay's *The Lady and the Mute* made up for its literary limitations by being advertised as

a powerful, uncompromising, almost harrowing study of the brutality and blind stupidity underlying primitive life in a country village. The clock is set back a little, for it was sixty years ago that the Greens came to Wheatfield, an East country hamlet on a hill, where the feudal tradition still lingered, and squire and parson ruled the roost. Agatha Green was a little girl then, and, as fate ordained it, she was destined to live a long and lonely life in the same surroundings, closed in on every side by half-suppressed cruelties, and torturing inhibitions, born of thwarted desire. There is a wretched dumb man in the village, the butt of all the children and fools, and Agatha gives him a home in her house. Out of this friendly gesture spring complications yet more tragic; and the picture gains a lurid emphasis, as the shadows of fate close in. It is a terrible witness to the degree of Paganism still possible in neglected corners of Christian England.[76]

The usual elements are all in this summary: 'fate', cruelty, backwardness, remoteness, 'paganism' – a view of rural existence mediated through an outsider, written sometimes for urban self-assurance, that reinforced stereotypes of rural workers as primitive and unenlightened, and that hinted strongly at the cultural advances attained by those who had migrated from the land. Similar themes exist in many other regional novels, influenced by Hardy, Kaye-Smith, Constance Holme,

---

[75] S. Gibbons, *Cold Comfort Farm* (1932).
[76] As advertised at the end of M. E. Lambe, *Crag's Foot Farm: a Novel of Leicestershire* (1931).

John Trevena, Phillpotts or Mary Webb, although the locale and characterisation may be better developed. One may date the heyday of the 'rural-as-primitive' regional novel from perhaps 1878 (the date of *The Return of the Native*, as well as the foundation of the Folklore Society in London, and the start of the collapse of agricultural prices) to the Second World War, its perspectives accentuated by the depths of rural decay and depression that afflicted many agricultural regions in the late nineteenth century and in inter-war years.[77]

Yet, today and in retrospect, it is the intensity and regional range of fiction on British rural societies over this extended period that is most striking. Some of these rural novels, like those in other countries on comparable themes, can be read almost as informal ethnography.[78] The decades after 1880 – in so many ways an evening for rural history and one of the final British phases of what later came to be seen throughout Europe as *la fin des paysans* – saw the greatest analytical writing on the history of agrarian communities in England, by scholars such as Slater, Hasbach, Seebohm, Vinogradoff, Garnier, Green, Heath, the Hammonds, Gonner, Sturt, Collings, Robertson Scott and many others. This was a time of persistent and often nostalgic interest in rural culture and its demise, in small-holdings, allotments, vernacular architecture, folk song and dance, communal games, folklore, and agrarian craft traditions. But for the most sensitive, humanly-scaled and perceptive interpretations of the rural exodus from the mid-nineteenth-century – of the decline of pervasive rural understandings, traditions and regional ways of life – it is to this remarkable body of rural fiction and its assumptions that one should turn.

TRENDS IN OUTPUT AND MODERN DEVELOPMENTS IN THE GENRE

The growth of regional fiction was closely tied to the expansion of the reading public in the later nineteenth century. There was a massive increase in demand for fiction, associated mainly with improved levels of literacy. The Reform Act of 1867 had made the passing of a measure along the lines of the 1870 Education Act desirable, which considerably

---

[77] For discussion of this genre, see especially Keith, *Regions of the Imagination*; G. Cavaliero, *The Rural Tradition in the English Novel* (1977); J. Alcorn, *The Nature Novel from Hardy to Lawrence* (1977); R. Ebbatson, *Lawrence and the Nature Tradition: a Theme in English Fiction, 1859–1914* (Brighton, 1980).

[78] Compare A. Waswo's preface and introduction to Nagatsuka Takashi, *The Soil: a Portrait of Rural Life in Meiji Japan* (1910, 1993 edn), pp. vii–xvii.

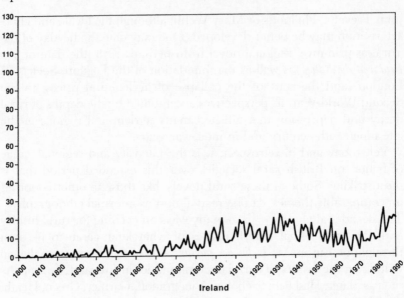

Ireland

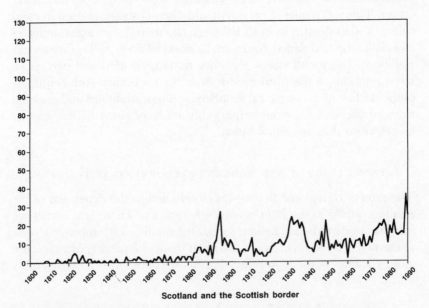

Scotland and the Scottish border

1 Numbers of regional novels published every year for Ireland, Scotland,
Wales and England, 1800–1990.

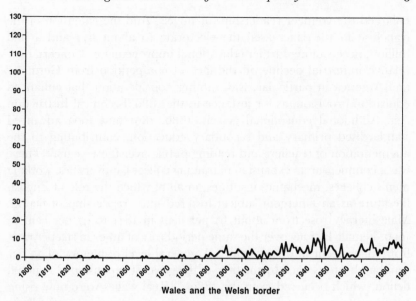

Wales and the Welsh border

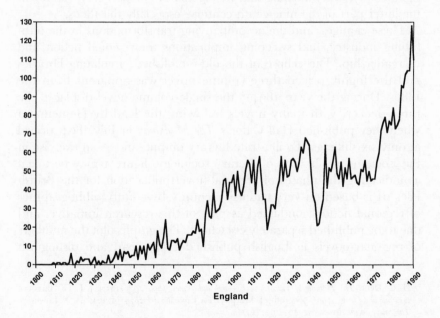

England

enlarged the younger readership for novels. And the extension of the franchise in 1884 increased the electorate to about five and a half million, necessitating further educational improvements. Concern over relative industrial decline, in the face of competition from Germany and America in particular, was another consideration that enhanced education provision, as for instance in the 1889 Technical Instruction Act. Additional educational acts in 1880, 1891 and 1902 advanced standardised primary and secondary education, contributing to the augmentation of teachers and reading public over these years.[79] There was a commensurate expansion of training colleges, universities, working men's colleges, mechanics institutes, in all of which the role of English literature as an emergent subject fostered mass readership of fiction. Male literacy rose from about 67 per cent in 1841 to 97 per cent in 1900. Female literacy over the same period rose at an even steeper rate, from 51 per cent to 97 per cent.[80] A general level of literacy of 75 per cent had been reached by the time of the greatest expansion of regional fiction, which occurred from the 1880s.[81] Real wages were now rising significantly, and matching this, newspaper circulation grew rapidly in the latter part of the nineteenth century, especially the 1890s.[82]

These changes, and the accompanying transformations in the publishing industry, had sweeping implications for regional fiction and its readership. The eclipse of the old-established circulating libraries and the highly priced three-volume novel was apparent from the 1880s. During the years 1894–7 the single-volume novel displaced the three-decker, with many novels following the lead by Heinemann when they published Hall Caine's *The Manxman* in July 1894, priced at only six shillings. To illustrate literary output, and as an exercise in the 'sociometric' branch of literary sociology, figure 1 may be taken as indicating the phases of regional-novel publication for the British Isles. It is based on very extensive county-by-county bibliographies of regional fiction conducted as part of this research initiative, and due to be published separately elsewhere. The graphs plot the numbers of regional novels in English published every year, and distinguish

[79] H. C. Dent, *The Training of Teachers in England and Wales, 1800–1975* (1977); J. F. C. Harrison, *Learning and Living, 1790–1960* (1961); J. Murphy, *The Education Act, 1870* (1972); G. A. N. Lowndes, *The Silent Social Revolution, 1895–1935* (1972).

[80] J. A. Bull, *The Framework of Fiction: Socio-cultural Approaches to the Novel* (1988), p. 150.

[81] J. Hall, *The Sociology of Literature* (1979), p. 129.

[82] R. Williams, *The Long Revolution* (1961), ch. 3; Keating, *The Haunted Study*, p. 34.

between the four countries concerned.[83] The general trends are shared across Britain and Ireland. After a slow and gradual growth from the 1820s, output of regional novels then expanded rapidly from about 1885. This upsurge of regional fiction was probably a Europe-wide phenomenon, and it also accompanied a growing interest in local and regional history.[84] In Britain as a whole, the figures indicate that unprecedentedly high levels of output were reached in the years immediately before the First World War. These fell markedly during that war, then rose to higher levels in the 1930s. Output plummeted again as private and public resources and loyalties shored up wartime effort, and as books were subject to authorised economy standards. The numbers published then returned to slightly below pre-war levels in the post-war period, before rising to ever greater number from the early 1970s.

One point in particular may be made. In recent years it has sometimes been suggested that the regional novel is obsolete – that it had its heyday between the mid-nineteenth century and the early twentieth, and that its future now, like that of regionalism itself, is bleak.[85] No one can doubt the significance of regional writing during that earlier period; and yet, qualitative judgements aside, such generalisation about decline seems questionable, especially if one considers non-rural fiction. As can be seen from figure 1, the genre as a whole has expanded in output since the Second World War, and noticeably during the later 1970s and 1980s. Probably more British regional novels were published in 1989 than in any previous year. There have been evident fluctuations. Regional-novel publishing fell markedly during times of war – during periods of nationalistic emphases – and emerged most strongly during periods when older interior ways of life were being threatened economically, and when changes in familiar and psychological 'landscapes' affected even those who were economically secure, who comprised the

---

[83] Further discussion of this data is forthcoming in a separate book, containing the county-by-county bibliographies of regional fiction that the graphs are based on. These also include collections of regional short stories. No such bibliographical work can be exhaustive, and it is possible that there has been a greater likelihood to miss items before the late nineteenth century than after, but the general trends are certainly as indicated here.

[84] F. W. Morgan, 'Three aspects of regional consciousness', *Sociological Review*, XXXI, no. 1 (1939), p. 78.

[85] See in particular Keith, *Regions of the Imagination*, ch. 11, 'The passing of regionalism'. Keith's perceptive comments are made largely with regard to rural regional fiction, using a slightly different definition of regional fiction than that employed here. From a rather different perspective and view of the 'regional novel', see R. Williams, 'Region and class in the novel', in his *Writing in Society* (1983, 1985), e.g. pp. 230, 238.

majority readership. The most obvious periods were the late nineteenth century, the 1930s, and especially the 1980s. This is true to a lesser extent in Ireland, where political developments have had such an impact on regional fiction. Superimposed and related to this pattern has been the effect of the trade cycle on the publishing industry, although it is notable how little this affected the genre during the great slump after 1929. Perhaps one has here a process of alternation: each swing being then succeeded by the revival of the previously discarded mode – nationalism and regionalism being experienced alternatively and not simultaneously.

However the trends may be explained, it is the case that in none of the four countries of the British Isles has such fiction been in decline. Among the best selling British authors of recent years are regional novelists: Cookson, Middleton, Sillitoe, Doyle and many others come to mind. The popularity of literary pilgrimages, to the Lakes, 'Hardy country', the Brontë parsonage and Haworth (the 'Blackpool of Literary Heritage'),[86] 'Mrs. Gaskell's country', Lawrence's Eastwood, George Eliot's Nuneaton, Joyce's Dublin, and so on, and the many 'guides' written for such travellers, 'to make it easy for the literary pilgrim . . . to follow up the associations of writers',[87] all attest to a strength of interest in the genre today that publishers, and others, have readily appreciated. Commentators on the fiction of particular areas have stressed the vitality of modern regional writing. For example, in her valuable account of the Glasgow novel, Moira Burgess discussed 'the remarkable increase in both the quantity and quality of Glasgow novels published since World War II'. 'At the moment of writing, in 1985,' she continued, pointing to the growing individuality and diverse creativity of regional fiction set in the city, 'the Glasgow novel is in full flower'.[88] The same statement could be made of many other areas of the British Isles in the past twenty years.

This persistence or growth of regional fiction is found in many other advanced countries. In Germany, where political entities and questions of unification have never been taken for granted, novelists like Siegfried

---

[86] The Brontë parsonage registered 221, 467 visitors in 1974, an average of over one person every minute during opening hours.

[87] For example, J. Freeman, *Literature and Locality: the Literary Topography of Britain and Ireland* (1963), p. vii – only one of many such works which are often focused on particular authors, especially the Brontës, Eliot, Hardy, Lawrence or Joyce. On Hardy, see in particular W. J. Keith, 'Thomas Hardy and the Literary Pilgrims', *Nineteenth-Century Fiction*, 24 (1969), pp. 80–92.

[88] M. Burgess, *The Glasgow Novel: a Survey and Bibliography* (1972; Glasgow, 1986), pp. 56, 62.

Lenz (on East Prussia and the North Sea Coast), Hermann Lenz (the Stuttgart area), Marie Beig (the Stuttgart-Constance region), or Max von der Grün (and some of the writers who were associated with his pro-East German stance), are unquestionably regional novelists, despite the reluctance in many German academic circles to view them in that light. Perhaps even Martin Walser, whose writing is predominantly concerned with middle-class life, might be thought a regional writer because his fiction is set in the rural area around Lake Constance. German dialect writing, for example in Plattdeutsch or Bavarian, remains very prevalent.

Among French regional novelists, one thinks of Pierre-Jakez Helias's writing on Brittany, or Michel Ragon, whose historical-regional novels are set in the Cholet area. Other regional authors, recently dead, include Jean Giono (on Provence), or Henri Bosco (on the Cévennes). Marcel Pagnol is still very widely read. Italian regional novelists publishing works after 1950 have included Vasco Pratolini, Elio Vittorini, Leonardo Sciascia, Ignazio Silone, Giorgio Bassani or Alberto Moravia, and the extensive earlier traditions of such Italian writing includes many of these as well as authors like Cesare Pavese, Grazia Deledda, Federigo Tozzi, Matilde Serao, Federico De Roberto, Edoardo Calandra, Remigio Zena, Mario Pratesi, Giovanni Verga (whose translators include D. H. Lawrence), Luigi Capuana and Francesco Mastriani.

In New Zealand, where authors tend to define themselves or be seen as 'New Zealand' writers rather than 'regional novelists', there have nevertheless been obvious examples of regional fiction – I think of the *The Bone People* by Keri Hulme, or the writers Maurice Gee, the late Ronald Hugh Morrison, Karl Stead, or Rosie Scott. In Japan, the fiction of the late Sawako Ariyoshi and Kenji Nakagami (on the Wakayama Prefecture), Sei Ito and Takiji Kobayashi (on Hokkaido), Osamu Dazai (on Tsugaru), Sakunosuke Oda (on the Osaka region), Sakae Tsuboi and Junichiro Tanizaki (on the Kansai area), or Yasushi Inoue and Yasunari Kawabata (on the Izu Peninsular) is strongly regional in the sense defined here. Their novels are very widely read (and some have been translated into English). In the former USSR and the countries replacing it, there is strong resurgence of such writing – for example, the Russians Valentin Rasputin, Vladimir Soloukhin, and Yuri Trifonov, or Chinghiz Aitmatov (from Kyrgyzstan), or Yuri Rytkheu (from Chukchi) – with much of this work increasingly dealing with the tensions of the break-up of the USSR, and the emergent nationalisms of its hitherto component parts.

The political impetus behind such work is often very clear, as it has been in Bohemia, Wales, Ireland, Catalonia, Croatia, Slovenia and other such countries now or in the past, although the implications for regional fiction of national political circumstances are highly complex and varied. This warrants detailed comparative study. There is the example of Fazil Iskander, writing on the so-called republic of Abkhazia, which lies next to Georgia on the Black Sea. His work *Sandro of Chegem* is concerned with 'The history of a clan, the history of the village of Chegem, the history of Abkhazia, and all the rest of the world as it is seen from Chegemian heights – that is the concept of the book, in broad outline'.[89] Regional fiction in this case appears akin to patriotic local history. In Canada there is a definite regional sense to the urban or rural novels that deal with the Maritimes, the Prairies, or British Columbia as well as smaller areas and towns. Indeed, the vastness of this country has meant that its fiction might generally be labelled as regional, with many regional novelists producing outstanding work in recent decades, such as Rudy Wiebe, Matt Cohen, or Margaret Laurence.[90] And in the United States (where pressure for national unity has probably exceeded that in Canada) regional writing flourishes, so much so that one can barely hint at its scope and importance here.[91] Like in Canada, the late twentieth-century American examples have been conspicuous in describing life in the large urban centres, as in the writing of Richard Price,[92] or in works like Tom Wolfe's *Bonfire of the*

[89] Fazil Iskander, *Sandro of Chegem* (1983), Foreword.
[90] L. Hutcheon, 'The novel', in W. H. New (ed.), *Literary History of Canada: Canadian Literature in English* (1990 edn), vol. 4, p. 78. On the importance of regional fiction in Canada see D. Harrison, *Unnamed Country: The Struggle for a Canadian Prairie Fiction* (Edmonton, 1977), and his (ed.) *Crossing Frontiers: Papers in American and Canadian Western Literature* (Edmonton, 1979); L. Ricou, *Vertical Man, Horizontal World: Man and Landscape in Canadian Prairie Fiction* (Vancouver, 1973); G. Woodcock (ed.), *The World of Canadian Writing: Critiques and Recollections* (Vancouver, 1980), and his *The Meeting of Time and Space: Regionalism in Canadian Literature* (Edmonton, 1981); W. Toye (ed.), *The Oxford Companion to Canadian Literature* (Toronto, 1983); B. Proulx, *Le roman du territoire* (Montreal, 1987); G. Dusterhaus, *Canada, Regions and Literature* (Paderborn, 1989); W. H. New (ed.), *Native Writers and Canadian Writing* (Vancouver, 1990); D. Jordan, *New World Regionalism* (Toronto, 1994).
[91] For discussions of American regional fiction see note 137 below, and C. B. Brown, *Regionalism in American Literature* (Heidelberg, 1962); W. T. Pilkington, *My Blood's Country: Studies in Southwestern Literature* (Fort Worth, 1973); G. W. Haslam, *Western Writing* (Albuquerque, 1974); R. Gray, *Writing the South: Ideas of an American Region* (Cambridge, 1986); H. P. Simonson, *Beyond the Frontier: Writers, Western Regionalism and a Sense of Place* (Fort Worth, 1989); S. Manning, *The Puritan-provincial Vision: Scottish and American Literature in the Nineteenth Century* (Cambridge, 1990); D. M. Holman, *A Certain Slant of Light: Regionalism and the Form of Southern and Midwestern Fiction* (Baton Rouge, 1995).
[92] See for example his first novel, *The Wanderers* (1974).

Vanities: the latter contributing to a genre between journalism and the regional novel, tackling political, urban and ethnic life with much local realism and Dickensian scope.[93]

In England too, particularly in the 1980s, it has been remarkable how much regional writing has been concerned with London, specifically with the City of London and its associations, which became a key area in projections of 'England'. For an extended time there was an aversion to representing urban life in regional novels, which is one reason why some cities (like Birmingham) have such slight coverage within the genre.[94] However, in almost all countries, the urban regional novel has now taken over the rural, although we still have a rather vague sense of when this occurred, or how it may be related to rural depopulation, urbanisation and other cultural changes. In Canada for example, this development took place rather later than in England. Whatever the country, one conclusion seems clear: the desire of authors to create their own region, almost to assert their own uniqueness in not sharing too much space with other writers, is probably stronger today than ever before.[95]

ETHNICITY AND REGIONAL FICTION

One important modern development in regional fiction in Britain, as in countries like Canada or the United States, has been the burgeoning of a variety of 'black' and 'ethnic' writing since 1945, which in Britain has usually been centred upon particular urban areas. In defining some such work as 'regional' I do not wish to pre-empt alternative categorisation for this writing. Further, there are particular difficulties in categorising such regional writing that is significantly mediated through very varied cultural backgrounds and traditions that are Afro-Caribbean or West Indian, Asian, Chinese, South African and so on. There are also problems here in the definition of ' "black" or "ethnic" British writers', some of whom certainly would question their inclusion

---

[93] For a study of such urban writing, see B. H. Gelfant, *The American City Novel* (Oklahoma, 1970).

[94] On Birmingham, see K. Pagett, *Image Problems: the Ambiguous Identity of Birmingham as Represented in Novels set in the City, 1870 to 1950* (Department of English Local History, University of Leicester, unpub. MA dissertation, 1992).

[95] For two recent discussions of regional fiction in other countries, see R. T. Sussex, *Home and the Homeland Novel: Studies in French Regional Literature* (Queensland, 1979), and C. J. Alonso, *The Spanish American Regional Novel: Modernity and Autochthony* (Cambridge, 1990).

in this or similar categories.[96] The sense of place in much of this (often autobiographical) literature is permeated and influenced by the memory of sometimes distant cultures, traditions and countries. This is true in probably different ways for so-called first, second or third generation 'immigrant' authors. The same applies for European, Jewish, Irish, Welsh or Scottish authors, setting their fiction in regions of the British Isles other than those in which they grew up, although I can think of few examples of English equivalents set in Ireland, Scotland and Wales. In such writing one often finds representation of 'community' (or the idea of one, for such writing can be isolated and desolate) and its associations, which are regional even though they may be heavily influenced by distant memory, removed networks of social and personal relations, and the idea of a foreign past and culture. These features, alongside the often cultural self-preservational and dignifying qualities of such fiction, have contributed to the frequent richness of its dialect (for example, the work of Buchi Emecheta or David Simon),[97] as well as to its formal structure, senses of community and personal relations, and political intent. These may sometimes have an ironic bearing on local traditions of fiction, and on the common racial assumptions in supposedly indigenous fiction. This writing includes some of the most salient, spirited and promising developments in regional fiction, often innovative in form, a development in which the relationships between fiction and ethnic community are prominent, opening up many possible questions for study and appreciation.

LOCAL LANGUAGE, DIALECT AND REGIONAL FICTION

I mentioned earlier that one defining feature of regional fiction is attempted realism in dialogue. The regional dialect novel in particular treats language not only as representational, but as a living form integral and distinct to the people using it, although this form is represented and compromised in many artistic ways. There was considerable growth in dialect fiction during the nineteenth century, particularly in Scotland and England, and an earlier tradition of dialect writing expanded

---

[96] On questions of definition of 'black British writers', see Prahbu Guptara, *Black British Literature: an Annotated Bibliography* (Oxford, 1986), pp. 14–16. On black women's writing in Britain, see Lauretta Ngcobo (ed.), *Let it be Told: Black Women Writers in Britain* (1987). More generally on post-colonial and immigrant writing in Britain, see A. R. Lee (ed.), *Other Britain, Other British: Contemporary Multicultural Fiction* (1995).

[97] See for example Buchi Emecheta, *In the Ditch* (1972); David Simon, *Railton Blues* (1983).

self-confidently after about 1850.[98] It developed at the same time as dialect societies were formed to study and preserve regional dialects. This writing was local, often domestic and oral in purpose and appeal, influenced by ballads and almanacs; but, whatever the ubiquity of dialect itself, such writing was by no means universal. In England, for example, it had its centres in the north-east and north-west, in Yorkshire, and to a lesser extent in the Potteries and the Black Country. It extolled regional values and aspirations shared by rich and poor. It assumed the superiority of the ordinary people reading or hearing it, and it was commonly anti-metropolitan.[99] Its study should occupy the historian or cultural geographer as well as the literary critic. For representations of local language and speech, particularly before the advent of modern oral history, there can be few sources to compare with regional fiction. There are, for example, the greatly diverse technical and other languages of occupational cultures, as illustrated in novels like *Anna of the Five Towns, Love on the Dole, The Lonely Plough*, or *Whisky Galore* – in these cases covering the Staffordshire potteries, engineering works in Lancashire, a Westmorland rural community and the Hebridean islands.[100] Or there are the descriptions of the terminology of fishing communities along the English north-east coast in the work of Leo Walmsley,[101] or of the Derbyshire lead and coal-mining districts by Walter Brierley, Nellie Kirkham and Albert Rhodes.[102] Fictional representation of rural speech is extraordinarily rich in the British Isles, even if it is often relayed by outsiders. Whatever one's verdict on the historical accuracy of such dialect, language and description, a language of period is well conveyed by such works, whether captured at the time, or retrospectively in fine historical regional novels like *Waterland* or *Ulverton*.[103] A statement like this, on the temporal specificity of language and the possibilities of studying it, should imply shared work by historians and literary critics.[104]

---

[98] P. Joyce, *Visions of the People: Industrial England and the Question of Class, 1848–1914* (Cambridge, 1991), chs. 11–12, contains an interesting discussion relevant here.

[99] *Ibid.*, p. 294.

[100] A. Bennett, *Anna of the Five Towns* (1902), W. Greenwood, *Love on the Dole* (1933), Constance Holme, *The Lonely Plough* (1914), Compton Mackenzie, *Whisky Galore* (1952).

[101] L. Walmsley, *Three Fevers* (1935), *Phantom Lobster* (1948), *Sally Lunn* (1967), *Foreigners* (1967), *So Many Lovers* (1969).

[102] W. Brierley, *Means-Test Man* (1935); N. Kirkham, *Unrest of their Time* (1935); A. Rhodes, *Butter on Sundays* (1964).

[103] Graham Swift, *Waterland* (1983); Adam Thorpe, *Ulverton* (1992).

[104] For interesting discussion of a closely related subject, see P. Burke & R. Porter (eds.), *The Social History of Language* (Cambridge, 1987).

Dialect used by so many authors, particularly after Scott, has been fundamental in fictional characterisation, for speech is the firmest expression of emotion, variously carried by dialect and its regional and class associations, stereotypes and emotional expectations. In many novels idiolect (a character's aggregate features of speech) may bear a complex relation to dialect (the group features of speech), adding a further level of interest. Behind dialect, in obvious linkages, lies the idea of region, with crude or sophisticated understandings of it and of the regional societies it contains. Some fine work has been done on dialect and speech in fiction, notably by Norman Page, which deserves close attention from historians.[105] Fictional use of such speech epitomises one of the most prominent attempts made in any medium to handle questions of class difference in regional contexts. Think for example of the alternating, contextualised speech of Mellors in *Lady Chatterley's Lover*. But further questions remain. Dialect is frequently used by authors to indicate how closely tied to a locality specific characters are. In an appreciation of the social status of these characters (who are usually but not always of low social standing) there lies an opening to the question of the social and status connotations of regionality itself, in different periods, and with reference to varied regions. Such investigation parallels in an interesting way the study of the frequently pejorative or inferior status of 'regional', with its many cultural, political and indeed literary connotations. There is the need to make explicit the bases of dialect: to research in detail the relation between dialect and place in fiction, much as a dialect cartographer might do (for speech and dialect in fiction cannot be studied without reference to the region they supposedly pertain to).[106] One needs then to use such information to ask why an

---

[105] N. Page, *Speech in the English Novel* (1973); M. Sabin, *The Dialect of the Tribe: Speech and Community in Modern Fiction* (Oxford, 1987); R. Chapman, *Forms of Speech in Victorian Fiction* (1994); R. Golding, *Idiolects in Dickens: the Major Techniques and Chronological Development* (1985); P. Ingham, 'Dialect as realism: *Hard Times* and the industrial novel', *Review of English Studies*, 37 (1986). Compare also E. M. Burkett, *American English Dialects in Literature* (New Jersey, 1978); S. W. Holton, *Down Home and Uptown: the Representation of Black Speech in American Fiction* (1984). Careful note needs to be taken of Page's warning: 'It is dangerous to use literary dialogue, in fiction or drama, as a basis for assumptions about the prevailing features of common speech in earlier periods, even though this has been a frequent practice of historians of the spoken language. The nature of the written medium makes it inevitable that there should be considerable adaptation of the features of actual speech, by omission, modification and exaggeration, in the process of transposing it into visible form. Such terms of praise as authentic and realistic are to be understood, therefore, in a strictly relative sense . . . for most novelists the primary aim is not linguistic accuracy'. (Page, *Speech in the English Novel*, p. 86).

[106] Much work has been conducted on dialect situation and boundaries. See for example M. F. Wakelin (ed.), *English Dialects: an Introduction* (1972); his (ed.) *Patterns in the Folk Speech of the British Isles* (1972); D. J. North and A. Sharpe, *A Word Geography of Cornwall* (Redruth, 1980);

author has found it necessary to depart from the ascertainable social realities of such a relation. It is of further interest to study reviewers' and readers' responses to representations of dialect, which in some cases have been angry and dismissive.[107] To consider such questions is to open up significant areas of interpretation and judgement, and has broader possibilities beyond the study of dialect. The conclusions one might reach when assessing fictional verisimilitude against alternatively evidenced regional history – and the seeming disjunctures between the two – can suggest many further hypotheses about the author's position over putative subject matter, and the anticipated readership for the fiction. In the study of readerships in particular, such a method has much to offer.

REGIONAL STEREOTYPE, IMAGE-MAKING, READERSHIPS AND FICTION

Many regional novels use region or place in crucially important ways, to explain or interpret, to develop characterisation, to indicate how character grows out of certain occupied localities, how people respond to particular circumstances and environments, to evoke good and evil through landscape contrasts, or to intensify mood or convey a sense of irony, as is so often the case in a novel like *Tess of the D'Urbervilles*. Hardy, like others, also used legends of place for similar purposes, with Tess, for example, being equated with the White Hart of Blackmore Vale. The use of local elements, in a closely known place or region, respective to each character – for example, in *Ulysses* – is a dimension that might be, and indeed, usually is, studied within the terms of the novel only. Yet these fictional allusions cannot be fully interpreted without knowledge of the popular associations and symbolism of such local elements or legends in a wider public consciousness or contemporary readership beyond the novel. This then is an agenda for the local historian, for the historian of popular culture, for the social historian, and when conducted with subtlety and reference to other sources, it is one that could enhance all the relevant areas of study.

P. Trudgill, *On Dialect: Social and Geographical Perspectives* (Oxford, 1983), and his *The Dialects of England* (Oxford, 1990); J. M. Kirk, S. Sanderson and J. D. A. Widdowson, *Studies in Linguistic Geography: Essays on English Dialect Study* (1985); P. Trudgill, *Dialects in Contact* (Oxford, 1986); C. Upton, S. Sanderson and J. Widdowson, *Word Maps: a Dialect Atlas of England* (1987); B. Strang, *A History of English* (1970).

[107] For example, the award of the 1994 Booker Prize to James Kelman for his *How Late it Was, How Late* was publicly condemned by one of the judges who felt that the novel's use of Glaswegian speech made it inaccessible to a broader readership.

An important effect of regional fiction has been the articulation of
regional stereotypes, particularly of regional character and behaviour.
Regional writers have created or (more commonly) perpetuated such
stereotypes for the sake of sales, through disinclination to break with
tried and tested formulae, for ideological or racial reasons, or through
attachment to literary clichés. This is inevitable, and perhaps even art-
istically desirable in some fiction, for it is often the clichés that induce
emotion in readers. This is as true for fiction as it is for music, or indeed
religion. People respond to narrative structures, imagery, formulaic
phrases and terms that are known either from other fiction or from
different genres or contexts. 'Regional fiction' without these elements
might not exist as such a popular concern. To point to literary use of
such formulae is not necessarily to minimise any author. It ought rather
to open up new ways of analysing regional fiction. Even Hardy –
having argued against the view that 'novels that evolve their action
on a circumscribed scene . . . cannot be so inclusive in their exhibition
of human nature as novels wherein the scenes cover large extents of
country'[108] – perpetuated views of the rustic chorus, of 'Hodge' and of
the 'dialect'-using yokel. These figures served to clarify or comment on
events in his novels, but they also contributed a comic and particular
'Wessex' colouring for something akin to a sidestepping ideological
dodge.[109] Whatever the form it takes, stereotype or cliché may lead to
the rejection of information contrary to it, and it can have far reaching
if intangible consequences, for example on regional prejudice, political
policy, and economic decision-making. In Dorset and the surrounding
counties a dismissive and literary view of 'Hodge' allayed many contemporary worries over extreme low wages, poor health and rural
poverty. Furthermore, cultural ascriptions of this sort underlie self-
perceptions in deeply felt ways. Throughout nineteenth-century southern
England, the attempts of rural workers to build self-respect through
organisations like friendly societies, the Primitive Methodist and Wesleyan
Churches or the rural trade unions become intelligible when we think
of the prevailing stereotypes that these people were subjected to. Comparable situations and responses could be multiplied endlessly. In all

---

[108] See the General Preface to the 1912 Wessex edition of his works.
[109] K. D. M. Snell, *Annals of the Labouring Poor: Social Change and Agrarian England, 1660–1900*
(Cambridge, 1985), ch. 8. As N. Page commented, in George Eliot or Hardy, as indeed in
many other novelists, 'regional speech is largely reserved for comic, pathetic or sentimental-
nostalgic purposes. For more heroic or dramatic effects, standard speech is a *sine qua non*.'
N. Page, *Speech in the English Novel* (1973), p. 126.

cases regional fiction was a key medium in the display of cultural ascriptions and the responses to them. It carried interpretations of the regional or ethnic past and present that contributed to personal and collective identities, and it highlighted artifacts, symbols or episodes of the local past that had significant influence upon current life.

No one can doubt the prevalence and influence of such literary stereotypes, images and formulae purporting to account for and describe people from different areas, and the reactions these may produce. The history of regional clichés – their forms, derivations, mutations and perpetuations, and (closely related to these) their artistic effects on different readerships – remains to be written.[110] Clearly some regions or districts have tried hard to modify or reject, as well as to capitalise on, the reputations given them by certain regional novelists. One thinks of the complaints against D. H. Lawrence's representation of morals in Eastwood and its surrounding area: 'We are trying to forget him', objected one resident, as outsiders to the community inaugurated their commemorations. 'Why must the people of Eastwood be classed with this type of filthy literature?' asked one local councillor in 1974, as he denounced a proposal to rename one of the town's streets as 'Chatterley Mews'.[111] Or there have been Brighton's efforts to shake off the influence of *Brighton Rock*. Some Dorset people felt that Thomas Hardy had ridiculed them, had made fun of them or presented them as miserably gloomy. Such antagonism to him can still be found in Dorchester. Lewis Grassic Gibbon's characters hardly endeared him to people in the Mearns.[112] In Wales, Richard Llewellyn's *How Green Was My Valley* appeared in 1939, and had sold 150,000 copies within a few months. The novel's 'clichés about the Welsh miner and his society spread to the ends of the earth', complains one of Wales' most outstanding modern historians.[113] A remarkable novel, it was nevertheless slated by some, lampooned for example in Harri Webb's poem 'Synopsis of the

---

[110] See in particular P. Dodd, 'Lowryscapes: recent writings about "the North"' *Critical Quarterly*, vol. 32, no. 2 (1990), for a discussion of how 'the "North" of the present continues to be haunted by an earlier "North" which it cannot escape'. On regional characterisation in America, see H. S. Fiske, *Provincial Types in American Fiction* (New York, 1968).

[111] Quoted, with other such comment, in C. I. Bennett, '*A Devouring Nostalgia and an Infinite Repulsion': the Impact of D. H. Lawrence on the Town and Country of Eastwood* (Department of English Local History, University of Leicester, unpub. M. A. dissertation, 1994), pp. 30, 45.

[112] L. G. Gibbon, *A Scots Quair* (1946). And see I. Carter, 'Lewis Grassic Gibbon, *A Scots Quair*, and the peasantry', *History Workshop*, 6 (1978), pp. 175, 182.

[113] John Davies, *A History of Wales* (1990; Harmondsworth, 1993 edn), p. 589. I can confirm this: my Welsh mother used to discuss *How Green Was My Valley* with me when I was a child growing up in tropical Africa.

Great Welsh Novel'. Very different in tone was the hostile reception
in west Wales to Caradoc Evans. Rhys Davies has written of a deep-
seated suspicion of regional novels in Wales, of Welsh reluctance to
tolerate criticism, and the resulting difficulties for Welsh writers faced
with controversy over their regional novels.[114] With the exception of
Allen Raine, in whose work Welsh culture was slight, novels with Welsh
settings have often sold poorly, and been well-thrashed with leeks upon
publication. Welsh Calvinistic Methodism, with its enormous influence,[115]
was almost as discouraging of plays and the dangerous snare of novels
as it was of folklore, the harp, folk tunes, popular dancing and Sunday
games. Such a religious ethos probably restricted both potential Welsh
readership and the country's regional fiction.[116] In Scotland, a large body
of literature has depicted an aggressive, 'gangland' Glasgow, notably
Alexander McArthur and H. Kingsley Young, *No Mean City* (1935), but
also many works by John McNeillie, George Friel, Alan Spence, Bill
McGhee, William McIlvanney and others. *No Mean City*, wrote Moira
Burgess, 'has cast a particularly long shadow', and huge sums have been
spent in controverting 'shadows' like this.[117] Advertising by the City
Council and other bodies (promoting 'Glasgow – City of Culture') has
tried hard to rise above such gang-warfare images of the city. Some
regions have perhaps been better served. Fiction from Walpole to
Bragg has extolled the 'yeoman' hardiness of Cumbria's independent
'statesman farmers' and their workers. Popular images of 'Yorkshire'
cannot be conceived without reference to the Brontës, Winifred Holtby,
Phyllis Bentley, Storm Jameson, the harder hitting realist novels of the
1960s, like *Billy Liar* or *This Sporting Life* (and the films based upon them),
and some more benign media creations.[118]

---

[114] R. Davies, *My Wales* (London, 1937 edn), pp. 204–14.
[115] See K. D. M. Snell and P. S. Ell, *Rival Jerusalems: Land and Religion in England and Wales* (provisional title, forthcoming), on the cultural distinctiveness of Wales in religious terms.
[116] I. C. Peate, *Tradition and Folk Life: a Welsh View* (London, 1972), p. 84. Or see R. S. Thomas,
'The Minister', in *Selected Poems, 1946–1968* (1946, Newcastle upon Tyne, 1986 edn), e.g. p. 32.
The idea that fiction-reading was sinful had largely disappeared elsewhere by 1900. It would
be interesting to know more about the relation between Welsh revivalism and the writing and
reading of novels.
[117] M. Burgess, *The Glasgow Novel: a Survey and Bibliography* (1972, Glasgow, 1986 edn), p. 44. On
images of Glasgow and their ramifications, see J. R. Gold and M. M. Gold, *Imagining Scotland:
Tradition, Representation and Promotion in Scottish Tourism since 1750* (Aldershot, 1995), ch. 9.
[118] For example, 'The Last of the Summer Wine', or the James Heriot inspired television series of
a rural Yorkshire veterinary practice. For Scotland, there has been *Dr Finlay's Casebook*, *Whisky
Galore*, the films of *The Thirty-Nine Steps*, or those based on Neil Munro's Para Handy. On
images of Scotland in film, including the adaptation to the screen of regional novels, see E.
Dick, *From Limelight to Satellite: a Scottish Film Book* (1990). Other publications have dealt with the
conversion of regional novels into film – for example, R. Ellis, *Making Poldark* (Bodmin, 1978).

The broader cultural and historical influences impinging on regional fiction are little examined, although more critical attention has been paid in media studies to their role in advertising and regional 'image-making'. Often these originated long prior to forms they took in regional fiction: in folklore, chapbooks and *blason populaire*, in proverbial sayings, in images created or perpetuated by characterisation in the picaresque novel, or in the popular perceptions of antiquarian local history and regional political association and tradition. Yet there has been no regionally-based historical study of how such assumptions, motifs, presuppositions about character and landscape were translated from folklore or regional oral traditions into new fictional forms, how they influenced such fiction, how fiction replaced or supplemented them, or how those fictional forms were themselves subject to redefinition or changing improvisation over time – that is, how the evolution of certain regional identities was staged, and how the montage of associations and formulae has been managed.

The pervasive social and economic ramifications of these associations is overwhelming, very visible in what we may think of as the 'management' of regional fiction. Appropriation of literature by local authorities, environmental pressure groups, local societies and other parties is increasingly common. One sees this in the cases of Thomas Hardy, George Eliot, Mary Webb, Eden Phillpotts, James Joyce, Brett Young, Dickens, and many others. 'Dylan Thomas Country' demonstrates how some poets have also been claimed in this way. This is noticeably so for Wordsworth, who has even had the Department of the Environment intervene to maintain the view from the house that he lived in. One could also mention Stratford-upon-Avon. These commercial locales with their visitors' centres are sometimes significant branches of the publishing industry, in some cases funded by that industry, outlets for sales of books and tapes, but they are more than that. The phenomenon of 'literary pilgrimage' has already been touched upon. Almost all County Councils have a variously named 'Department of Heritage'. Statues and plaques on buildings commemorate literary figures associated with the district. Local history is rewritten as the history of the author, not of the place. Author's faces appear on mugs, tea-towels and bookmarks. Postcards provide maps of Hardy's 'Wessex', and Wessex, Casterbridge, Mellstock and so on provide names for local businesses and amenities.[119]

[119] M. Millgate, 'Unreal estate: reflections on Wessex and Yoknapatawpha', in R. P. Draper (ed.), *The Literature of Region and Nation* (Basingstoke, 1989), p. 67.

The continuous 'Blue Line' appears on Eastwood pavements, to guide 10,000 annual visitors around significant 'Lawrence sites'.[120] Hospital wards are named after George Eliot novels. Schools and hospices also take her name. Coventry has its Marner and Garth Crescents, its Middlemarch, Lydgate, Barton and Bede Roads, and its Tulliver Street. The 'Middlemarch Business Park', owned by P. & O. Properties Ltd., tells me that it has close connections with 'Middlemarch School'. Maps of 'George Eliot country' (which adjoins so-called 'Shakespeare country') are separately produced by the Tourist Board and by Nuneaton and Bedworth Borough Council, thus 'putting Nuneaton on the map' via the author, allowing people to partake of 'the George Eliot tourist experience'. George Eliot's 'birthday' is re-scheduled from November to June, so that the 'festival of her birth' (started in 1919) may coincide with the tourist season.[121]

There has never been a time in which local residents have been made more aware of authors somehow associated with their district. However, much of this is directed at the outsider, the businessman, the tourist, at the agent of change and uniformity. Cultural expression that once celebrated distinctiveness or even a local attachment to place is now eroding much of its own principle. These tendencies appear to be stronger in Britain than in Europe or America, and much stronger than in Japan (where the idea of a literary pilgrimage has yet to depose that of a religious one). In this regard the conception of de-industrialised Britain as museum and historical theme park is one that overspills to its regional literature, that literature which can most easily be 'placed' and therefore 'visited', as well as to its material 'museable' artifacts. Thus a new cultural cytology develops from a once living literature, as a new commercial structure thriving in dead tissue.

Or is this too critical a judgement? For this predisposition and com- mercial usage is not only backward-looking, but has strong implica- tions for cultural progression. Many areas, cities, and local companies or Chambers of Commerce have temporarily funded particular writers, partly in the hope that certain representations, or regional muses, could benefit the pursuit of industrial or commercial investment and

---

[120] Bennett, 'A Devouring Nostalgia', pp. 63–74. This was apparently inspired by the 'Red Line' tourist trail of Boston in America.

[121] J. King, George Eliot's Legacy: Local History Revisited (Department of English Local History, University of Leicester, unpub. MA dissertation, 1992), pp. 34, 37, 52–4. The attempt to generate tourism in Nuneaton through the Eliot association has had limited success compared with other 'literary' areas.

location.[122] Authorial success is in some cases highly dependent upon such patronage, seemingly turning the writing of fiction, as well as the retrospective assessment of authors, into a branch of the advertising industry. The region of the north-east in which Catherine Cookson's novels are said to be situated is openly advertised as 'Catherine Cookson Country'. Yet the moral, commercial, historical and future-oriented purpose of identification like this is little considered, necessitating, as it does, close attention to how such a novelist is perceived among her readers, or even perhaps among those who have no immediate familiarity with her pages. Among the many issues that ought to be pursued here is an evaluation of the *effects* of literary appreciation, including its more conservative forms. In this as in the study of readerships one looks for participation from literary critics, and the adoption by them of social-science methods not often associated with their own discipline. As with the sociological study of individual authors and their relation to more general regional categories and contexts, it is indeed possible that the priorities of more conservative critics would benefit, at a later stage of assessment, from a fuller appreciation of these wider contextual issues and from the adoption of these methods.

There has as yet been no significant study of local readerships, and of how regional novelists have been locally received. Nor have the various societies associating themselves with some regional novelists been given much attention.[123] The issues arising here are historical as well as literary and sociological. One may use questionnaires and other such approaches to pursue the questions today, but it is a more problematical matter to press this issue in the past, to see how readers interpreted fiction then. The questions become all the more interesting when one considers our position now, standing (as we probably do) on the threshold of the electronic 'interactive novel'. It needs to be asked why and how regional novels came to mean something to people. To what extent do readers belong to a community of interpretation,

---

[122] On this general issue, see J. R. Gold and S. V. Ward (eds.), *Place Promotion: the Use of Publicity and Public Relations to Sell Towns and Regions* (Chichester, 1994); G. Kearns and C. Philo (eds.), *Selling Places: the City as Cultural Capital, Past and Present* (Oxford, 1993).

[123] It needs to be borne in mind that there is much variety in these local societies. Some of them were initiated by local people eager to keep familiar the achievements of writers who chronicled their area – for example, those connected with John Clare, Edward Thomas, Mary Webb, Henry Williamson, or the Richard Jefferies Society in Swindon. Most of them have expanded outwards as interest in the authors has grown. Many of course (e.g. the Thomas Hardy Society, founded in 1968) post-date the main upsurges of interest in the author concerned.

and what are or were those interpretative communities? How far did texts themselves create their readerships, and define a role for them as *regional* readers? In any period, local readers who know the areas supposedly described respond differently, and with different imaginative resources, to those who do not share their local knowledge, or to those who do not share such knowledge but who *believe* that they do. They may cross-relate information in a novel, of whatever sort, to other locally acquired references in ways that will also be unique to themselves. Their demands and expectations of such fiction may also be distinctive, like their reactions to it. Although not a homogeneous group, but one that reflects local social, ethnic, gender-based, or political differences, they may still share certain as yet undefined characteristics, mentalities and values as a specific regional (or associatively regional) readership.

One way of putting these points is to express them as the coupling of reception theory to the perspective of the regional historian. The literary critical stress in recent years (particularly in Germany) on the reader, or the readership, on the expectations directed at a text in the past, and the effects that it has on readers, on the uses of reading such a text, bodes well for the type of work advocated here. Furthermore, and to reverse the issue, there is the question of whether and in what ways a readership is envisaged by the author as 'regional'. This issue may be tied to the more empirical question of whether, for certain authors, readerships *are* regional. Both within social history and literary criticism there is increasing interest in the ways in which texts like regional novels have changed the horizons of readers. The 'regional novel' itself is an ideal starting point for such investigation. It is here that the sociological term 'horizon' takes on its most literal meaning: the regional novel in many of its forms provides a focus for the study of readers' expectations about the locality or region *vis-à-vis* a wider area such as the nation state, and for the study of those elements (e.g. speech, dialect, social relations, topography, local tradition) that form the basis for local consciousness and a sense of attachment. How can literary works be said to be 'representative' of the regions they purport to describe? In addition, the role of the reader in 'producing' the final text is crucial in the understandings of regionality at issue here. Many authors have been pre-empted as 'regional' at the behest of certain readerships, a process that has had ramifications for the development of particular novelists' work, for the ideologies they have become associated with, as well as for their retrospective interpretation.

A further question which emerges in this connection is that of the association of particular authors with the areas they describe. What is the nature of a novelist's loyalty to a region, and what are his or her motives when writing about it? Who indeed *are* the regional novelists, as a question of regional biography? Who do they believe themselves to write for? Of course, many write from within a community, almost as its spokespersons. However, just as in the folk song and dance revivals, or in the collection of folklore, the needs and expectations regarding regional fiction have often come from *outside* the community concerned. A recurring phenomenon has been the regional novelist as outside witness, in some cases almost as anthropological visitor, participant-observer and investigator, in others as having been displaced by education and mobility from the people and landscape the fiction describes, experiencing a sense of dislodged or multiple belonging. There have been many examples: Edgeworth, R. L. Stevenson, Hardy, Brett Young, W. Riley, Arnold Bennett, Lawrence, Henry Williamson, H. E. Bates, Raymond Williams or Cookson. In some cases the sense of place became more poignant the further the novelist was from the place concerned, as with Stevenson in the Pacific.

In many novels, key fictional characters have also been outsiders, like the English heroes of Scott's 'Jacobite' novels, David Balfour in *Kidnapped*, or Lydia Lensky in *The Rainbow*, even disruptive outsiders (as for example in *Shirley*), carrying certain moral connotations. In much regional fiction insider–outsider tensions are central to the plot. Such ambivalent stresses are persistent in Hardy, for example. While much eighteenth-century fiction was based around the portrayal of individuals in some kind of anomalous social position (often with some mystery over their birth or social status, for example Joseph Andrews, Tom Jones, Roderick Random or Humphry Clinker), the regional novel seems to give this anomaly a spatial dimension. Clym Yeobright, Grace Melbury and so many others have been taken away from the landscape of their birth – they are from it but not of it – enabling the author to explore the relationships between the individual, the community and the landscape, as the eighteenth-century writers were able to explore social relationships.

The frequently distanced relationship between author and subject matter points to a central theme in the interpretation of much regional fiction: that it has often been a complex product of nostalgia, partial recollection, regret, ambivalence, uncertainty, guilt, hesitantly assumed superiority, recognition or reconciliation, brought about by the losses and gains associated with mobility and new horizons, and by the consequent difficulties in communicating feelings to those who become the authors' subjects. Academic commentators, above all, are well qualified to discuss such issues. These relationships between authorial biography and the structures of regional fiction add a further dimension to the study of readerships, in this case to the relation between author and reader. For the regional novel is partly a communicative form that mediates between them, sometimes in the absence of any other possibility, and the subtle complexities of this relationship raise many issues about the passivity, viability and activity of readerships both within and outside the region described.

NATIONALISM AND REGIONAL FICTION

Jeremy Hooker, writing in his *The Poetry of Place* about the poet Ivor Gurney, spoke of how

identifications of place or region with nation were common then; with individual and historical differences, they have been common in England from its beginnings as a nation, for England has always been characterized by physical, cultural, and social variousness, forming a mosaic of individual localities within the larger regional differences; and appeals to unified national feeling have invariably used images either of this variousness or of a locality or localities presented in *their* particularity and variety as *essence* of the whole. The identifications of part with whole are naturally felt with special intensity at times of national crisis . . .[124]

Now these observations were seemingly made here for England only, but they are of considerable relevance to the interpretation of regional fiction, to the questions surrounding its emergence, and to the forms it has subsequently assumed.

We saw earlier the connotation in Phyllis Bentley's definition of the regional novel, which related regional writing to national issues, to the 'motherland' as she put it in 1941. It was not just the wartime context of her book that may have suggested such an emphasis, important though that seems to have been. 'Regionalism' itself, on the literary and broader artistic scale that developed from the early nineteenth century, to be thought of as such, was arguably inconceivable in a context in which questions of nationality – of what it was to be Irish, Scottish, Welsh or

---

[124] Jeremy Hooker, 'Honouring Ivor Gurney', in his *The Poetry of Place: Essays and Reviews, 1970–1981* (Manchester, 1982), p. 121. (I quote Hooker here for his general sentiment, rather than for the strict accuracy of his statement on the Anglo-Welsh poet Ivor Gurney.)

English – were irrelevant or minor. Those questions contributed in both negative and positive ways to focus attention on particular localities and cultures, taken rightly or wrongly to be either representative of key elements in nationalistic self-identity, or to be threatened by it. Without a concept of nationhood, it was perhaps impossible, or unnecessary, to conceive of 'regions' in the usual sense.

One commonly found a (regionally contested) emphasis in late eighteenth- and early nineteenth-century literature in Britain upon the fundamental importance of folk art and regional tradition as supplying the roots of national identity and human experience. Much of the Romantic movement and the forms of nationalism emerging at that time were affected and ostensibly inspired by such folk idioms. One finds this too in many other European countries – in for example the emphasis on nationalistic song as being based upon regional folk traditions, as being fundamentally *volkslieder*, songs of the people. This was stressed rather earlier by such writers as the German philosopher Herder, and was found in Johann André, the songs of Reichardt and Schulz from the early 1780s, and most markedly in composers like Carl Maria von Weber, Crusell, Beethoven, Berlioz, Chopin, Liszt, Glinka, Bortniansky or Johann Carl Löwe. In many languages 'folk music' and 'national music' have, or have had, the same names, and while the regional aspect of much folk music contributed to debates about 'authenticity' (about how truly a song reflects the spirit and personality of the people who sing it, and how far it may be said to belong to them), this has not detracted from willingness to define such music as 'national', and to alter its functions and form accordingly. The influence of folk music and regional traditions on musical composition at this time was as pervasive as regional folk traditions were to literature, to such figures as Scott, and to the nationalistic use made of much regional fiction. It is worth stressing how European-wide this phenomenon was, across different artistic idioms. As in Germany, Poland, France, Russia, Bohemia, or Hungary, so in Britain too such artistic developments were accompanied by a return to popular sources, from Shakespeare (now being set to song, and characters like Falstaff being widely engraved in prints), to the collections of older songs, narratives, regional artistic and oral traditions, which were to be restored in the sense that they were reinterpreted, reintroduced in different forms to 'the people', and to a gradually more democratic understanding of the latter. In many cases the reinterpretation was complex and multi-layered, speading into other genres, and this was not exclusively national. Scott, like

Shakespeare, was a widely influential example of this, and his material was often set to music. In addition, the ever-wider readership encompassed by market expansion, coupled with imperatives of patriotism and national alliance (especially during extended war-time mobilisation), required the pragmatic abandonment of official, polite, classical, politico-mythological themes in favour of the real, the recognisable, the regional and even the humble.

This argument was well made by Wordsworth in 1798, and elaborated to become the famous 1802 preface to the *Lyrical Ballads*, where he defended his use of 'the real language of men': a language recognisable to middle and lower classes in society, a more conversational and vernacular language. His subject matter complemented this, being of 'low and rustic life', grounded in the domestic and working cultures of particular landscapes. The poet, after all, expressed 'the general passions and thoughts and feelings of men'; so how then, Wordsworth asked, 'can his language differ in any material degree from that of all other men who feel vividly and see clearly?'[125] He wrote elsewhere of how 'local attachment . . . is the tap-root of the tree of Patriotism', a theme common to Burke and many others.[126] The emergence of the regional novel at this time – catering to an ever wider readership, revolving regional traditions into new and often nationalistic forms, interpreting character in personal or generic types but stressing common people and their local cultures and history – may be taken as a key element in the changes of focus and theme epitomised by Wordsworth.

In subsequent periods too, regional writing has reflected such nationalistic impulses, and this occurred in different ways in all four British countries. One sees this in the literary flowering of the Welsh industrial valleys from about 1830 to 1870. It was notable in those regions where a fundamentally Welsh character was being most threatened by Anglicisation and English immigration, as in the western Gwent poets and other writers like John Davies of Tredegar, Thomas Price, T. E. Watkins of Blaenafon, the writers of the Abergavenny Cymreigyddion Society founded in 1833, or William Thomas the poet of Newport and Tredegar. The reaction against the 1847 educational commissioners gave further purpose to this. Similarities arose in the early 1890s, with Cymru Fydd, the Wales to be, and its emphases on

[125] The 1802 Preface to *Lyrical Ballads* is reprinted in H. Bloom and L. Trilling (eds.), *Romantic Poetry and Prose* (London, 1973), and see especially pp. 596, 605–6.
[126] W. J. B. Owen and J. W. Smyser (eds.), *Essays upon Epitaphs, 3, The Prose Works of William Wordsworth* (Oxford, 1974), 2, pp. 93, 495–6.

Welsh Home Rule, on Welsh education and literary culture. There were parallel developments in the mid 1930s, when revived stress on Welsh-language fiction followed the events connected with Saunders Lewis, himself strongly associated with nationalistic literature, 'against Philistia and her mire'.[127] These cultural developments were compounded by the resentment stockpiled in Welsh 'depressed areas' over the previous decade, a resentment and experience that produced a remarkable body of fiction, usually and significantly in English, from such authors as Kate Roberts, Gwyn Jones, Jack Jones, B. L. Coombes, Rhys Davies, Lewis Jones, Gwyn Thomas, and most popular of all, Richard Llewellyn.[128] The literary magazines *Wales* and *The Welsh Review* were inaugurated in 1937 and 1939. Many such nationalistic associations have been apparent also in the resurgence of English regional writing since the late 1970s, marked by a search for the meaning of 'Englishness' – initially in part response (often in antagonism) to centralising measures and their effects on local government, on local productive ways of life and their traditions, on regional cultures more widely understood. At times, regional fiction might be said to have fulfilled an eclectic role as comparative and self-assessing dialogue between regions. Such ferment overspilled to become one element in debates about Britain's position *vis-à-vis* European integration.[129] In other words, regional fiction cannot be interpreted without reference to the problems or even failures arising in different periods of formulating and imposing national programmes or ideologies. These have included problems of regional consensus, of incorporating diverse regional cultural traditions and political sensibilities within enveloping policies of the state, as well as the threats to regional landscapes, to local 'heritages' however and for whomsoever defined, and to local ways of making a living, so often perceived to be endangered from outside.

There has also been a demand, sometimes explicitly made (especially in the late nineteenth and early twentieth centuries), that literature should eschew the local and regional, and should impart a sense of nationality and of national ideals. For example, many educationalists were strongly resistant to dialectal expression of any sort, found most

---

[127] Idris Davies, 'Saunders Lewis', in D. Dale-Jones and R. Jenkins (eds.), *Twelve Modern Anglo-Welsh Poets* (London, 1975), p. 30.

[128] On these novelists, see in particular Glyn Jones, *The Dragon has Two Tongues* (1968).

[129] On 'Englishness' during this period, see in particular R. Colls and P. Dodd (eds.), *Englishness: Politics and Culture, 1880–1920* (1986); R. Samuel (ed.), *Patriotism: the Making and Unmaking of British National Identity* (1989), 3 volumes.

notably in many regional novels, seeing it as one aspect of cultural degeneracy, wherever it was encountered, and as a challenge to a unified
national language. The rigid vision of a standardised English that
encapsulated supposedly common aims, that served as a vehicle for
'national efficiency', and a cultural nationalism expressed in centralising
attempts to standardise language and literary expression, have a long
history. They led to the reformulation of the educative role of 'English
Literature' as a unifying expression of a shared culture.[130] As Crawford
writes, 'anti-provincial linguistic prejudice . . . found its voice not just
in singing the merits of one dominant cultural tradition, but also in its
silencing of others'.[131] There was usually little place here for analysis of
the regional diversity of fiction, let alone its relation to regional speech,
cultural traditions and ways of life. Literary criticism was slow to shed
the nationalistic coats in which the discipline had once justified itself.
Such an academic ethos, however, seems not to have retarded the
remarkable effervescence of regional, dialectal and ethnic writing.

'PROVINCIALISM' AND CENTRALISM

One issue bound up with my concerns here is the disparagement of
regional literature as essentially an expression of the local, regional or
'provincial'. This has been a persistent influence in critical neglect,
from which many novelists, of lesser stature than 'little Thomas Hardy',
have suffered. The term 'provincialism' is open to varied understanding, but it usually involves belittlement of any form of cultural life
other than that supplied by the metropolis. It assumes metropolitan
arbitration of taste, the superiority of metropolitan people and expression over that of the merely 'local' person, whose criteria are 'only'
those of locality – as though metropolis and locality were mutually
exclusive terms. There have been qualitative assessments implicit here

---

[130] B. Doyle, 'The invention of English' in Colls, *Englishness*; on 'national efficiency' see G. R.
Searle, *The Quest for National Efficiency: a Study in British Politics and British Political Thought, 1800–
1914* (Oxford, 1971). For discussion of the linguistic issues in an earlier period, see J. Barrell,
English Literature in History, 1730–1780: an Equal Wide Survey (1983), ch. 2; R. Crawford, *Devolving
English Literature* (Oxford, 1992), esp. ch. 1; O. Smith, *The Politics of Language, 1791–1819* (Oxford,
1984); J. M. S. Tompkins, *The Popular Novel in England, 1770–1800* (1932, 1969), p. 188, citing the
Monthly in 1784: 'Readers of taste will be disgusted at descriptions which enter too minutely
into vulgar scenes, and at dialogues which are degraded by the cant of provincial speech'.
Compare the desire for centralisation and uniformity in France during and after the Revolution, and the consequent surveys of rural patois, as discussed in M. De Certeau *et al.*, *Une
politique de la langue: la révolution française et les patois* (Paris, 1975).

[131] Crawford, *Devolving English Literature*, p. 43.

in the types of people being compared as well as the artistic merits of 'provincial' production. 'Provincialism is the residuum which remains after the course of events has drawn the ablest local men away', wrote James Hannay in 1865, commenting on an increasing frequency of the term in popular literature.[132] He continued: 'Provincial politics are the politics of men who know nothing of any other. Provincial wit and literature are the wit and literature of those who, if they had more of both, would carry them to a better market, but who have just enough to make them distinguished where they are'.[133] 'Provincialism, in fact, may be defined as the counterpart of cockneyism, – as the cockneyism of country towns. For every city has its own cockneys. There are Liverpool, Manchester, Edinburgh, and Dublin cockneys, just as London produces the typical breed from which they all derive the name. The local man, the man whose prejudices are bred in him by the place, and who measures everything by the place's standard, is and must ever be a cockney.'[134]

The 'cockney' here – and remember the start of *Alton Locke* – stood not only for a certain London dialectal 'breed', the supposedly hidebound inhabitants of Mayhew's East End 'tribal' ghettoes. It stood also for its regional counterparts. This was a style of thinking not necessarily tied to conventional 'class'. It was one in which regional differences, the expansive variety in regional popular cultures, could be passed over by emphasis upon class separateness: that supposed difference whereby provincial cultures, including the provincial press, could be termed 'cockney' (the cultural equivalent and symbol for Hannay of the working class). By comparison the 'cultured' classes of the metropolis epitomised cosmopolitan and truly accomplished man, no longer 'intensely local', no longer 'jealous' of other provincial centres,[135] able to view with 'amusement' a provincialism that was as regionally provincial as the working class itself was felt to be. Hannay looked forward to the day when 'cockneyism and provincialism may be expected to recede together into the past'.[136]

Hannay was only one example among very many. The dismissive attitudes he and others expressed are less fashionable today, although one readily finds examples. More commonly now 'provincialism' is viewed as a frame of mind that accepts and relishes its 'marginality'

---

[132] J. Hannay, 'Provincialism', *Cornhill Magazine*, 11 (June, 1865), pp. 673, 675.
[133] *Ibid.*, p. 675.　[134] *Ibid.*, p. 674.　[135] *Ibid.*, p. 679.
[136] *Ibid.*, p. 681. See also Keating, *The Haunted Study*, p. 331, on 'the distinctly pejorative connotations' that were now habitually attached to the words 'regional', 'provincial', and 'local'.

from the 'centre', using this in original ways rather than deferentially following a habit of thought that is itself, after all, utterly parochial in its metropolitan location. Evidently, parochialism in the sense of antiquarianism in imaginative writing is of limited use, and (like its historiographical counterparts) it usually has slight attraction beyond the neighbourhoods that it addresses, despite the success of writers like Galt. Yet in choice of universal or wide-ranging themes, interpreted against a particular locality, regional writing assuredly has wide appeal, as has been demonstrated in the reception of writers from Scott through to the Brontës, Mrs. Gaskell, George Eliot, Hardy, Lawrence, or more recently Llewellyn, Middleton, Gunn, Cookson, Plunkett, Sillitoe, Toulmin, George Mackay Brown, Doyle and so many others. The regional imagination of such writers is a crucial element in their art. This dimension has not been neglected in appreciations of American authors like Faulkner.[137] The critical indifference to this theme in Britain surprises social or local historians, cultural geographers or anthropologists. From their perspectives, there is great scope for interdisciplinary work of a wider nature, that supplements de-contextualised analysis and assessment of literary value. Nowhere is this more obvious than for the regional novel: widely neglected as such, and so frequently studied in guises other than its regional aspect, despite the regionalism that it addressed, perpetuated and helped to reformulate in a variety of ways that require close attention.

Many regional novels are present-day or historical affirmations of the regional life described, in direct antipathy to more metropolitan styles, to the cultural influence of London, or even other areas of England. Compton Mackenzie's *Whisky Galore*, for example, ends with the approbation of an old woman from Nottingham ('that peculiar place where she lives')[138] for the life of the Hebridean islands of Great and Little Todday. There are references throughout the novel to 'barbarous places like Africa and Devonshire',[139] and value judgements of the form: 'People in London thought I was mad when I came to live up here, but I've never regretted it. Not once'.[140] In William Riley's *Windyridge* the narrator, Grace Holden, leaves London for rural Yorkshire, taking a yearly tenancy in a cottage by the edge of a moor

[137] W. T. Ruzicka, *Faulkner's Fictive Architecture: The Meaning of Place in the Yoknapatawpha Novels* (Ann Arbor, 1987, 1992 edn); R. G. Deamer, *The Importance of Place in the American Literature of Hawthorne, Thoreau, Crane, Adams, and Faulkner* (New York, 1990); R. Rabbetts, *From Hardy to Faulkner: Wessex to Yoknapatawpha* (New York, 1989).
[138] C. Mackenzie, *Whisky Galore* (1955), p. 223. [139] *Ibid.*, p. 34. [140] *Ibid.*, p. 56.

– 'these wild parts which are as bad as a foreign country'.[141] Needless to say, she ends by controverting the way Londoners refer to 'the character of the heathen in whose midst I dwelt'.[142] These are sentiments much repeated in the extra-metropolitan regional novel: asserting a superiority and richness of that life and language thought to be condescendingly seen as 'regional' or 'provincial' by many in the metropolis.[143] This conflictual tension and interplay between supposedly subordinate and superordinate regions, and the morals and cultural norms associated with them, is a recurring element in such writing. It is related to, but goes beyond, the country–city tensions that are so common a feature in virtually all eighteenth-century and many nineteenth-century novels. The fiction may highlight the scarcely contained antagonisms between London and other regions. It may suggest comparisons of a more undecided nature.[144] Or the tension may be between England and the other three countries of the British Isles. 'We are fighting to preserve England, I mean Britain', proclaims Compton Mackenzie's Captain Waggett, an outsider commanding the 'home guard', a character incongruous and unpopular in Great Todday.[145] Mackenzie's Hebridean islanders display scant regard for the 'national' war effort, blaming it for the whisky shortage and then pinching the whisky bound for America to pay for that war. They assert their autonomy over central government and its agents, the latter represented as officious buffoons and snoopers, reporting unfavourably on islanders' attitudes to the war effort. Those islanders resent military titles, and do not respond to them, thus downplaying the standards and efforts of the wider nation during the Second World War.[146] A novel entitled *The Garrotted Announcer* is recommended by one of Mackenzie's cast – ostensibly for the inside view it gives of life in the BBC, perhaps also for its unconscious cathartic potential for those distanced from the centres of cultural and governmental influence.[147] Major Quiblick, by contrast, 'regarded all Gaelic Christian names as a threat to Security Intelligence'.[148]

[141] W. Riley, *Windyridge* (1913), p. 34.   [142] *Ibid.*, p. 177.

[143] See for example the series of articles published by the *Yorkshire Post* in February 1930 by Yorkshire novelists. One such, Gordon Stowell, complained angrily of 'the arrogant, ignorant pretence that London is the only town in the world, or at least the only place fit for the heroes of novels to live in. It is a form of snobbery not confined to literature. There are too many people who can only conceive of life outside the Metropolis in terms of agriculture or slums.' 19 February 1930.

[144] For example, J. L. Carr, *A Month in the Country* (Brighton, 1980).

[145] Mackenzie, *Whisky Galore*, p. 68.   [146] *Ibid.*, p. 163.   [147] *Ibid.*, p. 56.   [148] *Ibid.*, p. 201.

Much of the humorous potential of a novel like this, modest and dated though it now is, is contained in the relation between insider and outsider, and their respective regional associations. The use of dialect and of the Gaelic language reinforces this. It is worth recalling how such regional emphasis and approbation were reversed by Stella Gibbons. In *Cold Comfort Farm* the apparent distance between the rural and urban worlds was magnified: like a modern anthropologist, the urbane heroine finally leaves the earthbound churlish boors and returns to the metropolis by aeroplane.[149] In the novel's rural characterisation any suggestions of urban degeneracy and rural purity received short shrift. Joanna Godden, by contrast, was dismayed by the vulgar superficiality and rowdy triteness of the smoky London music hall, and sought rapid rural escape from it and from her little London clerk: 'I tell you, you ain't man enough for me'.[150] These themes have many forms and intentions, whether nationalistic, politically regionalistic, competitive, moral or gendered. Where they are found, their implied stance in fiction is usually in opposition to the standards and power of the metropolis, part of a long anti-centralist tradition, even if sometimes (as in *Whisky Galore*, with its Gaelic glossary) the novel appears to be partly directed to a metropolitan readership, and even if such fiction itself sometimes seems to acquiesce to a condescending understanding of the 'provincial'.

CONCLUSION

I have emphasised the remarkable absence of study of 'the regional novel'. To some extent I have accounted for this neglect by drawing attention to the fenced characteristics of the relevant academic disciplines, the way that their enclosures have developed, and how such development has been affected by cultural and political relations between the earlier metropolitan centre and the larger countries and regions of the British Isles. It is hard to conceive of a subject that has been more paralysed by disciplinary boundaries than the study of regional fiction. In the course of this introduction, certain themes and questions have emerged as being worth close attention. These are almost invariably of an interdisciplinary nature. The essays that follow have been written by leading literary critics, historians and geographers, and many further

---

[149] The novel was published in the same year as the famous photographs of Amy Johnson, before her flight to South Africa.
[150] Sheila Kaye-Smith, *Joanna Godden* (1921), pp. 285–98.

issues will arise from these analyses of selected aspects of the regional novel. The genre is today an even more widespread and international phenomenon than hitherto. Its artistic and regional diversity is certainly expanding, and its political relevance is conspicuous. Levels of readership are unprecedented. There is huge interest in regional authors from Hardy to Cookson, and thriving fluidity and reworking of the genre across various media. This most popular literary form can extend, confirm, deepen, question, refine or co-ordinate people's notions of belonging and region, affecting readers personally, and influencing their understanding of others. Above all, the issues of nationalism, centralism, regionalism and localism – of local distinctiveness or uniformity, and related questions about loyalties, personal identities and the meaning of 'community' – have rarely been so prominently discussed. What it is to be 'British' or 'Irish', and the issue of whether these are still relevant questions at all, now preoccupy a great many people. 'Britain' may be a political reality, but for many it is not a cultural one. There is perhaps a growing cultural and ecological sense that identity and senses of place can only be established locally or regionally, rather than nationally.

One sees here how literary analysis extends to matters of great private and public importance. In addition, there has been acceptance of self-reflexive attitudes in historical writing, as well as in fiction and autobiography. Fiction and non-fiction have now interpenetrated to the extent that we are seeing growing flexibility of form and a breakdown of conventional artistic and disciplinary boundaries. If the literary genre that concerns us is to be studied with the resourcefulness that it deserves, there must be academic open-mindedness, and inventive re-application of methods and questions found in the disciplines of literary criticism, cultural, regional and social history, cultural and media studies, geography and literary sociology. The many possibilities invite rethinking of disciplinary boundaries, adventurous approaches and fresh questions. I hope therefore that the scholarly essays of this book, and the extensive bibliographies of regional fiction due to follow, will help to promote creative, sympathetic and innovative approaches to the subject.

CHAPTER 2

Regionalism and nationalism: Maria Edgeworth, Walter Scott and the definition of Britishness

Liz Bellamy

The origins of the regional novel have conventionally been traced back to Maria Edgeworth and Walter Scott.[1] Yet Edgeworth's Ireland and Scott's Scotland are hardly regions comparable to Hardy's Wessex, Blackmore's Exmoor, or Arnold Bennett's potteries, for as well as being emotional or literary units, they are nations. I want to suggest, however, that the fact that the form of what we know as the regional novel was developed by writers exploring national rather than purely local or provincial cultures has important implications for the political status of the genre, and for the construction of literary histories of Ireland and Scotland.

Edgeworth and Scott responded in rather different ways to the peculiar histories of their respective countries, but many attempts have been made to develop broad generalisations about the two writers and the circumstances in which their regional works were produced.[2] This approach has the sanction of almost two centuries of criticism, and the parallel was originally drawn by Scott himself. In a well-known passage in the General Preface to the 1829 edition of *Waverley* he explained that one of the reasons for writing the novel was that he 'felt that something might be attempted for [his] own country, of the same kind with that which Miss Edgeworth so fortunately achieved for Ireland'. He therefore sought to produce 'something which might introduce her natives to those of the sister kingdom, in a more favourable light than they have been placed hitherto, and tend to procure sympathy for their virtues and indulgence for their foibles'.[3]

---

[1] George Watson, introduction to Maria Edgeworth, *Castle Rackrent: An Hibernian Tale* (1800; Oxford, 1964), p. vii; Avrom Fleishman, *The English Historical Novel: Walter Scott to Virginia Woolf* (London, 1971), p. 22.

[2] Anonymous review of *Waverley* in *The British Critic*, August 1814, no. 2, 189–211; Donald Davie, *The Heyday of Sir Walter Scott* (London, 1961), pp. 65–77; James M. Cahalan, *Great Hatred, Little Room: The Irish Historical Novel* (Syracuse, 1983), p. 2.

[3] Walter Scott, *Waverley, or, 'Tis Sixty Years Since*, Claire Lamont (ed.) (1813; Oxford, 1981), pp. 352–3. There is no authorised edition of Scott's novels. References to *Waverley* will be to the Oxford edition. References to other novels are to The Edinburgh Waverley (47 volumes) (Causewayside, 1902).

Scott's words can be read in the context of a prevalent early nineteenth-century belief that the Irish Act of Union of 1801 would follow the pattern established by the Union with Scotland of 1707. Comparisons between the condition of eighteenth-century Scotland and that of nineteenth-century Ireland were commonplace at the time at which Scott wrote, but the closeness of the comparison depended on the maintenance of a particular geographical as well as political perspective. It is from the point of view of the English – of those natives of the 'sister kingdom' to which, Scott suggests, not only his own works but Edgeworth's were directed[4] – that Scotland and Ireland can be seen to have comparable status. Implicit in Scott's reference to Edgeworth, and in the critical tendency to relate the writings of the two, is the suggestion that behind the notions of Irishness and Scottishness is the construction of an Englishness that constitutes the position of the reader. The novels are therefore identified as tacit explorations of what it is to be British, as well as what it is to be Scottish or Irish; they are explorations of colonialism, as well as of the cultures of the colonised.

IDEAS OF NATIONAL IDENTITY IN EIGHTEENTH-CENTURY BRITAIN

Framed by the two Acts of Union, punctuated by the Jacobite Risings of 1715 and 1745, and the Wolfe Tone Rebellion of 1798, the eighteenth century was a period in which issues of national identity were high on the political agenda. Within the nascent bourgeois culture there was considerable anxiety about manifestations of cultural and geographical diversity, particularly within the realm of language. Robert Crawford has indicated how the Enlightenment preoccupation with improvement and progress amongst Scottish writers such as Adam Smith, Adam Ferguson and John Millar generated an interest in the purification of English, and the removal of the primitive Scots or Gaelic voice, which ultimately led to the emergence of English Literature as a discipline within Scottish Universities.[5] At the same time, lexicographers such as Samuel Johnson sought to undermine the disintegrative potential of regional dialects and tongues, by establishing an invariant national vocabulary.[6] This was the declared motive for the publication

---

[4] Cf. Edgeworth, *Castle Rackrent*, pp. 96–7.
[5] Robert Crawford, *Devolving English Literature* (Oxford, 1992), pp. 16–43; see also Olivia Smith, *The Politics of Language 1791–1819* (Oxford, 1984).
[6] John Barrell, *English Literature in History, 1730–80: An Equal Wide Survey* (London, 1983), pp. 110–75.

in 1780 of the *General Dictionary of the English Language* by the Anglo-Irish Thomas Sheridan. The subtitle explained that *One main object of [the work] is, to establish a plain and permanent standard of pronunciation*, and Sheridan outlined in the preface the benefits that the nation would accrue from the fulfilment of his task. In his *Rhetorical Grammar of the English Language* he rhetorically apostrophised in the same vein:

Whether it would not greatly contribute to put an end to the odious distinction kept up between the subjects of the same king, if a way were opened by which the attainment of the English tongue in its purity, both in point of phraseology and pronunciation, might be rendered easy to all inhabitants of his Majesty's dominions, whether of South or North Britain, of Ireland, or the other British dependencies?[7]

In the episodic or picaresque novels of writers such as Henry Fielding or Tobias Smollett, the heroes were made to experience the range of characters that existed within a complex and diffuse society, but this representation of regional difference was underscored by an impulse towards the construction of a concept of national identity. Smollett was a lowland Scot,[8] and Fielding was the author of the *Jacobite's Journal*, utilising the spectre of Jacobitism to unify the country behind the administration. Both writers were therefore acutely aware of the extent and dangers of social and cultural difference within the state, but they also recognised how the threat of disunity and disintegration could serve to stimulate a sense of identity. Their novels represent at once the perception of diversity, and the desire for unity, that can be taken to characterise at least the first three-quarters of the eighteenth century.

By the end of their novels, the eponymous heroes of Fielding and Smollett are endowed with wealth and status. They have become gentlemen, and have thereby achieved a perspective which will enable them to make sense of the world through which they have travelled and suffered. Once they have become the standard against which others can be judged, they can identify as alien or other all departures from this norm. So while the world of the eighteenth-century picaresque novel is as richly diverse as the critical clichés claim, this diversity is structured around a search for ideas of national identity which would make it possible to explain and characterise a disparate and seemingly incomprehensible age.[9]

[7] Thomas Sheridan, *A Rhetorical Grammar of the English Language* (Dublin, 1781), Preface, xv–xvi.
[8] See Crawford, *Devolving English Literature*, pp. 55–75.
[9] Cf. Barrell, *English Literature in History*, pp. 179–209.

Towards the end of the eighteenth century it is possible to detect a certain lessening in the insistence of the impulse towards the national within the interest in the regional or local. The 'topographic' poems of the sixteenth, seventeenth and early eighteenth centuries have conventionally been read as vehicles for the exploration of aristocratic, and therefore national, values.[10] But by the end of the eighteenth century there was an increasing interest in the local, the vernacular, and in the symbols of cultural difference. This was manifest in the upsurge of interest in local history, archaeology, folklore, folksong and dialect that was satirised by Scott in *The Antiquary*. The cult of primitivism maintained the idea that rural society was some kind of 'other', but the other was sanitised into a romantic ideal which could challenge the values of the present, instead of being a dangerous and destabilising force. In Ireland this interest in the indigenous culture corresponded with the golden years of the Ascendancy.[11] The protestant landowners, self confident in their rapidly expanding Georgian capital, looked out to the provinces and cultivated an interest in things Irish which served in part to legitimise their colonial role.

Under the penal statutes of the 1690s the majority Catholic population was virtually excluded from the ownership of land, and Catholics were debarred from holding public office by the Test Act of 1673. Edmund Burke characterised the penal laws as 'a machine of wise and elaborate contrivance; and as well fitted for the oppression, impoverishment and degradation of a people, and the debasement, in them, of human nature itself, as ever proceeded from the perverted ingenuity of man'.[12] But in late eighteenth-century Dublin, the burgeoning interest in an Anglicised version of Gaelic culture gave the dominant English-speaking classes a sense that they had some understanding of the land over which they ruled. In 1776 the actor Robert Owenson (father of Sydney Morgan) had been criticised by *The Freeman's Journal* for singing the savage and guttural songs of Connaught.[13] By 1786 the publication of Joseph Cooper Walker's *Historical Memoirs of the Irish Bards* was greeted with considerable critical and social acclaim, and was followed by Charlotte Brooke's *Reliques of Irish Poetry* of 1789, Edward Bunting's *The Ancient Music of Ireland* of 1796, and Thomas Moore's extensively

---

[10] Raymond Williams, *The Country and the City* (London, 1975), pp. 40–7
[11] Thomas Flanagan, *The Irish Novelists, 1800–1850* (New York, 1959), p. 111.
[12] Edmund Burke, Letter to Sir Hercules Languishe, in *The Works of Edmund Burke* (London, 1826), vol. 6, p. 375.
[13] Flanagan, *Irish Novelists*, p. 111.

Anglicised *Irish Melodies* of 1808. In 1792 the vigorously Presbyterian city of Belfast hosted a festival of Irish harp music.

In Scotland, the gradual fading of memories of the Jacobite risings, and the progress of the Highland clearances, encouraged the celebration of the culture of the clans, epitomised most famously in the pan-European popularity of James MacPherson's versions of the Ossianic legends. The primitive simplicity of the Highlander's life began to be romanticised as an indictment of the complexity of commercial society, while the political philosophers and economists of the Scottish Lowlands developed models to suggest that the destruction of this way of life was inevitable.[14] At the same time Robert Burns developed a poetry which was identified as an authentic Scottish voice, even though modern commentators have discerned a bastard blend of English, Scots and invented idiom.[15]

MARIA EDGEWORTH

Although the regional novel needs to be seen against this background of general interest in 'folk culture', the terms of its portrayal of national character and colonial conflict ensured that it fulfilled rather more complex functions than the legitimation of a dominant colonial class. This is particularly evident in Edgeworth's *Castle Rackrent*, a novel which discloses the inapplicability of simple models of the colonial relationship to nineteenth-century Ireland, and explores the role of literature within a colonial context.[16] Although the cultural lions of eighteenth-century Dublin were anxious to display their acquaintance with the airs and legends of their native bogs, outside the protestant strongholds the landowners were rather less confident of their position within a population of alien values and different religion. The cultural imperialism of the polite societies for the study of Gaelic was juxtaposed against the nervous uncertainty of the Protestant militias, manifested in their brutal

---

[14] Adam Ferguson, *Essay on the History of Civil Society* (1767), Duncan Forbes (ed.) (Edinburgh, 1966); David Hume, 'Of Refinement in the Arts', in *Essays, Moral, Political and Literary* (1777), T. H. Green and T. H. Grose (ed.) (1874–5, 1882, 1889), revised with variant readings, Eugene F. Miller (ed.) (Indianapolis, 1985).

[15] Carol McGuirk, *Robert Burns and the Sentimental Era* (Athens, Georgia, 1985), p. xxii; Raymond Bentman, *Robert Burns* (Boston, 1987), p. i.

[16] There has been no collected edition of Maria Edgeworth's novels in this century. References to *Castle Rackrent* are to the Oxford edition. References to other works are to the Longford Edition of the *Tales and Novels*, 10 vols. (Manchester and New York, 1893).

suppression of the United Irishmen, and in the foundation of the Orange Orders.[17] *Castle Rackrent* embodies this ambivalent attitude towards indigenous culture, but it also embodies the often equally ambivalent position of the Irish landowners.

Notwithstanding a number of critical representations, *Rackrent* does not portray a simple relationship between protestant Anglo-Irish landowners and their Irish retainers.[18] The novel's narrator, Old Thady Quirk, explains that 'the family of the Rackrents is . . . one of the most ancient in the kingdom. – Every body knows this is not the old family name, which was O'Shaughlin, related to the Kings of Ireland', but on the death of Sir Tallyhoo Rackrent the estate passed into the hands of Sir Patrick O'Shaughlin 'upon one condition, which Sir Patrick O'Shaughlin at the time took sadly to heart, they say, but thought better of it afterwards, seeing how large a stake depended on it, that he should, by Act of Parliament, take and bear the sirname and arms of Rackrent'.[19] The implication of this passage is that Sir Patrick O'Shaughlin was obliged to change not only his name but also his religion. As a scion of one of the oldest families in Ireland, he converted to protestantism in order to inherit the Rackrent estate. So that, while in some respects the Rackrents represent the class of protestant landowners, their origins are in the old Irish catholic gentry. They are in the anomalous position that was to be explored in Anthony Trollope's *The Macdermots of Ballycloran*, and insofar as they can be classed as Anglo-Irish, they embody the crisis of identity that characterised many within that group.

The first Rackrent we meet, Sir Patrick, is celebrated by Thady as the upholder of the traditional behaviour of the Irish overlord – he is a thoughtlessly extravagant drunken glutton. His son, Sir Murtagh, is of a rather different cast, and Thady ruefully recounts how under him 'the cellars were never filled . . . and no open house or anything as it used to be – the tenants even were sent away without their whiskey – I was ashamed myself, and knew not what to say for the honor of the family' (p. 12). Yet it would not really be correct to characterise Sir Murtagh as a more progressive or more Anglicised landlord than his father. He is intimately involved in the administration of the estate,

---

[17] David Cairns and Shaun Richards, *Writing Ireland: Colonialism, Nationalism and Culture* (Manchester, 1988), p. 24.

[18] See, for example, Robert Tracy's introduction to the Oxford edition of Anthony Trollope, *The Macdermots of Ballycloran* (Oxford, 1989), p. xiii; Flanagan, *Irish Novelists*, p. 67.

[19] Edgeworth, *Rackrent*, pp. 8–9. Subsequent references will be incorporated in the text.

but his preoccupation is not with efficiency or innovation, but rather
with the exploitation of the rights and levies enshrined in customary
Irish tenancies:

He was always driving and driving, and pounding and pounding, and canting
and canting, and replevying and replevying, and he made a good living of
trespassing cattle – there was always some tenant's pig, or horse, or cow, or
calf, or goose, trespassing, which was so great a gain to Sir Murtagh, that he
did not like to hear me talk of repairing fences. Then his herriot and duty
work brought him in something – his turf was cut – his potatoes set and dug
– his hay brought home, and in short all the work about his house done for
nothing; for in all our leases there were strict clauses with heavy penalties,
which Sir Murtagh knew well how to enforce. (pp. 14–5)

The next in line, Sir Kit Rackrent, commences his career as an absentee,
gambling away his rents in Bath, and leaving the management of the
estate to his agent. After attempting to repair his fortunes in a marriage
to a rich Jewess, he returns to Ireland to imprison and oppress his wife.
Both he and his successor, Sir Condy, can be taken to symbolise the
negligence of the Anglo-Irish elite in their failure to play any part in the
administration of their lands, and the estate is gradually engrossed by
the swindling and acquisitive agent. But the great irony of *Rackrent* is
that the agent, who, if the novel can be taken as embodying any kind of
historical dialectic must be taken as the representative of the new, com-
mercially minded class, is none other than Jason Quirk, son of the faithful
(and Catholic) old retainer, Thady. Behind the genial irresponsibility
of the improvident Sir Condy Rackrent, who never pays his tradesmen's
bills, can be read a heartless exploitation of the trading classes that is
explored in detail in Edgeworth's moral tale *The Dun*. But in *Rackrent* it
is not the unpaid craftsmen or the rackrented tenants who are portrayed
as the victims, but rather the landowners themselves, as the Rackrent
estate is gradually taken over by the increasingly wealthy, powerful and
assertive Jason Quirk.

Few of the Anglo-Irish families could trace their origins back to the
Old Irish families as the Rackrents do, but many had been in Ireland
for a considerable time, and had adopted some of the ways of the place.
Thomas Flanagan has written of the cultural divide in nineteenth-
century Ireland that:

On one side stood 'native' Ireland. It had become a nation of peasants,
fiercely Catholic, indifferent or hostile to statute law, Gaelic-speaking or at
least heavily influenced by the traditions of Gaelic society, nourished by dark

and sanguinary resentments and aspirations. On the other side stood the nation of the Anglo-Irish, land-owning, Protestant, and, of course English-speaking. Though this nation aspired, intermittently, to political independence, in point of fact, its culture and its modes of thought were indisputably English.[20]

Flanagan delineates the picture of Irish 'Barbarism' which Seamus Deane has identified as characteristic of English representation over three centuries.[21] Yet despite Edgeworth's position as a member of the culturally oppressive colonial class, her formulation of the uncertainty of Irish identity undermines the simple distinction between dominant and subservient culture, and underlines the complexity of the impact of colonialism on language and literature.[22] While the voice of Edgeworth's landowners is not authentically Irish in Flanagan's terms, Edgeworth suggests that it is certainly not English either. The Anglo-Irish exist in a cultural no-man's land, rejected by the English for their Irishness, and by the Irish for their Englishness. This point is dramatised in *The Absentee*, where the desperate attempts of Lady Clonbrony to become accepted in London society only serve to reinforce the extent of her Irishness, while her husband's intemperate habits are identified as vulgarity.[23]

The Absentee is an appeal to the Anglo-Irish to embrace their responsibilities as landowners, but also to embrace a 'polite' and sanitised version of Irish culture. As such it functions to legitimate the social and economic dominance of the protestant elite,[24] but complementary to this project is a genuine search for a cultural identity. Edgeworth sought to resolve that feeling of cultural displacement which characterised her class, and which was experienced so strongly by Jonathan Swift. Swift always felt like an Irishman in England and an Englishman in Ireland, and constructed various accounts of his birth and early years which manifested his ambivalent attitude to his native land.[25]

In *Ennui* and *The Absentee*, Edgeworth exposed the misery that she believed resulted from the negligence of absentee landowners, and set out a fictional blueprint for the efficient and paternalistic organisation

[20] Flanagan, *Irish Novelists*, pp. 35–6.
[21] Seamus Deane, 'Civilians and Barbarians', in Field Day Theatre Company, *Ireland's Field Day* (London, 1985), pp. 33–42, p. 33.
[22] For an analysis of the cultural impact of colonialism see Terry Eagleton, Fredric Jameson and Edward Said, *Nationalism, Colonialism and Literature* (Minneapolis, Minnesota, 1990).
[23] Maria Edgeworth, *The Absentee* (1812), *Tales and Novels*, volume 6, pp. 1–2, 21–2.
[24] Cairns, *Writing Ireland*, pp. 20–1.
[25] David Nokes, *Jonathan Swift, A Hypocrite Reversed: A Critical Biography* (Oxford, 1985), pp. 5–9.

of an Irish estate. In *Rackrent*, however, and to some extent in *Ormond*, she sought to explore the essence of the Ireland of the landed estate. In doing so she did not participate in the construction of a bourgeois counter culture, nor did she contribute directly to the cultural hegemony of the colonisers. For while in relation to the peasantry, the Anglo-Irish might be seen to constitute a class of colonial exploiters, in relation to the English they could be seen as the colonised – an alien other sharing much of the culture and assumptions of their tenantry. The cleverness of the basic text of *Rackrent* lies in the fact that the fictional perspective is that of the reader. We are expected to read through the words of Thady, and put our own construction on the actions of the Rackrents, and on Thady's attitude to them. And this is a far more complex process than might at first be imagined.

Thady's narrative is more than merely a transparent device to convey an authorial line, and can be seen as fundamentally ambiguous. The reader has to decide to what extent Thady is the credulous old retainer that he would have us suppose. To what extent has he connived at the actions of his son in ruining his masters? Is the ultimate irony that Thady, far from being the representative of an alien and bygone era, is connected by more than blood to the new acquisitive society, and shares the reader's mockery of the system of deference and blind obedience that his tale appears to embody? It is certainly the case that Thady is instrumental in bringing down the Rackrents (pp. 58–9), and there are numerous occasions where the irony of his words appears to be conscious rather than unconscious (e.g. pp. 61–2).

While the ironic structure creates a sense of readerly independence, the location of the novel in the exploration of the character of the Irish landed elite suggests that the posited reader is an interested outsider, someone who can provide a judicious and impartial assessment that will be in striking contrast to the narrative of Thady. S/he is, as Walter Scott recognised, an inhabitant of England rather than Ireland. Edgeworth is not so much writing with an English voice, as writing for English ears.

The popularity of *Rackrent* needs to be seen not merely in the context of an Anglo-Irish desire to legitimise its position, but also in relation to an English desire to legitimise the assumption of control over Irish affairs by the parliament in Westminster. *Rackrent* serves to satisfy this desire by constructing an image of the Irish landowner that will help the English to feel that they understand the nature of the Irish. 'What what', said George III, on reading the novel 'I know something now of my Irish subjects' – or so Richard Lovell Edgeworth claimed.[26] But *Rackrent* went beyond introducing the Irish landowner to the natives of the sister kingdom, for Edgeworth used her considerable satirical powers to present the Irish in such a way as virtually to justify the removal of political influence from their hands. The Rackrents are feckless, thoughtless and improvident, and entirely lacking in political integrity. The novel has an elegiac tone but it also suggests that this is a world well lost. The foibles of the Rackrents may be satirised because they no longer pose a direct threat, having been undermined by the combined actions of Jason Quirk and the Act of Union.

The historical processes represented within the book's plot were further embodied in the circumstances of its publication and reception. As the Irish became full subjects of the British monarchy, so they also became the subject matter of an English ruling class. This ethnographic or anthropological aspect was brought out by the addition of the Glossary to the basic text of *Rackrent* in 1799. This contained a mass of information on Irish manners and language which Maria and Richard Edgeworth felt would be of interest to their English readers. Marilyn Butler has suggested that the glossary was added as 'a means of introducing more serious sociological information about Ireland' because the novel itself did not represent a clash of values of the kind portrayed by Scott in *Waverley*.[27] This may be true in the sense that the complexities of the relationship between the Rackrents and the Quirks ensure that the conflict between the two does not constitute a true dialectic, but a clash of values is nonetheless present within the novel in the juxtaposition of the ideology of the Rackrents, not with that of Jason Quirk, but with that of the implied reader. The process of reading is necessarily a process of historicising the Rackrents. As such the novel fulfils a very different function from *The Wild Irish Girl* of Sydney Morgan, with which it is occasionally compared.

Morgan's heroine, Glorvina, is a romanticised remnant of the Old Irish nobility, living in a picturesque ruined castle with her father 'the Prince'. Glorvina is ultimately able to regain her ancestral lands, through marriage to the son of a protestant absentee who has become a devotee of Irish culture. This unproblematic union of Ireland with England provided an allegorical celebration of the political union while it suppressed the hegemonic implications of the latter act. As such it can

---

[26] George Watson, introduction to *Rackrent*, p. xvii.
[27] Marilyn Butler, *Maria Edgeworth: A Literary Biography* (Oxford, 1972), pp. 356–8.

be seen as a sentimental distortion of the recurrent image of Gaelic folk tradition which represents Ireland as an impoverished woman, raped and betrayed by a wealthy nobleman, who symbolises England. This long established trope of Dark Rosaleen and Kathleen ni Houlihan was picked up by Swift in his prose allegory, *The Story of an Injured Lady*. It is also invoked in Anthony Trollope's first novel, *The Macdermots of Ballycloran*, in which Feemy Macdermot, the young and credulous daughter of a ruined and demented representative of the Old Irish elite, is seduced by the dashing Captain Ussher, protestant upholder of British law. Edgworth's image of Ireland lacks the bitterness of Trollope's portrait of cultural conflict and change, but it goes beyond Morgan's evocation of harmonious marriage to embody some of the tensions and complexities of the colonial relationship.

SIR WALTER SCOTT

Scott's publishing history demonstrates the location of his work in the oral, vernacular tradition of the Scottish borders. His early efforts collecting ballads for his *Minstrelsy of the Scottish Borders* led to the composition of ballads of his own, such as *The Lay of the Last Minstrel*, and ultimately to the construction of a version of Scottish cultural identity in the *Waverley* series of novels. But Scott was not a straightforward romantic, harking back to an earlier, simple age. Virginia Woolf is said to have described him as 'the last minstrel and the first chairman of the Edinburgh oil gas company', and for all its mock medieval charm, Scott's house at Abbotsford was one of the first in the country to be lit by gas lighting.[28]

In the Victorian period Scott tended to be seen as a fairly uncomplicated figure who presented a nostalgic evocation of a pre-commercial past.[29] But this image was overturned first by George Lukács and later by David Daiches. Coming from rather different political perspectives, these writers highlighted the concept of historical process which lay within the novels.[30] Lukács emphasised Scott's role as an historical novelist, showing how his utilisation of mediocre heroes (often previously

[28] A. N. Wilson, *The Laird of Abbotsford: A View of Sir Walter Scott* (Oxford, 1980), pp. 55–6.
[29] See John O. Hayden (ed.), *Scott: The Critical Heritage* (London, 1970).
[30] David Daiches, 'Scott's Achievement as a Novelist', in *Literary Essays* (Oliver and Boyd Ltd., 1956) reprinted in D. D. Devlin (ed.) *Walter Scott: Modern Judgements* (London, 1968), pp. 33–62; Georg Lukács, *The Historical Novel* (1937), H. and S. Mitchell (trans.) (London, 1962), pp. 30–63.

identified as one of his main weaknesses) enabled him to present the effects and implications of the social revolution of the rise of commercial society. David Daiches argued in a similar vein that:

Underlying most of these novels is a tragic sense of the inevitability of a drab but necessary progress, a sense of the impotence of the traditional kind of heroism, a passionately regretful awareness of the fact that the Good Old Cause was lost forever and the glory of Scotland must give way to her interest.[31]

These essays stimulated a general review of Scott's literary status, and, despite a few dissenting voices, encouraged a widespread acceptance of the image of Scott as an important historical novelist. In this essay I want to examine the implications of translating the terms of the Lukács/ Daiches analysis into the debates over Scott's role as a regional writer, and his relationship to the literature of nationalism and colonialism. For while Scott's celebration of the society of the past can be seen to be coloured by an acceptance of the changes of the present, it is also possible to see that his presentation of indigenous culture has been affected by a recognition that this culture has been subsumed within a larger social and political entity.

Scott's Scottish novels typically begin with the portrayal of a young, talented, but impressionable hero, anxious to escape from the humdrum existence and learn something of life. This figure, characterised by Lukács as a 'more or less mediocre, average English gentleman',[32] finds his way from England to Scotland, or from metropolitan or civilised lowland Scotland to either the Borders or the Highlands, so that the process by which he comes to know himself and life becomes tied up with the process of getting to know a countryside in which he is a stranger, but to which he usually has some kind of emotional or ancestral tie. The hero then finds himself enmeshed in a series of events (either historic or fictional) which can be seen to symbolise the clash between the old traditional culture and the structures and systems of a new commercial society.

The conflict between the Jacobite cause and the Hanoverian regime served, in particular, as the supreme example of this cultural clash, and provided the vehicle for what Lukács identified as a dialectical affirmation of the middle way.[33] In the portrayal of the 1715 rising in

---

[31] Daiches, 'Scott's Achievement', p. 36. [32] Lukács, *Historical Novel*, p. 33.
[33] Walter Scott, introduction to *Redgauntlet: A Tale of the Eighteenth Century*, *Waverley Novels*, vols. 35 and 36, vol. 35, p. xi; Lukács, *Historical Novel*, pp. 53–5 and *passim*.

Rob Roy, the 1745 revolt in *Waverley*, and the fictional and doomed conspiracy portrayed in *Redgauntlet*, the hero has to confront first the nature and appeal of traditional cultures and values, then the strength and inescapability of the forces of modernity that are destroying the old order. The process by which he resolves this conflict symbolises the process of history itself. The point that cultural critics have to settle is precisely how this resolution is formulated. What is the nature of the 'middle way'? Does the moral message lean towards the present? Or does it lean towards the past? Do the novels celebrate the culture of the local community? Or do they accept the destruction of this culture in the face of an emergent concept of national identity? On the whole critics assessing the historical perspective have emphasised the final commitment to the forces of modernity,[34] whereas when critics have assessed the attitude towards local and national culture, they have tended to emphasise the importance of regional tradition.[35]

The schema outlined above is, of course, a gross oversimplification of the variations and complexities in the plots of Scott's various novels. The attitude to events is complicated by the use of a range of mediating narrative perspectives, and the precise period of the historical setting has a considerable influence over the way that Scott weights the balance of power between the forces of old and new. The location of the novels affects the terms of the portrayal of character, in that the wildness of the Borders is rather different from that of the Highlands, or the Shetlands portrayed in *The Pirate*. Nonetheless it is possible to detect considerable common ground not only within the Scottish novels, but also in works such as *Anne of Geierstein* and *The Talisman*. Local and regional culture are not so much explored for their own sake as used as vehicles for the analysis of certain themes and ideas about the nature of social change, the process of cultural imperialism, and the relationship between local and national character. These issues are embodied, in some degree, within the essential structure that forms the basis for so many of Scott's narratives.

In the eighteenth-century fictional tradition of Fielding and Smollett, the hero leaves the safe community of the countryside, and journeys through the dangerous and morally unstable world of the town, before finding his place in the country estate. Scott's heroes share the sense of

---

[34] Fleishman, *English Historical Novel*, pp. 100–101; Cahalan, *Great Hatred*, p. 5; David Brown, *Walter Scott and the Historical Imagination* (London, 1979), pp. 204–5; Daiches, 'Scott's Achievement', p. 36.

[35] P. H. Scott, *Walter Scott and Scotland* (Edinburgh, 1981), p. 90.

dispossession that characterised their picaresque predecessors, but they journey in the opposite direction. The plot structure has undergone a very significant reversal. Edward Waverley, Francis Osbaldistone, Darsie Latimer, Guy Mannering etc. set out from a complex, commercial society which may be conceived as restrictive, but is ultimately comprehensible and reassuring, and journey through an unstable rural environment which does not adhere to the established rules of the civilised community. The heroes have to comprehend a new set of values and givens before they can return to the modern world, and accept, with a new understanding, its nature and structure. This is not to say that they necessarily return to take up residence in the counting house or the tenement block. The final resolution is usually a return to the same environment that creates a sense of order in the eighteenth-century novel – the country house with its estate, and its established social hierarchy. But the country house in Scott's novels is clearly identified as part of the civilised commercial state. It gains its meaning and its security through its connection with the exchange network, and is a world away from the society of the Highlands or the lawless Borders, where social status is measured by power rather than by property.

Scott is well aware of the appeal of the primitive, pre-commercial society, and the image he constructs draws heavily on the models of the Scottish school of philosophers. As Waverley approaches Glennaquoich, the redoubt of the Highland chieftain, Fergus Mac-Ivor:

There was a sight . . . before the gate, which perhaps would have afforded the first owner of Blenheim more pleasure than the finest view of the domain assigned to him by the gratitude of his country. This consisted of about an hundred Highlanders, in complete dress and arms; at sight of whom the chieftain apologized to Waverley in a sort of negligent manner. 'He had forgot' he said, 'that he had ordered a few of his clan out, for the purpose of seeing that they were in a fit condition to protect the country'.[36]

Waverley then attends a vast feast, shared by all the clansmen, from the chief at the head of the table to the humblest peasants at the end:

Mac-Ivor, indeed, apologized for the confusion occasioned by so large a party, and pleaded the necessity of his situation, on which unlimited hospitality was imposed as a paramount duty. 'These stout idle kinsmen of mine' he said 'account my estate as held in trust for their support; and I must find them beef and ale, while the rogues will do nothing for themselves but practise the

---

[36] Scott, *Waverley*, p. 94. Subsequent references in text.

broadsword, or wander about the hills, shooting, fishing, hunting, drinking and making love to the lasses of the strath. (p. 97)

This is the organic, primitive community described by Adam Ferguson in his *Essay on the History of Civil Society* as part of a debate about the relationship between the primitive and the civilized which Robert Crawford has identified as particularly pertinent to Scottish culture.[37] The heroic code of values embodied in *Waverley* in the figures of Fergus Mac-Ivor and his sister Flora, forms a striking contrast to the complex political and administrative systems of the commercial state. It is Waverley's romantic fascination with Highland culture, combined with the apparently arbitrary injustice of the British army, which encourages his desertion to the Jacobite cause. Waverley journeys into the Highland landscape of Glennaquoich, to learn about the people and their manners, but he then accompanies the Highlanders in their movement south, as they attempt to overthrow the established government.

As the fortunes of the insurrectionists begin to wane following the retreat of the Jacobite forces from Derby, the strength of Waverley's commitment to the cause is increasingly put into question. This is dramatised by Scott through the juxtaposition of the character of Fergus Mac-Ivor with Colonel Talbot. Crawford has suggested that Talbot symbolises 'oppressive prejudice', particularly because of his imperialistic dismissal of the Scots tongue as 'gibberish'.[38] Yet although the initial presentation of Talbot is unprepossessing, he becomes an increasingly sympathetic figure, as his staid and prosaic dependability are contrasted with the mercurial Mac-Ivor:

Colonel Talbot was in every point the English soldier. His whole soul was devoted to the service of his king and country . . . Added to this, he was a man of extended knowledge and cultivated taste, although strongly tinged with those prejudices which are peculiarly English. (p. 246)

Despite his position as prisoner, Talbot exerts increasing influence over Waverley's mind. As Mac-Ivor is shown to be singlemindedly thoughtless almost to the point of cruelty (p. 238), Talbot comes to symbolise the solid and reliable values of the modern state. As the undisciplined heroism and irrascibility of the Highlanders begins to undermine their endeavour, the discipline of the British troops is revealed as a manifestation not of mindless regimentation, but of thoughtful humanity. Waverley and Talbot together uncover a trail of deceit which shows

---

[37] Crawford, *Devolving English Literature*, p. 16.   [38] *Ibid.*, p. 130.

that the former's dismissal from the army was a consequence not of British high-handedness, but of the treachery which the Jacobites regard as a legitimate weapon in their campaign. Waverley is left paying only lip service to the justice of the venture in which he is engaged (p. 258).

Waverley's recognition of the inapplicability and even undesirability of the Highland way of life is tinged with romantic regret, but it is also accompanied by a more positive appreciation of the values of complex society. With the execution of Fergus Mac-Ivor and his faithful retainer Evan dhu Maccombich we are led to feel that an unfortunate era has been brought to a close. Mac-Ivor himself, when condemned to death, can look forward to a time 'when there are no longer any wild High-landers' (p. 326), and while there is some implicit censure of the barbarity of the punishment for treason, there is also a sense that this was the inevitable end for such anachronistic figures. When offered the chance of pardon by the judge, the response of Evan dhu is an assertion of the brutal Highland values, and an illustration of the impossibility of reconciling them with the judicial institutions of the complex state:

'Grace me no Grace', said Evan; 'since you are to shed Vich Ian Vohr's [Fergus'] blood, the only favour I would accept from you, is bid them loose my hands and gie me my claymore, and bide you just a minute sitting where you are.' (p. 321)

This may be heroism, but it is heroism of an anachronistic and un-desirable cast. It is not to this that we look at the end of the novel for stability and resolution. Like Waverley, we are expected to come down from the Highlands, and recognise the way that the progress of society has transformed the ethical code and the idea of public virtue. Waverley's ontogeny reproduces phylogeny. His experience demon-strates how society has moved away from an ethos of heroic individu-alism, towards a more corporate system, based on the interdependence of the parts within a complex whole. The regional culture of Highland society is shown to have been superseded by more civilised, national – British – codes of behaviour, and the structures and institutions of the complex commercial state. For from being the 'target' of the text,[39] the English officers, Colonel Talbot and Major Melville, almost end up as the heroes. They do not seek egregious eminence, but rather aim to play their part within the institution of the British army. Their

[39] *Ibid.*

example is far more appropriate to the undistinguished and easy-going Waverley, than that of the redoubtable Chief of Glennaquoich. The end of the novel, with the union of Rose Bradwardine and Edward Waverley, of the estates of Scottish Tully-Veolan and English Waverley Honour, overseen by Colonel Talbot and Major Melville, provides an allegorical idealisation of the Union of Scotland with England.

The main themes and ideas of *Waverley* are reaffirmed and reworked in *Rob Roy*, where the conflict between ancient and modern values is represented in terms of a Highland/Lowland as much as Scottish/English clash. The English hero, Frank Osbaldistone, is confronted with two images of Scotland, the heroic Jacobite outlaw, Rob Roy, and the honest Glasgow merchant, Bailie Nichol Jarvie. Jarvie is proud of his Scottish origins and his Highland ancestry, and suspicious of English ways, but his interest in commercial prosperity makes him an enthusiastic supporter of the Act of Union and the spread of those economic ties that will bind the two countries together. He emphasises the distinction between the heroic and the commercial ethos in his words to Osbaldistone that:

'I maun hear naething about honour – we ken naething here but about credit. Honour is a homicide and a bloodspiller, that gangs about making frays in the street; but credit is a decent honest man, that sits at home and makes the pat play'.[40]

Jarvie is a comic character, with his Glaswegian accent and dialect, and his plans to drain and 'improve' the picturesque Highland lakes, but he nonetheless embodies values of loyalty, honesty and integrity. In the course of the novel, these virtues are shown to be backed up by physical strength, and a cautious courage and generosity. As the symbol of the new morality, the stout bailie lacks the romance of his mysterious kinsman, Rob Roy, but his 'credit' is shown to be a surer route to happiness than the bloody honour of the Highlanders, and a more appropriate code for an essentially unheroic age.

Duncan Forbes has indicated the connection between Scott's rationalist model of social progress, and the Enlightenment tradition of philosophy and political economy that he imbibed during his education in Edinburgh.[41] This insight into the theoretical basis of Scott's work was to some extent anticipated by Walter Bagehot. Bagehot observed that:

[40] Walter Scott, *Rob Roy*, *Waverley Novels*, vol. 8, p. 122.
[41] Duncan Forbes, 'The Rationalism of Sir Walter Scott', *Cambridge Journal*, 7 (1953), pp. 17–32.

When Sir Walter's own works come to be closely examined, they will be found to contain a good deal of political economy of a certain sort – and not a very bad sort. Any one who will study his description of the Highland clans in *Waverley*; his observation on the industrial side (if so it is to be called) of the Border life; his plans for dealing with the poor of his own time, – will be struck not only with a plain sagacity, which we could equal in England, but with the digested accuracy and theoretical completeness which they show. You might cut paragraphs, even from his lighter writings, which would be thought acute in the *Wealth of Nations*.[42]

In Scott as in Adam Smith, romantic and philosophical regrets over the lost values of an earlier, simpler age are portrayed as understandable, but ultimately pointless. We cannot go back to an age based on the exchange of deer and beavers,[43] and society cannot be run like a Highland clan. Indeed, in some of Scott's bleaker novels, such as *Redgauntlet* and *The Bride of Lammermoor*, the redundancy of the heroic ethos is exposed in terms that display its inherent undesirability.

In *The Bride of Lammermoor*, the values espoused by the old and now impoverished family of Ravenswood are shown to be brutal and vengeful, but Scott also destroys the myth of the organic community by exposing the exploitation of the peasantry that lay at the heart of the concept of feudal dependence. The old retainer of the young Lord Ravenswood, Caleb Balderstone, attempts to maintain the 'honour of the family' by repeated exactions from the villagers of Wolf's Hope. But although the inhabitants 'paid a kind of hereditary respect to the Lords of Ravenswood' they:

Had contrived to get feu-rights to their little possessions, their huts, kail-yards, and rights of commonty, so that they were emancipated from the chains of feudal dependence, and free from the various exactions with which, under every possible pretext, or without any pretext at all, the Scottish landlords of the period [around 1710] themselves in great poverty, were wont to harass their still poorer tenants at will.[44]

The villagers of Wolf's Hope are able to seek redress against continued levies through a legal system which, while often arbitrary and unjust, is identified as a mechanism for the institution of social order and justice. The perspective of the narrative voice not only emphasises the benefits of this system of law, but also identifies it as a product of the Union of Scotland with England. The Lord Keeper, Sir William Ashton, who

[42] Walter Bagehot, *Collected Works* (1965), pp. 416–19.
[43] Adam Smith, *An Inquiry into the Nature and Causes of the Wealth of Nations*, Book I, chapter 6.
[44] Walter Scott, *The Bride of Lammermoor* (1819), *Waverley Novels*, vol. 14, pp. 184–5.

has taken over the Ravenswood estate, expresses anxiety lest his loss of political influence should lead to the loss of his lawsuit:

Judging, though most inaccurately, from courts which he had himself known in the unhappy times preceding the Scottish Union, the Keeper might have too much right to think that, in the House to which his lawsuits were to be transferred, the old maxim might prevail in Scotland which was too well recognised in former times – 'show me the man, and I'll show you the law'. The high and unbiassed character of English judicial proceedings was then little known in Scotland, and the extension of them to that country was one of the most valuable advantages which it gained by the Union.[45]

The judicial system, like the British army, may have its problems and iniquities, but it is represented as a fundamentally stable institution which spreads itself through a formerly diverse society, bringing order and a degree of harmony. Scott's model of social progress emphasises the homogenising effect of recent political and economic changes. He sees himself as charting systems of manners and morals which have now disappeared,[46] and this ethnographic function was recognised by contemporary reviewers. An anonymous review of *Waverley* in *The British Critic* noted that the work was not to be considered as a common novel, but as:

A vehicle of curious accurate information upon a subject which must at all times demand our attention – the history and manners of a very, very large and renowned portion of the inhabitants of these islands; of a race who, within these few years, have vanished from the face of their native land.[47]

The regional novel developed by Scott was located in a time of historical crisis, in which regional identity could be shown to be threatened by a hegemonic national culture. The fact that the moment of demise was identified at various different historical junctures comes as no surprise, since regional culture is firmly placed on that historical escalator which Raymond Williams identified as bearing images of the rural past. The escalator is always moving, and 'Old England' is always behind us, just a generation away.[48] And sitting next to it can be discerned the lean figure of 'Old Scotland', always on the point of being crushed by its more prosperous and assertive neighbour.

---

[45] Scott, *Bride*, p. 231.   [46] Scott, *Waverley*, p. 340.
[47] Anon., *The British Critic*, August 1814, 2, pp. 189–211. A similar point was made by Francis Jeffrey in *The Edinburgh Review*, November 1814, 24, pp. 208–43.
[48] Williams, *The Country and the City*, pp. 18–20.

The regional novel is thus inseparable from the historical novel; the terms of Scott's celebration of Scottish tradition constitute an elegy on its destruction. This was necessitated by Scott's dialectic narrative method, but it was also in part due to the fact that local and regional diversity could only be a subject of polite enjoyment when it was no longer perceived as a threat. In the century in which the Jacobite risings actually occurred, the emphasis was on a Britishness that suppressed national difference. It was only with the growing sense of the economic strength and political coherence of the British state that came in the nineteenth century, that the disparate characteristics of the constituent nations could be romanticised.

It was only when the Hanoverians were entirely confident of 'the fidelity of the millions' that they could exercise clemency towards the last remaining scheming Jacobites, forcing Redgauntlet to exclaim that 'the cause is lost for ever'.[49] In the same way, the evolution of the regional novel stands as a symptom of the emergence of a sense of British identity confident enough to seek legitimation in the propagation of images of Irishness and Scottishness. Implicit in the texts is the concept that these national characters have been subsumed within the normative perspective of a Britishness which is often equated with Englishness. The fictional portrayal of Ireland and Scotland is precisely regional – not because Edgeworth and Scott concentrate on particular areas and particular local variations of the culture of the country concerned (although this is often the case),[50] but because these countries are not considered independently, but as constituent parts of the broader national entity of Britain. This is not only manifested in the plots of Scott's works, but is also enshrined in the structure of the genre which he uses. The language and traditions of Scotland are identified as other, a subject of entertainment and curiosity for those who are assumed to be divorced from the values they embody, and endowed with wider, less distinctive, but more discriminating views.

The regional culture portrayed by Scott is distanced temporally, through its location at various points in the past, and geographically, through the presentation of Scottish tradition as a feature of marginal areas, such as the Borders and the Highlands. But it is also socially distanced to some extent. The most powerful evocations of the traditional way of life and language tend – particularly in those novels set

---

[49] Scott, *Redgauntlet*, vol. 36, p. 364.
[50] Cf. W. J. Keith, *Regions of the Imagination: The Development of British Rural Fiction* (Toronto, 1988), p. 20.

in the more recent past – to be those characters at the bottom of the social scale, the itinerant beggars and minstrels, such as Wandering Willie (*Redgauntlet*), Edie Ochiltree (*The Antiquary*) and Meg Merrilies (*Guy Mannering*), or peasants and servants such as Cuddie Headrigg (*Old Mortality*) and Caleb Balderstone (*Bride of Lammermoor*). Those of more elevated status, such as Fergus Mac-Ivor or Redgauntlet, may be prepared to identify themselves with the political cause associated with traditional culture, but they do not constitute an authentic regional voice. They speak a pure and sophisticated English, and maintain a certain ironic distaste for the activities of their more lowly born compatriots.

The presentation of 'folk' characters accords with Scott's belief, outlined in the advertisement for *The Antiquary*, that this 'class of society . . . are the last to feel the influence of that general polish which assimilates to each other the manners of the different nations'.[51] With the progress of time and society, regional culture is increasingly identifiable with peasant culture, as the middle and upper classes become absorbed into a general civilised, polite society. Scott's mysterious itinerants are celebrated as repositories of traditional culture, but they have to be sanitised by juxtaposition with 'ordinary', non-regional characters with whom the sophisticated reader may be expected to identify. The 'regional' characters are pre-commercial and have a child-like unreality about them which reinforces the undercurrent discernible in Scott's work that marginal, local culture is some kind of escapism from the real issues of life. As Waverley somewhat ruefully ponders how he is to extricate himself from his involvement with the Jacobite cause:

He felt himself entitled to say firmly, though perhaps with a sigh, that the romance of his life was ended, and that its real history had now commenced. (p. 283)

For Scott, the modern commercial world is the world of real history. The world of the regional novel is a world of romance which we may indulge as long as it is kept in perspective.

CONCLUSIONS

Scott has received a more general acceptance as a Scottish writer than Edgeworth has as an Irish one, but this identification has tended to rest on the view that Scott constructs an exploration of Scottishness.

---

[51] Walter Scott, *The Antiquary*, *Waverley Novels*, vol. 5, p. 1.

Insofar as he is seen to have failed in this, his work has been censured by many nationalist critics.[52] The political overtones of Scott scholarship were graphically demonstrated in the 1930s by the storm that greeted the publication of Edwin Muir's *Scott and Scotland: The Predicament of the Scottish Writer* in 1936. Muir's book was essentially a polemic work that used Scott to argue against the possibility of an autonomous Scottish literature in order to undermine the political aspirations of Scottish nationalists, and the attempts of writers such as Hugh MacDiarmid to construct a new Scottish tradition. Muir identified 'a very curious emptiness behind the wealth of Scott's imagination' and 'was forced to account for the hiatus in Scott's endowment by considering the environment in which he lived, by invoking the fact – if the reader will agree it is one – that he spent most of his days in a hiatus, in a country, that is to say, which was neither a nation nor a province, and had, instead of a centre, a blank, an Edinburgh, in the middle of it'.[53]

There were many who quite emphatically did not agree with the contention that eighteenth-century Scotland was a hiatus and Edinburgh a blank, and Muir's suggestion that Scott's novels could be generally accepted as flawed was considerably weakened by the general revaluation that took place following the publication of the essays of Lukács and Daiches. Yet the strength of the reactions against Muir's slim volume[54] may be a testament to the validity of his belief that the critical status of the works of Sir Walter Scott is of fundamental importance to the definition of the Scottish literary tradition. More recently, Robert Crawford has broken away from the traditional emphasis on the autonomy of Scottish culture, to stress Scott's role in the emergence of definitions of Englishness and Britishness.[55] This prioritisation of Scott's role as a regional writer – that is, a writer examining Scotland as a region of the greater entity of Britain – rather than a national – a Scottish – writer causes a considerable reorientation of the terms of the argument put forward by Muir. From this perspective, Muir's arguments about the absence of an autonomous Scottish culture may be read not as an indictment of Scott's artistic method, but as a consequence of the model of social progress conveyed within the fictional structure. For Scott, the absence of a contemporary and vital Scottish culture is not

[52] David Craig, *Scottish Literature and the Scottish People, 1680–1830* (London, 1961), pp. 145–55.
[53] Edwin Muir, *Scott and Scotland: The Predicament of the Scottish Writer* (London, 1936), reprinted with introduction by Allan Massie (Edinburgh, 1982), p. 2.
[54] Allan Massie, introduction to Muir, *Scott and Scotland*, pp. i–v.
[55] Crawford, *Devolving English Literature*, pp. 130–4.

evidence of social decay, but a sign of the progress of civilised values, and a blessing, though it may not be unalloyed.

This interpretation may not be popular with those readers who emphasise the counter hegemonic potential of the regional novel. But it is not intended as a direct reflection on contemporary literary and political movements. Instead it aims to indicate the diversity of the cultural and political functions of 'regional' literature. Scott and Edgeworth presented images of their native characters which were rendered safe through being historicised, and presented within fictions which displayed their inapplicability to the modern world. The irony is that the very fact of the dialectical narrative structure ensured that the resultant versions of Scottishness and Irishness could be embraced by those members of the middle and upper classes whom the model of historical process portrayed as progressively divorced from traditional culture. The regional novel made possible the reconstruction of regional culture by dramatising the fact of its disappearance as a real social and political threat. The emblems of Scottishness and Irishness could be reinscribed with new systems of values, appropriate to the bourgeois descendants of Nichol Jarvie and Jason Quirk.

It may be no coincidence that the first half of the nineteenth century saw not only the emergence of the genre of the regional novel, but also the first systematic attempts to map the British Isles. In 1792 Daniel Beaufort (Richard Edgeworth's father in law) noted in his *Memoir of a Map of Ireland* that:

It is to be lamented that the astronomer and the engineer have been so much less employed in settling the geography of the British Isles, than in ascertaining that of our distant possessions. The coasts and harbours of India and America are better known, and more correctly laid down, than those of Ireland or even Great Britain.[56]

Sentiments of this kind stimulated the project that became known as the Ordnance Survey. The publication of maps commenced in 1801, but it was not until 1824 that the survey of Ireland was begun.[57] Through the process of mapping, the British Ordnance were able to stabilise territorial boundaries that had previously been enshrined in local tradition, and through the incorporation of local names and knowledge

---

[56] Daniel Beaufort, *Memoir of a Map of Ireland: Illustrating the Topography of the Kingdom, and Containing a Short Account of its Present State, Civil and Ecclesiastical with a Complete Index to the Map* (1792), Preface, p. iii.

[57] J. H. Andrews, *A Paper Landscape: The Ordnance Survey in Nineteenth-century Ireland* (Oxford, 1975).

they could provide an authorised version of a sense of place.[58] This could fulfil the desire of the English authorities to feel that they 'understood' the subject peoples, but it also gave the native members of the middle and upper classes a sense of national identity and cultural distinctness that was rendered safe through being validated by written forms which were clearly dissociated from the popular, unwritten codes of naming and folk tradition, by very reason of their connectedness with hegemonic national/British forces.

The process of mapping may be interpreted as an imperialistic exercise in legitimation, but in practice its effects, like those of the regional novel, were complicated by the complexity of the relationship between the constitutent elements of Great Britain, but also of the structure of class relations within each of those elements. Scotland and Ireland cannot be easily accommodated within simple models of the colonial relationship,[59] because the centuries of cultural interchange between these countries and England, and the way in which the amalgamations took place, ensured the existence of substantial sectors of the native populations who identified their interests at least to some extent with those of Britain, and who shared some of the English suspicion of the expression of cultural traditions identified with the lower classes of society. The development of fictional and cartographic representations of cultural identity reinforced the regional status of both Ireland and Scotland, and thus had hegemonic implications. But the omission of such representations from the literary histories of these countries, because of their absence of a sense of cultural autonomy, serves to exclude those elements of the population who identified to any degree with the structures and institutions of the British state, and thus to erase from history precisely the social tensions which Edgeworth and Scott identified as the essential subject of the regional novel.

[58] Cf. Brian Friel, *Translations* (London, 1981).   [59] Cairns, *Writing Ireland*, pp. 8–17.

CHAPTER 3

The deep romance of Manchester:
Gaskell's 'Mary Barton'

Harriet Guest

LIVING IN MANCHESTER

Elizabeth Gaskell's first novel, *Mary Barton* (1848), might seem to be determinedly regionalised or localised: it claims a local character for itself in its sub-title, *A Tale of Manchester Life*, and in the copious use of Lancashire dialect, supplemented and weighted with explanatory foot-notes.[1] Elizabeth Gaskell explained in her Preface that:

Three years ago I became anxious (from circumstances that need not be more fully alluded to) to employ myself in writing a work of fiction. Living in Manchester, but with a deep relish and fond admiration for the country, my first thought was to find a frame-work for my story in some rural scene; and I had already made a little progress in a tale, the period of which was more than a century ago, and the place on the borders of Yorkshire, when I be-thought me how deep might be the romance in the lives of some of those who elbowed me daily in the busy streets of the town in which I resided. (p. xxxv)

These opening sentences emphasise that what Gaskell wanted to write, as a result of her personal circumstances, was what might readily be defined as a regional novel, a novel set 'on the borders', beyond the pur-view of the metropolis. Yet the phrase, 'Living in Manchester', hangs oddly, perhaps ambiguously, in this account of the narrator's intentions:

---

[1] All quotations are from *Mary Barton* (ed.) and intro., Edgar Wright (Oxford, 1987). Page references to this edition will be given in the text. Jack Culross suggests that Gaskell's working title for the first drafts of the novel was 'A Manchester Love Story', see '*Mary Barton*: A Revaluation', *Bulletin of the John Rylands University Library of Manchester*, vol. 61, no. 1, Autumn 1978, pp. 42–59. The notes on dialect were contributed by William Gaskell, who 'was an able authority on the Lancashire dialect, and it is said that he never lost an opportunity of hearing it spoken by the native. One of his old pupils tells of seeing him leave a first-class railway carriage and join a number of Lancashire workmen in a third-class compartment, in order to hear them speak in the true Lancashire dialect', Mrs Ellis H. Chadwick, *Mrs Gaskell: Haunts, Homes, and Stories*, rev. edn (London, Pitman, 1913), p. 210. My discussion of regionalism takes as its starting point the arguments of Raymond Williams's essay, 'Region and Class in the English Novel', in his *Writing and Society* (London, Verso, 1983).

it might implicitly justify that 'first thought', of finding a frame in rural Yorkshire, as the result of living in urban Lancashire. Or it might explain the second thought, and that apparently accidental and yet convoluted process in which 'I bethought me' of a deep romance made remote by its very familiarity and proximity. Through a curious dialectic of presence and absence, the syntax seems to regionalise Gaskell's Manchester, the town in which she resided, from which she escapes, to which she escapes, in fiction.

Most explicitly in the Preface, deep romance is attributed to the familiar remoteness produced by class difference, the mundane disjunction and contrast between the 'even tenor' of the 'seemingly happy lives' of the rich, and the 'anguish caused by the lottery-like nature' of the lives of the poor. Living in Manchester, anxious from circumstances that will be more fully alluded to in the novel, Gaskell writes that she:

> had always felt a deep sympathy with the care-worn men, who looked as if doomed to struggle through their lives in strange alternations between work and want; tossed to and fro by circumstances, apparently in an even greater degree than other men. (p. xxxv)

Class difference invokes deep sympathy. The apparently random vicissitudes of the lives it makes strange promote looks and feelings, the sentimental projections of sympathy that create deep romance. And the romance of estrangement and sympathy seems to displace the original need for distancing by time and place. So that perhaps the placing of Manchester, and the localisation that implies, is a manifestation not so much of that idea of regionalism which emphasises topographical enclosure and the emotional depth it produces, as of class imagined as producing a regionalised form of social space.[2]

The regional novel is often thought of as rural, and as distinguished from urban narratives of class difference, or from novels which dramatise the 'condition of England' – industrial capitalism and the urban poverty it produced. So it may not obviously seem appropriate to look at *Mary Barton* as an example of the regional novel. Manchester in the 1840s

---

[2] Williams writes that: 'Through all the observable ideological manoeuvres and shifts, Elizabeth Gaskell, Dickens, Kingsley, Disraeli, George Eliot and others were continuously and intensely concerned with the active relations between as well as within classes. A problem in the definition of 'class' is then especially relevant. A class can indeed be seen as a region: a social area inhabited by people of a certain kind, living in certain ways . . . [But] to see a class on its own . . . is subject to the same limitations as seeing a region on its own, and then to some further limitations, in that certain of the crucial elements – that it is formed in and by certain definite relations with other classes – may then be missed altogether'. ('Region and class', p. 234).

is above all else the modern industrial city, 'the great METROPOLIS of LABOUR', as Disraeli called it,[3] though it was not the capital seat of government, not metropolitan in that sense. And it seems set in stark contrast to those enclosed and rural regions in which human relations and human verities are imagined to achieve a particular depth, duration and intensity. Regionalism seems to imply that placid milky sense of time suspended that Hardy's Tess enjoys at Talbothays, released from the dreamy spell of a changeless pastoralism only when she and Angel travel to the railway station and see the trains that engirdle and fitfully intrude upon the outer limits of the Great Vale of Dairies. It seems to involve that isolation of locality, and innocence of change, that informs the exclusive and shared identity of Heathcliff and Catherine Earnshaw as children, and which they attempt to perpetuate, to regress to through starvation, in *Wuthering Heights*. And the contrast between those fantasies – visions which focus on place with an intensity that is almost hallucinatory or ecstatic in its myopic exclusiveness – and the urban 'reality' of Manchester, seems explicitly to be emphasised in *Mary Barton*. Gaskell writes that for the heroine, alone in the city night:

There was little sympathy in the outward scene, with the internal trouble. All was so still, so motionless, so hard! Very different to this lovely night in the country in which I am now writing, where the distant horizon is soft and undulating in the moonlight, and the nearer trees sway gently to and fro in the night-wind with something of almost human motion . . . The sights and sounds of such a night lull pain and grief to rest.

But Mary re-entered her home . . . with a still stronger sense of anxiety, and a still clearer conviction of how much rested upon her unassisted and friendless self, alone with her terrible knowledge, in the hard, cold, populous world. (p. 290)

The contrast between the humanised dim sympathies of the country, and the antipathetic harshness of the populous city seems to confirm the hackneyed polarisation of rural richness and urban etiolation of feeling. Manchester seems to lack specificity and uniqueness, to be different and enclosed only in those characteristics that make it the exemplary forerunner of other industrial cities. It seems to lack even the native or indigenous population that might articulate its authentic character

---

[3] Benjamin Disraeli, *Coningsby, or The New Generation*, ed. Sheila M. Smith (Oxford, 1982), p. 133. For discussion of the representation of Manchester in these terms, see Alan J. Kidd, 'Introduction: The middle class in nineteenth-century Manchester', in Alan J. Kidd and K. W. Roberts, (eds.), *City, Class and Culture: Studies in Social Policy and Cultural Production in Victorian Manchester* (Manchester, 1985), pp. 5–7.

– for most of the characters of the novel are first or second generation immigrants, or, by the end of the novel, have left the city.

Yet the strength of feeling, for place and for community, that regionalism may imply seems produced in Gaskell's Manchester precisely by those characteristics – of accident and mobility as opposed to permanence – that apparently deny or disavow its possibility. When Mary leaves Manchester for Liverpool, the narrator writes that she:

> looked towards the factory-chimneys, and the cloud of smoke which hovers over Manchester, with a feeling akin to the 'Heimweh.' She was losing sight of the familiar objects of her childhood for the first time; and unpleasant as those objects are to most, she yearned after them with some of the same sentiment which gives pathos to the thoughts of the emigrant. (p. 333)

It's not the vision of Manchester itself, but the smoke obscuring that vision, that makes possible Mary's sentimental apprehension of this 'hard, cold, populous' place as home, and her attachment to that idea of it. Her identity is so vested in the idea of its 'familiar objects' that her transportation to Liverpool seems a threat to her sanity, her personal coherence and integrity. In Liverpool Mary cannot understand what is said to her, and her 'very words seemed . . . beyond her power of control' (p. 350).[4]

The narrator seems concerned to emphasise that the attachment of her characters to their locality does not only involve a kind of private and asocial fetishism. When she details how John Barton, thinking of leaving his home, 'seemed to know every brass-headed nail driven up' there (p. 132), she points out that this is not just a possessive attachment to things, but the expression of a more generalised sense of place:

> The agricultural labourer generally has strong local attachments; but they are far less common, almost obliterated, among the inhabitants of a town. Still there are exceptions, and John Barton formed one. (p. 131)

The sympathetic representation of class relations seems almost to depend, at moments like this, on a kind of displaced expression of a more usually rural intensity of attachment. It depends on the transposition into the regional key of some of the conventional tropes of metropolitan representation. Manchester, in Gaskell's writing, seems to be both the

---

[4] In Liverpool, Mary is taken for a street-walker. For discussion of this, and of the significance of the parallel between Mary and her aunt Esther, see Jenny Uglow, *Elizabeth Gaskell: A Habit of Stories* (London, 1993), pp. 207–9. The contrast between Liverpool and Manchester is marked, perhaps most notably, by the dominance of men in the society Mary encounters in the port.

metropolis of cotton – the prototype of the modern city – and a location on the borders, the site of regional codes of feeling and behaviour.

'COMMON RULES OF STREET POLITENESS'

The implications of this ambivalent position can perhaps be seen most
clearly if we juxtapose the narrative of John Barton's experience of
the city streets with that described in the Preface, which I began by
discussing.

It is a pretty sight to walk through a street with lighted shops; the gas is so
brilliant, the display of goods so much more vividly shown than by day, and
of all the shops a druggist's looks the most like the tales of our childhood,
from Aladdin's garden of enchanted fruits to the charming Rosamond with
her purple jar. No such associations had Barton; yet he felt the contrast
between the well-filled, well-lighted shops and the dim gloomy cellar, and it
made him moody that such contrasts should exist.

Barton is hostile to the 'hurrying crowd' that surrounds him, and the
narrator rebukes him for the anger that he feels at what he takes to be
its joy:

he could not, you cannot, read the lot of those who daily pass you by in the
street. How do you know the wild romances of their lives; the trials, the temp-
tations they are even now enduring, resisting, sinking under? You may be
elbowed one instant by the girl desparate in her abandonment, laughing in
mad merriment with her outward gesture, while her soul is longing for the
rest of the dead, and bringing itself to think of the cold-flowing river as the
only mercy of God remaining to her here. You may pass the criminal, medit-
ating crimes at which you will to-morrow shudder with horror as you read
them. You may push against one, humble and unnoticed, the last upon earth,
who in heaven will for ever be in the immediate light of God's countenance.
Errands of mercy – errands of sin – did you ever think where all the thousands of people you daily meet are bound? (p. 70)

The account of the shops, with their Arabian-nights associations,
repeats the dominant structural trope of the novel, in the contrast
between the rich world of literary fantasy made available as a luxury of
middle-class culture, and the impoverished bare necessities that dictate
the language of working-class desires. The radiance of the gas-lit shops
of the modern city is specifically textualised, their allure made specifically dependent on a cultural education that Barton has not received.
It seems to be as much because of that lack, as because his progress
is purposive and not leisurely or idle, that he cannot acknowledge the

'wild romances' that might differentiate the 'hurrying crowd'. For those romances are textualised fantasies that emphasise the connection between the radiant commodity displayed in the shop window and the individual in the crowd. In the terms suggested by Walter Benjamin, the individual in the crowd is also a commodity insofar as they are identified with their labour power, and participate in the romantic and complex exchanges of desire and projection that commodities stimulate and focus.[5] Though the reader is assured that neither Barton nor they could 'read the lot of those who daily pass you', the obstruction to doing so is certainly not the obscurity or unpredictability of the narratives of prostitution, crime, or salvation available. Barton might be thought of as proletarianised in Benjamin's terms because he is conscious of the 'mode of existence . . . imposed upon him by the system of production': he does not 'feel like empathizing with commodities', with the people in the crowd, because he is bitterly conscious that he is 'gripped by the chill of the commodity economy'.[6] But the readers' incapacity to read these narratives seems to mark their exclusion in different terms. The anonymity of the crowd, which seems as alien to Barton as does the allure of the shops, may be typical of the modern city, but the readers' exclusion from the romance in which shops and crowd are involved may mark their exclusion from the network of local attachments and sympathies peculiar to 'Living in Manchester'.

For what is most intriguing about the comparison between this narrative of walking the street and that of the Preface is not so much the suggestion that Barton's class position makes the city crowd illegible to him, but the emphasis on the physical proximity of the crowd that both passages share. In the Preface, the narrator was almost forcibly distracted

[5] Walter Benjamin, 'The Paris of the Second Empire in Baudelaire, II, The Flaneur', in *Charles Baudelaire: The Lyric Poet in the Era of High Capitalism*, tr. Harry Zohn (London, 1983), see especially pp. 55–58, and the argument that: 'The *flaneur* is someone abandoned in the crowd. In this he shares the situation of the commodity. He is not aware of this special situation, but this does not diminish its effect on him and it permeates him blissfully like a narcotic. . . The intoxication to which the *flaneur* surrenders is the intoxication of the commodity around which surges the stream of customers. If the soul of the commodity which Marx occasionally mentions in jest existed, it would be the most empathic ever encountered in the realm of souls, for it would have to see in everyone the buyer in whose hands and house it wants to nestle' (p. 55). And see Judith R. Walkowitz, *City of Dreadful Delight: Narratives of Sexual Danger in Late-Victorian London* (London, 1992), on 'the flaneur's propensity for fantasy': 'As illusionist, the flaneur transformed the city into a landscape of strangers and secrets. . . Always scanning the gritty street scene for good copy and anecdote, his was [a] quintessentially "consumerist" mode of being-in-the-world, one that transformed exploitation and suffering into vivid individual psychological experience' (p. 16).
[6] Benjamin, 'Paris of the Second Empire', p. 58.

back to urban Lancashire from the rural regions of Yorkshire by the thought of the deep 'romance of some of those who elbowed me daily', and here the generalised 'you' is again elbowed and pushed against. The evidently feminine narrator, and her potentially feminine reader,[7] are both constructed as experiencing some obligation to project sympathising romances into the crowd they are immersed in, and physically forced up against.

Gaskell's capacity to write this politically charged tale depended of course to some extent on her distance from the more usually masculine subject position that might articulate a directly political discourse. The positioning of the narrator in the street makes available to her a capacity for individual and depoliticised sympathy, perhaps a '"consumerist" mode of being-in-the-world',[8] that is important to the expression of liberal concern. But it is not a position one can readily imagine a feminine narrator adopting in a novel set in London in this period. As Janet Wolff, among others, has pointed out, 'Women could not stroll alone in the city' if they wished to maintain a respectable middle-class identity.[9] That identity is of course critical to the production and reception of the sympathetic romance of *Mary Barton*. The position of the narrator, in the Preface and in the account of John Barton's shopping trip, is that of a woman at home in the streets, enjoying the lure of the gas-lit shops, and yet capable of maintaining her distance from that lure. She seems detached from the degree of absorption in the world of the commodity that makes prostitution and suicide the only narrative available to the women in the crowd of passers-by. The narrator's position is voyeuristic in so far as it implies her presence in the crowd that elbows her, but also her detachment from its commodified and commodifying imaginary. That gendered position in Gaskell's novels is made possible specifically by the regionalisation, or perhaps provincialisation, of Manchester, by its being perceived through the lens of contrast with London.

---

[7] I do not wish to imply that the novel was exclusively addressed to women. George Sand commented that: 'Mrs Gaskell has done what neither I nor other female writers in France can accomplish – she has written novels which excite the deepest interest in men of the world, and yet which every girl will be the better for reading' (Quoted in Chadwick, p. 171).

[8] Walkowitz, *Dreadful Delight*, p. 16.

[9] Janet Wolff, 'The Invisible *Flâneuse*: Women and the Literature of Modernity', in *Feminine Sentences: Essays on Women and Culture* (Oxford, 1990), p. 41. My discussion is also indebted to Rachel Bowlby, 'Walking, women and writing: Virginia Woolf as *flâneuse*', in *Still Crazy After All These Years: Women, Writing and Psychoanalysis* (London, 1992), pp. 1–33.

In an intriguing passage from *North and South* (1855), the narrator reflects on the heroine Margaret Hale's experiences of walking in London, the New Forest, and 'Milton' or Manchester. Margaret had been able to walk freely, and at her own pace, in the Forest, but in London, her aunt's 'ideas of propriety and . . . helpless dependence on others, had always made her insist that a footman should accompany Edith [her daughter] and Margaret, if they went beyond Harley Street or the immediate neighbourhood'.[10] Margaret finds walking 'something of a trial' in Milton, 'this busy bustling place' (p. 109), but it is unclear, because of the triangular structure of the contrast, whether the ordeal is produced by walking alone in the urban streets, after the protection she had grown used to in London, or by having to adopt 'the even and decorous pace necessary in streets' (p. 110), in contrast to the freedom of the forest.

The ambivalence of Margaret's reaction to walking in the street is compounded when her encounters with 'factory people' are described:

Until Margaret had learnt the times of their ingress and egress, she was very unfortunate in constantly falling in with them. They came rushing along, with bold, fearless faces, and loud laughs and jests, particularly aimed at all those who appeared to be above them in rank or station. The tones of their unrestrained voices, and their carelessness of all common rules of street politeness, frightened Margaret a little at first. The girls, with their rough, but not unfriendly freedom, would comment on her dress, even touch her shawl or gown to ascertain the exact material; nay, once or twice she was asked questions relative to some article which they particularly admired. There was such a simple reliance on her womanly sympathy with their love of dress, and on her kindliness, that she gladly replied to these inquiries, as soon as she understood them; and half smiled back at their remarks. She did not mind meeting any number of girls, loud spoken and boisterous though they might be. (p. 110)

I have quoted the passage at length because the relation between the first sentence and last is curious and complex. Initially it seems that it will be only a matter of time before Margaret learns to avoid these very unfortunate encounters, and her alarm at her unprotected exposure to them seems paramount. The proprieties appropriate to her gender and class seem violated by the 'independence' which Gaskell, like other commentators, attributed to women earning mill wages. At first Margaret seems to fear these women as representatives of a marginalised and

---

[10] Elizabeth Gaskell, *North and South*, ed. Dorothy Collin, intro. Martin Dodsworth (Harmondsworth, 1970), p. 109.

alien sub-culture, transgressors of 'all common rules of street politeness'. The transformation is not so much in their behaviour, though they do become more individualised as their threatening noise is articulated and broken up into speech she begins to understand. The change is in Margaret's perception of the implications of her own class and gender position. Her defence of her own proper invisibility in the street gives way to 'womanly sympathy'; a kind of 'maternal complaisance' in 'love of dress' which marks her out for an appropriately extensive and generous benevolence.[11] The women share an interest in dress that restates class difference in terms appropriate to the distinction between their fragile economic independence and her private independence of mind, or between their position as wage earners, and hers as a consumer – she possesses the clothes they desire.[12]

That her encounters with these factory women do involve a substantial recasting of Margaret's understanding of her own position in the street is apparent from the continuation of the passage. Margaret

did not mind meeting any number of girls . . . But she alternately dreaded and fired up against the workmen, who commented not on her dress, but on her looks, in the same open, fearless manner. She who had hitherto felt that even the most refined remark on her personal appearance was an impertinence, had to endure undisguised admiration from these out-spoken men. (p. 110)

Though the perception of a common interest is what makes it possible for Margaret to accept the factory women's version of street politeness, there's clearly a significant difference between her clothing being made visible, as it were, by comment in the street, and her body becoming the focus for explicit sexual admiration. Here class difference, and the privacy implicit to middle-class feminine identity are her resource. The narrator comments on the behaviour of the men that:

[11] Middle-class women did of course expect to be looked at in the street, as objects of curiosity or desire, but they do not seem to expect comments on their appearance, let alone comments that demand some response; and they are therefore invisible as potential subjects. Both situations contrast with Margaret's earlier (pre-adult?) 'free walks' in the New Forest, where it is implied that she had enjoyed a more absolute and almost extra-social invisibility: 'She went along there with a boundless fearless step, that occasionally broke into a run, if she were in a hurry, and occasionally was stilled into perfect repose, as she stood listening to, or watching any of the wild creatures who sang in the leafy courts, or glanced out with their keen bright eyes from the low brushwood or tangled furze' (pp. 109–10).

[12] Within a few sentences the text juxtaposes references to 'the greater independence of working in a mill', and the way London propriety had 'circumscribed Margaret's independence', as if to emphasise the possibility of comparison between the notions of independence available to different classes of women.

the very outspokenness marked their innocence of any intention to hurt her delicacy, as she would have perceived if she had been less frightened by the disorderly tumult. Out of her fright came a flash of indignation which made her face scarlet, and her dark eyes gather flame, as she heard some of their speeches. Yet there were other sayings of theirs, which, when she reached the quiet safety if her home, amused her even while they irritated her. (pp. 110–1)

The passage as a whole suggests the pleasure of the street-wise narrator, enjoyably excited and secure in her understanding of the sometimes startlingly different rules of street behaviour that apply in Manchester. These crowds seem legible in terms of a specifically local knowledge, though the registering of fear and indignation as a kind of necessary prelude to a condescending pleasure (in the comments of the women), and a more secretive, partly disavowed pleasure (in the remarks of the men), indicates that for her these local rules must be juxtaposed with and cannot replace gendered codes of propriety derived from metropolitan London.

The regionalised pattern of street behaviour that the heroine learns to accept in *North and South*, and that may distinguish the position of the narrator of *Mary Barton*, does not, of course, ungender the masculine identity of the urban spectator,[13] by whom so many nineteenth-century accounts of metropolitan life are authorised. For it is central to the voyeurism of that masculine identity that the spectator should remain anonymous, and not be drawn into the kinds of exchanges described in *North and South*.[14] Those exchanges described the pleasure the narrator or heroine experienced in assuming the identity of a consumer or commodity among commodities, and in exercising the sympathy or empathy that position made available. But the narrator maintained a gendered identity set apart from those exchanges, and which marked pleasure in them as somehow licensed by the northern or more specifically the Mancunian nature of the experience. In Manchester, the narrator assures us, male outspokenness to women is a sign of innocence of intention, even though it violates the proper invisibility

---

[13] I borrow the phrase from the title of Judith Walkowitz's first chapter, in *Dreadful Delight*. There it describes a category that is always masculine, and that includes but is not confined to that of the *flaneur*.

[14] See Bowlby, 'Walking, Women and Writing', pp. 6–10. In Caroline Arscott and Griselda Pollock with Janet Wolff, 'The partial view: the visual representation of the early nineteenth-century city', in Janet Wolff and John Seed (eds.), *The Culture of Capital: Art, Power and the Nineteenth-century Middle Class* (Manchester, 1988), pp. 191–233. A range of representations of northern industrial towns from the first half of the nineteenth century are discussed. The authors point out that in a number of street scenes 'ladies walk alone' (p. 202) but, disappointingly, they do not discuss what these women are doing there.

of middle-class women in the streets: the rules of street politeness are different, exceptional and regionalised.

'COTTONOPOLIS'

The obvious distinguishing feature of Manchester, compared to other growing industrial cities, is, of course, the economic dominance of cotton. Cotton manufacture and trade pervades and structures the representation of Manchester life in the 1840s. Cotton workers were said to be regarded by other workers as 'as a set of spiritless milksops – as soft and pliable as the woolly fibre which they twist'.[15] Seen in the streets, the male factory workers appeared 'in general undersized, sallow-looking', and the women were similarly 'stunted and paled' from mill work, and always 'speckled with flakes of cotton'.[16] Cotton 'impregnated' the air of the mills' blowing rooms with its 'flying dust and impalpable filaments', and filled the lungs and stomachs of those who worked in 'blowing' off its impurities and carding it.[17] Bessy Higgins laments, in *North and South*, that cotton fibre 'winds round the lungs, and tightens them up' till its workers fall 'into a waste, coughing and spitting blood' (p. 146). The cotton industry blanched and dyed its workers, recolouring them in the scarlet of blood, or of the exotic shades of the empire around which it wound, in, for example, the lyrical visions of the Manchester correspondent of the *Morning Chronicle*:

There is something curious, while walking through the stack of coloured stuffs with which the rooms of a great warehouse are heaped, in the reflection that . . . the piles of fabric which surround you will form the clothing and household drapery of half the nations of the east and south. This piece of gaily-tinted cloth will cover a divan in a Turkish harem – this other will flutter across the desert in the turban of an Arab sheik. Here is the raw material of a garment which will be stitched up by Hindoo fingers – there a web which will be 'made up' by a Chinese tailor, while beside there may, perchance, be the staple of the flowing robe which the Tahiti girl doffs when she laves her limbs in the pellucid depths behind the coral reefs in the South Seas.[18]

[15] Angus Bethune Reach, 'Manchester', in *Labour and the Poor in England and Wales, 1849–1851: The Letters to The Morning Chronicle from the Correspondents in the Manufacturing and Mining Districts, the Towns of Liverpool and Birmingham, and the Rural Districts, vol. I: Lancashire, Cheshire, Yorkshire*, J. Ginswick (ed. and intro.), (London, 1983), p. 56. The importance of the cotton industry to Gaskell's representation of Manchester is indicated in her choice of the pseudonym 'Cotton Mather Mills' for the first edition of *Mary Barton*. For discussion of the representation of Manchester as 'Cottonopolis', see Kidd, pp. 7–9. Kidd argues that the importance of Manchester was for international trade in, rather than the manufacture of, textiles. This distinction seems blurred in the accounts of many nineteenth-century correspondents, reporters, and novelists, and for the purposes of this essay I have adopted the imprecision of their view.
[16] Reach, 'Manchester', p. 4.   [17] *Ibid.*, p. 11.   [18] *Ibid.*, p. 37.

What seems most obviously curious about this reflection is its juxta-position with the account of dying processes which involve 'degrading, stupefying and exhausting' labour. The correspondent comments that the boys employed in this work 'were the only species of labourers whose condition I pitied since my arrival in Lancashire',[19] but there remains an unspoken sense that this pitiable condition may be veiled and exoticised by the colourful romance of his speculations, like travel advertisements lighting up the inner city.

The imperial weave of industrialised Lancashire, in these decades, seems to leave its imprint in Dickens's account of Coketown, as 'a town of unnatural red and black, like the painted face of a savage',[20] and to be figured in the imperious dignity of the heroine of *North and South*, with her 'regal composure', like that of 'some great Egyptian statue'.[21] It colours commonplace perceptions of the exotic savagery of the mill workers.[22] Its incongruous implications of abandoned luxury and indolence seem to be figured in images of the excess, the 'over-loading . . . with colour', and 'gaudy patterns', that Gaskell represents as characterising the Mancunian 'taste that loves ornament, however bad, more than the plainness and simplicity which are of themselves the framework of elegance' (*North and South*, p. 98). What Gaskell saw as the childish taste of the Manchester workers who produce the cloth aligns them with its exotic consumers, in the account of the *Morning Chronicle*:

As a general rule, the Mediterranean and Levantine nations prefer the most glaring patterns. The manufacturer can never make his reds, oranges and yellows too bright for the taste of the archipelago, the Smyrniote cities, and the fashions prevalent among the African subjects of France.[23]

---

[19] *Ibid.*, pp. 37–8.

[20] Charles Dickens, *Hard Times*, Paul Schlicke (ed.) (1854; Oxford, 1989), p. 28.

[21] Margaret Hale's queenly air seems related to the exoticism of her clothes, which are not made of calico print: 'a large Indian shawl . . . which she wore as an Empress wears her drapery' (*North and South*, p. 99). But the representation of Margaret on her arrival in Milton from London seems, as it were, to close the circle of trade that the *Morning Chronicle* describes.

[22] 'For my part, I should much rather be exposed to the savages of New Zealand than to a community composed of the worst specimens of humanity to be found in the wynds of Glasgow, the cellars of Liverpool, and the Angel-meadows of Manchester', W. Cooke Taylor, *Notes on a Tour in the Manufacturing Districts of Lancashire*, ed. W. H. Chaloner (New York, 1968), p. 128.

[23] Reach, 'Manchester', p. 37. Reach writes of workers' homes that: 'A conspicuous object is very frequently a glaringly painted and highly glazed tea-tray, upon which the firelight glints cheerly, and which, by its superior lustre and artistic boldness of design, commonly throws into the shade the couple or so of tiny prints . . . suspended above it' (p. 21). Compare Gaskell's account of the Barton's furniture: 'resting against the wall, was a bright green japanned tea-tray, having a couple of scarlet lovers embracing in the middle. The firelight danced merrily on this, and really (setting all taste but that of a child's aside) it gave a richness of colouring to that side of

The cotton industry required the labour of women, which was perceived to result in a range of social problems. In accounts of these
women workers, it seems as though the tropical hues of the imperial
product wind round them, to license fantasies of lurid and exotic sexual
abandon, which must then be disavowed, bleached into credible and
depressing stains of dreary and pathetic realism. But to unpack that process a little: factory work was perceived to unfit women for domestic
life, because they lacked the opportunity to acquire the necessary skills,
and because they became accustomed to levels of disposable income
that they could not have if they stayed at home. And this lack of domesticity was perceived to be immanently scandalous. Engels recorded the
comment that 'most of the prostitutes . . . had their employment in the
mills to thank for their present situation', and endorses the view that
this resulted from the crowding together of people of different ages
and sexes in the work room, and the 'indecent' language employed
there.[24] The *Morning Chronicle* noted the 'sincere conviction' that 'there
is hardly such a thing as a chaste factory girl', though it commented
that 'this is an assertion the correctness of which is generally, and I
believe with truth, denied'.[25] The point is that mill work produces
women who are undomesticated and economically independent, and
who can therefore be most appropriately described in the pejorative
language of sexual abandon, even if the accuracy of this then needs to
be denied. As John Barton comments on his sister-in-law, 'the worst of
factory work for girls' is that it gives them a disposable income to
spend on luxuries such as dress, and the conclusion he draws seems
inevitable; 'I see where you'll end at with your artificials, and your fly-
away veils, and stopping out when honest women are in their beds;
you'll be a street-walker' (p. 6).[26] The implication that women workers

the room' (*Mary Barton*, p. 13; infantilism and exotic primitivism are, of course, overlapping
    discursive categories).
[24] F. Engels, *The Condition of the Working-Class in England: From Personal Observation and Authentic
    Sources* (London, 1973), p. 168.
[25] Reach, 'Manchester', p. 39.
[26] Compare the account of Harriet, in Disraeli's *Sybil, or The Two Nations* (1845), Bk 2, ch. 14. The
    assumption is that women's earnings are not used to purchase necessities. Esther comments
    that: 'I did not know the value of money. Formerly I had earned it easily enough at the factory,
    and as I had no more sensible wants, I spent it on dress and on eating' (*Mary Barton*, p. 188).
    For comment on the ideological nature of this assumption, see Jane Rendall, *Women in an
    Industrializing Society: England 1750–1880* (Oxford, 1990), pp. 58–64. The emphasis on the scan-
    dalous sexuality of women workers, despite evidence to the contrary, might be understood as
    compensating for the threat they were seen to pose to masculine identity, and to notions of
    sexual difference; see Barbara Taylor, *Eve and the New Jerusalem: Socialism and Feminism in the
    Nineteenth Century* (London, 1983), pp. 110–113.

waste their incomes on the luxuries of dress, which lead them into vanity
and sexual immorality, is associated for Barton with a freedom of movement which may not have been unusual for working-class women, but
which is cast, by the dominance of middle-class notions of street politeness and feminine domesticity, as a further intimation of immorality.

For Barton, the link between factory work and prostitution seems
so strong that he is prepared to undergo considerable sacrifice in order
to apprentice his daughter to a 'milliner and dressmaker' (p. 28). The
decision might seem surprising, for the connection between prostitution and working in the clothing trade was historically powerful: the
work was poorly paid and often seasonal, and, in as it were a different
register of causation, there was a strong discursive association of sexual
immorality and interest in dress.[27] Prostitutes were characteristically
represented in 'flashy' clothes[28] that travestied those perceived as
appropriate to a more affluent social class. Gaskell writes of the dying
prostitute in *Mary Barton*, that: 'fallen into what appeared simply a
heap of white or light-coloured clothes . . . lay the poor crushed Butterfly
– the once innocent Esther' (p. 462): the badge of Esther's profession
here seems to leave no other identity or presence available to her –
she becomes 'simply a heap' of inappropriate clothing. Milliners and
dressmakers seem to share access to this inappropriately fine, light, or
colourful clothing, and therefore to the profession it identifies. 'Lushing
Loo', one of the women interviewed for the survey of prostitution in
Mayhew's *London Labour and the London Poor*, seems to play ironically on
the overdetermined character of narratives of the descent of clothing
workers into prostitution in her response to questions about her history:
' "Oh I'm a seduced milliner," she said, rather impatiently; "anything
you like." '[29]

---

[27] See Judith R. Walkowitz, *Prostitution and Victorian Society: Women, Class, and the State* (Cambridge,
1980), pp. 26, 34, 195. The connection between interest in dress and moral abandon – light
clothing and light-mindedness – marks the character of Sally Leadbitter in *Mary Barton*. See in
particular ch. 25, where Gaskell writes that she 'flaunted into the little dingy room, making it
gaudy with the Sunday excess of colouring in her dress' (p. 323).

[28] Walkowitz, *Prostitution*, p. 26.

[29] Bracebridge Hemyng, 'Prostitution in London', in Henry Mayhew, *London Labour and the London
Poor, in Four Volumes, vol. 4: Those That Will Not Work, Comprising Prostitutes, Thieves, Swindlers, and
Beggars* (New York, 1968), p. 224. Hemyng lists 'milliners, dress-makers, straw bonnet-makers,
furriers, hat-binders, silk-winders, tambour-workers, shoe-binders, slop-women, or those who
work for cheap tailors, those in pastry-cook, fancy and cigar-shops, bazaars and ballet-girls' as
'trades that supplied women to swell the ranks of prostitution', p. 255. Compare Esther's
response to Jem's questions about her history: 'Where have I been? What have I been doing?
Why do you torment me with questions like these? Can you not guess?' (p. 187). The seduced
heroine of Gaskell's *Ruth* (1853) is of course a dress-maker's apprentice.

Once Mary has become an apprenticed milliner, she is caught up in the logic of the 'romances which [the milliner's] young ladies were in the habit of recommending to each other': she imagines herself as the consumer who 'would drive up to the door in her own carriage, to order her gowns from the . . . dress-maker', and she is positioned as an appropriate object of desire for Carson the mill owner's son, who sees 'the beautiful little milliner . . . while lounging in a shop where his sisters were making some purchases' (pp. 90–91). Because her work makes her movements predictable, Mary begins to experience walking the streets as a source of unavoidable persecution rather than freedom, for Carson lies 'in ambush' for her in shops and side streets. She is caught up in a commodity economy which projects her into romances like those which the narrator read in the faces of the crowd on London Road: she figures in the 'Jack Sheppard romances' of police detection (p. 258), in newspaper reports of crime and trial (p. 422), and in Sally Leadbitter's imaginary theatrical melodramas (p. 423). As a result, she is told that the dressmaker will be 'glad to have you back . . . by way of tempting people to come to her shop. They'd come from Salford to have a peep at you, for six months at least' (p. 422).

Work in the production of cotton cloth, or in the clothing trade, seems to involve women in a blurred and extensive discursive category that is more or less implicitly characterised by sexual abandon. Gaskell's writing about Manchester draws on, and to some extent intensifies, this characterisation. But I think her writing also sets it alongside a notion of the regional specificity of Manchester, and the almost exotic character of the cotton industry, in a way that may call into question the commonly received critical image of Gaskell as a defender of feminine domesticity. Margaret Hale's complex pleasure in the different rules of street politeness that she finds in Manchester, I suggest, may be taken to indicate the complexity of the gender politics of the 'deep sympathy' that animates *Mary Barton*.

The inexorable narrative that seems to structure the representation of working with cotton, or working with cloth, extends, in Gaskell's novel, to embrace Carson the mill-owner's son, who seems subject to the inevitable laws of its commodity economy: he is described by his sister as a 'masculine flirt' (p. 239), and is represented to the police detective after his death by his portrait in fancy-dress costume (p. 249). In what might seem to be a parody of his plans for Mary's seduction, he is shot through the head with the gun that Mrs Wilson believed might go off by itself (p. 261), though 'she seemed to think' her husband 'could manage it' (p. 450). Finally, in the little sentimental tableau which teaches his father to forgive his killer, young Carson is represented by the figure of a little girl whose white party dress is stained with blood – 'those scarlet marks so terrible to little children' (p. 434). The occasion for his death is that he believes himself to be in command of the economy of the factory, and he believes that this gives him the right to manipulate the complex business of representation. While arguing that the striker's demands should not be met, he draws a caricature of their representatives, which the men then use to draw lots to determine who shall be his assassin, each having 'sworn to act according to his drawing' (p. 224). Carson's drawing transposes the political representatives of the workers into the register of educated, literary representation in a gesture that indicates the luxury available to power, rather than the sympathy that, in Gaskell's terms, might license it. Carson's romantic representation reinforces the chill of the terrible reality of the commodity economy, and violently trashes the sense in which sympathetic romance may be necessary to the workings of that economy.

That second function of romantic representation seems underlined when, in the same chapter, Gaskell writes of the striking trades unionists being entertained by the delegate from London:

As the man who has had his taste educated to love reading, falls devouringly upon books after a long abstinence, so, these poor fellows, whose tastes had been left to educate themselves into a liking for tobacco, beer, and similar gratifications, gleamed up at the proposal of the London delegate. Tobacco and drink deaden the pangs of hunger, and make one forget the miserable home, the desolate future. (p. 218)

Here the hunger of the men can best be understood, or sympathetically apprehended, in terms of the apparently more common, or primary appetite for books. Representation is what makes their hunger and misery accessible, though representation, in the hands of young Carson, is also what belittles and does violence to the urgency of their needs. That ambivalence about the use of representation or fantasy, I suggested, colours the representations of women in the novel. The working women in Manchester, with their access to a street-life denied to metropolitan ladies, are represented as participating in romances that may identify them as commodities both in their labours and in their desires. Those narratives may imply sexual abandon in the transgression of 'common rules' – or middle-class and metropolitan rules – of feminine behaviour.

But romances are also necessary to sympathy, which makes partially legible, and even enviable, the local codes that structure what appear to be transgressions of the common rules of street politeness.

'UNSPEAKABLE TERRORS, PRICELESS TREASURES'

The importance of deep romance in Gaskell's representations of Manchester is more complex than, say, that of fantasy in Dickens's *Hard Times*. In *Mary Barton*, romance is what leads the heroine from the straight and narrow, and what characterises her sense of shameful exposure in the second half of the novel, though it also appears to be what enables the narrator to extend her sympathetic projections across the lines of class difference or into the anonymity of the crowd. In particular, I have suggested that romance was the genre appropriate to the narrator's pleasure in the 'pretty sight' of the gas-lit shops. The shops of Manchester acquired a particular importance in Engels' account of the city. He remarked that: 'I have never seen so systematic a shutting out of the working-class from the thoroughfares, so tender a concealment of everything which might affront the eye and nerves of the bourgeoisie, as in Manchester'. And he explained that:

the thoroughfares leading from the Exchange in all directions out of the city are lined, on both sides, with an almost unbroken series of shops, and are so kept in the hands of the middle and lower bourgeoisie, which, out of self-interest, cares for a decent and cleanly appearance and *can* care for it. True, these shops bear some relation to the districts which lie behind them . . . but they suffice to conceal from the eyes of the wealthy men and women of strong stomachs and weak nerves the misery and grime which form the complement of their wealth.[30]

Engels' account contrasts with these sheltered prospects the striking revelations of railways, cutting through previously concealed cross-sections of the city, and, most unknowable of all, the 'horrors which surpass all others by far' to be found beneath the railway bridges.[31] Gaskell's knowledge, as one 'Living in Manchester' rather than in the wealthy suburbs, extended well beyond the shop-lined thoroughfares,

---

[30] Engels, *Condition of the Working Class*, pp. 79, 78.

[31] *Ibid.*, p. 82, see also p. 92. It is intriguing to contrast with Engels' narrative strategy George Eliot's sense that the train is inimical to the production of narrative, and perhaps of the regionalised richness that requires, in the Author's Introduction to *Felix Holt, The Radical* (1866). See also the opening paragraphs to Gaskell's *The Life of Charlotte Bronte* (1857), and *My Lady Ludlow* (1859).

but Engels' account nevertheless suggests the extent to which the presence of shops structured the imaginative apprehension of the city by its middle class.

Representations of shops in *Mary Barton* seem to confirm Engels' implication of their importance in drawing lines of class ignorance and antagonism. The mill-owners are represented as happy consumers of luxuries, while necessities are denied to the increasingly embittered workers. Gaskell writes that 'the workman loiters away his unemployed time in watching' the rich shop, while he meditates on the deprivations of his own family; and for him the 'contrast is too great' (p. 24). But shopping is also represented as a source of peculiarly feminine pleasure. So, in the good times described in the opening pages of the novel, 'Mary ran off like a hare to fulfil what, to a girl of thirteen, fond of power, was the more interesting part of her errand – the money-spending part' (p. 16). The imagined pleasures of consumption – or perhaps more accurately, of money-spending, and the power that implies – are, as I have said, important to the progress of Mary's seduction. And it is that imaginary power of expenditure that the narrator appeals to in her account of the shops and crowds of London Road. In that account, the fantasy of expenditure becomes the expenditure of fantasy, of sympathetic projection. This act of imagination, the narrative implies, is not one in which John Barton can participate, partly because of his class, but partly also because of his gender.

At the beginning of this essay, I suggested that the regionalisation of Manchester in *Mary Barton* was constructed through a curious dialectic of presence and absence. Because she lives in Manchester the narrator thinks of writing a tale set somewhere else, and that thought somehow returns her to a Manchester transformed by sympathy into the stuff of romance. This curious process in a sense repeats Gaskell's account of the writing of the novel. The anxiety she alluded to in her Preface as having driven her to write the novel was caused by the death of her nine-month old son, William.[32] She explained to Mrs Greg that:

The tale was formed, and the greater part of the first volume written when I was obliged to lie down constantly on the sofa, and when I took refuge in the invention to exclude the memory of painful scenes which would force themselves upon my remembrance. It is no wonder then that the whole book seems to be written in the minor key; indeed, the very design seems to me to require

---

[32] For a fuller account of the personal circumstances in which the novel was written see Uglow, pp. 150–5, and Chadwick, ch. 12.

this treatment. I acknowledge the fault of there being too heavy a shadow over the book; but I doubt if the story could have been deeply realized without these shadows. The cause of the fault may be looked for in the design; and yet the design was one worthy to be bought into consideration. Perhaps after all it may be true that I, in my state of feelings at that time, was not fitted to introduce the glimpses of light and happiness which might have relieved the gloom.[33]

This letter, like so much of Gaskell's prose, is difficult to summarise because its argument is mobile and ambiguous. She both defends and apologises for the 'gloom' of the book, which she claims is the fault of the design and of her 'state of feelings'. But what seems to emerge most strongly is the ambivalence of the sense in which she was able to take 'refuge in the invention', for the book seems to function for her both as an escape from 'the memory of painful scenes', from loss and guilt, and as a means of reinscribing them, forcing them 'upon my remembrance'.

More than half way through *Mary Barton*, when Gaskell had perhaps felt able to leave her sofa, the text refers explicitly to the loss that drove her to find employment in writing. At this point in the story, Mary, dazed by the revelation of her father's guilt, is watching over the sleep of Alice and Jane Wilson. Mary fears the changes that sleep may bring in the condition of the two women, for Alice is dying, and Jane Wilson is 'dateless' with anxiety for her son, who has been charged, partly on the basis of her evidence, with the murder John Barton committed (p. 305). The narrator adds, on the state of Jane Wilson:

Already her senses had been severely stunned by the full explanation of what was required of her, – of what she had to prove against her son, her Jem, her only child . . . and what if in dreams (that land into which no sympathy nor love can penetrate with another, either to share its bliss or its agony, – that land whose scenes are unspeakable terrors, are hidden mysteries, are priceless treasures to one alone, – that land where alone I may see, while yet I tarry here, the sweet looks of my dear child), – what if, in the horrors of her dreams, her brain should go still more astray, and she should waken crazy with her visions, and the terrible reality which begot them? (p. 316)

The paragraph repeatedly insists on the isolation of the dream state, but in the same movement, and perhaps most emphatically in the way that the narrator's confessional moment is encompassed about in the almost incoherent extensions of the sentence, it links her dream to the

[33] *The Letters of Mrs Gaskell*, (eds.) J. A. V. Chapple and Arthur Pollard (Cambridge, Mass., 1967), Letter 42, pp. 74–5.

visions of Jane and Alice Wilson, and with the 'terrible reality' they inhabit.

By this stage of the novel, the women involved in the narrative have almost all suffered some loss, some mental or physical impediment, which in a sense removes them from immediate contact with their surroundings, from 'Living in Manchester'. Alice has gone blind, and imagines herself in the rural scenes of her childhood – in a country which, the other characters agree, she would no longer have been able to find had she travelled there as she wished. Jane Wilson had an injury which prevented her from working in the factory, her infant sons and her husband have died, and she has now become 'dateless' with anxiety for her surviving son. Mary's friend Margaret is blind, which prevents her from sewing and allows her to take her singing seriously. Mary believes that Margaret has acquired a kind of instinctive sensitivity and 'new charm' in place of her sight (p. 205), so that her 'blindness almost appears a blessing' (p. 226). Esther, who has also lost her child, is confused and sometimes consoled by the effects of drink. She is feverish from the consumption which is killing her, and as a result speech is difficult for her, as it also becomes for Mary. As a result of these different forms of loss and deprivation, the narrative represents each of these women as having access to romances and fantasies, or inhabiting a kind of dream-land that obscures yet reinscribes 'terrible reality'.

In the letter to Mrs Greg, in which she described writing the novel, Gaskell explained that John Barton 'was my hero, *the* person with whom all my sympathies went, with whom I tried to identify myself at the time'. He is, however, progressively excluded from the narrative, as critics have frequently pointed out. As the degree of Gaskell's prostration diminishes, he becomes peripheral to the action, and the women take over his central role. In her letter Gaskell wrote that Barton was animated by a 'sympathy for suffering' that, in the novel, makes him increasingly a figure of melancholy isolation. His sympathies confine him in an inexorable narrative that is likened to the shrinking room of the Borgias, whose walls finally crush their prisoner (p. 198). Gaskell's account of the living conditions of the workers of Manchester does not emphasise the physically oppressive proportions of the spaces they inhabit as insistently as does, say, Engels', but nevertheless Barton's shrinking prison seems to echo his experience of fetid cellars and basement areas, spaces he could measure 'without the least motion of his body' (p. 66). Gaskell writes that the opium he uses to suppress his

hunger and his sense of despair reinforces his 'monomania', producing: 'Days of oppressive weariness and langour, whose realities have
the feeble sickliness of dreams; nights, whose dreams are fierce realities
of agony' (p. 198). As a result of his sympathetic sorrow and guilt, Barton
is confined within a prison of insistent realities, alternately 'feeble' or
'fierce'. His sympathy oppresses him, and leaves no room for what
Freud identified as 'the work which mourning performs' in enabling a
'compromise in which the command of reality is carried out piece-
meal':[34] it is not coloured by that dialectic of presence and absence that
identified the narrator's deep sympathy with deep romance.

The difference between the representation of John Barton and of
the women in the novel suggests again that interplay between romance
and reality, need and desire, that is so important to the narrative.
The romance that characterises *Mary Barton* as 'A Manchester Love
Story'[35] is the specific and determined product of a region dominated
by cotton; and of a narrator who takes pleasure in the Manchester shops
and the fantasies they market, but who also observes the 'terrible reality'
of the workers' lives, which the shops both conceal and re-emphasise
through contrast. Fantasy and romance mark the narrator's distance
from that reality, which is a measure of her class-difference from those
she writes about, but they are also the means of projecting her sympathy into that reality, especially as it is imagined to be experienced
by the women in the novel who have suffered loss. Romance allows
the narrator to escape from the confinement of Manchester, from the
hardships she observes and from the 'painful scenes' they force upon
her remembrance, but romance also insistently reinscribes that confinement. It constantly calls to mind the loss that makes the luxury of fantasy
a necessity; and the forms taken by fantasy are the forms of Manchester
itself, or visions of a world elsewhere constructed entirely in terms of
what Manchester is not. The terrible reality of loss makes possible,
indeed makes necessary, the 'deep sympathy' that animates Gaskell's
writing. She projects that sympathy in forms of deep romance that
mark her sense of the remoteness produced by class difference and the
regional specificity of the cotton industry.

[34] Sigmund Freud, 'Mourning and Melancholia', in *The Pelican Freud Library, vol. 11: On Metapsychology:
The Theory of Psychoanalysis: Beyond the Pleasure Principle, the Ego and the Id, and Other Works*, Angela
Richards (ed.) (Harmondsworth, 1984), p. 253.
[35] *Letters*, Letter 23, p. 55, and see n. 1 above.

CHAPTER 4

Geographies of Hardy's Wessex

John Barrell

I

When I wrote this essay, I had never been to Dorset. But I make that confession, not to disqualify myself from writing but to indicate at the outset the sort of essay it will not be. It will not be concerned with the identification of places in the Wessex novels with their possible originals in Dorset and the neighbouring counties. That task has already been performed more than a few times, most convincingly by Denys Kay-Robinson, and by Andrew Enstice whose work is especially useful where it points out how Hardy manipulated the geography of Dorset to create the imaginary space called Wessex.[1] Nor am I offering – I would be equally incompetent to offer – the sort of study that H. C. Darby has made of the regional geography of Hardy's Wessex – a study whose implications have still to be taken up by literary critics and humanist geographers, in that it would seem possible to base upon it an understanding of how the plots and the narrative structures of Hardy's novels might have been to a degree determined by their various settings.[2]

This essay sets out instead to examine how localities and spaces in Hardy's novels are constructed, are mapped, by the characters in the novels, and therefore also by Hardy in his narrative and by us as we read. I am concerned, then, with different, subjective geographies, and with geographies as modes of cognition. This is a topic we can approach, traditionally enough, through a consideration of the development of

---

[1] Denys Kay-Robinson, *Hardy's Wessex Reappraised* (Newton Abbot, 1972); Andrew Enstice, *Thomas Hardy: Landscapes of the Mind* (London, 1979). Earlier studies include B. C. A. Windle, *The Wessex of Thomas Hardy* (London, 1902); Hermann Lea, *Thomas Hardy's Wessex* (London, 1913); R. T. Hopkins, *Thomas Hardy's Dorset* (London, 1922); D. Maxwell, *The Landscape of Thomas Hardy* (London, 1928). Also relevant are F. B. Pinion, *A Hardy Companion* (London, 1968); Robert Gittings, *Young Thomas Hardy* (London, 1975). References to other studies of the 'real' settings of Hardy's novels will be found in the bibliography to Enstice, *Thomas Hardy*.

[2] H. C. Darby, 'The Regional Geography of Thomas Hardy's Wessex', *Geographical Review* 38 (1948) pp. 426–43.

theme and character in the novels, but it also has implications for the study of Hardy's narrative method, particularly the problem of who speaks what in the narrative – a problem more salient, perhaps, in Hardy than in any other nineteenth-century novelist, and one well-described by David Lodge in some remarks on *Tess of the d'Urbervilles*.[3] It is to *Tess* (1891) and to *The Return of the Native* (1878) that this study will address itself.

The context for my discussion (particularly of *Tess*) will be Hardy's concern with the mobility of agricultural labourers in Dorset in the second half of the nineteenth century by the system of annual hirings at statute fairs, described in *Far from the Madding Crowd* and referred to in *Tess*; and, in Hardy's essay 'The Dorsetshire Labourer' (1883), represented as so well-established that it was not uncommon for a labourer to change his farm and master each year.[4] It is this, not as it may or may not have been common in Dorset, but as it occurs in the Wessex of the novels, that is crucial to the different representations of space I am concerned with. It is an experience which produces a change from the sense of space that Hardy describes in *Tess*, where he writes that 'to persons of limited spheres, miles are as geographical degrees, parishes as counties, counties as provinces and kingdoms' – a change from that sense, which can hardly have survived as unadulterated in Dorset as it survives in Wessex, to the geography of those whom he describes, in 'The Dorsetshire Labourer', as the new 'inter-social citizens' of the county.

Dorset labourers now look upon an annual removal as the most natural thing in the world, and it becomes with the younger families a pleasant excitement. Change is also a certain sort of education. Many advantages accrue to the labourers from the varied experience it brings, apart from the discovery of the best market for their abilities. They have become shrewder and sharper men of the world, and have learned how to hold their own with firmness and judgment. Whenever the habitually-removing man comes into contact with one of the old-fashioned stationary sort, who are still to be found, it is impossible not to perceive that the former is much more wide awake than his fellow-worker, astonishing him with stories of the wide world comprised in a twenty-mile radius from their homes.[5]

[3] David Lodge, *Language of Fiction: Essays in Criticism and Verbal Analysis of the English Novel* (London, 1966) chapter 4.
[4] Hardy, *Tess of the D'Urbervilles*, P. N. Furbank (ed.), (1891; London, New Wessex, 1974) 400; P. N. Furbank, 'The Dorsetshire Labourer', *Longman's Magazine* (July 1883), pp. 252–69, reprinted in Harold Orel (ed.), *Thomas Hardy's Personal Writings: Prefaces, Literary Opinions, Reminiscences* (London, 1967), pp. 168–91.
[5] Hardy, *Tess*, p. 136; Orel, *Personal Writings*, p. 180.

As long as Hardy is talking primarily, as here, about the expansion of mental, consequent on that of geographical, horizons he clearly welcomes it; the fact of the labourers becoming less 'local in feeling', however – the essential condition for the development of sharpness, of judgement – is presented with rather less equanimity, and especially in the novels. For it involves, in *Tess* particularly, not so much the exchange of one, 'local', for another, 'regional', sense of space, but the destruction of a local sense and the substitution of nothing in its place; for the new, regional geography of the migrant labourer, at ease with a knowledge of the world comprised 'in a twenty-mile radius from his home', can be acquired, it seems, only on terms that Tess herself cannot manage. In 'The Dorsetshire Labourer', the 'migration' of labour suggests to Hardy the image of the labourers as 'birds of passage', a phrase used to indicate that 'nobody thinks whence or whither' they come and go, but which still serves to remind us that, in moving from place to place, they are searching for the environment most congenial to them.[6] But the phrase occurs again, in *Tess*, to put an entirely negative valuation, as we shall see, on Tess's migrations.

II

I want now to give a sense of the local geography Hardy attributes to the 'old-fashioned stationary sort' of Dorsetshire labourer, and in particular to those whom, in *The Return of the Native*, he describes as the 'heathfolk'. Egdon, we are told, is a place 'away from comparisons';[7] and the sense of place indicated by that phrase involves, in its ideal state, no clear sense of relations of difference or similarity between the place one knows – the only place – and other places; and thus no sense of a place as belonging by such relations to a definable geographical or geological or economic *region* – 'Wessex' itself implies a notion of geography quite unavailable to the 'heathfolk' or to the youthful Tess. The local geography involves instead a knowledge, and a way of knowing, so intense, so full, so detailed, that it cannot be acquired in more places than one, and cannot be exported from one place to another: it is not knowledge elsewhere. And what *is* knowledge elsewhere may not be on Egdon: take for example this passage from *The Return of the Native*,

---

[6] Orel, *Personal Writings*, p. 181.
[7] Hardy, *The Return of the Native*, Derwent May (ed.), (1878; London, New Wessex, 1974) p. 131.

where the mummers assemble for a rehearsal of their Christmas play
'St George':

> The next evening the mummers were assembled in the same spot, awaiting
> the entrance of the Turkish Knight.
>   'Twenty minutes after eight by the Quiet Woman, and Charley not come.'
>   'Ten minutes past by Blooms-End.'
>   'It wants ten minutes to, by Grandfer Cantle's watch.'
>   'And 'tis five minutes past by the captain's clock.'
>   On Egdon there was no absolute hour of the day. The time at any moment
> was a number of varying doctrines professed by the different hamlets, some of
> them having originally grown up from a common root, and then become
> divided by secession, some having been alien from the beginning. West Egdon
> believed in Blooms-End time, East Egdon in the time of the Quiet Woman
> Inn. Grandfer Cantle's watch had numbered many followers in years gone
> by, but since he had grown older faiths were shaken. Thus, the mummers
> having gathered hither from scattered points, each came with his own tenets
> on early and late; and they waited a little longer as a compromise.[8]

The mummers, it seems, have no sense that there is a national, or a
longitudinal time, of as much authority on Egdon as at Greenwich. It
is out of no determination to preserve the individuality of their sense of
place – of what would then be, for them, the uniqueness of Egdon –
that they defer to one or another of the local times rather than to what
is, absolutely, the time; for they evidently have no notion that Egdon
falls within a segment of the globe whose time has already been defined for it. In making the point, of course, Hardy writes with that distanced tone of amusement which so often, in spite of his protestations,
clothes his 'rustics' in the comic uniform of 'Hodge' that, in *Tess*, he
writes so eloquently against;[9] but elsewhere, in both novels, he attempts
to make good his protestations by revealing that what I have called
the fullness of the local knowledge possessed by the heathfolk, for
example, is beyond anything that his polite audience could acquire.
For the heathfolk, as also for the woodlanders and for Tess, knowledge
of place is given not by the eye alone, perhaps not even primarily by
the eye, as is our extended and picturesque geography, but by smell,
by tread – the feel of the earth underfoot – and by sound – the wind in
the vegetation of Egdon or in the woods around Little Hintock.

I should make it clear at this point that I am not convinced of the
historical truth of Hardy's account of the local geography of the

---

[8] Hardy, *The Return*, p. 154.   [9] Hardy, *Tess*, p. 156; also Orel, *Personal Writings*, pp. 168–71.

heathfolk, nor am I particularly concerned with that issue. I suspect, of course, that the 'primal' unity of the senses, by which they understand the place they live in, is a myth, a nostalgic fiction of Hardy's own, but to amplify that suspicion I would have to use evidence from outside the novel, from social history and from the history of literary representations of primitive man. But what particularly interests me about the novel is that, within it, we are given no position from which we can argue that what Hardy announces as a fact of life on Egdon is, in fact, a fiction. By representing the geography of the heathfolk in terms of what we may suspect to be a myth, of primal unity, the novel constructs us, its readers, as alienated observers of their sense of place, who are thus *obliged* to understand the process of our alienation in terms of the correlative myth, of history as the progressive differentiation of a lost, an original unity[10] – and who cannot therefore describe that unity as 'mythical', because, from the alienated viewpoint we have been assigned, we cannot know the minds of the heathfolk, and can assert nothing about how they work.

For this reason, we cannot describe this idea of a local geography; and the words we reach for, and that Hardy often reaches for, in attempting to comprehend it, instead conceal it from us. We may think of labourers working in the fields of their native village as 'at one with', or 'in harmony with', or 'a part of' something we describe as 'the landscape' or as 'Nature' (the 'n' capitalized), but these words and phrases can make sense, in such contexts, only to those whose experience is wide and therefore de-localized. 'Nature' refers to a notion of the *essential* that we abstract from the range of her *accidental* manifestations, but for that local sense that Hardy tries to apprehend, the local is at once accidental only, and yet not perceived as such by those for whom it is the whole. 'Landscape' implies the detached experience of an observer who arrives from some place other than the landscape itself, and it implies a habit of pictorialising based on, among other things, the opportunity of comparing different places with an abstract,

---

[10] This point, to which I return at the end of this essay, seems to me to be one which has been insufficiently taken into account in recent work on literature by geographers. I am thinking for example of Catherine A. Middleton, 'Roots and Rootlessness: An Exploration of the Concept in the Life and Novels of George Eliot', and David Seamon, 'Newcomers, Existential Outsiders and Insiders: Their Portrayal in Two Books by Doris Lessing', both in Douglas C. D. Pocock (ed.), *Humanistic Geography and Literature: Essays on the Experience of Place* (London, 1981). In both essays an analysis in terms of 'at home-ness' and its opposite, rootedness and rootlessness, insideness and outsideness, seems to be simply *applied* to the novels discussed as if those terms themselves were not susceptible (and badly in need) of analysis as ideology.

picturesque ideal. No less than 'Nature', then, 'landscape' is a concept produced by the comparison of the diverse, the accidental; whereas, for the 'heathfolk' of Egdon, where the local geography is represented as surviving least adulterated by intimations of a world outside than anywhere else in Hardy's Wessex, the heath is a place, as I have said, 'away from comparisons'. But we should be careful before deciding what such reflections can tell us about our relation to the heathfolk: for if words like 'nature' and 'landscape' put an unscaleable wall between our language and theirs, our mode of knowing and theirs, they do so only within the context of the myth and of the novel – they do nothing to assert, as the novel asserts, that the heathfolk *really did* have such and such a sense of place, or that we *really are* incapable of knowing, and Hardy of representing, what they knew. Nor, of course, do they tell us anything to the contrary.

I shall return to this question at the end of my discussion and mean- while try to define more of this, as it were, primal sense of place that is attributed to the heathfolk, in whom the eye has not yet dissociated itself from the other senses, and asserted its authority over them as the chief inlet of knowledge; and we can get an idea of what more there might be by looking at some of the writing which describes the cere- mony of the bonfire on Rainbarrow.

While the men and lads were building the pile, a change took place in the mass of shade which denoted the distant landscape. Red suns and tufts of fire one by one began to arise, flecking the whole country round. They were the bonfires of other parishes and hamlets that were engaged in the same sort of commemoration. Some were distant, and stood in a dense atmosphere, so that bundles of pale strawlike beams radiated around them in the shape of a fan. Some were large and near, glowing scarlet-red from the shade, like wounds in a black hide . . . Perhaps as many as thirty bonfires could be counted within the whole bounds of the district; and as the hour may be told on a clock-face when the figures themselves are invisible, so did the men recognise the locality of each fire by its angle and direction, though nothing of the scenery could be viewed.

'It seemed', continues Hardy, a paragraph or so later,

as if the bonfire-makers were standing in some radiant upper storey of the world, detached from and independent of the dark stretches below. The heath down there was now a vast abyss, and no longer a continuation of what they stood on; for their eyes, adapted to the blaze, could see nothing of the deeps beyond its influence. Occasionally, it is true, a more vigorous flare than usual from their faggots sent darting lights like aides-de-camp down the inclines to some distant bush, pool, or patch of white sand, kindling these to replies of the same colour, till all was lost in darkness again. Then the whole black phenomenon represented Limbo as viewed from the brink by the sublime Florentine in his vision . . .'[11]

This is a rich passage, and so let me apologize in advance for the fact that I will have to ignore much of what it does, and invite it to be seen, for the moment, as a metaphor for the local sense of space I am trying to define.

By this metaphor, then, the immediate locality of the heathfolk is the lighted circle around their fire, which is surrounded by a darkness made the more impenetrable precisely by the intense clarity with which they see what is in that circle: 'their eyes, adapted to the blaze' can 'see nothing of the deeps beyond its influence'. And so the place they do see is quite 'detached from, and independent of, the dark stretches below', except when 'a more vigorous flare than usual' illuminates, but only momentarily, a slip of land nearby. Intimations of a wider geography are offered by the fires of other, invisible settlements which the men recognise by their 'angle and direction', 'as the hour may be told on a clock-face when the figures themselves are invisible' – and that image suggests that, beyond the lighted circle they do occupy, there is for the heathfolk another, a wider circle at whose circumference are situated the parishes that surround their own. The image suggests, therefore, that to the heathfolk those other parishes are all in some sense *equidistant* from Rainbarrow, for a place is either *here* or it is *there*, and it is the *direction* from their own parish to another, rather than the distance between the two, that is of concern to them, when all parishes not their own are distant.[12] Intimations of distance, it is true, are said to be given by the size and clarity of each fire, but this is not apparently something the heathfolk take account of in identifying the fires, and it seems that these distances register not with the furze-cutters but with the narrator, whose language, characteristically at such moments, obtrudes upon the circular, local geography of the men – a geography, in the literal sense, self-centred – a wider, a regional geography of his own, in such a way as to produce a continually evident disjunction between his (and our) experience of place, and that of the characters he is describing. I shall say more about this later.

---

[11] Hardy, *The Return*, pp. 42–3.

[12] Compare John Clare's reference to Maxey, the next settlement to the north of his own parish, Helpston, as a 'distant village' – quoted and discussed in my *Idea of Landscape and the Sense of Place 1730–1840: An Approach to the Poetry of John Clare* (Cambridge, 1972), p. 122.

The geography of the heathfolk, as it is imaged in this passage, is the absolute opposite of Eustacia's, who sees the world as landscape, with Egdon as the dark and featureless foreground of a painting organized in such a way as to attract the eye to a distant central area of illumination. Her eye passes hurriedly, impatiently over Egdon in search of a glittering distance in Budmouth or Paris. There is, writes Hardy, 'no middle distance in her perspective: romantic recollections of sunny afternoons on an esplanade, with military bands, officers and gallants around, stood like gilded letters upon the dark tablet of surrounding Egdon':[13] a sentence that manages to convey, at once, the impatient seeking of the distance in past recollections or future hopes, and the consequent reversal of what is near and what is far, so that the gilded letters stand 'upon', and as if in front of, the 'dark tablet' of Egdon. It is the sense of space symbolized by the telescope she constantly carries, which frames the distance, converts it instantly into a near but unattainable foreground, and which carves through the circular space of the Egdon of the heathfolk a single straight line from herself to the far distance.

Clym, on the other hand, is 'permeated' with the scenes, and also with the odours and substance of the heath: he acquired in childhood that unified and complete knowledge of it, so that 'he might be said to be its product';[14] he *is* what he knows, or what he knows, at least, with that intense local knowledge, for his knowledge of elsewhere is a disguise which falls from him when the native returns. The contraction of his geographical horizons, the effacement of Paris from his concerns, is confirmed by his developing myopia, as the persistence of Paris in Eustacia's vision is confirmed by her telescope. When his sight begins to fail him, and he decides to stay and work on the heath, his 'daily life', says Hardy, became 'of a curious microscopic sort, his whole world being limited to a circuit of a few feet from his person'[15] – his horizon thus confined to the small circular space of his immediate environment as was the horizon of the heathfolk of whom he is now, in some sense, one. If we regard Clym's reoccupation of that circular space as a regression into the past, into the self-contained and self-centred world of childhood, we will perhaps find support for that judgment in Hardy's remark that Egdon was 'obsolete', belonging to what he describes in *Tess* as 'the days before the habit of taking long views'. For the modern world is rectilinear: *these* are the days 'of square fields, plashed hedges,

---

[13] Hardy, *The Return*, p. 95.   [14] *Ibid.*, p. 197.   [15] *Ibid.*, p. 273.

and meadows watered on a plan so rectangular that on a fine day they look like silver gridirons'.[16]

III

If Clym willingly allows his short-sightedness to contract the horizons of his mind as well as of his vision, Tess's experience might, in the terms of 'The Dorsetshire Labourer', invite itself to be understood as an expansion, as she becomes after her marriage to Angel Clare an itinerant farm-worker. This is how Hardy describes the geography that she constructs as a child, or that is constructed for her by the limits of the horizons of her childhood:

> The Vale of Blackmoor was to her the world, and its inhabitants the races thereof. From the gates and stiles of Marlott she had looked down its length in the wondering days of infancy, and what had been mystery to her then was not much less than mystery to her now . . . only a small tract even of the Vale and its environs being known to her by close inspection. Much less had she been far outside the valley. Every contour of the surrounding hills was as personal to her as that of her relatives' faces; but for what lay beyond her judgment was dependent on the teaching of the village school . . .[17]

Tess, it seems, had not at sixteen progressed far beyond a child's sense of place, as we might put it: 'what had been mystery to her then was not much less than mystery to her now'. She knows only a small portion of the vale, and the hills that surround it she has seen only from below, only from Marlott, so that, familiar as their contours are from there, the hills have as it were only two dimensions, they are a flat wall on her world beyond which she knows only what she has learned at school.

In her early excursions from Marlott – to Trantridge, and, after the death of her child, to Talbothays in the Vale of Froom – she is represented as apprehending those places entirely in terms of the differences they exhibit from the one place she knows well, her portion of the Vale of Blackmoor. For her, the Vale of Froom

> was intrinsically different from the Vale of Little Dairies, Blackmoor Vale, which, save during her disastrous sojourn at Trantridge, she had exclusively known till now. The world was drawn to a larger pattern here. The enclosures

---

[16] *Ibid.*, p. 198; Hardy, *Tess*, p. 40. For an analogous contrast between a modern, improved landscape as expressive of a 'linear' geography, and an old-fashioned landscape as expressive of a 'circular' sense of space, see my *Idea of Landscape*, pp. 98–109.

[17] Hardy, *Tess*, p. 65.

numbered fifty acres instead of ten, the farmsteads were more extended, the
groups of cattle formed tribes hereabout; there only families. These myriads
of cows stretching under her eyes from the far east to the far west outnumbered
any she had ever seen at one glance before . . . The bird's-eye perspective
before her was not so luxuriantly beautiful, perhaps, as that other one which
she knew so well; yet it was more cheering. It lacked the intensely blue
atmosphere of the rival vale, and its heavy soils and scents; the new air was
clear, bracing, ethereal. The river itself, which nourished the grass and cows
of these renowned dairies, flowed not like the streams in Blackmoor.[18]

The experience of elsewhere, then, is constructed in terms of its difference from the constant in Tess's system of geography, Blackmoor Vale
as seen from Marlott; and as long as she can still believe she has some
geographical centre, some home, the experience of being elsewhere, at
some point on the circumference of the circle whose centre is known,
can be managed. It does not threaten her identity, whatever else does,
for the habit of contrasting what she does not know, with what she
does, is a mode of cognition by which she can adapt to the unknown
as well. This adaptation is facilitated at Talbothays by Hardy's extravagant representation of the life there as one so sustaining that it is
two months before it occurs to Tess to make any excursion beyond the
immediate environs of the farm. Tess, says Hardy, was 'physically and
mentally suited among these new surroundings'; she re-rooted herself
there – had been 'transplanted to a deeper soil';[19] and by her marriage,
of course, she seems to have the opportunity of making this vale her
new home, the new constant by which other places will be known in
the future – so that when the marriage collapses, and she can no
longer live in the Vale of Froom, she returns to a Marlott which is now
strange to her. The turnpike gate on the highway to the village is
opened to her by a stranger, not 'by the old man who had kept it for
many years', and his reassurance that 'Marlott is Marlott still' serves
only to remind that for Tess this is no longer home, which should be,
but is not, with her husband in the vale she has been obliged to leave.[20]
'Where do we d'Urbervilles live?' her father had asked the parson who
informed him of his illustrious ancestry, and who had replied, 'You
don't live anywhere'.[21]

[18] *Ibid.*, pp. 139–40.   [19] *Ibid.*, p. 168.   [20] *Ibid.*, p. 299.
[21] *Ibid.*, p. 36. For an illuminating discussion of this passage, see Tony Tanner, 'Colour and movement in *Tess of the D'Urbervilles*', *Critical Quarterly* 10 (Autumn 1968) reprinted in R. P. Draper
(ed.), *Hardy, the Tragic Novels* (London, 1975), pp. 182–208. Tanner's essay remains by far the
best discussion of *Tess* that I am aware of.

It is this loss of a home, of a centre by which Tess might come to apprehend her migrations as movements along the radii and circumference of a circle, which makes her subsequent travelling, from Marlott to Port Bredy to Flintcomb-Ash to Emminster and back to Flintcomb-Ash, and then again to Marlott, not 'a sort of education', but a destruction of her way of knowing and of her identity alike. To some extent, of course, this loss of identity is willed, or at least an acceptance of necessity: at Marlott and Talbothays, Tess had always been distinguishable, from other women and from the landscape alike, by articles of clothing – a red ribbon, a pink jacket, a white collar – which did not allow her to be assimilated into the mass of either.[22] But on the road to Flintcomb-Ash, to discourage the attentions of the men she meets, she dresses herself as 'a fieldswoman pure and simple', in the grey, buff and whitey-brown of the chalk upland itself, and she becomes 'a thing scarcely percipient, almost inorganic', 'part of the landscape'.[23]

The monotony of this new landscape, its 'blank agricultural brownness', facilitates Tess's disguise: the 'long and unvaried road' from Port Bredy to Flintcomb-Ash, or the road from Long-Ash Lane, whose 'dry pale surface stretched severely onward, unbroken by a single figure, vehicle, or mark'.[24] At Flintcomb-Ash, there is 'nothing but fallow and turnips everywhere; in large fields divided by hedges plashed to unrelieved levels'[25] – the trees and shrubs, which were born to rise vertically from the landscape, cut down and flattened until there is, almost literally, 'no relief' in the landscape. Its anonymous character, and its power of conferring anonymity on those who work it, is perhaps best evoked in this extraordinary paragraph which describes the field in which Tess and Marian are set to hack swedes: it was

a complexion without features, as if a face, from chin to brow, should be only an expanse of skin. The sky wore, in another colour, the same likeness; a white vacuity of countenance with the lineaments gone. So these two upper and nether visages confronted each other all day long, the white face looking down on the brown face, and the brown face looking up at the white face, without anything standing between them but the two girls crawling over the surface of the former like flies.[26]

The absolute, unrelieved featurelessness of the landscape, insisted upon by the reminder that when we speak of the 'features' of a landscape we

[22] Hardy, *Tess*, pp. 42, 124, 328; for a valuable discussion of this topic, see Tanner's essay, section 3.
[23] Hardy, *Tess*, p. 326.   [24] *Ibid.*, pp. 361, 322, 354.   [25] *Ibid.*, p. 329.   [26] *Ibid.*, p. 331.

think of it as a face, contrasts quite evidently with the hills at Marlott, 'as personal to her as . . . her relatives' faces' – hills which, as if by confirming their personal relation with her, confirmed her identity in the vale they surrounded. But in these featureless fields on the chalk upland, where even the rain 'had no occasion to fall, but raced along horizontally upon the yelling wind',[27] Tess and Marian cannot make the simple act of self-assertion involved in standing upright – or they appear, briefly, as 'standing' between earth and sky, only to be crushed between the two 'visages' and to be set 'crawling' over the field 'like flies'.

The mechanization, too, of the modern farm at Flintcomb-Ash contributes to deny identity: Marlott had only a 'rickety' reaper, but to Flintcomb-Ash comes an itinerant steam threshing-machine, the identity of whose operator has been consumed by the engine he serves: 'if any of the autochthonous idlers asked him what he called himself, he replied shortly, "an engineer" '. But it is not simply that he serves a machine, that he is 'in the agricultural world, but not of it', that has left him with no name and with no identity beyond his occupation.[28] It is also the fact that he must be, for the engine *is*, itinerant; and his travelling has bred out of him the habit of noticing, so that he hardly perceives the scenes around him, or distinguishes one from another. The idlers who ask his name are distinguished from him, not simply by being idle, and thus not, for the moment, involved, as he is, in the industrialization of agriculture; they are also *autochthonous* – and to be so, the implication is, is to expect people to have names, which those who are itinerant, as we shall see, may not have.

For, beyond the conspiracy of Tess and the blank landscape to deny her identity, lies the fact that her identity has been destroyed by her new habit of travelling without reference to a constant centre in Marlott or Talbothays, so that she and the landscape merge and disappear: the landscape, existing in no relation to her knowledge of place, is no longer seen by Tess in terms of similarity and difference, and so no longer seen at all. Now all roads are long, unvaried, undifferentiated: this is the account of Tess's journey from Flintcomb-Ash towards Emminster:

[27] *Ibid.*, p. 322.
[28] *Ibid.*, pp. 123, 373. It may be worth pointing out that if Denys Kay-Robinson is right in his suggestion that the most likely original for Flintcomb-Ash is the village of Plush in the parish of Alton Pancras, *Wessex Reappraised*, pp. 126–7, then Flintcomb-Ash may be appropriately represented by Hardy as a farm on which mechanization was unusually far advanced; for Christopher Taylor, *Dorset* (London, 1970), p. 153, notes that in 1866 'one of the first steam ploughing-engines in the county was used to break up the downland at Alton Pancras'.

Keeping the Vale on her right she steered steadily westward; passing above the Hintocks, crossing at right-angles the high road from Sherton-Abbas to Casterbridge, and skirting Dogbury Hill and High-Stoy, with the dell between them called 'The Devil's Kitchen'. Still following the elevated way she reached Cross-in-Hand . . . Three miles further she cut across the straight and deserted Roman road called Long Ash Lane; leaving which as soon as she reached it she dipped down a hill by a transverse lane into the small town or village of Evershead, being now about half-way over the distance.[29]

There seems almost nothing to notice, here, but distances and directions, the intersection of one straight road with another: none of the features, the colours, the *differences* that marked the accounts of Tess's apprehension of places earlier in the novel. And yet, what has replaced that earlier mode of cognition is not the extended, educated, inquisitive geography of the tourist or traveller. The point is best made, perhaps, in a passage I referred to at the start of this essay:

After this season of congealed dampness came a spell of dry frost, when strange birds from behind the North Pole began to arrive silently on the upland of Flintcomb-Ash; gaunt spectral creatures with tragical eyes – eyes which had witnessed scenes of cataclysmal horror in inaccessible polar regions of a magnitude such as no human being had ever conceived . . . [they] retained the expression of feature that such scenes had engendered. These nameless birds came quite near to Tess and Marian, but of all they had seen which humanity would never see, they brought no account. The traveller's ambition to tell was not theirs, and, with dumb impassivity, they dismissed experiences which they did not value for the immediate incidents of this homely upland . . .[30]

Enough has been done, earlier in the novel, to identify Tess, by a series of images, as a bird, for us to see now in this passage a close relation between what Tess has suffered and what has been suffered by these 'birds of passage, whose expressions reveal that they have survived journeys of which they will not speak, and which, not valuing, they dismiss'.[31] So little time do they spend in one place that the process of moving, of migration, has left them 'nameless' – just as Tess's name has been made doubtful, and her identity destroyed, by her homelessness. For the birds, change has not been 'a sort of education' as it had been for the 'birds of passage' in 'The Dorsetshire Labourer': if they have not lost the capacity to learn, they have lost the will to do so, and

---

[29] Hardy, *Tess*, p. 343.   [30] *Ibid.*, p. 334.
[31] Passages in which Tess, with varying degrees of directness, is compared with a bird, will be found on pp. 105, 138, 161, 183, 238, 263, 332, 337.

to tell what they may have learned. They do not have the traveller's
sense of geography which Hardy recognised, in the essay, from the
eagerness of the migrant labourers to 'astonish' their fellow-workers
'with stories of the wide world comprised in a twenty-mile radius from
their homes'; and simply to quote that sentence is to indicate why. For
those migrant labourers still think of themselves as having homes: they
experience other places, as did Tess once, as points at the ends of lines
radiating outward from that constant centre. Tess, and these nameless
birds, 'don't live anywhere'; and Tess, in becoming less 'local in feeling',[32] has become more nothing. The best that she and Marian can
do, working at Flintcomb-Ash, is look over to where on clear days, if
there were any, 'you can see a gleam of a hill within a few miles o'
Froom Valley'; but that centre, made ever absent, invisible, by the
'cloaking grey mist',[33] is not home for her, but only where home should
be, and where her name should be clear, and Clare.

IV

I want to conclude by turning back from the process by which the
local, circular and self-centred sense of space is destroyed in Tess, to
look at the ways in which Hardy attempts to communicate a notion of
that primitive geography, as it inheres in its purest form in the consciousness that he attributes both to the heathfolk and to Tess before
her marriage. The geography of the reader that Hardy constructs,
perhaps particularly in these two novels, is regional, pictorial and linear; and to that consciousness of space as it might have been acquired
by such a reader, from books and by the opportunity to travel, Hardy
appeals with a language rich in cartographical, geological and pictorial
reference. Here is his description of the Vale of Blackmoor in the
second chapter of Tess:

The traveller from the coast, who, after plodding northward for a score of
miles over calcareous downs and corn-lands, suddenly reaches the verge of
one of these escarpments, is surprised and delighted to behold, extended like
a map beneath him, a country differing absolutely from that which he has
passed through. Behind him the hills are open, the sun blazes down upon
fields so large as to give an unenclosed character to the landscape, the lanes
are white, the hedges low and plashed, the atmosphere colourless. Here, in
the valley, the world seems to be constructed upon a smaller and more delicate

---

[32] Orel, *Personal Writings*, p. 180.   [33] Hardy, *Tess*, pp. 332, 333.

scale; the fields are mere paddocks, so reduced that from this height their hedgerows appear a network of dark green threads overspreading the paler green of the grass. The atmosphere beneath is languorous, and is so tinged with azure that what artists call the middle distance partakes also of that hue, while the horizon beyond is of the deepest ultramarine.[34]

'Calcareous downs', 'escarpments', a 'map', a landscape that has 'a character', the 'atmosphere', 'azure', 'what artists call the middle distance', 'hue', 'ultramarine': words and phrases such as these identify the reader as a literate traveller whom Hardy is to introduce to the consciousness of those who do not read about, who do not travel over, the various landscapes of Wessex, but who inhabit just one of them. This language constructs the reader as an Angel Clare, who first encounters Marlott, and Tess, on a walking tour through Blackmoor. The invitation the novels extend is that he should stop, observe, penetrate and 'read the secrets'[35] of a place he would usually pass through; but the secrets of the Vale of Blackmoor cannot be 'read', or certainly not by such a reader as this language constructs, one whose knowledge is customarily derived from reading. It is not *what* but *how* we learn that is at issue, and how we learn determines absolutely what we learn. If the vocabulary of the reader contains such words and phrases as I have just picked out, and by which he is able to understand the Vale of Blackmoor as occupying a place in a broad, regional geography, and among a wide range of possible landscapes, which he has encountered in books, pictures and by travelling, he will not be able to suspend that knowledge, but will understand the local only as a more detailed form of general knowledge – he will fail, if you will forgive the cliché, to grasp its absolute otherness. He will be able, indeed, only to characterize it *as* 'local', which is all I can do – and not as a knowledge which is, for those who have it, so inherent in their living in *this* place and no other, that it is not knowledge elsewhere, or for anyone whose knowledge is not so completely *of* that place, and so completely learned *in* it, that the local is all they know. The reader can certainly grasp from *Tess* that there is such a local knowledge, in Hardy's Wessex if not in nineteenth-century Dorset; but he can grasp only the notion of its existence, not the knowledge itself.

And so the opposition, between a local, and a wider geography and consciousness – between Clym's myopia and Eustacia's telescope, between 'the old-fashioned stationary sort' of labourer and 'the

---

[34] *Ibid.*, p. 39.   [35] *Ibid.*, p. 141.

habitually-removing man', between what Tess learns by living in Marlott and what she learns at school, between Tess and Angel – that opposition appears in the novels not simply as a *theme*, but as a problem of epistemology which must question the terms on which the novels can be written at all. As they construct a reader who has to be invited to suspend his general knowledge to discover the local – but for whom, however willing he is to make it, that suspension is impossible – they construct also a narrator who must claim, if he is somehow to mediate between the general and the local, that he is capable of performing that act of suspension that the reader cannot perform. He must appear capable of knowing what the heathfolk know, and what the reader knows, and of representing the local in the language of the novel without appropriating it to the general. He must be able to write the local in the language of the local, the general in the language of the reader, while performing the same act of separation that Tess performs, in speaking dialect at home and a version of standard English abroad;[36] but not only must these languages co-exist, neither appropriating the objects of knowledge that properly belong to the other, but the transitions from one language to the other must enable the reader to cross over from the sort of knowledge he has to the sort of knowledge he has not, and which, I have suggested, he *cannot* have.

I have defined the problem of knowledge in the novels, it may seem, too hastily, by announcing it as impossible of resolution as soon as I announced what it was; that happened, I suppose, because re-reading *The Return of the Native* and *Tess* before writing this essay, it was the grand impossibility of the narrator's task that struck me most forcibly. For the transitions I have spoken of, which, properly concealed (the fiction is) should enable the reader to step innocently over into the consciousness of the characters, seem quite impossible to conceal, and so work only to insist upon the disjunction between the two sorts of knowledge. The act of concealment that the narrator must try to pull off requires him to call no attention to the most obvious fact about the local, that of its nature it cannot be *written*; but he calls attention to that fact continually, as he represents the speech of the locals in a language which hovers between one degree or another of dialect, their thoughts in a language which hovers no less uncertainly between what we might imagine as appropriate to their thoughts, and one appropriate only to the thoughts of the reader which the novels construct. Let us look back,

---

[36] *Ibid.*, p. 48.

for an example, to the passage describing the bonfire on Rainbarrow – a passage introduced by a most elaborate pictorialising of the scene, and yet it is not at all clear to whom it thus appears as a picture.

To begin with, it *is* clear. It is the scene 'before the reddleman's eyes';[37] the eyes of the character who – described immediately afterwards as 'the traveller' – seems to represent the possibility of the reader, as traveller, penetrating the secret knowledge of Egdon even though he is an outsider. This possibility is quickly obviated by the impossibility of attributing the command of the language of the reader to the reddleman without forfeiting our belief in the local knowledge that he so insistently displays. And so the scene disappears from the reddleman's eyes to be rediscovered in what 'an imaginative stranger' 'might have' seen, and thereafter the description moves as often as not into a conditional mode, as if searching for a viewer who might combine the possibility of knowing both the local and the general without appropriating either to the other. To see the figure on the barrow 'move' 'would have impressed the mind as a strange phenomenon'; or else things *seem*, they *appear*, but to whom is not specified. The reddleman re-emerges, briefly, as 'the observer', in such a way as to change the character of his knowledge entirely: for he of all those unengaged in the bonfiremaking, would have been able to interpret the scene before him, which for this 'observer' still remains a mystery to be deciphered. Then, finally, the attempt to represent the scene through the eyes of the reddleman, however disguised as 'the traveller' or 'the observer', is abandoned, and the conditional is resorted to again: 'Had a looker-on been posted in the immediate vicinity of the barrow, he would have learned', and so on. That conditional depends for its fulfilment on exactly what I have said to be impossible, the simultaneous *presence* of someone within the centre of knowledge at the top of the barrow, and his *absence* from it, in a position from which he observes but does not participate – an impossibility dramatized by the disjunction between being, at once, 'in the immediate vicinity of the barrow', and yet remaining 'a looker-on', 'posted' there as if as a spy, still unobserved, and yet able to examine as the narrator does the smallest details of the faces of the bonfire-makers.

The disjunction is repeated in the language of the description of the bonfire ceremony, in the attempt to facilitate a transition from absence to presence that only underlines its impossibility. I have already referred to the problem of knowing for whom the other fires in the

---

[37] All quotations in this paragraph come from Hardy, *The Return*, pp. 41–3.

landscape were 'near' or 'distant'. More striking, perhaps, is the problem of the representation of space as seen or imagined from within the lighted circle of the bonfire. 'The heath down there', says the narrator, 'was now a vast abyss' – and the phrase 'down there' situates him in 'the immediate vicinity of the barrow', within the lighted circle whose limits he defines for us. Occasionally 'a more vigorous flare than usual' illuminates a portion of the middle distance, 'till all was lost in darkness again'; and then 'the whole black phenomenon beneath represented Limbo as viewed from the brink by the sublime Florentine in his vision'. The word 'beneath' again invites us to situate the narrator within the lighted circle at the top of the barrow; but his immediate displacement, in favour of Dante, at once introduces a mode of knowing this landscape obviously inappropriate to those within the circle, and effectively reintroduces the conditional: had Dante been there, which he was not, he might have been able to repeat the trick he performed in the *Divine Comedy*, of seeing on our behalf what is invisible to us, the invisibility of the heath to those whose eyes see only the radiant circle round the fire.

Or take the description of the Vale of Froom as it appeared to Tess on her journey from Blackmoor to Talbothays – in which she was represented as learning the geography of the new vale by comparing it with the old. When I quoted this before, I omitted a couple of sentences which I will now restore, and I will introduce them with the sentence that precedes them, to give an idea of the disjunction of the different modes of knowing they offer:

These myriads of cows stretching under her eyes from the far east to the far west outnumbered any she had ever seen at one glance before. The green lea was speckled as thickly with them as a canvas by Van Alsloot or Sallaert with burghers. The ripe hues of the red and dun kine absorbed the evening sunlight, which the white-coated animals returned to the eye in rays almost dazzling, even at the distant elevation on which she stood.

There is perhaps no need for any very lengthy analysis of this – the disjunction could not be more evident. For whoever it could be to whom the cows appeared like burghers in a Flemish townscape, it is evidently not Tess, and it is evidently not her sophisticated picturesque knowledge which distinguishes the tones of the cattle in terms of whether their skins absorb or reflect the light. And the pretence that it is – that this effect was noticeable 'even at the distant elevation on which she stood', just as evidently calls attention to the disjunction by the elaborate attempt to conceal it.

The chapter continues, a few pages later:

Tess Durbeyfield, then, in good heart, and full of zest for life, descended the Egdon slopes lower and lower towards the dairy of her pilgrimage.

The marked difference, in the final particular, between the rival vales now showed itself. The secret of Blackmoor was best discovered from the heights around; to read aright the valley before her it was necessary to descent into its midst.[38]

It is apparently only when Tess descends into the Vale of Froom that the marked difference between the two vales – the difference that will finally enable her to grasp what she does not know, here, in terms of what she does know, in Blackmoor – now 'showed itself' to her. This descent enables her to 'read aright' the new landscape – and if that phrase 'to read aright' manages to remain just about appropriate to Tess's mode of knowing, by a reflection that she is now outside Marlott, in a space she previously could have known only from the teachings of the village school, we must still ask, of Blackmoor Vale, for *whom* it contained secrets, and by *whom* they were best discovered 'from the heights around'? Apparently, the answer is Tess, for the tense – 'the secret of Blackmoor *was* best discovered' – must indicate that this is her internal *oratio obliqua*; but, equally apparently, the answer cannot be Tess, who learned the geography of the vale from within its depths, and who had access to knowledge of the vale which are secrets only to the traveller. It seems that the traveller who, in the description of Blackmoor I quoted earlier, comes northward over the calcareous downs to discover the vale 'extended like a map beneath him' – the traveller whom the novel constructs as its own inquisitive, alienated reader – has here attempted to penetrate Tess's consciousness of place, and to imprint upon it his own.

We can perhaps interpret such attempts at appropriation, according to Hardy's account in 'The Dorsetshire Labourer', as embodying the process in real history whereby the consciousness of the traveller imprints itself on that of the 'locals', and obliterates the local knowledge; and if we are disposed to believe in the existence of that local knowledge as a matter of historical fact, not fiction, so perhaps they are. But if we are more disposed to believe that primal, local knowledge to have

[38] Hardy, *Tess*, p. 141.

been a myth deployed by the novel to describe us, its readers, as alienated by the process of the differentiation of a primal unity, what will
strike us most is not that such moments of appropriation occur, but
that they occur so *evidently*. They jut out of the narrative as awkwardly
as do those, in *The Return of the Native*, where the narrator searches so
painstakingly for a viewpoint, with such an evident attempt to do the
impossible, that it is evidently impossible for us, too, to cross the space
between what we see and what the locals know. The striking incongru-
ity between Tess's view of the Vale of Blackmoor and the traveller's,
between her perspective on the Vale of Frome and his, and the obvious-
ness of the attempt to imprint his knowledge on hers, also emphasise
the impossibility of the traveller's crossing the space that separates him
from Tess, and preserve, on either side of that space, the twin myths of
an original, unified sense of place, and of an alienated geography. The
traveller can certainly attempt to print his consciousness on Tess, so
that Blackmoor, 'an engirdled and secluded region' at the start of the
novel, 'for the most part untrodden as yet by the tourist and the
landscape-painter'[39] will be trodden, penetrated (as Tess, the bird, is
'trodden'[40] and penetrated by Alec D'Urberville) and inscribed in the
list of the traveller's other conquests, Mellstock, Egdon, Little Hintock;
and so that Tess will be violated again, by a smart tourist who knows
about landscape-painting. But the attempt to do so will establish that
she, and the Vale, if they can be violated, must certainly once have
been intact; and if they can't be, still are.[41]

[39] *Ibid.*, p. 39.
[40] *The Complete Oxford English Dictionary* (Oxford, 1971), 'tread', B.8.
[41] I would like to acknowledge the help and advice given to me in the preparation of this essay by
     Stephen Daniels, Harriet Guest, Adrian Poole, Hugh Prince and Keith Snell.

CHAPTER 5

Gender and Cornwall: Charles Kingsley to Daphne du Maurier

Philip Dodd

If readers had to guess the content of Daphne du Maurier's two best-known novels, *Jamaica Inn* and *Rebecca* from the names of their locations – Jamaica Inn and Manderley respectively – what would they conclude? Taking the publication dates into account, they might surmise that the novels were late examples of Rider Haggard-like imperial fiction or a contribution to the tradition of women's imperial romance of which E. M. Hull's *The Sheik* is the most famous example.[1] It is hardly likely that the names of the locations would lead readers to assume that du Maurier's novels are predominantly set in Cornwall.

The 'odd' names given to the locations may be an example of du Maurier's historical literacy, and in the case of *Jamaica Inn* may allude to the sea traffic between the Caribbean and Cornwall. For instance, in a note prefacing *Jamaica Inn*, du Maurier makes the ritual claim that all characters and events are entirely imaginary, but she also claims that Jamaica Inn refers to an actual Inn of that name on the road between Bodmin and Launceston.[2] But even when one has reflected on possible explanations there seems at the very least something curiously and deliberately exotic about the choice of names – and even some of the descriptions: Bodmin Moor, for example, is referred to several times in *Jamaica Inn* as 'motionless as desert sand'.[3] There is nothing unique about the presence of exoticism in thirties works. For instance *Rebecca* shares with an even more unlikely 'regional' work – George Orwell's *The Road to Wigan Pier* – a fascination with colonial places. In a travel book absorbed in northern mining landscapes, Orwell retells a story of a train journey to Mandalay in Burma in which he and a fellow

---

[1] E. M. Hull, *The Sheik* (1919). For a discussion of the sexuality in imperial romance see Nicola Beauman, *A Very Great Profession. The Woman's Novel, 1914–39* (1983), pp. 188–197. Place of publication is London unless otherwise stated.
[2] Daphne du Maurier, *Jamaica Inn* (1936; 1992), p. 3.   [3] du Maurier, *Jamaica Inn*, p. 32.

colonial confessed their loathing of the empire, before leaving the train together like furtive lovers.[4]

To ponder the presence of 'elsewhere' and the exotic in du Maurier's novels is inevitably to consider the issue of whether her fiction counts as regional at all. According to the orthodox view, and even to the rigorous counter-orthodoxy of Raymond Williams, du Maurier's novels (and hence a tradition of fiction which her work exemplifies) are unlikely to be seen as regional.[5]

Williams is characteristically alert to the fact that the 'region' is not so much a category as a relationship with the metropolis, and that some writing from the regions is exempted regional classification (for example Home Counties writing). But he does believe that a kind of regional fiction has existed, although his descriptions and definitions would not accommodate du Maurier's fiction. For Williams, there is a kind of novel 'which is not only set in its own place but set in it as if there were no others', and that 'is indeed more about a region or a way of life than about those people in relationships that inhabit or constitute it'. This writing appears analogous to working-class writing insofar as a 'class can indeed be seen as a region: a social area inhabited by people of a certain kind, living in certain ways'. Both kinds of writing are, at their best, realist, and both are diluted when they they move near the historical romance. One crucial difference Williams sees between the two kinds of writing is that working-class writing has most often been written by a 'sympathetic outsider observer', while regional fiction is 'characteristically written by natives'.[6]

By these criteria du Maurier is ruled out as a regional writer. After all, her novels are – if these distinctions hold – more about relationships than about a way of life; they are not novels about the working class (and Williams seems to assume regional novels primarily are or ought to be so); and du Maurier is not a 'native' of Cornwall. But the riposte to all this is to say that, attentive as he is to issues of class and the regional novel, Williams is woefully indifferent to issues of gender – and his definition needs radical overhaul once this acknowledgement has been made. To stress the autonomy of the life of the region in novels

[4] George Orwell, *The Road to Wigan Pier* (1937; Harmondsworth: 1962) p. 177.

[5] In his essay 'Region and Class in the Novel', *Writing and Society* (1983; Verso, 1991), Williams claims that the regional novel only became significant in the late nineteenth century. If he is right this may be further confirmation of the adage that the owl of history flies only at dusk; the regional novel becomes important at the moment when a truly modern national identity was being forged.

[6] Williams 'Region and Class', pp. 230, 232, 234, 233.

is, for instance, to ignore the fact that it is a convention of fiction for women to be at the disposal of family or men. Women shed light on a place because of their 'strangeness' to it. In *Jamaica Inn*, for example, the heroine Mary Yellan is forced to live with her aunt after her mother's death:

A girl can't live alone, Mary, without she goes queer in the head, or comes to evil. It's either the one or the other. Have you forgotten poor Sue, who walked the churchyard at midnight with the full moon, and called upon the lover she never had? And there was one maid, before you were born, left an orphan at sixteen. She ran away at Falmouth and went with the neighbours.[7]

In *Rebecca* the heroine is plucked by marriage from her peripatetic life in Europe and the United States as a woman's companion, to live in Cornwall.[8] In Winifred Holtby's *South Riding* even though the novel is set in Yorkshire, its motor is the new feminist headmistress, Sarah Burton, who brings radical ideas to her pupils in Yorkshire from her successful teaching career in metropolitan London, and previous to that in South Africa.[9] Even Constance Holme's *The Lonely Plough* (which is cited by Williams in *The Country and the City* as an exemplar of regional fiction[10] provides evidence against his own thesis. Not only is the first chapter titled 'Across the Dub' (the Atlantic) – presaging a discussion of migration – but the subject of the chapter is prompted by a woman's refusal to move as she is expected to when offered marriage:

Round comes the agent, and it's, 'You're for getting wed, I reckon? Right!' (if it *is* right), and the contract's made. The lass goes into the contract along with the farm, and along at the beck of the three men to the church. Well, that's your way, but it's not mine, and you may as well know it first as last. I'll come when I'm ready, or I'll never come at all!'[11]

It is equally masculinist to assume, as Williams does, that a proper regional novel does not focus primarily on personal relationships. Much women's fiction – including regional fiction – is precisely so focused in order to interrogate certain issues around place and identity. To put it simply, power relations in regional novels are much more variously expressed than Williams' foregrounding of class conflict allows. It is equally limited to assume that romance, which historically has become

---

[7] du Maurier, *Jamaica Inn*, p. 10.   [8] Daphne du Maurier, *Rebecca* (1938; 1992), p. 27.
[9] Winifred Holtby, *South Riding. An English Landscape* (1936; 1988), pp. 22–27. During Burton's inter-view for the post of headmistress, one of the members of the appointing committee pronounces '"London" as though it were an obscure village of whose name he was uncertain.' p. 23.
[10] Raymond Williams, *The Country and the City* (1973; St Albans, 1975), p. 304.
[11] Constance Holme, *The Lonely Plough* (1914; Oxford, 1931), p. 10.

identified as a women's form, is necessarily less available to the regional imagination than Williams' chosen realism. It is of course the romance form of du Maurier's fiction that partially sanctions the 'exoticism' of Manderley and Jamaica Inn.

Williams' rigidity also suggests a diminished sense of the various perspectives that are available to the regional writer – constructed as either the 'native' or of the outsider. There seems no place in his scheme for the migrant's vision, the richness of which has been eloquently articulated by Salman Rushdie.[12] At one level, there is of course no comparison between the migration of which Rushdie writes and the Hampstead/Paris/Cornwall movement of a writer such as du Maurier. But the migrant's vision – that of someone who both belongs and does not belong – can be an important element of one tradition of the regional novel, and more generally, the regional imagination.

In revising Williams' argument, one might go so far as to argue that there is at least as much congruence between women's fiction and the region as there is between region and working-class writing – after all, womens' fiction (like working-class writing) has often been considered as something apart and inferior.

Rather than pursuing Williams' arguments on the regional imagination any further, it might be more profitable to borrow the idea from Edward Said that fiction is always a matter of 'overlapping territories and intertwining histories'. As he argues, 'it is the case that no identity can ever exist by itself and without an array of opposites, negatives, oppositions: Greeks always require barbarians, and Europeans Africans, Orientals etc.'.[13] One might also add that the masculine always requires the feminine.

The regional novel and gender intersect in a number of ways, that can be summarised as follows. There is the fact that gothic fiction and the romance (including the historical romance), both of them seen increasingly as 'women's forms', have had 'place' at their centre – whether one thinks of Emily Bronte's *Wuthering Heights* or Catherine Cookson's *oeuvre*. Equally important is the way that place can be gendered in fiction. Small geographical areas, cities, counties or generalised regions such as 'the North' can all be given different gendered characteristics. Take for example the contemporary novelist David Storey who wrote two first-person novels, *This Sporting Life* and *Flight to*

[12] Salman Rushdie, *Imaginary Homelands: Essays and Criticism, 1981–1991* (1991), p. 20 and *passim*.
[13] Edward Said, *Culture and Imperialism* (1993), p. 60.

Camden, one narrated by a man, the other a woman. There is no doubt that Storey imagined places in terms of masculinity (the North) and femininity (the South):

It was in order, so it seemed, to accommodate the two extremes of this northern physical world and its southern, spiritual counterpart that I started making notes which two years later, while I was still at the Slade, resulted in the writing of a novel which I called *This Sporting Life* . . . In this way, the northern terminus of that journey became associated with a masculine terminus, and when I came to write about its southern counterpart – the intuitive, poetic and perhaps precious world to which I felt I had escaped – I immediately associated it with femininity and a woman's sensibility and responses. The north–south dichotomy became a masculine–feminine one. The second novel, *Flight into Camden*, was written in the first person by a woman.[14]

A glimpse at British cinema of the sixties – which drew on and developed out of the fiction of Storey's generation – shows the literalisation of the relationship between masculinity and northern landscapes. In films such as Lindsay Anderson's *This Sporting Life* and Karel Reisz' *Saturday Night and Sunday Morning*, a new generation of actors including Albert Finney and Richard Harris, were inserted into the 'masculine' industrial landscapes of Yorkshire and Nottingham. Of course this identification of 'north' and masculinity is not confined to fiction, as can be seen in E. P. Thompson's *The Making of the English Working Class*, a regional work *par excellence*, with its 'discovery' of a radical northern (male) working class and its author's deliberate affiliation with the north in the book's signature – 'Halifax, August 1963.'[15] Thompson's history is no less a regional work than E. M. Forster's 'southern' and 'feminine' novel *Howards End*, with its signature 'Weybridge, 1922'.[16]

Of course there is no necessary relationship between particular regions and gender, as this relationship is constantly ravelled and unravelled by history. In his fine essay, 'The Discovery of Rural England', the historian Alun Howkins shows implicitly how the apparent 'common-sense' notions of place and gender that a writer like David Storey can draw on, were 'invented' in the late nineteenth and early twentieth century, when the 'south' and its landscape of smooth and bare (never rocky or craggy) hills came to be described in feminine terms.[17]

---

[14] David Storey, 'Journey Through a Tunnel', *Listener*, 1 August 1963, pp. 159–60.
[15] E. P. Thompson, *The Making of the English Working Class* (Harmondsworth, 1963), p. 15.
[16] E. M. Forster, *Howards End* (Harmondsworth, 1989), p. 332.
[17] Alun Howkins, 'The discovery of rural England' in R. Colls and P. Dodd (eds), *Englishness. Politics and Culture, 1880–1920* (Beckenham, 1986), p. 64.

In this as well as other regards, the West Country is an interesting test case regarding the stability of a region's identification with gender. Du Maurier's *Rebecca* – perhaps the most famous example of a popular novel set in Cornwall – will be the central focus of the discussion, but other works to be considered here will inevitably include work from other arts, since for the last century it has been not only fiction, but painting that has helped to give Cornwall a visibility and representational identity. For instance, without its own indigenous artists, Cornwall was particularly indebted to visiting painters for creating its iconography: J. M. W. Turner visited the region in 1811 and created *Picturesque Views of the Southern Coast of England*; other painters of the region included William Daniell and Thomas Lumley.[18]

Many writers also helped to construct the region in particular ways, including Tennyson, who went in search of the legends surrounding Tintagel castle for the Arthurian *Idylls of the King*, and Charles Kingsley who published *Two Years Ago* in 1857. It is clear from the early chapters of *Two Years Ago*, that the region is an important touchstone for Kingsley in relation to wider world events, including the American War of Independence and the Crimea–Sebastopol is the reference in the title:

Let us go on, and up the street after we have scrambled through the usual labyrinth of timber-baulks . . . and have stood the stares and welcomes of the lazy giants who are sitting about among them . . . men who are on their own ground, and know it; who will not touch their caps to you . . . but expect you to prove yourself a gentleman, by speaking respectfully to them; which if you ever do, you will find them as hearty, intelligent, brave fellows as ever walked this earth, capable of anything, from working the naval brigade guns at Sebastopol . . . God be with you, my brave lads, and with your children after you; for as long as you are what I have known you, Old England will rule the seas, and much else besides.[19]

Kingsley is not alone in his imaginative alignment of the region with war. A hundred years later, Winston Graham in *Ross Poldark*, began his series of novels with reflections on the protagonist, absent from his native Cornwall, fighting in the American War of Independence.[20] Given that the novel was published in 1945, it is hard not to see that it has an analogical cast, with its return of a soldier to his birthplace and

---

[18] Tom Cross, *Painting the Warmth of the Sun: St Ives Artists, 1939–1975* (Penzance and Guildford, 1984), p. 10.

[19] Charles Kingsley, *Two Years Ago* (1957, 1906), pp. 49–50.

[20] Winston Graham, *Ross Poldark, A Novel of Cornwall, 1783–1787* (1945, 1968).

his attempt to humanise and modernise both his personal and work relationships. The struggle over the ownership of the mines in the novel appears to be an analogy for the disputes over the coal mines that were to be settled by nationalisation in 1947. *Ross Poldark* is another example of a novel that may well be absorbed in a place – as Raymond Williams insists is the characteristic of regional fiction – but it is as haunted by other places as any of the other fictions we have mentioned.

Charles Kingsley and Winston Graham are also united by their explicit identification of the region with masculine virtues. In Kingsley's case the identification is clear in the whole tenor of the novel which counterpoints two men as representatives of the region: the 'manly' naturalist and 'warrior' Tom and the 'effeminate' poet Elsley Vavasour, the author of *A Soul's Agonies and other Poems*. Both have returned to the region, Tom from colonial adventures, Elsley from the literary world of London. It is true that Kingsley's novels set in other places are equally absorbed in separating out 'true' manhood from false and effete versions. Nevertheless it remains an important comment on the identity of the region that in the 1850s Kingsley could see the region as masculine, the proper home of the English imperial spirit ('will rule the sea and much else besides'), and as somewhere that guaranteed the future of England. To put it simply, Cornwall for Kingsley was the site of a forward-looking, confident masculinity. Without overstating the point, the West Country is not just one manly forward-looking world, but a manly Protestant one, unlike the London world of Elsley. This comparison prefigured Kingsley's attack on the 'effete' Catholicism of J. H. Newman, which provoked the cardinal's publication of his great self-defence, *Apologia Pro Vita Sua*.[21]

This identification of the West Country with manly Protestantism stretches into the early twentieth century, in Edmund Gosse's *Father and Son*. In his autobiography Edmund recounts his father's settling as part of the community of Plymouth Brethren and upholding a kind of Protestant manliness that Kingsley so admired.[22] (Kingsley himself features in the book as a family visitor.) This is not to say that there is not demonstrable historical support for the identification of Protestantism and the West Country, but that this theme was sustained and elaborated in fiction by a group of nineteenth-century writers.

---

[21] See Kingsley's attacks on Newman which were incorporated into J. H. Newman's *Apologia Pro Vita Sua* (1864).

[22] Edmund Gosse, *Father and Son* (1907; Harmondsworth, 1989).

There is a difference between Kingsley and Gosse, however. This is that the West Country for the latter begins to be associated with an 'old' world, in contrast to the 'new' one of London, and Gosse's perception is shared by a whole host of writers and artists. Without trying to explain this shift – which would be far beyond the brief of this essay – it is worth mentioning Matthew Arnold's argument in works such as *On the Study of Celtic Literature*. Although Cornwall is only implicit in his argument about Celtic culture, the association by Arnold of old traditions with the 'genuine' Celts, who 'cling' to the past, is highly relevant to the re-making of representations of Cornwall that were going on at the same time.[23] More specifically, there is the founding of the Newlyn School in Cornwall by Stanhope Forbes and others. These painters had begun to mourn the disappearance of painterly subjects, as the traditional attire of the fisherman 'was passing away' and the 'quaint old houses' were replaced by cottages that 'ape the pretentiousness of modern villadom'.[24]

It is from around this period, the turn of the century, that Cornwall in fiction and art becomes identified, not with a modernising and manly England, but with that which resists or is opposed to change. A late continuation of this identification can be found in Sven Berlin's *Alfred Wallis: Primitive*, a biography of the untutored, deeply religious St Ives painter, who was an important influence on the St Ives school of painters. Written during the war, in 1942 – but not published until 1948 – *Alfred Wallis* begins and ends with a reference to Sebastopol; Wallis was born in the year of the battle and, as the book's postscript says, he 'died of senile decay at Madron Institution on August 29, 1942. Within a year of that date Sebastopol had fallen again'.[25] There is no doubt that Wallis, the sailor, painter and religious man, and the world from which he grew, represents for the author a rare glimpse into an authentic pre-modern world:

Madron, indeed Cornwall itself, was a remote place in those days, quite untouched by modern civilisation ... An undisturbed sunlit root of England founded on a tradition that reached far back beyond medieval times to days when Iberians, Goidels and Celts were driven west by invading tribes, settled

[23] Matthew Arnold, 'On the Study of of Celtic Literature' in *The Complete Prose Works of Matthew Arnold* (ed.) R. H. Super (Ann Arbor, 1965), p. 291.
[24] Mrs Lionel Birch, *Stanhope Forbes ARA and Elizabeth Stanhope ARWS* (n.d.) p. 27, and Caroline Fox and Francis Greenacre, *Artists of the Newlyn School (1880–1900)* (Exhibition Catalogue of Newlyn Orion Galleries, 1979), p. 66.
[25] Sven Berlin, *Alfred Wallis: Primitive* (1948, Bristol; Redcliffe, 1992), p. 100.

in these parts, tilled the land and helped to lay the foundation of the Cornish race.[26]

Thus there is no way in Berlin's book of connecting either Wallis or his world to the modern one. The sea – critical to Kingsley as a material emblem of past and future progressive Imperial rule – has migrated into a metaphor for Berlin of the emotional force within the man. At one moment Wallis is described as follows:

Alfred Wallis was alive to the sap in his veins. He knew the rock was not barren, nor the hill childless. The roughness of the heather root was the texture of his being, the force and violence of the sea broke continually against the walls of his heart . . . The lie of civilised life as we have come to know it never gained precedence over these things in Wallis; it smashed the discipline already imposed upon him and his *innermost being flowed through*, creating, under terrible circumstances, the poet of a primitive and *oppressed people*.[27] (our emphases)

Something that could be 'observed' by Kingsley in the mid-nineteenth century is now something that has to be imagined by Berlin: it is a critical fact of the biography that Berlin never met Wallis.

The metropolitan painters who settled in Cornwall and 'discovered' Wallis, did not try to follow the sailor-artist in allowing the 'force and violence of the sea' to overwhelm them. The paradox of their achievement was to modernise English art by continuing to fix Cornwall as either a 'pagan' world – Barbara Hepworth often talked of the importance of pagan Cornwall[28] – or as a world of small isolated villages and fishing boats. One should add, though, that they did contribute to the feminising of the representation of Cornwall. Ben Nicholson, for instance, mixed the received inconography of Cornwall in his paintings with domestic and kitchen objects – viewing the landscape with which Wallis identified himself directly, through a homely window. For his pains, Nicholson has recently been condemned by one contemporary art critic for introducing an element of 'domestic idiocy' into his painting, a further sign perhaps that Cornwall is still identified with the masculine.[29]

Whilst 'domestic idiocy' is hardly an accusation to made against Daphne du Maurier – a novelist best known for her 'adventure stories' for women – it is nevertheless the case that du Maurier shares with

---

[26] *Ibid.*, p. 20.   [27] *Ibid.*, p. 45.
[28] Tom Cross, *Painting the Warmth of the Sun; St Ives Artists, 1939–1975* (Plymouth, 1982), p. 65.
[29] Andrew Brighton, 'Ben Nicholson: A New Monograph by Norbert Lynton', *Tate: The Art Magazine*, 1, Winter 1993, p. 37.

Nicholson some of the cultural responsibility for feminising Cornwall. While the reasons for the congruence between such apparently disparate figures is beyond the scope of this essay, it may be worth noting that both of them were in effect Bloomsbury figures – and children of noted artistic parents, the actor George du Maurier and the painter William Nicholson – who both led cosmopolitan lives, moving between London and Paris, before settling in Cornwall.[30]

But what distinguishes du Maurier, even from Nicholson, is her attempt not only to feminise Cornwall but to align the modern and the feminine. Du Maurier's novels are as haunted by the sea and the Cornish coast as *Two Years Ago* or *Alfred Wallis*. But where those other works saw the sea as the site of a desirable English manhood – whether of a proud imperial 'Jack Tarr' or an anguished and oppressed artist – Du Maurier does not bestow any of these 'manly' assocations on it. The sea in her work is a place of terror, murder and criminality; it is a place prior to the modern world of decency and order. For instance, in *Jamaica Inn* – set around the beginning of the nineteenth century – the seashore is a lawless place, where wreckers lure ships on to the rocks before stripping them of their cargo. In the more contemporary *Rebecca*, the sea is equally 'dark' in its implications. Only from the west wing of Manderley, where Rebecca, the first, dead wife, had her bedroom, can the sea be heard, 'black, pitiless and cruel'.[31] And it is by the sea that Rebecca conducts her affairs in the beach cottage, where we later learn that she was murdered by de Winter; her body taken into the bay and her boat skuttled to make it look like a drowning. The only residual representative of the brave Cornish sailor in *Rebecca* is an 'idiot', a simpleton, who spends his aimless life on the local beach (p. 270).

Du Maurier's 'distanced' way of seeing one of the sites of Cornish (and English) masculinity is undoubtedly complex, and the fact that she is a migrant into the region is no doubt relevant. But there can be little doubt that a major determinant is the fact that as a woman, du Maurier would inevitably have found it much more difficult than Kingsley to acknowledge the sea as the site of a triumphant English masculinity. It is not simply that she could never be one of 'England's sons', but that her relationship to region and nation as a woman is much more unstable than a man's. As Virginia Woolf would write in *Three Guineas*, the year

[30] Philip Dodd, 'How Ben Nicholson Proved That You Can Be British and Modern', *Tate: The Art Magazine*, 1, Winter 1993, pp. 30–36.
[31] du Maurier, *Rebecca*, pp. 95–6. Subsequent page references to *Rebecca* appear in parenthesis in the text.

after *Rebecca* was published, women were only ever step-daughters of England – liable to change their identity on marriage.[32]

It is this social location of du Maurier – a member and yet not a full member of an elite – that allows her to scrutinise the identification of masculinity, the past, and Cornwall in such illuminating ways. In *Jamaica Inn*, there is the critical scrutiny by the young heroine, Mary Yellan, of both Jos Merryn, the murderous landlord and wrecker who is both a type of surrogate father and possible lover, and of the 'manly Protestantism' of the vicar Francis Davey – an albino and wholly corrupted figure whose celebration of Cornwall's pagan past is to be one of the most chilling sequences of the novel.[33]

Whilst it would be possible to construct an argument about du Maurier's work, region and gender, either in relationship to *Jamaica Inn* or across a wide range of her work, I have decided to give prominence to *Rebecca*. Formally, *Rebecca* sends out complex signals about who should be the centre of the reader's attention. The title would lead us to expect Rebecca to be the heroine, but she is already dead when the novel opens, her life reconstructed by the narrator, a woman who never met her. If the narrator is the protagonist, then it is strange that she remains unnamed throughout the novel. Perhaps the protagonist then is Maxim de Winter, the husband of both the women and the owner of the estate and house of Manderley? The truth is that the novel focuses on a triangular relationship: the representative masculinity of Maxim de Winter, the scion of Cornwall, coming under scrutiny from two female points of view. The site of masculinity has shifted however. It is no longer founded in a Protestant progressive manliness, a confident and stalwart fisherman or in a 'primitive' oppressed artist. In *Rebecca*, it is located in a representative of the landed gentry, in a man of property who not only inhabits the landscape but whose male ancestors have owned it for centuries. In the description of his house Manderley, du Maurier offers us a vision of an exclusively masculine world that stretches from the past and still haunts the present. It is a world of unencumbered appetites:

It was as if the house remembered other days, long long ago, when the hall was a banqueting hall indeed, with weapons and tapestry hanging upon the walls, and men sat at a long narrow table in the centre laughing louder than

---

[32] Virginia Woolf, 'A Room of One's Own', *'A Room of One's Own' and 'Three Guineas'*, intro. Hermione Lee (1938; 1984), *passim*.
[33] du Maurier, *Jamaica Inn*, p. 248.

we laughed now, calling for wine, for song, throwing great pieces of meat
upon the flags to the slumbering dogs. (p. 219)

When the narrator first meets Maxim, she feels that his look is attractively 'medieval' and hints at violence, chivalric rather than war-like,
reminding her of a portrait of a man in a gallery, with hat and cape,
who probably lived in a walled city in the fifteenth century. '[H]e would
stare down at us in our new world from a long-distant past – a past
where men walked cloaked at night . . . a past of whispers in the dark,
of shimmering rapier blades, of silent, exquisite courtesy' (p. 18). This
is a man's world, but not immune to certain kinds of feminine influence; later, as the unnamed protagonist and de Winter begin to fall in
love, she notes a softening, a new expression, 'less fettered . . . more
modern, more human'.[34] Very early in the novel there are, then, hints
of what is crucial throughout, a dialogue between the old, traditional
masculinity and the new, modernising feminine. The question is: can
Cornwall be either modernised or feminised?

   The dark, handsome, rather secretive and tragic male landowner
who owns Manderley and whose family forms part of the dominant
history of Cornwall is a recognisable type in romance fiction – whether
we are thinking of Rochester in *Jane Eyre*, or Carne of Maythorpe in
Winifred Holtby's *South Riding*, published just a year before *Rebecca*.
Like Maxim de Winter, these others are tied to the past, to a place or
region, an identification which is reasserted by the apparent certainties
of patriarchal power when threatened or thwarted by uncontrolled,
passionate female sexuality. In this sense the romance provides du
Maurier with a set of conventions through which to interrogate both
gender and place.

   But du Maurier is acutely aware of how new places and identities be-
come available. If *Two Years Ago* sets up a dialogue between Cornwall,
London and the Americas in order to articulate exactly what Cornwall
represents, so *Rebecca* sets up a dialogue between Cornwall, London and
Monte Carlo, the place from which the narrator starts her journey to
Cornwall, with her courtship by de Winter. At one level Monte Carlo

---

[34] du Maurier, *Rebecca*, p. 28. Beauman, *A Very Great Profession*, notes the definition of a popular
romantic novel given by the Boots First Literary Course for librarians in the inter-war years
included 'a strong and silent hero' from a good family but cut off from society. The heroine is
well-bred but 'delicately nurtured', so needing someone strong to lean on. Her delicate charms
brings out the soft side of his nature and 'the story ends with a fervent embrace' p. 197. Du
Maurier was always adamant she was not a 'romantic' writer in this mould, see Alison Light,
Forever England; Femininity, Literature and Conservatism Between the Wars (1991), p. 159.

operates as a simple geographical contrast to Cornwall. Nothing could be further from the wet and wild climate of Cornwall and Manderley, with its grey-stoned 'symmetry and grace' hidden by the dark woods and guarded by a menacing sea (pp. 6, 142, 373), than the Mediterranean with its 'ornate and ostentatious' hotels and with its impersonal 'glittering sun' and 'hard, clean sky' (pp. 8, 11, 14).

To use the terms of Edward Said that were quoted earlier, a geographical contrast is always more than that; there is also the question of power. Monte Carlo is new, and modern; and de Winter's class, wealth, sports car, and his ability casually to pick-up women, all at first suggest Monte Carlo as his 'natural home'. The south of France and later London, are seen as arenas for a loose-living, detached masculinity, epitmomised most particularly by Rebecca's lover, Favell. He is 'flashy in a sunburnt way', with 'hot' blue eyes and red hair and his mouth is 'sensual and horrible' (pp. 166, 350). Clearly this new masculinity is seen as debased and hardly the site of proper modernisation or renewal.

Monte Carlo and the Mediterranean signal not only a certain kind of masculinity but also, as Alison Light suggests – in the best commentary on one strand of 'conservative' women's literary writing between the wars – a flight from femininity. She notes that the construction of English life between the wars as feminine and domesticated, was partly the result of the many male writers who chose to travel and live abroad rather than suffer the humiliations of what they saw as middle-class English stuffiness and domesticity.[35] As Paul Fussell has also shown in *Abroad*, travelling was an outlet for the cogniscenti to express their repulsion for an 'effeminate' England, and to indulge in the pleasures of the detached male. The post-First World War retreat of masculinity, the sense of exhaustion, the feeling that peacetime was effeminate, and the alarm about changing relationships between the sexes, all led to the exploration of other places, as more hospitable to manliness.[36]

It soon appears that de Winter is not part of this exiled masculinity, and he is as much out of place in this new cosmopolitan world as the female protagonist. De Winter assures his future wife – who seeks out the oldest part of the town to sketch and who neurotically worries that only experienced women dressed in black satin and pearls belong there – that a modern woman is the last person with whom he wants

---

[35] Light, *Forever England*, pp. 6–7.
[36] Paul Fussell, *Abroad: British Literary Travelling Between the Wars* (New York and Oxford, 1980), *passim*.

to commune, and quickly persuades this unchallenging companion to marry him and return immediately to Manderley. De Winter identifies the modern woman with his first wife and her sexual licentiousness; he is not aware that another more domesticated woman might be just as modernising – if in a radically different way.

De Winter's love of his Cornish property is his only sense of stability and certainty, and it is equally his undoing. He talks of land as the greatest love a man can have, a secular male passion never discussed in the Bible: 'Christ said nothing about stones, and bricks and walls, the love that a man can bear for his plot of earth, his soil, his little kingdom' (p. 286). When he discovers Rebecca's disloyal nature very soon after his marriage, murder immediately occurs to him but he settles initially for an unmanly bargain; she will not tamper with the public dignity of his formal position, and in return will be able to flee him whenever she likes to her lover in London, where gendered certainties are loosened and where all kinds of illicit interminglings are possible (p. 286). Only when she begins to threaten the hypocrisy by bringing her lovers to the house, by invading its old male space with her new female sexuality and by casting doubt on the legitimacy of any heirs, does Maxim assume his patriarchal rights and kill her. He is prepared to murder to eradicate the threatening power of a sexualised, feminine force and to retain both his sense of an inviolate place and his masculinity.

But the masculine has not had it all its own way at Manderley. The feminising, modernising process had been set in train some time in the eighteenth century: '[Manderley] would still be gay, but with a certain grace and dignity, and Caroline de Winter . . . would walk down the wide stone stairs in her white dress to dance the minuet' (pp. 219–20). Rebecca later identifies with this feminine power and chooses Caroline's dress from a portrait in the house as her fancy dress costume for the annual ball at Manderley. She also puts in place other 'reforms', transforming the 'wilderness' of the inherited house by replacing much of its contents with carefully chosen, exquisite furniture, tapestry, and porcelain and extending the gardens. Max de Winter ruefully admits that 'Half the stuff you see here in the rooms was never here originally. . . . The drawing-room as it is today, the morning-room – that's all Rebecca' (p. 287). The protagonist had already guessed the source of the feminine distinctiveness of the morning-room. It was a

woman's room, graceful, fragile, the room of someone who had chosen every particle of furniture with great care . . . There was no intermingling of style, no confusing of period, and the result was perfection . . . (p. 89)

The only place completely untouched by this modernising femininity is the library, a traditionally masculine place, which has the deathly atmosphere of a sepulchre. It has 'an old quiet smell . . . an ancient mossy smell, the smell of a silent church where services are seldom held', and is darkened by the wood panelling and heavy curtains. Anything new, even the freshness of the garden air, is instantly aged, 'becoming part of the unchanging room itself' (p. 73). The protagonist feels excluded from the public business of the estate that her new husband conducts from the desk in the room. Only in her fantasies is she able to feminise the library and it is not insignificant that her longings are resolutely domestic. If Rebecca continues the general modernising cultural work of Caroline de Winter, the second wife longs to give it a contemporary inflection by making the house, this incarnation of old Cornwall, domestic. She imagines herself in the library as the mother of three sons and even more poignantly, from her position of exile after the house has been destroyed, she fantasises that the library has become the domestic setting for the most conformist type of middle-class gentility:

The room would bear witness to our presence. The little heap of library books marked ready to return, and the discarded copy of *The Times* . . . And Jasper, dear Jasper, with his soulful eyes and great, sagging jowl, would be stretched upon the floor, his tail a-thump when he heard his master's footsteps. (p. 7)

Since this image is somewhere between memory and desire, it is difficult to decide if it is intended as a gentle parody of both middle-class companionate marriage and a certain form of feminised 'southern' Englishness, echoed later with evocation of cricket, the English countryside, country sports, 'dripping crumpets' and 'fresh rasberries for tea' (pp. 10, 11, 12). Alison Light in her discussion of the late thirties 'Mrs Miniver' articles in *The Times* notes exactly the same kind of conservative, celebratory, domestic iconography: 'Tea was already laid: there were honey sandwiches, brandy-snaps . . . and crumpets. Three new library books lay virginally on the fender-stool . . .'.[37] It is perhaps more likely that du Maurier's vision of domestic quietude is, as Light says, double-edged; the apparent urging towards the acceptance of the controls of the solid and familiar are constantly undermined by other characters in her novels who are unbridled and free.[38] Whichever is

[37] Light, *Forever England*, p. 117.   [38] *Ibid.*, p. 158.

the more persuasive interpretation, it remains true that the masculine world of Manderley cannot accommodate the modernising feminine, whether it is the sexualised feminity of Rebecca or the domestic femininity of the narrator. It is not inappropriate that Manderley itself is destroyed, burnt down by Rebecca's outraged lesbian housekeeper.

What is fascinating are the terms in which masculinity, deprived of any feminine influence, is described. In order to grasp its power – which was simply celebrated by writers such as Charles Kingsley – du Maurier has to go outside the terms set by romance and draw on a vocabulary derived from imperial literature. Here is a description of the abandoned Manderley, bereft of feminine nurture:

The woods, always a menace even in the past, had triumphed in the end. They crowded, *dark and uncontrolled*, to the borders of the drive. The beeches with *white, naked limbs* leant close to one another, their branches intermingled in a strange embrace . . . squat oaks and tortured elms that straggled cheek by jowl with the beeches, and had thrust themselves out of the quiet earth, along with monster shrubs and plants . . . Scattered here and again amongst this *jungle* growth I would recognise shrubs that had been landmarks in our time, things of culture and grace . . . *had gone native* now, rearing to monster height without a bloom, *black and ugly* as the nameless parasites that grew beside them. (pp. 5–6, our emphases)

This use of an 'imperial language' was common in the thirties. It is present in Evelyn Waugh's *Handful of Dust* where the author makes all kinds of connections between the apparently 'civilised' English world and the jungle life of South America, and in Graham Greene's *Journey Without Maps*, where connections are made between early English rituals and the 'native' rituals of Liberia.[39] But what is important in *Rebecca* is that this language is drawn upon in order to picture Cornish manhood at its most predatory:

some half-breed from the wood, whose seed had been scattered long ago beneath the trees and then forgotten, and now, marching in unison with the ivy, thrust its ugly form like a giant rhubarb towards the soft grass where the daffodils had blown. (p. 7)

[39] Evelyn Waugh, *A Handful of Dust* (1934; Harmondsworth, 1975). He also wrote two travel books about Africa in the thirties, *Remote People* (1931) and *Waugh in Abyssinia* (1936). For a discussion see Martin Stannard, 'Debunking the jungle: The Context of Evelyn Waugh's Travel Books 1930–9' in Philip Dodd (ed.) *The Art of Travel: Essays on Travel Writing* (1982), pp. 105–126. Graham Greene, *Journey Without Maps. The Collected Edition of Graham Greene* (1978). For a discussion see Philip Dodd, 'The Views of Travellers: Travel Writing in the 1930s', in *The Art of Travel*, p. 130.

Femininity in sharp contrast is represented by 'whiteness', which is always at risk from the dark and monstrous:

> It was dark, much too dark. That naked eucalyptus tree stifled by brambles, looked like the white bleached limb of a skeleton, and there was a black earthy stream running beneath it, choked with the muddied rains of years . . . I should have stayed on the other beach on the white shingle. (p. 164)

This threatening masculinity is something persistent in du Maurier. It is just as visible in *Jamaica Inn* where the moors, as I have suggested earlier, are often described as a desert, with the implication that Joss Merlyn is analogous to some sheik ruling over them; he certainly imagines Mary as part of his harem. It is now possible to see why, in her two most famous novels, du Maurier should give Jamaica Inn and Manderley the names they have; they are part of her attempt to be able to imagine the power of the traditional male, identified with the untamed nature of the Cornish landscape, that has such a stranglehold over the modernising women who struggle within the novels. It is a wonderful irony in *Rebecca* that Maxim tells the unnamed protagonist when he first meets her in Monte Carlo that a woman's companion – the job she has – is analogous to the servant of an eastern potentate.

In conclusion, it is apparent that du Maurier's imaginings of Cornwall are important for a number of reasons. In thinking about the regional novel, du Maurier's work shows the limitations of the influential definitions offered by Raymond Williams, and reveals how gender and region are just as powerfully conjoined as region and class. Second, they show a female novelist trying to modernise 'old' Cornwall and challenge its dominant masculine identity which is so closely tied to the representation of Cornwall as a site of English masculinity. Of course, that the novels which challenge these dominant versions always end with the departure of the 'victorious' heroine suggests that the power of old masculine Cornwall was able to resist modernisation. This is clearly not a matter of the 'failure' of du Maurier. The thirties, when she was at the height of her fame, was the period when Cornwall was developing as a site for serious tourism and in that sense it was precisely the 'old' rugged masculine world of the sea and the sea stories that the tourist wished to find recreated in Cornwall. Who, after all, would want to travel to deepest Cornwall to find what the unnamed narrator of *Rebecca* so desired, English middle-class gentility, when it was precisely such a life from which the tourist wanted, at least temporarily, to escape?

CHAPTER 6

James Joyce and mythic realism

Declan Kiberd

Joyce's *Ulysses* is often treated as a definitive account of the mind of modern Europe in 1922, the year of its publication: but, for that very reason, it is also a recognition that Europe itself was nothing without its colonial holdings. *Ulysses* is one of the first major literary utterances in the modern period by an artist who spoke for a newly-liberated people. The former provost of Trinity College Dublin, J. P. Mahaffy, clearly sensed Joyce's disruptive power when he lamented that his publications proved beyond doubt that 'it was a mistake to establish a separate university for the aborigines of the island, for the corner-boys who spit into the Liffey'.[1] That use of the word *aborigines* captures a central truth about James Joyce: outcast from Ireland, scornful of Britain, and uneasy about the humanism of a Europe to which he could never fully surrender, he became instead a nomad, a world author.

Virtually alone among the great post-colonial writers, he did not head for the imperial city or the lush landscapes of the parent country: for him, there would be no Naipaulean 'enigma of arrival',[2] no pained discovery that the culture to which he had been assimilated lacked, after all, a centre. He took this as understood from the start and cut himself adrift from all cosy moorings: it was his strange destiny to be a central figure in world literature, whilst yet being somehow tangential to the cultural life of both Ireland and England. Though he jokingly saw himself as the most recent of the *Wild Geese* – the Irish rebels who sought training in the armies of Catholic Europe after 1691 in hopes of returning to expel the occupier – he was, in truth, a sort of *gastarbeiter* from a peripheral country with a chronically depressed economy.

Like many migrants in the decades since, Joyce performed his own research and field work in central Europe, his own reverse anthropology,

[1] Gerald Griffin, *The Wild Geese* (London, 1938), p. 24.
[2] V. S. Naipaul, *The Enigma of Arrival* (Harmondsworth, 1987).

while perpetually fretting that the homeland he had abandoned was about to disappear.[3] 'If she is truly capable of reviving, let her awake', he wrote in 1907, 'or let her cover up her head and lie down decently in her grave forever'.[4] The migrant intellectual is forever assailed by the feeling that he or she is speaking before a tribunal, and so it was with Joyce. He tried in journalistic articles to convey something to the developed world of his people's desolation. He had no great faith that his meaning would be understood. Adopting, for strategic purposes, the urbane tone of a central European, he described a bizarre and unjust murder-trial of a speechless defendant back in Ireland. 'The figure of this dumbfounded old man, a remnant of a civilization not ours, deaf and dumb before his judge', he told his Triestine readers, 'is a symbol of the Irish nation at the bar of public opinion'.[5]

That old prisoner's problem was a version of Joyce's own: how to express the sheer fluidity and instability of Irish experience in a form which would still be comprehensible to the arbiters of international order. Ireland was indeed a precarious invention, a fiction which might yet be sufficiently imagined to become a fact: but in 1907 its people were estranged from the past, a nation of exiles and migrants, caught on the cusp between tradition and innovation. They were in but not of any situation in which they might find themselves, their reality being the experience of perpetually crossing over from one code to another. The shortest way to Tara, the ancient centre of Celtic civilisation, was indeed through Holyhead, that clearing-house for exiles *en route* to the cities of England and continental Europe. Yet Joyce took into exile the notion that only in literature can the consciousness of a people be glimpsed.

There were so many different levels of national experience for Joyce to comprehend: and yet there was no overarching central image, no single explanatory category, no internal source of authority available to him. Too mobile, too adaptable, the Irish were everywhere and nowhere, scattered across the earth whilst feeling like strangers in their own land. The fear which gripped Pearse, MacDonagh and Desmond FitzGerald in 1914 – that a great historic nation was about to disappear as tens of thousands of its men went willingly to the slaughter of another

---

[3] For a contemporary parallel see Gayatri Chakravorty Spivak, *The Postcolonial Critic* (London, 1990), p. 165.

[4] Ellsworth Mason and Richard Ellmann (eds.). *The Critical Writings of James Joyce* (New York, 1959), p. 174.

[5] *Ibid.*, p. 198.

country's war – had also assailed Joyce. He began *Ulysses* in the hope of discovering an adequate form to this strange experience, one which might allow him eventually to proclaim the tables of a new law in the language of the outlaw, to burrow down into his own 'Third World' of the mind. For an audience in the made world, he wished to evoke a world still in the making.

He was, in that sense, one of those migrants who create newness out of the mutations of the old. The novel in the hands of a Rushdie or a Naipaul has come to be seen as a form through which the members of an educated native élite address their former masters: but, decades before they wrote, Joyce had used prose narrative to capture the jokes, oral traditions and oratory of a people, who might never have committed these to print themselves, unless they had been part of a more achieved, self-confident culture. Though *Ulysses* is indeed the collective utterance of a community, it is hard to imagine anyone within the world of the book (except possibly Stephen) actually writing it all down. 'I have put the great talkers of Dublin into my book', boasted Joyce, 'they – and the things that they forgot'.[6] For all that, there will be few to imagine either a Leopold or Molly Bloom *reading* it, which makes it in this respect also a supreme instance of the post-colonial text.

Yet these characters are in no way unmodern or unsophisticated. Joyce set his book in the 'centre of paralysis' that was Dublin in 1904, in the conviction that if he could get to the dead heart of that city, he could render the discontents and estrangements of the modern world. As an Irishman, he could never condone the glib assumption that 'undeveloped' countries like his own were like the developed ones at an earlier stage of their growth: not for him the easy evolutionism of Darwin or Marx. Joyce was radical enough in *Ulysses* to present Mr Deasy's optimistic Christianity and the socialist's vision of a classless society as two sides of the same oppressive coin. He knew better than that. He knew from personal experience that to be modern is to experience perpetual disintegration and renewal, and yet somehow to make a home in that disorder. The Irish, through the later nineteenth century, had become one of the most deracinated of peoples; robbed of belief in their own future, losing their native language, overcome by feelings of *anomie* and indifference, they seemed rudderless and doomed. Though *Ulysses* is set on a day in 1904, it is necessarily a portrait of the late-Victorian Ireland which went into its making and, as such, a remarkable outline of colonial torpor.

[6] Djuna Barnes, 'James Joyce', *Vanity Fair*, XVIII, April 1922, p. 65.

George Bernard Shaw read it in exactly this way and wrote rather ambiguously to Joyce's publisher:

I should like to put a cordon round Dublin to gather up every male person in it between the ages of fifteen and thirty, force them to read it, and ask them whether on reflection they can see anything amusing in all that foul-mouthed, foul-minded derision and obscenity. You are probably a young barbarian beglamoured of the excitements and enthusiasms that art stirs up in romantic youth, but to me it is all hideously real: I have walked those streets, and known those shops, and taken part in those conversations. I escaped from them to England at the age of twenty, and forty years later I have learned from the books of Mr Joyce that slack-jawed blackguardism is as rife in young Dublin as it was the 1870s . . . It is, however, some consolation to find that at least one man has felt deeply enough about it to face the horror and write it all down . . .[7]

Shaw recalled that the Dublin which he had abandoned in 1876 offered its young men a life that was hardly bearable, producing in them 'a certain futile derision and belittlement that confuses the valuable and serious with the base and ludicrous'.[8] What Shaw ignored was the fact that Joyce had deliberately composed his exposure of the torpor in those very years when it was being challenged and brought to an end.

The Easter Rising was a protest against this paralysis, 'a last desperate attempt to save Irish nationality from the obliteration that appeared to them to face it in the final years of the Great War'.[9] Its leaders concurred with the diagnosis which had been made by Joyce back in 1907: one of their sons later wrote that 'for them the alternatives were national extinction or, by a supreme effort on their part, the possibility of another lease of life for Irish nationality, out of which a free Ireland might somehow, some day, emerge'.[10] A full reading of *Ulysses* must take account not only of that torpor, but of the protest against that provincialization, as Joyce warmed to his task in 1916. Ireland in those years was indeed a crucible of modernity, a place of uneven development: desperate in the ways that colonies always are, but also a laboratory which enjoyed the effects of a streamlined educational and communications system long before imperial England. It was, in that sense, a land where the Immaculate Conception and *Das Kapital* existed side by side.

What had happened in Ireland was what would happen across the world in the later nineteenth and early twentieth century: traditional

---

[7] Letter to Sylvia Beach, in Beach, *Ulysses in Paris* (New York, 1956), p. 21.

[8] G. B. Shaw, preface, *Immaturity* (London, 1921).

[9] Garret FitzGerald, 'The Significance of 1916', *Studies* (Spring, 1966), LV, no. 217–29.

[10] *Ibid.*, p. 29.

patterns of living had been gravely disrupted, but without the material compensations which had elsewhere helped to make such losses tolerable. The people were suffering from that most modern of ailments: a homeless mind. Their small but persistent hope was that they might somehow yet manage to modernize in a human fashion and put an end to the loss of meaning which was all they knew. Whilst very few of them nursed regressive dreams of a return to the past, many did yearn for a more bearable version of modernity. Against that backdrop, both the 1916 Rising and *Ulysses* can be interpreted in rather similar ways: as attempts to achieve, in the areas of politics and literature, the blessings of modernity *and* the liquidation of its costs. In other words, the Irish wished to be modern and counter-modern in one and the same gesture. Fredric Jameson has argued that it is precisely this feature which Third World politics has in common with cultural modernism: it offers consolation for all that reification brings with it, assuring its devotees that the qualities of archaism and beauty which appear to be threatened by consumer capitalism can indeed be salvaged from its wreckage.[11]

By the time that Joyce began writing *Ulysses* in 1914, most of the industrial world, and not just its colonial outposts, was overcome by a sense of *anomie*: indeed, the Great War was proposed by many as a heroic alternative to such meaninglessness. Joyce's project of recounting 'the dailiest day possible' takes on a radical significance in that context: he wished to reassert the dignity of the quotidian round, to reclaim the everyday as a primary aspect of experience. But this was in no way intended as a surrender to the banality of that colonial life which had been evoked so unerringly in *Dubliners*. There Joyce had described an Ireland filled with echoes and shadows, a place of copied and derived gestures, whose denizens were turned outward to serve a distant source of authority in London. Such a collection of prentice stories would be written in later decades by many another member of an emerging national élite ashamed of his or her colonial setting, and taking bitter consolation in an ability to render all the futility with a wicked precision. Writing it all down may well have been Joyce's personal alternative to acts of political violence, his way of seizing power, for certainly his anti-English comments were more frequent and more bitter than those which came from the leaders of the Easter Rising.[12]

[11] Fred Jameson, *The Political Unconscious: Narrative as a Socially Symbolic Act* (London, 1981), p. 236.
[12] Richard Ellmann, *James Joyce* (London, 1966), pp. 226, 427, 436, 440, 441, 455.

Each of the stories in *Dubliners* chronicles an abortive attempt to achieve freedom, an attempt which is doomed precisely because it couches itself in the forms and languages of the enemy. In 'An Encounter', for instance, a group of boys play truant from school with all its boredom and whippings; but their outing leads to a meeting with a strange man who talks incessantly of chastising errant boys. Worse still, the whole enterprise demands an oppressive degree of planning (faking excuses, forging letters, saving money, squaring up sisters, etc.), which is just as banal and wearisome as the classroom routine to which it had initially seemed such a glamorous alternative. All this drilled conformism is necessary, in the words of one critic, so that this gesture of defiance will not be comprehended as such.[13] The act of rebellion is taken away from the boys even as they seek to perform it, prophesying the failure of a nationalism which would insist on confining its definitions to the categories designed by the colonizer.

Each narrative in *Dubliners* tells a similar tale, of an impulse arrested or else enacted to a point where it becomes self-negating: in either case, the gesture of revolt is fated always to have the old, familiar tyranny inscribed in it. Perhaps the most graphic image of this self-effacement is that of the monks who sleep in their own coffins discussed by the party-goers in 'The Dead': Joyce uses this story to evoke a world of martyrs and death-cults. If the past cannot be confronted or worked through, then the future is not feasible: that is the meaning of history, unconstrued history, as nightmare. What the culture worships is not so much the dead as its power to contain them. The monks in their coffins are Joyce's warning of the dangers of a death-cult, which contains the springs of life by converting its foreseeable death into a constant part of it. If the monks epitomise a sort of death-in-life, the statues in the story signalize a kind of life-in-death: but they are always evoked in a climate of mockery. The Morkans' workhorse – who walks in endless, aimless circles around the statue of King Billy – is caught in one kind of paralysis, whilst the snow-capped stone figure of Daniel O'Connell is frozen into another. The living protagonist, Gabriel Conroy, is himself covered in patches of snow which approximate him to the dead statue.

The short-story genre promised Joyce an escape, a line of flight from the formal inappropriateness of the novel, which was calibrated to a

---

[13] Clive Hart (ed.), *James Joyce's 'Dubliners': Critical Essays* (London, 1969): section on 'An Encounter'.

settled society rather than one still in the settling. But the escape-route which it offered Joyce proved just as illusory, just as self-defeating as that which beckoned and then frustrated his characters. When he had finished the stories he was rewarded by no sense of difficulties overcome:[14] though they are bound together by themes, symbols, even characters, the collection does not quite become a novel. Each story moves to an epiphanic revelation of an impasse, a paralysis which marks its termination, because if it were to proceed any further it would exfoliate into a much more extensive and unlimited type of narrative: the process which was allowed to happen just once when 'Mr Hunter's Day' became *Ulysses*. This vast and multi-faceted assemblage was latent in *Ulysses* and, as Yeats shrewdly observed, the stories contained the promise of a new kind of novelist.[15] However, their author was at that early stage no more able than his characters to fit that narrative together. All he could work with were shreds and patches, assembled to no clear overall purpose other than the revelation of such fragmentation to its victims. As Deleuze and Guattari were to write of Kafka's stories in a somewhat similar context: 'never has so complete an *oeuvre* been made from movements that are always aborted, yet always in communication with each other'.[16]

The style in which the stories of *Dubliners* were written was one of famished banality, whereby Joyce found his own appropriate level of linguistic under-development, taking Hiberno-English in its post-famine, post-Gaelic disorder to a degree of 'scrupulous meanness'. Irish was no longer a feasible literary medium for him, but a means whereby his people had managed to reshape English, to a point where their artists could know the exhilaration of feeling estranged from *all* official languages. Joyce never felt tempted to try to write in Irish, and he affected to scorn its senile folk narratives on which no individual mind had ever been able to draw out a line of personal beauty: but deeper than the disdain went a kind of fear, a sense of shared trauma at the loss, in most parts of Ireland through the nineteenth century, of the native language.

The fate of a sullen peasantry left floundering between two official languages, Irish and English, haunts the diary entries by Stephen Daedalus in *A Portrait of the Artist as a Young Man*:

---

[14] James Joyce, *Letters: 2* (ed.) R. Ellmann (London, 1966), p. 134.
[15] Quoted by Ellmann, *James Joyce*, p. 403.
[16] Gilles Deleuze and Felix Guattari, *Kafka: Toward a Minor Literature*, translated by Dana Polan (Minneapolis, 1986), p. 41.

John Alphonsus Mulrennan has just returned from the west of Ireland. European and Asiatic papers please copy. He told us he met an old man there in a mountain cabin. Old man had red eyes and short pipe. Old man spoke Irish. Mulrennan spoke Irish. Then old man and Mulrennan spoke English.[17]

Joyce there mocks the widespread hopes of a language revival, of opening the lines of communication to a Gaelic past: but it is obvious from *A Portrait* that he was not fully happy with the English-speaking Ireland of the present. Though the old peasant might struggle to recall a few phrases of Irish for the Gaelic Leaguer's notebook, the truth (as Joyce saw it) was that English did not provide a comprehensive expressive medium for Irish people either. That is part of the tragicomedy of non-communication pondered by Stephen Daedalus during a conversation with the Englishman who is dean of studies at his university:

The language in which we are speaking is his before it is mine. How different are the words *home, Christ, ale, master*, on his lips and on mine! I cannot speak or write these words without unrest of spirit. His language, so familiar and so foreign, will always be for me an acquired speech. I have not made or accepted its words. My voice holds them at bay. My soul frets in the shadow of his language.[18]

The death of language takes many forms besides fatigued cliché, and one of them – in Ireland, at any rate – was the loss of the native tongue.

The moment when Joyce wrote in English, he felt himself performing a humiliating translation of a split linguistic choice. In his writings, he seeks to express that sundering; and, eventually, in *Finnegans Wake* he would weave the absent texts in the space between standard Irish and standard English. But in the passage just quoted, he posits a harassment of the Irish student's emotional nature by the Englishman's intellectual culture. On such a subject, Joyce was resolutely conservative. He knew that the colonial education system offered Irish children an alien medium through which to view their native realities. To interpret those realities through literary forms which were similarly alien to them would serve only to make the people seem even more unknown and unknowable. Hence Stephen's unrest of spirit.

No matter how brilliant Joyce's use of English, it would always run the risk of being seen as his way of serving his colonial master: English

---

[17] James Joyce, *A Portrait of the Artist as a Young Man* (ed.), Seamus Deane (Harmondsworth, 1992), p. 274.
[18] *Ibid.*, p. 205.

would be the perceptual prison in which he realized his genius, and the greater his achievements, the greater the glory reflected on the master language. In *A Portrait*, Stephen goes on to complain to a Gaelic Leaguer: 'My ancestors threw off their language and took another . . . They allowed a handful of foreigners to subject them. Do you fancy I am going to pay in my own life and person debts they made'.[19] The hatred in that sentence is not so much for the Irish language as for the fact of its humiliation and repression: but Joyce does pay the debt. Shreds of Irish would turn up repeatedly in *Ulysses*: and by the time he wrote *Finnegans Wake*, Joyce had learned to emphasise the ways in which Irish caused its speakers to rework English, so that the book's underlying idiom is his own idiolect of Hiberno-English. But his treatment of the language and its speakers is never confident or final: beneath the pose of disdain lies a real fascination and an even deeper fear. In 'The Dead' Gabriel Conroy is forced to come to terms with the spiritual gulf between himself, a sophisticated Dublin intellectual, and his homely wife from the west. He is chided by a young woman named Miss Ivors for holidaying on the Continent rather than on Aran. As the story closes, his thoughts are moving west, across the Central Plain over a snow-bound Ireland, to the peasant boy whom his wife had once loved.

The ambiguity of Gabriel's feelings about the west is reflected in the predicament of his author, elaborated with an almost unbearable clarity in the treatment of Mulrennan in Stephen's diary at the close of *A Portrait*. There Gabriel's split-mindedness has grown to near-hysteria:

I fear him. I fear his red-rimmed horny eyes. It is with him I must struggle all through the night till day come, till he or I lie dead, gripping him by the sinewy throat till . . . Till what? Till he yield to me? No. I mean no harm.[20]

Joyce turned his back on Gaelic Ireland with mixed feelings, and no final certainty that silence, exile and cunning were answers to the challenge posed by the native tradition. And well might he have been afraid:

Mulrennan spoke to him about universe and stars. Old man sat, listened, smoked, spat. Then said:
   – Ah, there must be terrible queer creatures at the latter end of the world.[21]

This is not just a caustic parody of Synge's peasants, but a terrified recognition that Joyce's liberation from Ireland was more apparent

---

[19] *Ibid.*, p. 220.   [20] *Ibid.*, p. 274.   [21] *Ibid.*, p. 274.

than real: it haunted him forever in the form of his wife. He knew in his heart that the writing of a post-colonial exile is a satanic pact, a guilty compromise, a refusal of a more direct engagement. As he wrote in near-confessional mode in *Finnegans Wake*: 'he even ran away with hunself and became a farsoonerite, saying he would far sooner muddle through a hash of lentils in Europe than meddle with Irrland's split little pea'.[22]

Joyce may well have left Ireland because he sensed that it was a country intent on using all the old imperialist mechanisms in the name of a national revival. In *Dubliners* he offered the people a look at themselves in his nicely-polished looking-glass: but his enraged audiences broke the mirror, only to find their rage fruitless, since they were left with only a fragmented mirror and a broken image of themselves. The gesture of revolt merely deepened the crisis of representation. Salman Rushdie has said that the exiled writer is 'obliged to deal in broken mirrors, some of whose fragments have been irretrievably lost'.[23] For Joyce, writing was not only a measure of his own exile from Ireland, but also of that Ireland from its past, of Hiberno-English from standard languages, and of writing itself as a fall from oral culture – emigration simply emblematized these denials. Joyce remained most anxious to publish *Dubliners* in Ireland, however, because he was convinced that it represented a necessary first step 'in the spiritual liberation of my country'.[24] He was well aware of what happens when a colonial writer loses contact with his native audience and writes only for an international élite: he wanted to mediate between Ireland and the world, but most of all he wished to explain Ireland to itself.

When the Dublin printer refused to reproduce vulgar words, Joyce persisted bravely rather than place his work elsewhere. His struggles with censorship were intensely patriotic, for what he sought was the heart's desire of every provincial intellectual: 'permission to narrate'.[25] The use of the diary at the end of *A Portrait* may actually tell us less about Stephen's narcissism than about the censorious attitudes which drove a youth to that most solitary form of literary activity. In these moments, Joyce was a critic of a nation-state which had not yet fully formed itself, but whose putative sponsors were already trying to muzzle himself, Synge, Yeats and others.

---

[22] James Joyce, *Finnegans Wake* (Harmondsworth, 1992), p. 171.
[23] Salman Rushdie, *Imaginary Homelands* (London, 1992), p. 11.
[24] James Joyce, *Letters*, I (London, 1966), p. 63.   [25] The phrase is Edward Said's.

If *Dubliners* was Joyce's *exposé* of an Ireland frozen in servitude, *A Portrait* was his exploration of the revivalist illusion. It offers the first major account in modern English literature of the emergence of a post-colonial élite. The fat young man in the final chapter who rapidly listed the results of the examinations for 'the home civil' and 'the Indian' was the living incarnation of those forces which made it imperative for Joyce to emigrate.[26] The emerging middle-class did not see literature as something which might be made an element of daily vision: for them an education was the gateway to an administrative post. The civil service would be swollen with recruits, even as native industry continued to fail in the new state, because its administrative structures left traditional Catholic codes more intact than they might have been in a wholly industrialized society. In this, too, Ireland had much in common with the experience of other emerging nations, where traditional codes often happily accommodated themselves enough to administrative mechanisms.

In his 1907 essay entitled 'Home Rule Comes of Age', Joyce painted a devastating picture of the new comprador middle-class, the constitutional nationalists whom he portrayed as working hand-in-glove with the imperial exploiters:

the Irish parliamentary party has gone bankrupt. For twenty-seven years it has talked and agitated. In that time it has collected 35 million francs from its supporters, and the fruit of its agitation is that Irish taxes have gone up 88 million francs and the Irish population has decreased a million. The representatives have improved their own lot, aside from small discomforts like a few months in prison and some lengthy sittings. From the sons of ordinary citizens, peddlers, and lawyers without clients they have become well-paid syndics, directors of factories and commercial houses, newspaper owners, and large landowners. They have given proof of their altruism only in 1891, when they sold their leader, Parnell, to the pharisaical conscience of the English Dissenters without extracting the thirty pieces of silver.[27]

Joyce was scathing about the kind of revival which would be possible under such leadership at home: more torpor, more betrayal, more unconfessed self-loathing. He foresaw the plight of an 'independent' state under the constraints of neo-colonial economics: 'the Irish government about to be born will have to cover a deficit ably created by the British treasury'.[28] Nobody should be fooled or persuaded by 'the fact that Ireland now wishes to make common cause with British democracy'.[29]

[26] Joyce, *A Portrait*, p. 228.   [27] James Joyce, *Critical Writings*, p. 196.
[28] *Ibid.*, p. 224.   [29] *Ibid.*, p. 212.

In essay after essay written in the first decade of the century, Joyce asserted his conviction that the Irish were understandably disloyal to the British monarch because they were the victims of misrule. 'When a victorious country tyrannizes over another, it cannot logically be considered wrong for that other to rebel',[30] he told Triestine readers, adding that nobody could any longer believe in purely Christian motives for such policies. 'A conqueror cannot be casual, and for so many centuries the Englishman has done in Ireland only what the Belgian is doing today in the Congo Free State. . . .'[31] In one of the earliest and most accurate predictions of partition, Joyce forecasted that the same divide-and-rule policy which had carved up Africa would lead British conservatives to incite Ulster Unionists to rebel against any settlement with the leadership in Dublin. Ireland remained poor, he averred, because English laws had been systematically designed to ruin the country's industries. The Irish Parliamentary Party might pursue reconciliation with unionists for its own Home Rule purposes, but ordinary Irish men and women could never forget the centuries of broken treaties and industrial sabotage: 'can the back of a slave forget the rod?[32] Nor was Joyce at all convinced by the good intentions of enlightened British liberals: in an essay called 'Fenianism' in 1907 he brutally declared: 'any concessions that have been granted to Ireland, England has granted unwillingly, and, as it is usually put, at the point of a bayonet'.[33] Three years later, he was even more coruscating in his critique of the Liberal strategy, 'which aims to wear down the separatist sentiment slowly and secretly, while creating a new, eager social class, dependent, and free from dangerous enthusiasms, by means of partial concessions'.[34]

All this is worth reviewing, because Joyce has too often been portrayed as a cosmopolitan humanist with an aversion to militant Irish nationalism. In fact, he was in full agreement with the Fenian diagnosis and remarked rather savagely of a constitutional nationalist like Stephen Gwynn MP that if Westminster were to grant Ireland the status of Canada, 'Mr Gwynn becomes an Imperialist at once'. He also endorsed the idea of the spiritual superiority of Ireland as opposed to 'the incurable ignobility of the forces that have overcome her'.[35] However, when it came to prescriptions, he parted with the irreconcilables, seeing in their ideals nothing but a point-for-point contradiction of English Tory thinking. If the constitutional nationalists were in danger

[30] *Ibid.*, p. 163.　[31] *Ibid.*, p. 168.　[32] *Ibid.*, p. 188.
[33] *Ibid.*, p. 212.　[34] *Ibid.*, p. 90.　[35] *Ibid.*, p. 105.

of being co-opted by empire, the militants were at grave risk of embracing the imperial psychology in a reworked form. Joyce heaped repeated mockery on the imitation of English models by Irish revivalists. Joyce did not fail to note in the young Patrick Pearse a hatred of those English whom he was, quite unconsciously, so keen to emulate.[36]

The closing sections of *A Portrait* raise sharp, difficult questions about the meaning of a Gaelic culture which had been 'lost', a loss which can be established by the revivalists only in terms of a valued English scheme of things. What the revivalists sought to rediscover was merely a projection of imperial fantasy, eventually embodied in the person of Haines in *Ulysses*. The mistake of the revivalists would be repeated in Africa and India in later decades: too often an 'African' or an 'Indian' culture would simply be one which could be easily translated into forms comprehensible to European imperial minds. The revivalists failed to recognise that tradition in that sense is always syncretic: only a 'tradition' which was the invention of the colonisers could so facilely disintegrate to be supplanted by a ready-made modern equivalent. The question put by Mazzini to the Irish – what distinctive civilisation justifies your separatist claim? – would be raised again and again. Joyce had his own reply and it was not the expected one: 'if an appeal to the past in this manner were valid, the *fellahin* of Cairo would have all the right in the world to disdain to act as porters for English tourists'.[37] His claim would base itself not on the past but on the future: Ireland's conscience was yet 'uncreated'.[38] Stephen Daedalus in *A Portrait* rejects all calls to a loveliness which has long faded from the world and prefers to seek a loveliness which has not yet come into the world. In Joyce's hands, the *bildungsroman* was an instrument with which to investigate the Irish experience, and the ensuing self-understanding was a discovery of the real Ireland of the present. After the famines and the decline of the Irish language, the autobiographical narrative became doubly important in explaining to a baffled people who they were.

What Mulrennan's encounter with the peasant told them was not comforting: it would be impossible to reclaim whatever had been lost. The very construction of a *Gaeltacht*, a zone of pristine nativism, might itself be an effect of colonialism rather than an obvious answer to it. In Joyce's text, there is a double exposure: he indicts colonialism, as do the revivalists themselves, but he then proceeds to indict the native culture for not living up to expectations of it, for not being an authentic

[36] *Ibid.*, p. 195.   [37] Ellmann, *James Joyce*, p. 62.   [38] Joyce, *A Portrait*, p. 253.

elsewhere. The revivalists feel this lack, too, but they respond by making the peasant the embodiment of sacred values which the peasant himself would never claim to uphold,[39] converting him into a fetish of unsatisfiable desire. The revivalist thus comes to know the 'melancholy of the collector', the tantalizing hope that the next salvaged lyric, the next native speaker, will perhaps reveal the holy grails that he seeks. Yet these cultural trophies can offer no more than a fleeting charm, for to linger over any for too long would be to confront in them the selfsame emptiness which led the revivalist, in desperation, to evoke them. The tragic knowledge which awaits the revivalist is that also which attends the imperialist, who comes to the native quarter in search of the authenticity of the exotic. Desiring a pristine experience, Mulrennan is thwarted: hoping to recover the scope of an ancient culture from which he was cruelly separated, he finds instead a peasant whose inheritance is as broken as his own. There is no absolute *elsewhere* to be found, not even a final frontier where the theory of Irish innocence and the discontents of English civilisation could come to a competitive point.

This was Joyce's perception: that Ireland is just another of those modern places, where there is no *there* any more. The nationalists who denounced England were, more often than not, denouncing an England inside each one of themselves. Their search for a pristine 'Ireland' was a quintessentially English search, because it involved them in the search for a corresponding 'England' as well, if only so that they might repudiate it. Since 'Ireland' in such a construction was largely an English invention, those who took upon themselves the burden of having an idea of Ireland were often the most Anglicised of the natives.[40] The devising of the ludicrous category *un-Irish* was among their strange achievements, although in actual practice, nothing could have been less typical of the Irish than this attempt to form an ideology out of Irishness and with it to combat un-Irish behaviour.

Joyce was perhaps the first major cultural critic to intuit that dogmatic assertions of Irishness were an ill-judged attempt by their makers to cope with the fear of hybridity. The problem of the Irish was not so much rootlessness as the fact that they had roots in too many different places at once. He wrote: 'To tell the truth, to exclude from the present nation all who are descended from foreign families would be impossible'.

---

[39] This was the central allegation made by John Eglinton against revivalist representations of the western peasant.

[40] Vincent Tucker, 'The Myth of Development' unpublished paper, Dept. of Sociology, University College Cork, March 1993.

In the face of such variousness, a unitary racial nationality could never be more than 'a convenient fiction', and that fiction would only be convenient if it could evolve a form hospitable to the many strands that made up Irish experience: 'Do we not see that in Ireland the Danes, the Firbolgs, the Milesians from Spain, the Norman invaders and the Anglo-Saxon settlers have united to form a new entity, one might say under the influence of a local deity?'[41] This would demand a rejection of nationalist singularity, something which the Latin American example had suggested would happen only after independence, 'when society really decides to break through its veneer of westernization and look at itself – in its plurality and traditions – straight in the face'.[42]

The need was to find more open forms, which would be a prey to neither western structures nor to the mystique of indigenous identity. Mulrennan's encounter had shown that the architects of Ireland could not know it except as a possibility, glimpsed from the perceptual prison of imperial fantasy, whose ideal peasant was indeed 'a man who does not exist, a man who is but a dream'.[43] This representational debacle arose from the impossibility of rendering a consciousness which, being uncreated, did not exist as such. 'Nothing kills a man off', wrote the novelist Julio Cortazar, 'like having to represent a country':[44] yet Joyce knew that the men most ignorant of a country were invariably the ones to believe that they could represent it. Even the leaders of political nationalism early this century had, in effect, to bluff the new state into being, proclaiming unification in the name of an Ireland or an India yet to follow. The more scrupulous among them, like Mahatma Gandhi, realising that the unity which had proved invaluable in the struggle against empire might become a denial of difference after liberation, urged that the national congress should liquidate itself after independence.

Neither in Ireland nor in India were internal minorities much regarded, and so movement was frozen in its nationalist stage. The fragility of state borders (artificially designed by the colonial power), the uncertain legitimacy of state forms (borrowed wholesale from the colonial system) meant that its best energies went into securing its stability. The obsession with territorial integrity, with policing borders,

[41] Joyce, *Critical Writings*, p. 166.
[42] 'Carlos Fuentes: An Interview', *Modern Latin American Fiction: A Survey*, John King (ed.) (London, 1987), p. 144.
[43] W. B. Yeats, 'The Fisherman', *Collected Poems* (London, 1950), p. 167.
[44] Julio Cortazar, epigraph to *Hopscotch* (New York, 1966) from a letter from Jacques Vaché to Andre Bréton: 'Rien ne vous tue un homme comme d'être obligé de réprésenter un pays'.

led the new states to define themselves reactively in terms of what they were not. In Ireland a shaky state sought legitimation by placing itself under the aegis of the Catholic Church, thereby ensuring the defeat of many marginal groups: the landless labourers, the urban poor, feminists, Irish speakers, creative artists. By censorship and theocratic law, it defended itself against the fragility of its underlying structure, against the lack of a true point of origin. Christ and Caesar went hand in glove in this land, and Joyce, foreseeing what was to come, attempted in *Ulysses* to unleash a plurality of voices which would together sound the notes that moved beyond nationalism to liberation. After Mulrennan, there was no choice but to put oneself in the place of that absent Other that was the peasant, to take as one's own responsibility that emptiness and to fill it with the sound of voices. *Ulysses* would, like Joyce's earlier books, hold a mirror up to the colonial capital that was Dublin in 1904: but, unlike them, it would also be a book of Utopian epiphanies, hinting at a golden future which might be made over in terms of those Utopian moments.

Benedict Anderson has observed that the problem which besets many partitioned states is of having been 'insufficiently imagined'.[45] That is hardly surprising, for the builders of modern nation-states were expected to dismantle the master's house and replace it with a better one, using only those tools which the master cared to leave behind. A similar issue is raised in the opening chapters of *Ulysses*, where Stephen's problem is a version of Joyce's: he wears the second-hand trousers cast off by Mulligan, and yet he must learn to cut a dash in them. The search for a true home is conducted in inappropriate, inherited forms. The first chapter of *Ulysses* is set in the Martello Tower in Sandycove, built by the British authorities to forestall a possible French invasion in support of Irish republicans. A colonial structure, it nonetheless allows the youths to improvise what freedoms they can. If Joyce adopts a somewhat incongruous scaffolding of Homer's *Odyssey* for a subversive narrative, then Stephen and Mulligan attempt a similar transformation of the tower, which they plan to make the centre of a modern Irish culture. All are compelled to reshape past forms in keeping with the needs of the present. Joyce's initial chapter is named for Telemachus, the embittered son in *The Odyssey* who was angry because the land of his father was occupied by foreign warriors: in the story, false suitors of his mother shamelessly waste his patrimony, while

---

[45] Benedict Anderson, *Imagined Communities* (London, 1983), pp. 127–46.

the goddess Athene (disguised in *Ulysses* as an old milkwoman) advises him to leave his mother and seek the absent father.

Even at this early stage, Joyce employs the technique of mythical realism, juxtaposing Odyssean marvels against the Irish quotidian. This method has been shown to have been implicit in many texts of the Irish revival, especially the early plays of the Abbey Theatre, whose writers were among the first to grasp that fantasy, untouched by any sense of reality, is only a decadent escapism, whilst reality unchallenged by any element of fantasy, is a merely squalid literalism. Joyce's early books, with their unusual blend of symbolism and naturalism, added much to this method: but it was in *Ulysses* that it reached its apogee. Henceforth, Joyce would equate realism with the imperial/nationalist narrative: it was the favoured mode for chronicling the fate of the European bourgeoisie. The Irish experience, however, was not fully comparable with the European in this respect, because the Irish middle class was not yet fully formed. The split between modernity and undevelopment was obvious to Joyce within Ireland itself in the almost surreal juxtapositions of affluence and dire poverty, of ancient superstition and contemporary *anomie*. No merely realist method could do full justice to that. A form had to be created which would, in the words of Salman Rushdie, 'allow the miraculous and the mundane to coexist at the same level – as the same order of event'.[46] That form was adumbrated in *Ulysses*.

Its introduction of mythic realism to prose narrative coincided with terminal diagnoses of the 'death of the novel' in English, French and German literature. The novel was calibrated to the layers, classes and institutions of a shaped society: what Joyce evolved was a form more geared to a society still in the shaping. He was, by virtue of his location, a leader of European modernism: but, by virtue of his example, he became a pioneer of mythical realism. He needed to invent very little, describing himself as a humble 'scissors and paste man'.[47] In this he had much in common with the writers of the Latin American boom, who had equally little to ask of their imaginations. Their common problem was a different one: to find a form which would render the colourful disorder and strange juxtapositions of life on the periphery. In the Latin America of later decades, Asturias would salute Joyce's 'magic wand', Carpentier his 'complex beauty', Borges his 'total reality'.[48] All

---

[46] Rushdie, *Imaginary Homelands*, p. 376.   [47] Ellmann, *James Joyce*, p. 538.
[48] All quotations from Gerald Martin, *Journeys through the Labyrinth: Latin American Fiction in the Twentieth Century* (London, 1989), p. 130.

of them identified with his cosmopolitanism, his exile, his Catholicism, his audacious remodelling of an imperial language, and, most of all, his utter conviction that the problems of his little land were in fact the central issues facing the modern world.[49]

The modernism of Joyce was not only that of Mann, Proust or Eliot: it also anticipated that of Rushdie, Marquez and the post-colonial artists. For them, modernism did not signalise a move from univocal realism to multivocal hyper-reality, but from a realism that never seemed real at all to a pluralism which did try to honour the many voices raised after independence.[50] European radicals still followed Rousseau in asking how it was that, born originals, people still died as copies. The post-colonial artists, however, born as copies, were determined to die originals. The modernisers from Europe sought to expose the myths of traditional societies to the scrutiny of analytic reason, but they never dismantled the myths which bound them to their own culture. Joyce's canny blend of myth and realism did just that, using each term as a critique of the other. His technique was not unlike that practised by many doctors in the new states, as they combined homeopathic and alleopathic medicine, nativist and western remedies. He was one of the earliest writers to realise that as long as he posed his questions to the west solely in the old, familiar terms of the west, he would be surrendering to the ends of its discourse, just as to resort to pure fabulism, untouched by any element of realism, would be to submit to the intentions of the native tribe. Mythic realism, by its subversive act of combination, disrupted the hegemony of both discourses, so that neither could achieve its goals. Rather than levelling all differences, however, he produced in *Ulysses* a genuinely multi-cultural text, which did more than simply redraw the boundaries between discourses at some other point. And he provided a model for the magic realists in the refusal of *Ulysses* to ground itself in a narrating subject or an identifiable author: instead he offered a text without any final authority.

The risks of such a venture are still huge, and must have been all but unimaginable when Joyce wrote. Octavio Paz has asserted that there are no safety-nets for authors who wish to dismantle the cultures into which they have been inserted, no ordered network of institutions underwriting the discourse which they throw into question.[51] 'If successful,

---

[49] Martin, *Journeys*, p. 206.
[50] On this I follow Gari Laguardia, 'Marvelous Realism/Marvelous Criticism', *Reinventing the Americas* (eds.), Bell Gale Chevigny and Gari Laguardia (Cambridge, 1986), p. 301.
[51] Quoted by Richard Wohl, *The Generation of 1914* (Cambridge, 1979), p. 216.

they run the risk of annulling, even silencing, themselves, or else becoming exotic offshoots of powerful western cultures' (in Joyce's case,
of English literature). In strict terms, there can be no national literature until there is first a liberated nation, so the challenge for Paz
is whether to invent reality by magic, or to rescue it by realism. The
answer, as always in these situations, is a little of both – to search for a
tradition and to invent it in that very act of searching. Such a tradition
exists more in its absence than in its presence: it is its very lack which
constitutes an artist's truest freedom, for nothing could be more deaden-
ing than the pull of the past. 'You can't lug the corpse of your father
around for the whole of your life',[52] wrote the poet Apollinaire; and
that is also the voice of Stephen at the start of *Ulysses*, denying the pull
of his dead mother ('Ghoul! Chewer of corpses! . . . Let me be and let
me live!')[53] and of his unvital father.

Yet the very denial of tradition can become the most potent tradition of all, the tradition of inherited dissent, which becomes all the more
powerful for being paradoxical. Borges proclaimed that the conceit of
his fellow-Argentinian writers that they were creating *ex nihilo* was
reminiscent of that moment in history when the Emperor of China
ordered the Great Wall to be built and all books written before its
commencement to be burnt.[54] He was quite open in his admiration
for, and rapturous devotion to, the European classics. 'Apart from a
few professors of philology, who receive a salary for it', writes Roberto
Retamar, 'there is only one type of person who really knows in its
entirety the literature of Europe: the colonial'.[55] These elements are present also in Joyce, but with a difference: he mocked them to perdition
in the bookishness of Stephen and, again, in the writerly exchanges of
the men in the National Library. In that scene, most of them speak in
dead quotations and citations, as they are surrounded by the 'coffined
thoughts'[56] of a cultural cemetery.

Joyce, therefore, adopted an attitude of lofty condescension to the
European realist novel. He sought a method which could treat of the
superstitions of a pre-modern community, which existed alongside and

---

[52] Octavio Paz, 'A Literature of Foundation', translated by Lysander Kemp in Jose Donoso and
William Henkins (eds.), *The Triquarterly Anthology of Latin American Literature* (New York, 1969),
p. 8.
[53] James Joyce, *Ulysses*, introduction and notes by Declan Kiberd (Harmondsworth, 1992), p. 11.
[54] Jorge Luis Borges, *Labyrinths* (Harmondsworth, 1970), pp. 221–4.
[55] Roberto Fernandez Retamar, *Caliban and Other Essays*, translated by Edward Baker (Minneapolis,
1989), p. 28.
[56] Joyce, *Ulysses*, p. 248.

within a society already developed beyond the confining outlines of the nation-state. He did this in the conviction that the religious sensibility can sometimes survive more honestly outside of church structures and official dogma: for him art could be the third principle which, mediating between the material and sacred worlds and incorporating both, offered that new thing, 'a secular definition of transcendence'.[57]

This was done by restoring a dimension of high seriousness to epic narrative, something which had been lost to most European writers since the time of Cervantes and Milton. The English novels of Henry Fielding in the eighteenth century had managed to evoke the epic codes only in a mode of prevailing parody: he called them 'comic epic poems in prose'. In these, Fielding's characteristic ploy was to mock the ancient classical formulae by a brutal act of domestication: a typical example would be a sentence which began with a heroic run 'hardly had the day dawned, than Caesar . . .', only to end with the words 'ran yelping from his kennel'.[58] Even the tragic novels of George Eliot in the later nineteenth century were concerned with the refusal of the English environment to allow characters equipped with epic desires to find a life commensurate with those high capacities. So, in *Middlemarch*, the epigraphs from *Paradise Lost* are strictly ironic, as are the repetitions of key moments from Milton's plot in the novel. The imperial nation-states of Europe, it seemed, could no longer sustain the heroic except in a mode of parody. In the developing countries, however, the form could be pursued with a sense of expanding possibility.

By setting the past and present into dialectical tension, the mythic method employed by Irish writers allowed for a critical investigation of the relation between ancient heroic values and the modern world. But it did something also to undermine the European enlightenment notions of time and linear progress. Instead, it evoked a world of cycles and spirals, which mocked the view of history as a straight line and set in its place another, very different model. Separate chapters of *Ulysses* overlap in chronology, and even separate sections of the 'Wandering Rocks' chapter narrate the same events in time as seen from different perspectives, rendering by this means a most varied set of voices and experiences. The linear time of the realist novel denied all this and sought to dispose of time in neat parcels, but Joyce, in restoring a sense of an Eternal Now, also restored time's mystery.

---

[57] Rushdie, *Imaginary Homelands*, p. 420.
[58] Henry Fielding, *Joseph Andrews* (New York, 1965), pp. vii, 279.

Ulysses includes many lines which predict its future composition as being latent in memories of a distant past. So Stephen in the National Library on 16 June 1904 predicts that 'in the future, the sister of the past, I may see myself as I sit here now but by reflection from that which I shall be':[59] a reminder that the entire book is a backward glance cast with the wisdom of much hindsight. This would also provide the time-structure for *One Hundred Years of Solitude* as well: 'the placing of a remembered past within a future which in a sense has already happened'.[60] Yet in no sense are such manoeuvres to be read as an attempted erasure of the past: on the contrary, the past and present are juxtaposed to constitute a comparison which may be the basis of an informed judgement. An assured sense of the past appears to Joyce as a condition of happy modernisation. Such writers favour modernisation, but fear that if it is introduced abruptly and without regard for local sensitivities, people will fail to adjust intelligently to it and lapse back into nostalgia and revivalism. If for a writer such as Joyce the past is forever present, then the present is also somehow past, always interpreted under the sign of goals that may supersede it. Stephen, in the Library, says to himself, with *Ulysses* already in mind: 'See this. Remember'.[61] *Lisant au livre de lui-même*, he construes himself with the knowledge of one who knows that the past is a handy fiction to serve current and future needs.

One explanation of this return to the mythical is the conviction that the enlightenment project in its merely European form was incomplete. Yeats, complaining that nineteenth-century meliorists lacked the vision of evil, prayed for delivery from a mechanistic rationalism. The darker forces thus excluded were bound to reassert themselves on the peripheries: Ireland – like Africa, India or Latin America – was bound to become a sort of fantasy-land, resulting from the psychological self-repression at the imperial centre, a repression crucial to the imperial enterprise. In Yeats and Joyce, and in many writers of the developing world, certain themes and images seem to recur, as if inevitably: the self as labyrinth, the notion of the environment as a place calibrated to solitude, the sense that all texts are psychological rather than social explanations.

The critique of imperial educational methods in the chapter known as 'Proteus' perfectly accords with Yeats's attack on rote memory-work

---

[59] Joyce, *Ulysses*, p. 249.
[60] Quoted by William Rowe, 'Gabriel Gárcia Márquez', *Modern Latin American Fiction*, p. 196.
[61] Joyce, *Ulysses*, p. 246.

and on that compilation of facts which excluded all feeling and emotion. In later sections of *Ulysses*, especially 'Circe', Joyce would explore the forbidden night-world of the dreamer whose censors have been freed. In a more general way, his book deliberately utilised all the discredited materials and despised potentials banished from the European mind-set, in a manner similar to the Abbey playwright's adoption of the superstitions and folk beliefs of a derided native culture. Clearly, a realist text, with its narrative stability and its depiction of intense personal relations in an ordered society, would have been inadequate to Joyce's needs: what he faced was an underdeveloped country under the yoke of empire and a people's culture which was oral rather than written in its predominant forms.

To understand the evolution of mythical realism, it must be seen as the outcome of a desperate refusal by native artists of the recommended European novel. In eighteenth-century Ireland, for instance, the tellers of romantic tales responded to the challenge in predictable ways. The anti-hero made his first appearance in Gaelic Ireland in *Stair Éamuinn Uí Chléire* (The Story of Eamonn O'Clery, 1710), a parodic reworking by Seán Ó Neachtain of medieval texts. The author, dissatisfied with the two-dimensional characters of the romances, seemed caught between the desire to mock them in a hilarious send-up and the wish to supply a more realistic motivation for the virtues and weaknesses of the central character. O'Clery is an innocent abroad in a corrupt world, which plays upon his weakness for alcohol. There are supernatural interventions of the kind commonplace in medieval folk tales, but the prevailing narrative strategy is closer to the novel, in ways which make O'Clery the Gaelic counterpart of a Quixote.

An even closer analogy can be found in *Siabhra Mhic na Míochomhairle* (The Spectre of the Errant Son, 1725) by Brian Dubh Ó Raghallaigh. Here, the anti-hero meets a warrior named Gruagach, who promises his daughter's hand if he will defend him in battle. The character finds the daughter attractive, but breaks into a cold sweat whenever he thinks of the coming fight, being the living antithesis of the ancient Fianna whose warriors never shunned a conflict. He also violates the troubadour code, dispensing with polite courtly preliminaries, as he attempts to bed the daughter on their very first meeting. Modern Gaelic scholars tend to see in the emergence of such an anti-hero 'a noteworthy phenomenon which suggests a decline in cultural standards',[62] but it really represents the attempt by artists in the Irish language to marry

---

[62] R. A. Breatnach, 'The End of a Tradition', *Studia Hibernica*, *1*, 1961, p. 87.

their oral narratives to the forms of Cervantes and Fielding. The attempt failed mainly because there were few Gaelic printing-presses in eighteenth-century Ireland. England was undergoing an industrial revolution and a massive growth in towns, as Fielding produced his masterpieces for the expanding middle class. In Ireland, speakers of the native language still told the old romantic tales, which were filled with supernatural wonders and were recited in public to a credulous audience. The European novel, on the other hand, was a realistic account of everyday life, to be read in silence and in private by the sceptical, solitary reader. It dealt in private emotions and psychological analyses which were lacking in the world of most storytellers.

Ó Neachtain and Ó Raghallaigh did their best to conflate the two modes, but could go no further without a printing-press;[63] and nineteenth-century novelists in English simply repeated the prevailing English methods, in a tradition which stretched from Edgeworth to Griffin, from Carleton to Moore. Only Joyce in *Ulysses* managed to take the form out of that rational, middle-class world and to restore some of the magical elements of the romances – as when Mr Bloom ascends into heaven, at the close of 'Cyclops', 'like a shot off a shovel', thereby escaping his pursuers. The deadpan narration of the attendant factual details ('at an angle of forty-five degrees over Donohoes' in Little Green Street')[64] anticipates by some decades the somewhat similar ascension of Remedios the Beauty in *One Hundred Years of Solitude*. In both cases, the writers achieve their characteristic effect by a subversive *combination* of the mythical and the real.

Whether the results of their labours should be called 'novels' is a highly debatable point: it is more likely that they are written in new forms for which there is, as yet, no agreed generic name. There is a strongly parodic element at work in *Ulysses*, mocking the heroic milit-arism of epic, the supernatural wonders of folk-tale, the psychological verisimilitude of the novel, but the form which results is in no way confined by these targets. Due homage is paid to those targets: their working conventions are laid bare, in an active exploration of each mode which is also an exercise in literary criticism: however, the parody is no merely temporary transgression, but a gesture which precedes a radical break.[65] *Ulysses* illustrates the dictum that every great work of

---

[63] On this see Cathal Ó Háinle, 'An tÚrscéal nar Tháinig', *Promhadh Pinn* (Dublin, 1978), pp. 74–98.
[64] Joyce, *Ulysses*, p. 449.
[65] Linda Hutcheon, *A Theory of Parody: The Teaching of Twentieth Century Art Forms* (London, 1985), p. 35.

literature not only destroys one genre but helps to create another. Radical parody of this kind has the effect of speeding up this natural development of literary form: its ensuing narrative frees itself sufficiently from the targeted texts to constitute a fresh and autonomous form, a further proof that (in literature, as in politics) the urge to destroy may also be a creative urge.

Indeed, the dialectics of decolonisation reproduce themselves in this progression too, reminding us of the analogies between radical parody and subversive mimicry. In this schema, the original author is analogous to the colonizer, the parodist to the nationalist-in-revolt, and the radical reader of these movements who can then proceed to shape a new form in these opened spaces becomes the harbinger of literary liberation. What is enacted in the third phase is an energetic protest against those who would convert a once-enabling form into a life-denying formula: and that protest is based on the conviction that all genres – not just the epic basis of *Ulysses* – are mere scaffoldings, which may permit a new text to be created, but which should be unsentimentally dismantled when the work is well done. On this marvellous mutation, Fredric Jameson has a pertinent comment:

The failure of a generic structure, such as epic, to reproduce itself not only encourages a search for those substitute textual functions that appear in its wake, but more particularly alerts us to the historical ground, now no longer existent, in which the original structure was meaningful.[66]

Yet even this statement is scarcely enough for, despite all the mockery of those superannuated militarist elements of *The Odyssey*, there is also in *Ulysses* a genuine refunctionalisation of other, less disposable aspects. If classical epic depicted an individual risking all for the birth of a nation, *Ulysses* will instead present a hero living as the embodiment of community values. If bodies were pulverized in ancient epic to support its ideals, *Ulysses* will, chapter by chapter, celebrate each distinctive organ, offering an 'epic of the body'[67] as an image of the restored human community.

A *part* of each earlier form survives in the assemblage that is *Ulysses*, but it would be foolish to name the book for one or other of these genres. Insofar as it is susceptible to generic analysis, it might be placed in vibration not just with Homer or Rabelais but also with Borges or Rushdie, serving as a rallying-point for the emergence of a new

---

[66] Jameson, *The Political Unconscious*, p. 146.
[67] Frank Budgen, *James Joyce and the Making of Ulysses* (London, 1972), p. 17.

narrative mode. For Joyce, the shattering of older forms permitted the breakthrough of a new content, a post-imperial writing. The danger, as always, is that conventional critics will seek to recolonise that writing, or any other baffling text by an Irish artist or a Latino or an Indian, translating its polyvocal tones back into the too-familiar, too-reassuring terms of the day-before-yesterday.

Alejo Carpentier said that new worlds had to be lived, before they could be explained. For him, part of the complex beauty of *Ulysses* was its fidelity to the 'Third World city without style', which was less an established city than an agglomeration of villages[68] (just as *Ulysses* is not so much a novel as a constellation of micro-narratives). Carpentier spoke of 'the style of things that have no style', as if to evoke the disappearance of a coherent narrating subject. The book, like any modern conurbation, could be entered or left at any point, for it was as open to experimental interpretation as any city.

Another, even greater, danger in interpreting *Ulysses* would be to treat it as a 'Third World' text which is, in *all* aspects, the very antithesis of a 'First World' narrative. Yet the Ireland which Joyce chronicled had its share in the making of empire, as well as of its victims. It was, in that respect, a vivid reminder of the relentless reciprocity by which one set of experiences is bound to the other. If Europe scarcely has any meaning without the suffering of the native peoples who contributed to its opulence, and if the 'Third World' is but an effect of European desires, then Ireland affords a field of force in which the relation between the two is enacted within the community.

Europe, after all, was the creator of both the dialectics of liberation *and* the ethic of slave-holding: what characterises Joycean modernism is its awareness of the need to write both of these narratives *simultaneously*. Each situation has its unique aspects and to construct the 'Third World' exclusively as a manageable other of the 'First' is, at a certain point, to submit to the very tyranny the phrase was designed to deplore. There is, however, a linked and even greater danger: that of conceiving the encounter as of two *distinct* worlds facing each other, rather than as social worlds which are part of one another, though differently constituted.[69] Ireland's historical disadvantage, being a European people who were nonetheless colonised, afforded it a remarkable *artistic* advantage. The country was, and still is, one of those areas

[68] Alejo Carpentier, 'Problematica de la actual novela latinoamericana', *Tientos y diferencias* (Havana, 1966), p. 15.
[69] Tucker, 'The Myth of Development'.

where two codes most vividly meet: and, as such, its culture offers itself as an analytical tool at the very twilight of European artistic history. It, too, was asked to remain marginal, so that other peoples could feel themselves central.[70] Now in a position to negotiate between coloniser and the colonised, it could be forgiven for strategically seeing itself as a centre. If the 'west' turns to the exploited peripheries in the desire for a return of all that it has repressed in itself, the post-colonies turn to the west as to yet another command. Ireland, in between, provided Joyce with a more visibly open site of contest, and a reminder that each side in that contest needed the other for a completed account of its own meanings.

The great absences in the texts of European modernism are those native peoples whose exploitation made the representations of European magnificence possible. Even writers such as Conrad or Forster who showed some awareness of the issue were unable to render with comprehensive conviction the lives of Africans or Indians. A curious paradox ensued. The suffering of such peoples kept the empires in business, allowing their more liberal servants to toy impressively with their own scruples in texts, just as surely as the masters relied for an identity on the slaves. Yet those slaves and all that suffering are largely a blankness in the pages of *Heart of Darkness*. Conrad could see only a world dominated by the west, or a world in which obsessive opposition to the west simply illustrated its cruel power: but, comments Edward Said, he could never see a life 'outside this cruel tautology'.[71]

Irish writers of the time gave English readers some inkling of the life behind that blankness: and they could do this because they wrote in the language of the imperialist, about what it was like to grow to maturity in an occupied country. Radical modernism, as practised by a Joyce or a Rushdie, has been a prolonged attempt to render this accounting, to write a narrative of the colonisers and colonised, in which the symbiotic relation between the two becomes manifest. This is usually based on a recognition by the members of a nomadic native intelligentsia of all that has been repressed in the imperial texts and all that has gone uncomprehended in the native fables. The two orders of reality, when taken together onto a third plane, make for a new level of meaning.

Irish writing has never sought to deny this stress in its history, but critics of Irish writing often do so. Yet its presence is insistent in works,

---

[70] Spivak, *The Postcolonial Critic*, p. 8.
[71] Edward Said, *Culture and Imperialism* (London, 1993), p. xix.

beneath the level of mere visibility, where it exists as an instance of the political unconscious. Seeking to unmask these stresses, Fredric Jameson has called Ireland an 'intermediate situation' embracing both metropolis and colony, lord and bondsman, simultaneously: and he has found in *Ulysses* one of the few narratives of European modernism which allow for an inspection of what is elsewhere suppressed. The national situation can reproduce the appearance of 'First World' relationships while being, deep down, much closer to a 'Third World' reality: 'a modernism arising in these circumstances could then be inspected and interrogated for its formal and structural differences from works produced within the metropolis'.[72] True enough: but it might be said that *many* colonial situations produce fictional characters and creative individuals who are 'intermediate' in exactly this way. It is the discovery that colonial crisis is just such an intermediate situation which leads to the moment of liberation, a truth revealed by Simón Bolivar to Latin Americans in his famous Jamaica Letter:

We are but a small human kind, a world apart . . . neither Indians nor Europeans, but a species half-way between the legitimate owners of the land and the Spanish usurpers.[73]

This theme would, much later, be extended beyond the colonial situation by Alice Walker to cover the experience of black Americans: she argued that they were often the descendants not only of slaves but of slaveowners:

We are the *mestizos* of North America. We are black, yes, but we are 'white' too, and we are red. To attempt to function as only one, when you are really two or three, leads, I believe, to psychic illness: 'white' people have shown us the madness of that.[74]

The notion would also be explored in Rushdie's celebration of the nomad and migrant as hybrids. Joyce felt himself to be such a person in whom contradictory forces met. However, he experienced this less as a pain than as a challenge to make something positive out of the mingled traditions of Celt, Viking, Norman and Anglo-Saxon which made up his Ireland.

[72] Fredric Jameson, 'Modernism and Imperialism', *Field Day Pamphlet*, no. 14 (Derry, 1988), pp. 19–20.
[73] Simón Bolivar, *The Jamaica Letter*; quoted Martin, *Journeys*, p. 14.
[74] Alice Walker, *Living the Word* (London, 1988), p. 82.

Ireland, in his schema, was one of those liminal zones, between old and new, where all binary thinking was nullified, and where there could be a celebration of manly women and of womanly men. He recognized the extent to which nationalism was a necessary phase to restore to an occupied people a sense of purpose: and he distinguished sharply between the xenophobic nationalism of the imperial powers and the strategic resort to nationalism by the forces of resistance. The men in the pub in 'Cyclops' are a case in point. They mimic English Francophobia ('set of dancing masters'), but are not anti-foreign, evincing a real sympathy for people of colour living under the lash in other corners of empire. Humanist critics like Richard Ellmann who castigate their chauvinism have failed to note that their range of reference is not Eurocentric, but far wider than that of most humanists.[75] The law, which seems established to many Anglo-American readers of *Ulysses*, did not appear as such to Joyce, being merely a tyranny based on official terror.

Nevertheless, Joyce in *Ulysses* never fell into the trap of equating nationalism with modernization: indeed, his spiritual project was to attempt to imagine a meaningful modernity which was more open to the full range of voices in Ireland than any nationalism which founded itself on the restrictive apparatus of the colonial state. If the patriots cloaked the fundamental conservatism of their movement in a rhetoric of radicalism, Joyce more cannily chose to dress his utterly innovative narrative in the conservative garb of a classical narrative. This led many critics to the mistaken view that he offered his critique of nationalism from the vantage-point of a European humanist. A close reading of *Ulysses* will, however, throw up far more evidence of its anti-colonial themes.

[75] For a more extended meditation on this point, see Emer Nolan, *James Joyce and Nationalism* (London, 1994).

CHAPTER 7

Cookson, Chaplin and Common: three northern writers in 1951

Robert Colls

The years 1950–1 saw the publication of three novels set in the North East of England. Catherine Cookson's *Kate Hannigan* (1950), was the first in a long line of novels about northern women who were to make their author the most famous 'regional novelist' in the world. Sid Chaplin's *The Thin Seam* (1950), was a short, incisive story about one night's coal-cutting on a Durham face. And Jack Common's *Kiddar's Luck* (1951), was the tale of Will Kiddar, a Newcastle lad growing up on the streets and corner-ends of Heaton just before and during the Great War. All of these fictions[1] would come to be seen as landmarks in writing the North East, and each of their authors wrote about the working-class experience from an autobiographical point of view. Just what that experience was, and how it was offered and received, is the subject of this essay.

Catherine Cookson was born on 20 June 1906, at 5 Leam Lane, Tyne Dock, South Shields. If there was a doctor present we don't know, but we do know that one was present when 'Kate Hannigan' gave birth. Indeed, in the manner of all Cookson's strong women and sensitive heroes, it almost seems as if it was he – Dr Rodney Prince – who gave birth, and not Kate:

Pulling, easing, pressing, it went on. The sweat was running into his eyes now and his shirt was no longer white.

Davidson's expression became pitying . . . Poor Kate! It was practically up. Still, this fellow was good; if she were paying hundreds she wouldn't have had anyone better . . . But these things happened . . .

---

[1] Catherine Cookson, *Kate Hannigan* (1950; London, 1976); Sid Chaplin, *The Thin Seam and Other Stories* (1950; Oxford, 1968); Jack Common, *Kiddar's Luck* (1951; Bath, 1971). Penny Smith reviews 'The Post-War North-Eastern Novel' in, 'Remembered Poverty: the North East of England' in Ian A. Bell (ed.), *Peripheral Visions. Images of Nationhood in Contemporary British Fiction* (Cardiff, 1995).

'A . . . ah!' It was an exclamation of triumph as much as relief. Rodney slowly withdrew the red body covered with silvery slime. For a second it lay across both his hands, a girl child . . . to be named Annie Hannigan, and who was to help make and to almost mar his career. (*Kate Hannigan*, pp. 27–8)

Born illegitimate, the woman who was later known as Catherine Cookson was named Kate, after her mother, and was brought up as a McMullen, after her step-grandfather. During her childhood she believed that her grandmother Rose and her step-grandfather John were her parents, and that her mother was her sister. After domestic service (as a 'lady's companion'), and about four years doing sweated work, painting cushion covers at home, which was now in East Jarrow, she found a job as a laundry-checker in the South Shields workhouse in 1924, where she worked for nearly five years. In 1929 she left the region: 'I told myself I was never going back. I had finished with the North East and all it stood for.'[2]

Jack Common had left the region too, the year before. Twenty-five years old and already with an unpromising future of dead-end jobs and dole queues behind him, Jack Common's luck had not been of the best. Nor had that of his fictional hero, Will Kiddar:

There were plenty of golden opportunities going that night. In palace and mansion flat, in hall and manor and new central-heated 'cottage', the wealthy, talented and beautiful lay coupled – welcome wombs were ten-a-penny, must have been. What do you think I picked on, me and my genes, that is? Missing lush Sussex, the Surrey soft spots, affluent Mayfair and gold-filled Golder's Green, fat Norfolk rectories, the Dukeries, and many a solid Yorkshire village, to name only some obvious marks, I came upon the frost-rimed roofs of a working-class suburb in Newcastle-upon-Tyne, and in the back-bedroom of an upstairs flat in a street parallel with the railway line, on which a halted engine whistled to be let through the junction, I chose my future parents. There, it was done. By the time that engine took its rightaway and rolled into the blue glare of the junction arcs, another kiddar was started, an event, one might add, of no novelty in that quarter and momentous only to me. (*Kiddar's Luck*, p. 7)

Common had left for London to ply his talent among left-wing literary circles. One of his earliest published pieces was for the *Manchester Guardian* of 27 October 1930, about loitering for his luck to change while in 'daily attendance at a hospital for financial incurables' – the dole office.

---

[2] Catherine Cookson, *Catherine Cookson Country* (London, 1986), p. 180.

Sid Chaplin was younger than the other two. Whereas McMullen had been brought up as the daughter of a Tyneside dock labourer, and Common was the son of a Newcastle railwayman, Chaplin was born into a mining family in 1916 in the South Durham pit village of Shildon. As Christopher Jack puts it in *The Thin Seam*,

I was born thirty-three years ago, coming contrariwise, as the old lady who assisted keeps telling me. This may be slightly symbolical. It is not for me to say. But I do persist in doing the wrong things. That's enough; let the rest seep through.

Let who I am and what I am be answered by the record of the journey. (*The Thin Seam*, p. 5)

When Jack and Kate had left the North East in 1928 and 1929, Sid was still at school. When Kate the laundry manager bought her big house, 'The Hurst', at Hastings in 1933, and while Jack the worker-writer was getting his foot in the door of *The Adelphi*, in 1935, Sid was nineteen and working underground at Dean and Chapter colliery, Ferryhill. By the time Cookson and Common's first novels were published, in 1950 and 1951, Sid had two books behind him, had won a writer's award, had just finished with the pit, and was living in London writing for *Coal News*, the National Coal Board magazine. Kate meanwhile was now Mrs Catherine Cookson, grammar school master's wife, and back in Hastings after various wartime moves. Jack was also in Sussex, at 32 Warren Hamlet, Storrington, a council house, and trying to earn money labouring by day, working on scripts and reviews by night, and writing for himself in between. They had all left and become distanced from their region, and they had all learnt their writer's craft the hard way – Catherine and Sid by themselves, or in adult education, and Jack the hardest way of all, by freelancing, for money and connections.

The region that these three people addressed in 1951 was at its urban-industrial peak. Census statisticians for that year tabulated the North East as a predominantly working-class region, with a relatively small upper and middle class. The vast majority lived in towns, although the landscape was characteristically hard to classify once beyond the urban fringe. Amidst a welter of county and municipal boroughs, and districts, the conurbations straggled into coalfield and the nucleated mining villages scattered into sparsely populated agricultural areas, and they extended westward into fell and moorland. Heavy industry dominated, and drew on the dense concentrations of skilled men on the steel river rims of Tyne, Wear and Tees, along the coast, and inland, into the pit villages. Far and away the biggest employers were metals and engineering, and coalmining, who had workforces of around 170,000 and 140,000 respectively. Between them these industries occupied over thirty per cent of the male work-force. The only female waged occupation which compared was, predictably, domestic service, employing 90,575. In terms of work that was felt to matter, the North East was a man's world and its people lived close. In Northumberland and Durham nearly forty per cent of dwellings consisted of only one to three rooms and high levels of overcrowding led to notoriously low levels of health.[3]

And yet, in 1951 things were improving. There was more or less full employment, a comprehensive system of welfare and national insurance was in place, vast new housing programmes were under way and, the most revealing test of all, the region's health was getting better. Newcastle Corporation had first investigated the health of children in 1934 and 1939 and, when it resumed its survey in 1947, could report upon a 'remarkable decline in disease and deaths in infancy over the past forty years'. Although 12 per cent of 'artisanal' and no less than 26 per cent of semi- and unskilled workers' households remained unfit for human habitation, nevertheless the early 1950s were still a time for optimism. In the Corporation's prize giving for better health, mothers and grandmothers were awarded bouquets, while welfare centres and health visitors were highly commended. Better housing came third. Doctors, one may add, had 'not been primarily responsible'.[4] So, when in these post-war years Kate Hannigan took her brave heart out into the struggle and spite of Edwardian Tyneside, and Will Kiddar ducked and dived before the mounting demands of capitalist civilisation, and Christopher Jack kicked and crawled his way across the face of a newly nationalised pit, it could be assumed that the North East of their fate was changing for the better.

These changes, however, were largely statistical, and the writers had their own 'North East' to consider. Never able, nor willing, to capture the wholeness of a place in the manner of the statistician, and unable to know that whole place personally, novelists need other literatures.

---

[3] General Register Office, *Census 1951*. County Report, *Durham* (London, 1954), pp. xlvi, xix, xxii; *Northumberland*, pp. xliii, xx. General Register Office, *Census 1951*. England and Wales, *Occupation Tables* (London, 1956), pp. 152–5, 620.

[4] James Spence *et al*, *A Thousand Families in Newcastle upon Tyne. An Approach to the Study of Health and Illness in Children* (London, 1954), pp. 175, 117.

'Regions' are unstable entities and we can no more infer from statistics and reports what a region means, than we can infer who writers are from what they write. The region which Cookson and Common and Chaplin wrote about existed in other realities too, and the optimism of 1951 must be seen in the light of other literatures and experiences.

In 1951 William Geenty produced his Durham Development Plan for Durham County Council.[5] Charged by the Town and Country Planning Act of 1947 to predict how the county would and *should* develop, the Plan was a watershed in the region's history. Not short of graphs and figures, and rich in historical memory, it saw a bright new dawn for the North East, if only the planners and politicians could have their way. Where the market had failed, state planning would succeed. Old regional meanings had centred on images of desolation and loss; the new depended on a clean break.

Geenty's hopes were shared by a post-war generation of Labour politicians and trade union leaders who had seen the bad old times and who were determined that they should not return. Just over thirty years before, in 1919, C. B. Fawcett had also displayed new hope in his call for 'provincial' self-government in this the most distinctive of English regions.[6] Fawcett, a geographer born in Staindrop, County Durham, was in turn the writer of a region which had recently redis-covered itself before the Great War, first in the leisure and scholarly activities of an intelligentsia devoted to an historic Northumbria, and second in the powerful political and cultural achievements of a liberal-labour progressivism which had tied class interests to civic pride. Fawcett's self-government idea had been prompted by Home Rule, originally a federalist policy for Ireland but capable also of Welsh and Scottish translations – 'Home rule all round'. If the Irish, Scots and Welsh dared to ask for it, why not 'The North Country'? Did not Fawcett's place have a language and a history, a distinctive territory, a booming imperial economy, an intelligentsia, and a politics within which, for a time, it looked as though radicals and socialists could find common cause? Newcastle was the capital of a natural and self-conscious region. It was time for recognition.

When Fawcett called for self-government in 1919 it was for a region which had re-invented itself in two generations. When Geenty called

---

[5] William A Geenty, County Planning Officer, *County Development Plan, 1951. Written Analysis prepared for The County Council of Durham* (Billingham, 1951).

[6] C. B. Fawcett, *Provinces of England. A Study of Some Geographical Aspects of Devolution* (1919; London, 1960), p. 88.

for planning and welfare in 1951 it was for a region which had dropped from high to low in one generation, from workshop of the world in a romantic Northumbria, to silent pits and rusting shipyards in a backward 'special area'. It was at this moment of post-war reconstruction, amidst the aerial photographs, the planners' maps and policy documents of a Welfare State, that these three novels were written. As regional novels, therefore, it is as well to ask 'which region?' From New Northumbrian romantics, to North Country home rulers, to inter-war Industrial depressives to post-war Brave New planners, including Socialist regionalists, not to say realists, there were at least five northern identities on offer.

If the region's past and present identities offered various opportunities for writing about it, then the sort of place it did become shaped the ways in which that writing was received afterwards.

Sid Chaplin was to become the author most at ease with the post-war 'regional writer' tag. At first, the regionality of Chaplin's writing was seen as a weakness as well as a strength. Friends and critics sympathetically urged that *The Thin Seam* was only the prelude to another 'fuller and more important novel', or that Chaplin would afterwards go on 'to *become* a great writer' but of course was not one yet. Sid was always being judged against the epithets 'great' and 'major'. Inevitably, if unfortunately, the comparisons were with D. H. Lawrence, a man who never wrote seriously about the work underground. Moreover, Chaplin's agents (Pearn, Pollinger and Higham, in the Strand) were pained to report ('Dear Chaplin') that the United States publishers would not take the novel because 'the mining terminology was too confusing to American readers'.[7] Even the Newcastle *Evening Chronicle*, in two published extracts which should have been three, took it upon itself to censor some of the more realistic dialogue.[8] However, this initial stumbling into mistaken comparisons and cautious marketing was not to last. In 1957 Chaplin came back to the North East, still working for the National Coal Board but now as a public relations officer. By the 1960s, Sid Chaplin the pitman's poet had become Sid Chaplin the regional pundit. With the remorseless decline of the old

[7] Bruce Barr, *Fircroft Magazine*, Autumn 1950. David Higham, author's agent, to Sid Chaplin, 12 September 1950: letter in possession of Mrs R. Chaplin.

[8] R. K. Gervie, London editor, to Sid Chaplin, 10 October 1950: letter in possession of Mrs R. Chaplin. Gervie explained that 'in cutting some of the strong language passages the result looked rather untidy and they decided the best thing would be to telescope the three into two. The total fee, of course, remains unaltered at 30 guineas.'

heavy-industrial North East, and with it the loosening of the old class
discipline (some were beginning to call it 'culture'), Chaplin became
the voice of 'the close knit community', the last man who could be
trusted to say something wise about all that was being lost. Regional
radio and television, and local and national newspapers, lined up for
pieces on how the North East used to be, and *was*. In 1968 *The Thin Seam*
along with some of Chaplin's other stories was turned into a musical
called *Close the Coal House Door*, with words by Alan Plater and songs by
Alex Glasgow. The values were Brechtian. Chaplin was awarded an
OBE for service to Northern Arts in 1977, and he received several
honorary degrees and fellowships, becoming something of a people's
remembrancer.

This is not to suggest that Chaplin had the role foisted upon him.
He said many times that he enjoyed his work and that he loved Newcastle, the region, and his life there.[9] A patriot of his land and people,
Chaplin took the chance to defend the achievements of his class as both
agents of decency and prefigurers of socialism. The pit village was his
emotional model. By the 1960s Chaplin deeply feared what was being
lost – the positive propensities to work hard, feel passionately, act
loyally; the negative uses of not being rich, pampered, or arrogant; the
open-handed resources of a popular wisdom garnered to live in ways
not possible in more cosmopolitan or alienated circles. And yet, it must
be said that no matter how honest his later response was, and no
matter how justified he was in regretting what he described in 1968 as
the demise of 'the old stable values',[10] this was not how he had represented his class and his region in *The Thin Seam*. In 1991 Chaplin's
family and friends met in the People's Theatre, Newcastle to celebrate
his life. *A Rich Seam* now, they came to honour a man with the knack of
seeing things in the round and aright.[11]

But this mellow Chaplin was not to be confused with the young
writer who had made Christopher Jack an ambiguous, tormented
stranger forty years before. Beguiled by his socialist hopes for a people

[9] See for instance, Michael Pickering and Kevin Robins, 'The Making of a Working-Class
Writer: An Interview with Sid Chaplin', in Jeremy Hawthorn (ed.), *The British Working-Class
Novel in the Twentieth Century* (London, 1984). Peter Lewis stresses the regionality in Chaplin and
uses it as a stick to beat what he sees as Marxist interpretations in 'Region and Class: An
Introduction to Sid Chaplin (1916–86)', *Durham University Journal*, 85, 1 January 1993.

[10] 'In *The Thin Seam* I was groping to a realisation that all the old stable values were going and
that we were in for disruption, unrest, disorder' – written in 1968 preface to *Thin Seam*, p. 3, 'A
Song Before The Stories'.

[11] *A Rich Seam*, celebration of Sid Chaplin's life and work at The People's Theatre, Newcastle
upon Tyne, 30 September 1991.

he thought he belonged to, but fearful that he, and possibly they, were unworthy of those hopes, Christopher Jack worked his coal shift in a state of deep personal anxiety. Chaplin later recalled that his writer's anxieties had related to the decline of working-class political culture. In retrospect, he tended to measure the disintegrative effects of that later decline against the more stable personal values of his own generation. But the young Chaplin had not been so self-possessed. In 1938 he had gone to Fircroft College for a year. Like his hero, he had come back with things on his mind. By having been away, and wanting to get away, Christopher Jack was himself part of the disintegration of working-class community, and his personal values are far from clear. It is only at the end that he is reconciled to his people, and only then in a blinding act of faith.

This mellowing appears to have begun soon after Chaplin left the coalfield. Absence may have made his heart grow fonder. He found London's anonymity very different to the life he had lived at 9 Gladstone Terrace, Ferryhill. Writing as a Coal Board journalist from Room 561, Hobart House, he was free to travel the coalfields and talk to miners. This gave him a new way of seeing – practically, from the air. Flying by light aircraft with his photographer colleague Harry Smead, and enjoying a new creative freedom, Chaplin was able to see the coalfields whole and compare them one to another. From such commanding heights, and with the story-teller's urge to make coherent, he was able to re-knit his sense of class and region. Those awkward, cross-grained anxieties of Christopher Jack – anxieties so knotted they could only be resolved by a miracle – became less intense. Seen in the round, and from the sky, high above the deep press of obligation, the pit villages could be re-invested with broader, more generous proportions. So handsome are these proportions in Chaplin's later writing, one wonders why these cultured terraces did not sprout a poet on every corner, a writer off every shift? (Chaplin's response would have been that they did.) A 'good forcing ground for the imagination', on the street, or in the kitchen, pub, pit, chapel, or lodge, he claimed that these places were schools of story-telling. Here he had learned 'the point and pith': 'folklore was not yet a subject but a second set of references'.[12] In *The Thin Seam*, Christopher Jack has to survive 'the hellish shift system', but in retrospect Chaplin came to believe that writing after an afternoon shift was 'so right for a spare time writer

---

[12] Pickering and Robins, 'Sid Chaplin', p. 140.

that it might have been designed for that purpose'.[13] And for the afternoon shift, one should read his North East as a whole. *The Thin Seam*
had a tortured and therefore exalted relationship with its region. Its
author survived to heal his wounds, to make ordinary his revelation.

Catherine Cookson is a publishing phenomenon. After *Kate Hannigan*,
came 94 novels at the last count, all but one set in the North East and
nearly all of them following the Hannigan way. Cookson's books have
been translated into a dozen languages. The brand name (and its
imitators) can be found at international airports and at the local news-
agent's alike. Easily Britain's most popular writer, she has sold well
over one hundred million copies, and her titles have always accounted
for more than one third of the top one hundred most borrowed library
books since records began. It may well be asked in what sense someone
who is amongst the world's most read authors in the English language
is a regional novelist, but it is as a regional novelist that she is known.
Indeed, if anyone ever had to demonstrate that regions are provinces
of the world and not just of nations, Catherine Cookson has done this.
The marketing people and popular press have said it all, of course:
'Born of Tyneside . . . acclaimed as a regional writer' she has 'made
the industrial North of England known and loved by a large public';
'A true tale of northern grit'; 'Tyneside can be proud to have such
a chronicler'.[14] South Shields used to bid welcome to careful drivers;
now it welcomes Cookson Trail hunters to 'Catherine Cookson Country'. She won the Royal Society of Literature Winifred Holtby Prize
for Best Regional Novel in 1968. She was made a Freeman of the
Borough of South Shields in 1974, and was awarded the OBE in 1983.
She received an Honorary Doctorate from Sunderland Polytechnic in
1991. In 1993 she was made a Dame. At her Honorary MA ceremony
at Newcastle, the University Orator said that 'the degree was being
conferred for her work dealing with the everyday lives and vicissitudes
of the people of this Northern area of England'.[15]

Even so, the selling of her first four novels made it plain at the outset
that the region was used only for background and atmosphere. 'Regional' marketing appears to have started in 1954 with *A Grand Man*,
set in the streets of Tyneside 'which Catherine Cookson knows and

[13] Chaplin, *Thin Seam*, pp. 17, 2.
[14] Macdonald dust jackets for *The Glass Virgin*, *Colour Blind* and *Our Kate*. See also features in *The
Daily Express*, 21 April 1973; *Liverpool Daily Post*, 2 February 1976; *The Daily Express*, 8 July 1976;
The Sunday Telegraph, 21 March 1993; *The Sun*, 23 September 1976.
[15] Cookson, *Cookson Country*, p. 10.

understands so well'. As late as 1966, with the first reprint of *Kate Hannigan* at the request of the London and Home Counties branch of the Library Association, the dust jacket simply said that Kate lived 'in the Newcastle slums' (which was inaccurate), and that the book was a 'deeply emotional, powerfully narrated human document'.[16] Her publishers do not seem to have been well informed about her market or their own history of supplying it,[17] but it seems likely that it was not until after 1969, with the publication of her autobiographical *Our Kate*, that the woman and the region became utterly and irrevocably synonymous.

Walter Pater once remarked that all art aspires to the condition of music. In Cookson's case it aspires to history. Contemptuous of romantic fiction, Cookson sees herself as a writer of social history.[18] Certainly her books, 'realistic' in content and predictable in outcome, matched trends in post-war radio and television serial drama. A mass-seller in an age of mass communications, Cookson's popularity stands four-square in the tradition of capitalist novel-making. Her kind of product is guaranteed by the gold embossed Cookson name: 'rich', 'northern', 'life'.[19] In an affluent post-war society, the pleasures of

[16] Macdonald's dust jacket for *A Grand Man* (1954), and Cedric Chivers' blurb for 1966 reprint of *Kate Hannigan*.

[17] As Wendy Tury, publicity manager for Transworld Publishers, said in 1977: 'Our products vary so much and appeal to such a wide range of tastes that it would be almost impossible to gain any very useful knowledge without spending a prohibitive amount of money.' She could only say that Mrs Cookson was their top-selling author and that they never print fewer than 250,000 copies for a new title – 'so you can understand her importance to the publishing world'. Transworld Corgi certainly do: they present her with expensive gifts for every million she sells. In 1997 Transworld Corgi were not sure how many novels she had written and had nothing to say to me about their marketing or publicity strategies. Her first publisher was Macdonald, who advanced £100 for *Kate Hannigan*. By 1972 publishers were bidding for her work at the Frankfurt Book Fair – Heinemann taking the hardback rights and Corgi the paperback. At the 1986 bidding, Transworld Corgi took all. Her biographer estimates that about £4m went to Mrs Cookson plus £400,000 for each new story, with print runs of 600,000. See Cliff Goodwin, *To Be A Lady. The Story of Catherine Cookson* (London, 1994), pp. 151, 269.

[18] 'Her Cookson novels were not romances, she said, but down-to-earth social histories of the north-east', *The Observer*, 29 September 1985, and, 'She has, in short, a good deal more in common with Emile Zola than with her fellow DBE, Dame Barbara Cartland', *The Sunday Telegraph*, 21 March 1993. In her novels, like those of Daphne Du Maurier, 'Families become the true histories . . .', Alison Light, *Forever England. Femininity, Literature and Conservatism Between the Wars* (London, 1991), p. 194. Bridget Fowler takes Cookson's claim to be a historian on its own terms and finds reformism: *The Alienated Reader. Women and Romantic Literature in the Twentieth Century* (Hemel Hempstead, 1991), pp. 78–82.

[19] Corgi do not know the region they profit by. They say their front cover illustration to the 1974 edition of *Our Kate* depicts Cookson as a young woman at Tyne Dock. In fact, it depicts her in Gateshead, with the Tyne bridges behind. The Macdonald's version of the same illustration says it shows Cookson age 24. If that was the case, then one of the Tyne bridges – and the most famous one – appears to be missing.

reading *Kate Hannigan* and her sisters could be enjoyed vicariously – hard times for sure, but not quite for these times. Cookson's blend of female protagonists and their hardships, with a dramatic style easily given to convenient reading, in an expanding market, was to prove an enormously successful formula. Whatever academic plaudits she missed, she no doubt rests content with a readership of tens of millions and a bank account not much smaller.

In Jack Common's diary for 1952, there is a cutting from the *News Chronicle* for 20 May. It tells the story of Mr Alfred Bayliss, thirty-nine, bricklayer of Harlow, Essex. Having borrowed £2 from his foreman, Bayliss went to the races and won on every race. He then threw himself under a bus because he believed, wrongly, that a track gang was after him. Unlike Chaplin or Cookson, Jack Common did not find the post-war world such an opportune place. After *Kiddar's Luck* he wrote one more novel, a sequel, *The Ampersand*, published in 1953. His publishers, the Turnstile Press, went into liquidation two years later, Common not having completed the trilogy with his long-promised *Riches and Rare*.[20] After that, he appears to have dried up and his published books were difficult to acquire. The 1950s found him writing, more or less as he had always written, lacking time and money, scraping advances, having to argue his worth. He finished *Kiddar*, he said, 'with people snatching the roof off my head and turning out the electric light and littering me with summonses . . . and lack of beer thinning my blood, lack of tobacco making my lungs transparent'.[21] And when the *Kiddar* came, it was at first as a prophet without honour. The Newcastle newspapers refused it, the city booksellers were apathetic. Turnstile only promoted the regional dimension after *Kiddar's Luck* had won critical praise.[22]

This was not Common's first book. He had won some admirers during the 1930s on John Middleton Murry's *Adelphi* and with the publication of two socialist compilations in 1938, *Freedom of the Streets* and *Seven Shifts*. During these years he had built a reputation as a 'proletarian'

---

[20] Common was offered £250 in four monthly instalments for 'the crowning volume' by 31 December 1954. By March 1955 Turnstile Press had decided to go into liquidation with no sign of Common's *Riches and Rare* manuscript: Michael Hodson to Jack Common, 11 August, 15 December 1954; 6 January, 29 March 1955 (*Jack Common Papers*, 29, University of Newcastle Library). The diary for 1952 is in *Papers*, 4.

[21] Letter to Irene Palmer, 2 April 1951, quoted in Eileen Aird, 'Jack Common': catalogue to 'Strong Words' Exhibition at Newcastle Central Library.

[22] Hodson to Common, 5 November 1951; John Roberts to Jack Common, 3 December 1951, 16 June 1953, *Papers*, 29.

writing-man in that salty, political, and universal way working-class writers were meant to be. E. M. Forster saw him as a 'warm-hearted, matey writer'.[23] Common knew George Orwell, kept his smallholding while the great man was in Spain, and received nice reviews from him. In the *New English Weekly* for 16 June 1938 Orwell referred to that 'innate decency' of the 'mass of the people', and it is hard not to see Common as his exemplar.

The trouble was that Jack Common went on believing in the working class while others did not. When he sent his friend Eric Warman the typescript of another unpublished novel, *In Whitest Britain*, in 1961, Warman replied, from Embankment Gardens, Chelsea, that although he was sorry that such 'a bloody good writer' could not 'make a big success at it', the book was out of place. There was too much 'class distinction':

If you will forgive me saying so, the cult of the good honest workman, down-trodden but golden hearted, is in itself a leading cliché and it has always surprised me that a man of your intelligence should be so determined to sustain it.[24]

Having been too late (and perhaps unwilling) for the Proletcult cult of the 1930s, and too early (and perhaps too old) for the Angry Young Man marketing of the 1950s, Common found himself too early again for the new left revivals of the 1960s. He died in 1968, without recognition.

Chaplin's *Thin Seam* is one man's story of a night at two hundred fathoms in 160 yards by 20 inches of County Durham. It is a journey in, and a journey out. Moving with his 'marras' to the coalface, Christopher Jack moves as well to the extremes of his own self-knowledge:

the first hundred yards or so was pretty good going. After that the girders begin to lower, bowing under the burden of stone, until they break and the jagged ends point to a lifting bottom. At the worst places I had to crawl. At the best places I could bend my back parallel with the gate . . . There are two ways of getting through . . . The first is to take it slowly and methodically, resting two or three times. This is the old men's system. You can find their camps, their regular camps, places where it widens a little, a plank with a chock-nob to sit upon. The second is to take it in one mad bull rush and get it over as quickly as possible. (*The Thin Seam*, pp. 44–45)

[23] E. M. Forster, in *New Statesman and Nation*, 10 December 1938.
[24] Eric Warman to Jack Common, 7 June 1961, *Papers*, 46.

Chalked on old girders, tunnelled in dark places, traced in dim corners, miners' history is written in the pit. The way is hard, the effort exhausting. Tense and awkward with all around him, and with all inside him, Christopher Jack's mind is on other things. But what is its message? He doesn't do his work properly, he insults and is assaulted for it, he thieves precious water. At the face, Jack knows he is not the man he imagined himself to be. Is this his place as well as theirs? Does he still know his 'marras'? Do they know him? Do they trust him? He should never have come back. Then, Art Lake is knocked by a fall of stone onto the shearing teeth of the coal-cutter. The final sequence, 'A Caravan to the Sun' is the journey outbye. Carrying Art on a bloody stretcher, the team rest and run, rest and run. The rests are stations of the cross, the runs are desperate kickings to the light. Death brings life. Crawling his way to the dying comrade, Christopher Jack is humbled into a personal reconciliation with his people, his history and his land.

This is the story of a man lost and found. What the miners have achieved before him is a history apart. Christopher Jack does, and does not, want to get back into relationship with it. Divided in his feelings, there is Jack-on-the-outside, the Durham pit lad who had been to college and come back bearing gifts, and Jack-on-the-inside, the scholarship boy doubting his decision to return. The two Jacks talk and feel differently: on-the-outside, a pitman in dialect and dress but missing his 'other world . . . books, good conversation . . . sunshine and lawns'; and Jack on-the-inside, a pen-man having 'lost something. My roots,' knowing only too well that 'all scholarship battens on the backs of the workers'.[25]

Then the real man is found, face to face, and darkly. A miracle of revelation, he realises the 'things in your blood',[26] not to be avoided. And the miracle does not come free floating from on high, but happens in this struggling place, from out of the darkest depths. Here, the bright Durham of beck and moorland is only a memory. The shrine is underground, the inner core of what Durham *is* to the men who have made it so. This is special. It is their place, a land beneath, hardly seen but smelled, and groped, and cut, and listened to, and squinted through to bring forth whole sight. Like some of the writing, this land is not open to outsiders. In Sid Chaplin's region, 'A man takes off his clean clothes and puts on his pit gear. That's all, but between the acts lies a lost world'.[27] The novel's last words:

---

[25] Chaplin, *Thin Seam*, p. 20.   [26] *Ibid.*, p. 37.   [27] *Ibid.*, p. 9.

Men do this. My folk. They pierce the fabric of His temple; make an incision into the heart of His mystery. And at the same time, unknowingly, they tend the hem of His robe and make most glorious the thin seam of His garment. (*The Thin Seam*, p. 108)

For a great industrial region in a state of dissolution, Chaplin's came to be *the* voice. His was the voice of what was being squandered. Embedding his story in the rock of Durham's labour traditions, and asking what a new generation could make of those traditions, the answer to Chaplin's dilemma is not to be found in *The Thin Seam*. Atonement it might have been, but for one man only and that man one of a company of special men. And for Christopher Jack, as for himself, Chaplin wanted it both ways: to fight for his people with the skills taken from the privileged, and also to belong, or to feel he belonged, to the class he no longer worked beside. By writing, part of Sid Chaplin even doubted his masculinity – 'Writing was very effeminate, so I said nothing about it'.[28]

Some of his friends did not want to share the burden. Chaplin's old adult college, Fircroft, sprang to his defence against patronising reviews in *The Times* and *Daily Worker* and yet criticised the novel for its 'battle-ground of the imagination',[29] even though the imagination was the very place where Chaplin's battle was being fought. The Fircroft reviewer still wanted his workers untroubled: solid simple hearts for solid simple duties.

So *The Thin Seam* took a class problem and solved it with an epiphany. By himself, and out of the pit, Chaplin had to cope when the ecstasy faded. He worked his own way through. After 1950 he was a professional writer, and after 1957 he found the time and the local connections to form a bulwark against the kind of snobbery which said that artistic and working-class aspirations were incompatible.[30] He was always on the lookout in defence of a popular culture that he saw as being as good as anybody else's culture. He found solace in a sense of place, more above ground now, which he cleaved to as a distinct territory encompassing many of the values he espoused. An emotional rather than a geographical place, this 'North East' was a land to be brave in,

[28] Quoted in Pickering and Robins, 'Sid Chaplin', p. 143.
[29] Bruce Barr, *Fircroft Magazine*, Autumn 1950.
[30] '... that to shape a fiction, however unconventionally, and however loyal the writer may remain to the people who have borne and sustained him, is an act that produces a result that is not in itself compatible with working-class aspirations.' C. C. Barfoot, *English Studies* 1983, quoted in Jeremy Hawthorn, preface, *British Working-Class Novel*, p. vii. For Tony Harrison's difficulty 'to speak "on behalf of" a group he no longer belongs to', see Bruce Woodcock, 'Classical Vandalism: Tony Harrison's Invective', *Critical Quarterly*, 32: 2, Summer 1990.

given the right emotional conditions, conditions bards like him would supply. This was a fertile plain and it also produced some very fine travel writing from him.[31] Another way through was achieved in Chaplin's rearguard defence of what his people had wrought in their making of a class counter-culture.[32] But these were only partial resolutions. By 'his people' Chaplin tended to mean men, North East men, and miners especially. As their numbers dwindled and the pit villages fell to grass, the odds moved against him. If the real Durham lay in its miners, what when the miners were few? In his later devotion to Newcastle, emotional place and class remnant came together. For here, like the pit, was a place 'you can touch and feel', 'I feel I belong'.[33] Its men were formidable, if still awkward. Its women, like his region and city, were to be enjoyed as his own creations. He loved words: a painstaking writer, he wrote for pleasure and enjoyed what he made. Pleasured by his inventions, secure in their presence, he drank them in:

The girls make a stunning spectacle when the shops turn out . . . they are the best and brightest image of a wonderful town. The challenge to the big river city planners is to provide the right setting for the girls. They will have a job on their hands. (*Terra Nova*, 1966)

Chaplin's resolution was personal. He made his own miracle. A happy man and a superb essayist, now trying to 'achieve a balance between my proper function as a member of society and a writer',[34] the North East came to feel like his home and not his battleground. Although Chaplin continued to worry about how working-class solidarity could survive, or adapt, in what he saw as a dislocated world – and he wrote two Newcastle novels in the 1960s to do with this – the point is that his protagonists stood their ground. Unlike a lot of other 'working-class' novels of the period, his young men did not seek resolution in flight. For Sid Chaplin, this was vital. Never flattered by any real national recognition, Chaplin's experience had taught him that it was only in their

---

[31] Beginning with, *My County – Durham*, Home Service BBC Broadcast, 12 August 1951. The producer was Denis Mitchell.

[32] Chaplin was interested in the social history of North East miners long before the academics. He would have been very comfortable with contemporary cultural and anthropological approaches to miners' history. On that history, the place to start would be David Levine and Keith Wrightson, *The Making of an Industrial Society. Whickham, 1560–1765* (Oxford, 1991), and Robert Colls, *The Pitmen of the Northern Coalfield. Work, Culture and Protest, 1790–1850* (Manchester, 1987).

[33] Sid Chaplin, 'Walking the Bounds', in *The Smell of Sunday Dinner* (Newcastle, 1971), p. 10; 'Back to Square One', *Terra Nova*, 17 October 1966.

[34] Sid Chaplin, 'The Power of the Word', *Sunday Dinner*, p. 24.

own place, nurtured and challenged by their own myths, that people like him would find themselves. Place and myth had always been in him, but in the end they predominated. Place moved to displace problem. Myth moved to displace miners. What else could he do? On 10 January 1986 Sid Chaplin died while staying at Grasmere, in Cumbria:

Then I knew that men like my Grandad who wrought in darkness never die. The life he gave to me lives on and will be my sons' in turn. The million pitmen will break through to daylight – they and their sons and grandsons. Swallows build instinctively. They will build – or know the reason why.[35]

For over forty years Catherine Cookson's writing has returned, time and again, to what she came to see as the humiliations of her own young life. This self-absorption has been so consistent that one can see all the great motifs of her subsequent writing in the first six pages of *Kate Hannigan*. Page one has Kate giving birth to her illegitimate child in illegitimate circumstances: the home is poor, there are sharp and wounding class resentments, the handsome doctor is in attendance, the midwife is unhelpful, and drunk. Page two introduces the child's grandmother and step-grandfather, whose house it is. Page three suggests the love-triangle that is to come: a virile professional man, his frigid snobbish wife, the lovely but humiliated Kate. Page four asks how the child will live – 'If it inherited her beauty and was brought up in these surroundings it was doomed from birth'. Page five has Kate troubled by her Roman Catholic guilt – 'her sins, the secret things she thought she was ashamed of . . .'. Page six reveals Kate knowing her true worth, certainly worthy of the child's father, an absent gentleman, and certainly better than her origins, 'fit to marry anybody'. And after chapter one, 'The Birth', there is chapter two, 'The Kitchen'. This is the hub of grandmother's quieter moments, where it seems that a woman's mind can wheel in and out from a very small universe:

Her mind wandered back and forth over the past, as she stared out into the dark day. Eleven o'clock and Christmas Eve, and you really needed a light, the sky was so low and heavy. Christmas had always brought trouble . . . She and Tim had married in Christmas week. She couldn't remember why she had married Tim . . . perhaps because she had wanted to get away from

---

[35] Sid Chaplin, 'Swallows Will Build', in *In Blackberry Time* (Newcastle, 1987), p. 229. The Newcastle novels were *The Watchers and the Watched* (1962) and *The Day of the Sardine* (1965). For an unusual approach to Chaplin's later novels, addressing sexuality and some Freudian motifs, see Michael Pickering and Kevin Robins, 'Between Determinism and Disruption: The Working-Class Novels of Sid Chaplin', *College English*, 51: 4, April 1989.

Mrs Harris's, where she worked for sixteen hours a day for seven days a
week . . . Now she was forty-two, and he was fifty-one; and all of her life she'd
had only three months happiness . . . And now things were changing, she
could feel the change. It wasn't that Tim had been a prisoner upstairs for six
weeks, or that there was a baby in the house; it was rather a premonition
. . . She'd better mash some tea and take him a cup . . . Presently her gaze
wandered around the kitchen. It was all beautifully clean for Kate's coming.
(*Kate Hannigan*, pp. 31–2)

Eighty pages later, 'Sitting before the kitchen fire, at three o'clock in
the afternoon, it was Kate's turn now to review the happenings of the
past year . . .'.

In 1945 Catherine Cookson lost her fourth baby in nearly as many
years and slid into a period of mental breakdown which was to last, on
and off, for over twenty years. She had to face up to who she was. *Kate
Hannigan*, her first novel, was one consequence of that.

First she had to face up to her mother. Catherine Cookson has said
that her mother was a liar, a drunk, a cheat and a ruthless exploiter of
her daughter's affections.[36] Her mother was called Kate and at first she
pretended that she was Catherine's older sister. But even when Catherine
discovered who her real mother was, she found it hard to call her
'mother' and was forty-seven years old before she could bring herself
to use the more endearing 'Mam': 'The only time she wanted to kiss
me was when she was drunk.'[37] Most importantly, there was Catherine's
illegitimacy, the low deception surrounding it, and a child's trauma of
finding-out the truth through back-lane gossip. Cookson could not bring
herself to write factually, or at least 'biographically', about her relationship with her mother until after Kate's death in 1956 and even then the
manuscript went through numerous drafts before she allowed its publication as *Our Kate* in 1969. Not that that is the whole story. It is only
a version, '*An* Autobiography'. Cookson has another manuscript 'upstairs, in the drawer',[38] which, she hints, is harsher still in its judgement
and might be published posthumously. Nevertheless Cookson's feelings for her mother were and are complicated. Over the years they
appear to have veered from love and gratitude to hate and disgust.
Kate Hannigan was dedicated 'TO MY MOTHER who has found expression through me'. *Our Kate* ends 'Good-bye, Kate, and thank you
for giving me life'.

---

[36] Catherine Cookson, *Our Kate* (London, 1974), pp. 27–28, 189; *Cookson Country*, p. 116.
[37] Robert and Rosie Colls, interview with Catherine Cookson, at her home, on 5 January 1989.
[38] *Ibid.*

Second, Catherine Cookson had to contend with her region. She has often remarked that right from an early age she did not feel that a dock labourer's Tyneside flat was her rightful place in life. Her Aunt had told her that when her natural father had come to do his courting he had sported an astrakhan collar, a high hat, and a silver-topped cane. Cookson says she spent much of her childhood and young womanhood dreaming of how to escape the working-class wretchedness of her native region. While working in South Shields she came upon Lord Chesterfield's eighteenth-century *Letters* to his son, not to his godson and successor, but to Philip Stanhope, illegitimate, and *filius nullius*:

In English law . . . the rights of the bastard were only those he could acquire: civilly he could inherit nothing, but he might gain a surname by reputation although he had none by inheritance. This meant, in Chesterfield's view, that Philip's effect on the people around him was of over-ruling importance.[39]

A 'practical manual' in the gentlemanly graces, Chesterfield's *Letters* were criticised by eighteenth-century critics as superficial, but they found a rising market among those intent on the arts of ambition.[40] In South Shields public library in the mid-1920s Catherine Cookson belatedly joined that market and found 'her Bible'. The noble Lord assumed the role of Catherine's personal tutor. Under his guidance she intensified her self-improvement, her serious reading, the phonetics and elocution lessons, the cold determination to expunge the North East, buy a big house and marry a gentleman worthy of her. In retrospect, Cookson makes it all sound so planned, as it probably was for a child who had carefully saved halfpennies from her train fare and who took out her first insurance policy aged eleven. And, after Cicero out of Chesterfield, Cookson learned the uses of *volto sciolto e pensieri stretti* – 'that is, a frank open and ingenious exterior, with a prudent and reserved interior',[41] or, the distinction between concealing a truth and telling a lie. The facade went up. There is not a word on the General Strike in *Our Kate*. The laundry checker ('St Catherine' to her workmates) went out with miners, 'real pit lads', and she worked just down the road from Harton Colliery, but she was thinking of fiddle, fencing, French grammar and Indian clubs while the miners were fighting for their lives. While the mining families of South Shields starved, St Catherine was reading a Lord and planning to marry a Duke. Despite

[39] S. M. Brewer, *Design for a Gentleman. The Education of Philip Stanhope* (London, 1963), p. 9.
[40] J. C. D. Clark, *English Society, 1688–1832* (Cambridge, 1987), p. 101.
[41] Brewer, *Philip Stanhope*, p. 197.

being a writer who extols strong northern women and, indeed, as someone who has come to exemplify their strength, she did not see them in
the way Ellen Wilkinson, for one, saw them: as political 'mothers in
Israel', 'indomitable', the Labour Party's 'backbone' through Jarrow's
bleakest times.[42] There were many reasons for this and in this connection it is worth remembering that while Catherine Cookson *is* the
North East to many people, not least the local Labour authorities who
sell her as a tourist industry, the fact remains that she has lived most of
her life outside the region and spent the first part of her life trying to
forget it, and the second part trying to remember it.[43]

In the same moment that she had to deal with her mental illness and
contend with her mother, she also had to come to terms with the North
East. Between 1945 and 1956, 'This was the bad patch . . . I knew that
I would have to come clean'.[44] 'Catherine Cookson', grammar school
master's wife of Hastings, County of Sussex, had been her first invention:
'Katie McMullen', poor unlettered girl of East Jarrow, was to be her
second.

She wrote obsessively about her origins, trying to make social and
psychological sense of her early experiences. She became a Geordie
again. She set about stripping facades and began liking northerners for
their supposed great openness of character. She persuaded herself that
she couldn't write about anywhere else. In one attempt, about south-
coast fishing families, 'The only thing in the story that had any guts
was the fish'.[45] 'Catherine' she came to see as the middle-class feminized
'south', 'Katie' she came to see as the working-class masculinized 'north'.
She came to wish that she had published under her maiden name.
'Katie' and 'Catherine' each became the self that writes, both of them
voracious characters forged over thirty years of fearful introspection
and made public in press releases, publicity blurbs, journalistic interviews

---

[42] Colls' interview with Catherine Cookson; Ellen Wilkinson, *The Town that was Murdered* (London, 1939), p. 195. Harold Heslop returned to Harton Colliery from the Central Labour
College in 1926, after the lock-out. Heslop went on to write novels, and would merit comparison with the writers discussed here, though he did not enjoy their post-war success: 'Almost
alone, Harry Heslop created the mining-novel in Britain, and won respect for it' – Andy Croft,
foreword, in Harry Heslop, *Out of the Old Earth* (Newcastle, 1994). p. 37.

[43] In 1985 South Tyneside launched a Tourism Development Programme which placed the
'Catherine Cookson Country' promotion at the centre of its policy. Connected to this programme was a major building and upgrading of facilities and infrastructure. Its success has
'exceeded all expectations' and 'couldn't and wouldn't have happened without her'. In 1990
and 1991, 481 coach groups took 'The Cookson Trail', and visitors to South Shields Museum,
where the Cookson display predominates, rose from 61,000 in 1985 to 198,000 in 1991: interview with Tom Fennelly, press officer for South Tyneside Council, 21 July 1992.

[44] Colls' Interview with Catherine Cookson.   [45] Cookson, *Cookson Country*, pp. 12–13.

and features. Her tale of two selves has a moral structure which shapes everything she writes. Her biographer found it difficult to tell any other tale but hers. Once he departs from that, to deal with recent times, the biography loses its coherence and disintegrates into a heap of clippings strung together by dates. Catherine Cookson desires it this way. Her will forbids her executors to inaugurate or authorize any biography. She has destroyed many personal papers. Not much of what she says happened in her young life can be checked. She admits to no other literary influence than Lord Chesterfield. She no longer appears to read other authors, or acknowledge them. Getting beyond her own self and the massive mythological edifice which has been built upon it, is very likely impossible.[46]

So, once upon a time there had been Katie, trailing to the pawn between Jarrow and Shields. Then there was Catherine who grew up to become mother to this child. Then the child grew up to become mother to Catherine. Both live as 'Catherine Cookson', world famous author, the woman who mothered herself. When my wife and I interviewed her in 1989 it was of course impossible to unravel the 'daughter' from the 'mother'. At first, we met Catherine, somewhat frail on a nurse's arm, but stately, and courteous, and promising only thirty minutes. Three hours later it was Katie, younger now, and stronger, holding forth by a friendly fireside. Either way, there was the impression of a performance. A woman who has 'pretended' from childhood, and fed her mind on the isolation that pretending required, she was, she told us, 'an inveterate, well we call it imagination, but me granda called it – I was a liar you see! (laughs)':[47]

---

[46] 'The self that writes', 'a subject bent on self-knowledge', 'especially women . . . You must have a self before you can afford to deconstruct it', Nicole Ward Jouve, *White Woman Speaks with Forked Tongue. Criticism as Autobiography* (London, 1991), pp. 1, 7. In *To Be A Lady*, Mr Goodwin is not much interested in getting behind the mythology, but he does make two incisions into Cookson's version. First, he suggests – albeit from 'little evidence' and with a lot of speculation – that her natural father may have been not so much a gentleman as a commission agent. Her mother registered her birth fifty-five days late and gave the date as 27 June, not 20 June, in order to avoid prosecution. Catherine was registered as Davies, and the father as Alexander Davies, while the mother gave her own name of Fawcett. Goodwin has found a Quayside firm of commission agents, E. F. Davis and Co, operating at the time out of Lombard Street, Newcastle. Cookson signed herself as 'Catherine Ann Davies, otherwise McMullen', in the church vestry on her wedding day in 1940 (pp. 62–63, 127). Second, Goodwin discovered that Cookson has expurgated the Eckford family from the memoir in spite of the fact that they were close neighbours and Belle the daughter and Jim the brother remained her friends well into Catherine's twenties. Belle, it appears, had been the girl who had famously refused the young Catherine entry to her party because 'me Ma says you haven't got no Da' (pp. 44–45, 196). The Eckfords are replaced in the memoir by the local shopkeeper, Cissie Affleck.

[47] Colls' interview with Catherine Cookson.

I was established as Catherine Cookson, the writer, yet to my ain folk I would ever remain Katie McMullen of the New Buildings . . . the truth was, I was still her . . . I was the North . . . Its people were my people. (*Our Kate*, p. 244)

To the literary theorists this is the 'split self', 'absolutely common-place, almost an identifying characteristic of women's writing in this century'.[48] For our purposes here, this split self produced a fiction that was forever cradled in darkest depression and the way out. Regardless of the actual stated chronology of her novels, emotionally it is always Katie's Tyneside in the 1920s, and Catherine's Sussex in the 1930s – the time of her struggle to leave and have done.

We still have some explaining to do. After *Kate Hannigan* in 1950, Catherine Cookson became locked into a market that was to make her a doyen of romantic fiction and Britain's most well-known regional novelist. But the truth is that she is only partially a romantic writer, and not at all a regional novelist.

When Cookson decided to renew contact with the North East some-time between 1945 and 1950, it must have been hard for her to see a way back. The region's dominant representations were male representa-tions. This was not just so in the political culture, a movement which Sid Chaplin tried to excavate from the inside, it was equally the case in popular culture. Bobby Thompson, born in 1909 at New Penshaw in County Durham, was a contemporary of Cookson's who left the pit to become the region's greatest comedian. Known on stage as 'The Little Waster', Thompson was a battered scrap of North East manhood in flat cap and ex-army battle blouse, tab stuck to lip, ready to take on a respectable world. In the pubs and clubs that were his natural medium, The Little Waster made mock of the very things which drove Cookson to distraction. Drink? 'Sup up lads, poverty's no disgrace.' Debt? 'There's plenty of money about . . . look at the amount we owe.' Fecklessness? 'He'll neither work nor want.' Thompson later recalled winning his biggest laugh in 1951, at the Miners' Welfare, Ferryhill, Sid Chaplin's place.[49] There wasn't much room in this club for a Sussex school-master's wife, just as there was not much room for her in the so-called working-class writing of the later 1950s and early 1960s. Both were largely men's stories and certainly not to be told by a posh lady in a

---

[48] Deirdre Burton, 'A Feminist Reading of Lewis Grassic Gibbon's *A Scots Quair*', in Hawthorn (ed.), *British Working-Class Novel*, p. 38.

[49] Richard Kelly, 'Survival of the Little Waster', *The Observer*, 4 November 1979.

hat.[50] One form which was open however, was women's romantic fiction, at this time a genre left over for women as seemingly not worthy of critical interest and, therefore, free from critical barriers. Moreover, this sort of writing carried, and continues to carry, the expectation that its authors could be recruited from its readers and that between the writing and the reading there was a similarity of experience and form.[51] In certain ways Cookson adhered to romantic fiction's expectations and conventions – in the formula, truly; in the love story, madly; in the marketing, possibly – but her personal craving to re-write herself broke with other aspects of a normally synthetic genre. Cookson grabbed those issues which women's romantic writers were not supposed to touch. Violence, alcoholism, rape, child abuse, incest, class division, history and politics all figure in her novels. *Fanny McBride*, one of her heroines, keeps the ladies' toilets.

It might be thought then that it was her desire to get back north which forced her to break with romantic sensitivities. This was not so. Cookson retained her romantic sensitivities but came to deploy them with full-force against a masculine represented region and, in doing so feminized the meaning of that region in a way that was truly unprecedented. Not that there was necessarily any grand strategy in this. Moreover, given the genre that was on offer and the personal torments she had to face and write about, it is difficult to see any other way she might have travelled. In her writing, public masculine identities are secondary, and it is in those detailed, personal and domestic arenas

---

[50] Mary Eagleton and David Pierce, *Attitudes to Class in the English Novel* (London, 1979), pp. 130–2, 137. For another reading of the 1950s which might be a way of placing Cookson's historical self-interpretation, see David Lodge, *Working with Structuralism* (London, 1981), pp. 6–9.

[51] It is reckoned that clever, or educated, people cannot like women's romantic fiction: see, for instance 'Ten well-known people – who have never before indulged – to delve between the book covers and admit if the earth moved', 'Love on the Shelf', *The Observer*, 7 April 1985. For the link between readers and writers see Jean Saunders, *The Craft of Writing Romance* (London, 1986), pp. 56–59; *Guidelines For Writers* (nd.); 'If you wouldn't dream of going on a job interview in a housecoat, with your hair up in curlers, take the time to be every bit as professional in appearance with your manuscript' – Yvonne MacManus, *You Can Write a Romance and Get It Published* (Severn House, 1983), p. 19.

In Cookson's case, it is possible to see a connection between inter-war 'working-class writing' and women's romantic fiction, and the generic opportunity it offered: 'By the mid-thirties publishers were actually advertising for working-class authors, and their books were marketed both as 'human interest' stories and as shocking revelations of the conditions of working-class life' – Janet Batsleer, Tony Davies, Rebecca O'Rourke, Chris Weedon, *Re-writing English. Cultural Politics of Class and Gender* (London, 1985), p. 45. See also ch. 5, 'Gender and genre: womens' stories'. Taylor opined: 'The best sellers of the thirties were predominantly realistic in tone. Priestley, Cronin, Louis Golding, offered chunks of ordinary life, usually in drab surroundings': A. J. P. Taylor, *English History, 1914–45* (Oxford, 1975), p. 312.

– where real life goes on, and is reproduced in body and feeling – that Catherine Cookson's North East has its being. Her strong women might break through, but they rarely seek to break-up, established structures. Catherine Cookson is a 'one off' but it is in this sense that she might usefully be seen as what Alison Light has called a 'conservative modernist'.[52] And it is in this sense also that she is not really a regional writer. Although there is a degree of topographical precision in her work, this does not of itself make that work 'regional'. Her characters move through named places. There are clear directions, accurate distances, factual events, proper nouns, and dates, and buildings. All this adds up to social history in the eyes of its author, a woman who can castigate D. H. Lawrence for his historical errors.[53] Yet in spite of her care to get details right (not always successfully, as it happens) there is no sense in *Kate Hannigan* for instance, as there is in *The Thin Seam*, of the North East constituting a culture, a civilization even, to be found inside its own territorial and emotional wholeness. Kate Hannigan's Jarrow could be anywhere hard and grimy. Cookson's topography merely serves as framework. It never really matters that this is the North East and not some other hard case.

The region Cookson knew from experience was tiny: three streets, two terraces, one house, one kitchen and a thousand journeys sliding a mile or so west to east by the river to Tyne Dock and back again. 'This is my world'.[54] Cookson will not admit to ever having left South Shields because she will not admit to ever having lived there. Shields was 'posh'. She claims that as a child she never went there beyond Tyne Dock, except to go to the sands, twice, which she didn't like. Harton workhouse and hospital, on the other hand, was well into town – down Stanhope Road and up Talbot. Moving half a mile outside this world in the wrong direction and she was lost, knowing little and remembering nothing.[55] Newcastle, which is often presented in her publicity, she never knew. And if her geographical region was small, there is also little affinity with how the North has expressed itself. Cookson does

---

[52] See Alison Light's interpretation of inter-war national identities in *Forever England*. Pat Barker has followed some of these female paths through the region in her *Union Street* (1982) and *The Century's Daughter* (1986). She has said that the women she writes about 'are highly articulate, but their problem is that nobody is listening to them': Lyn Pykett, 'The Century's Daughters: Recent Women's Fiction and History', *Critical Quarterly*, 29: 3, Autumn 1987, p. 72. Mrs Cookson's agent, Anthony Sheil, told me in 1997 that her early publishers had been badly mistaken to see her as a romantic novelist. To him, 'She is popular art'. At the risk of his client teasing him as 'la-tee-da', he said he thought she was 'a modern Homer'.

[53] Colls' interview with Catherine Cookson.   [54] *Ibid.*   [55] *Our Kate*, pp. 21, 101, 243.

not consider that she has written for the region in particular. She writes, she says, for anyone who will listen. She refuses the 'one of us' endearment. Wor Catherine is not a socialist, supports no political party, hates the grating of 'thick unintelligible Geordie'[56] and makes sure not to speak it herself. We can be sure that she would find the 'Wor' of that sentence as regrettable as the ascription 'conservative modernist'. Ah well, it's too late now. *The spuggies are fledged.*

Like all prominent writers of popular fiction, Catherine Cookson is held close by her readers, and no one has ever doubted that most of these readers are women. She reciprocates their feelings; women have 'eaten me alive'. She sees herself as a strong woman, is extremely proud of her huge correspondence and has been glad to be 'mother confessor' to thousands – 'I've had to be like iron'.[57] Her female protagonists have iron wills too and, through them, she has re-enacted some of the great moral themes of all art; namely virtue, talent, truth, and fulfilment.[58] Kate Hannigan lives, first and foremost, for virtue; she has a great talent for life itself and is driven, by necessity, to act upon it. With Rodney, Kate breaks the social taboos against their love and, by doing so, they affirm truth over all other considerations. If Kate finds fulfilment in Rodney then it works the other way as well. In fact, Rodney's need is the greater.

During the 1960s Cookson started writing with the help of a tape recorder. She believes this method most suited her creative processes: 'While talking my Northern characters down I could see them acting; I could feel through my voice their emotions', 'I put on a tape and sometimes I'm crying . . . sometimes I'm yelling'.[59] There are signs of this dramatic performance before the 1960s. Parts of *Kate Hannigan* read like treatments for movies. Cookson hates the word 'plot' almost as much as she hates the epithet 'romantic writer'.[60] To her, plots are unnatural because they contrive to manipulate how life is. And how life is has to do with what she sees as authentic settings: social problems, class divisions, people at the edge, holding on all bearing-inwards, the vortex of a woman's singular life. A strong believer in environmental determinants, once her characters are screened in the mind they are

---

[56] Colls' interview with Catherine Cookson.   [57] *Ibid.*
[58] Harriett Hawkins, *Classics and Trash. Traditions and Taboos in High Literature and Popular Modern Genres* (Hemel Hempstead, 1990). The interplay between 'high' and popular art Hawkins calls 'out-breeding'. (p. xvii)
[59] *Cookson Country*, p. 18; typescript of Catherine Cookson's interview with Melvyn Bragg for *Read All About It*, television programme, reel not televised, 13 May 1977.
[60] Interview, *Read All About It*.

let loose to interact with those determinants. Her female protagonists usually succeed in breaking out of social constraints. From the start, Cookson was clearly writing to a kind of formula, we could call it a series and, once successfully established, her procedures became standard. First, build the family trees by name, age, types, eye and hair colour. Second, put them in a distinct place and period. Third, grade them in their class relationships – the Poor, the Trades, the Professionals, the Uppers 'if it's a country house book'. Fourth, let them perform within a moral dualism of good and evil.[61] After she has acted out her own 'movies' of the mind and tape-recorded what she dramatises, the first drafts are typed.

It is in this sense that Cookson can be regarded more as a television 'soap' dramatist than as a writer of romantic fantasies, although there are overlaps between the two. Both have been seen as a women's form. Both are produced to be 'read' in short snatches, in the interstices of daily routines rather than in long concentrated passages. Both are emphatic in their line and characterization, and contract to shared understandings of what could happen in the story, each aiding memory and offering resolution.[62] But it is as a writer for women that Cookson comes nearest to the soap format. Once place has been indicated by an establishing 'shot', and character and dialogue by 'close-up' and 'two-shot', then real life can begin. In her novels the power to survive and change things is a feminist resource. Throughout *Kate Hannigan* it is Rodney who is given the usually 'feminine' unrequited feelings, while it is Kate who is more charged with fixed principle and ambition.

---

[61] Colls' interview with Catherine Cookson. Her husband, Tom Cookson, has been a modest but hugely influential figure from the beginning. He has always corrected proofs and latterly has taken a greater role in formulating the stories themselves.

[62] Resolution amidst domestic irresolution? 'Domestic life is dull and disorderly . . . The lives of housewives are sequences of disillusioned days in which order is established, then lost, then established and lost again . . . A novel, in which ordinary life is organized in an obviously provisional way, to be discarded at the end of the book, naturally attracts someone who spends her days, temporarily, provisionally organizing diurnal chaos: her life suits her to read novels, even to write them.' Rachel M. Brownstein, *Becoming a Heroine: Reading About Women in Novels* (Harmondsworth, 1984), p. 25. Key reading for understanding Cookson's sort of writing is Christine Geraghty, *Woman and Soap Opera. A Study of Prime Time Soaps* (Cambridge, 1991). Geraghty's treatment of soaps casts light on Cookson's writing form, her critical neglect, the emotional zones of her stories, her emphatic characterisation, the assumed link with the viewer/reader, and her self-estimation as a 'realist' writer dealing with history and 'ordinary' people's problems. What Geraghty says of episodes might be said of Cookson's individual novels which, to the uninitiated, can appear weak: 'Familiarity with the characters allows the viewer to bring meaning to the narrative rather than having to rely on what is shown in a particular episode. It is the viewer who brings richness and density to material which on the surface can look thin and unrewarding'. (p. 15).

Both have the capacity to give as one class and gender to another, yet by the end it is Kate who is the rescuer, the one who brings most:

In the second that it took Kate to reach him, she saw that he wasn't whole . . . his body seemed broken. She was at his feet and her arms were around him . . . there was a protective and maternal urge . . . as his lips gropingly sought hers, her whole being was transported, even while her heart was rent by his tears . . . (*Kate Hannigan*, pp. 221–2)

The only other man who invites real sympathy in the story is Stephen, Kate's natural father. He is a man unlike local men, a sensitive painter 'rather short and slim'. Other men hardly matter. They move coldly, like wraiths, in and out of a story which is bound by feminine feelings: Tim, useless and uncouth, usually out of the house; Alec and Pat, brief, inadequate; priests, bigotted and shadowy; the Tolemarches, kind but never shown; Annie's father, unkind, also never shown; Rodney's colleague, distant; lodgers and neighbours, fleeting, men we can do without. The male gaze may be unfocused but it remains a presence, and sets certain limits about what the women can do and feel. Within a male Roman Catholicism, an unhealthy spirituality has physical significance. In turn, unhealthy bodies have spiritual significance. Broken, tired, coarse, thin, sick, wounded, injured, vulnerable, but beautiful and virile too, bodies are a recurring metaphor for wholeness. When writing about her mother, Cookson draws on her mouth and limp to show the moral looseness: her 'foot flapped', 'It was the mouth that showed her weakness, with a top lip full of slackness'.[63] All four models of women's writing and the sexual difference[64] – biological, linguistic,

---

[63] Cookson, *Our Kate*, pp. 27–8. Cookson has suffered from serious health problems throughout most of her adult life, including double pneumonia, neuritis, phlebitis, nose bleeds, vascular disease, telangiectasia, anaemia, and since 1991, near blindness. There is the suggestion of sexual abuse as a child. In her early years she had a speech impediment. She has also suffered from problems to do with her mental health, including six weeks in a ward which involved electric shock treatment. The classic memoir of the health and maternity worries of working-class women of Cookson's generation and just before, is Margaret Llewelyn Davies, (ed.) *Life As We Have Known It* (London, 1931).

[64] Elaine Showalter, 'Feminist Criticism in the Wilderness', in, Elizabeth Abel, (ed.) *Writing and Sexual Difference* (Brighton, 1982). On the private self, and writing one's self into the text, see also Susan Gubar, '"The Blank Page" and the Issues of Female Creativity' in that volume. On the relationship of female illness to female writing, see Philip W. Martin, *Mad Women in Romantic Writing* (Brighton, 1987) – the mad woman is always a figure of incompleteness, 'Women, therefore, are naturally ill' (p. 45). And for a feminist reconsideration of romantic fiction, see the contributions by the editor, Terry Lovell, Elizabeth Cowie and Alison Light in Mary Eagleton (ed.), *Feminist Literary Theory. A Reader* (Oxford, 1986).

psychological and cultural – can be applied, in varying degrees, to Cookson's work:

> Time after time, both 'high' and 'popular' works in the artistic tradition . . . tend, whether explicitly or implicitly, to be far more subversive of gender stereotypes, and far closer to feminism in their sympathies . . . than either the (masculinist) critical tradition or the (Freudian) psychoanalytic tradition.[65]

Central to Cookson's work is the freedom to be as she likes. At one level, it is the struggle for subsistence, scrimping and saving, washing and cleaning. At another level, it is a battle of the imagination, a battle that Kate Hannigan finally wins. Everywhere that Kate's mind turns, Catherine's mind has been before. She too had to be strong, had to break away, had to labour, had to deal with her health. Suffering from nightmares from her first confession, Cookson turned Roman Catholicism into her own credo. Never able to pray to God, she prayed to Our Lady instead.[66] She insisted on the liberty to travel through her own thoughts. If Catherine Cookson is a regional novelist, then the region she had in mind when writing is the mental landscape of her female readers.

Kiddar's Luck is a song of innocence and experience. It is definitely more music hall than soirée though, as Will Kiddar looks back on all life's little jokes from the vantage of a bloke who knows the score now, even if he didn't know it then. *Seen it all, kid.*

A 'kiddar' from even earlier than an early age, the life chances that were offered to Will were no different from those that were offered to most. Here is Will's grandmother holding the spell between her front door and her back door. That she did so with the help of cape, trick and magic book will come as no surprise to those humorous enough to take Jack Common seriously:

> At her back door lay the middens of the Oystershell Lane slum but the front looked out on a row of freshly-whitened doorsteps and well-polished door handles. The family attitude had to be eyes front, while she kept the back door slum at bay with a Bible, a black cape, and a trick of grinding her teeth at anyone who crossed her. (*Kiddar's Luck*, p. 1)

Between his conception in 1903 and his first back-step foray into the labour market in 1917, Young Will lost his innocence, or at least he learned to keep it apart from his experience. He absorbs all that working-class Heaton has to offer. With 'the great sea glow' of the sky

---

[65] Hawkins, *Classics and Trash*, p. 90.   [66] Cookson, *Our Kate*, pp. 166, 208.

to his east and the wide-boy wonderful city of Newcastle upon Tyne
to his west, he knows his place only too well. As a toddler, Will lays
his cheek to warm summer pavements. As a youth, he strolls those
pavements in a setting which Common makes move as he moves:

From St Peter's you looked down a hillside of staggered roofs and cobbled
streets to where the river slid like new-boiled pitch under ships and quays
until it took the glitter of the lights on several bridges high and low, or
writhed with reflected flame as a train passed over. That was the basic scene,
but as you descended, its angles and emphasis shifted. Bridges moved their
relation to one another; quays and the shipping flattened out, losing the river
behind them; and the centre of the town began to rise up. (*Kiddar's Luck*, p. 179)

It is a tiered landscape, giving visions, and made for poets. Here,
Will *saunters* because he has learned to value his innocence. Those
more experienced know better, because industrial time-demands have
quickened their walk. At school, the golden rule is punctuality, the core
curriculum is boredom, the mental arithmetic is counting the minutes.
Later, the world of work will chew up what is left of innocence in a
mighty machine. All this inflicts grievous damage on what it is to be
human, damage which Will's mother drowns in drink and petty insub-
ordination against her railwayman husband – for, to be sure, if men are
the prisoners of capitalist time-discipline, they are its warders too. Before
conception there was only 'being', 'me and my genes . . . hanging about
on the other side of Time . . . corporeally uncommitted'.[67] After birth,
the time-training begins by the clock, graduating from child's potty to
railwayman's handbook. Thereafter, human values are streamlined
into measurements, time is handed-over for money and consciousness
of money is consciousness of time unto death. By contrast, childlike
instincts are whole because children have no property and need no time:
'Enormous summers dallied around' him. He was 'pavement free and
pal pleasured'. It begins to rain, a girl takes Will by the hand and the
memory is indelible because, in a moment, 'Everything stood still . . .
and all things were equally aware, not selecting, willing, making. Everything was in being, that only.' Against industrial-time, Will deploys
child-time. Dissolved into moments of permanent 'present', then and
only then does Will realize his self. This authentic self is found at play,
away from the speed-ups, turnovers and the time and motion men.[68]

---

[67] Common, *Kiddar's Luck*, p. 7.
[68] *Ibid.*, p. 25. It is a point given enormous significance in David Harvey's *The Condition of Post-
modernity. An Enquiry into the Origins of Cultural Change* (Oxford, 1990), p. 230.

It was out of such moments, when 'being is not transient', that Common wove his politics. The boy could simply desert the time money system, play truant, go outlaw in the park. Or he could form loyal oppositions, like The Sons of the Battle Axe with their rules and procedures, acting as adults but also weakening like them as private property (a stolen tin of corned beef) leads to internal wrangling and collusion with the adult enemy. Common's best solutions to capitalism were already quick within the culture. A socialist who believed that a new social order 'must be generally lived and common before it can be at all',[69] Common saw children's society as anarcho-socialist in the way that anarcho-socialist societies should be so – that is, conservatively, without knowing why:

the slow moving seasons brought each their distinctive sports and appropriate pestering of neighbours. Every one of these came in with the unannounced unanimity of an unconscious communal instinct. (*Kiddar's Luck*, p. 79)

a whooping, darting throng that multiplied itself in constantly changing combinations and recombinations like a sort of gnat dance of kiddy, or like a working model of the interior of the atom, electrons in knickerbockers weaving and charging among cloth capped neutrons, forming into groups or breaking off again on some principle of attraction and repulsion that no bystander was likely to find understandable at sight. After the first couple of minutes most of it was settling down though you might never notice it. (p. 116)

If there is a new civilization to build, he seems to say, shouldn't it resemble these free feelings of the street, these open structures of the playground?

Can he mean it? Or is he *kidding*?

Kidding can be the heaviest of ironies because it usually involves a conspiracy of those who know over those who do not. It can also be the most subtle because while it has to deny the irony, it simultaneously needs to affirm it. Following a fine line, kidding is the idiom of the dispossessed and Common uses it as a device to undermine authority. In the North East, the repartee of kidding is *the* distinctive oral humour.[70] Challenging straight at the centre without moving an inch

[69] '[S]omewhere in the apprehensions which moved these writers to experiment and expression is announced the coming of a life of complete social sanity, which they themselves could not have since it must be generally lived and common before it can be at all. It is still, in fact, being born.' Reviewing biographies of Thoreau and Jack London, in *New Statesman and Nation*, 23 April 1949.

[70] For a taste of shipyard humour in 1986, at Austin and Pickersgill's, Sunderland, see Tom Pickard's unique *We Make Ships* (London, 1989). Northern male kidding has much in common with 'rapping' and 'giving rag'. Both have been portrayed as vital to working-class male bonding, both demand an understanding which sets limits, both can be crudely sexual, and

from the periphery, it is about how to be serious without being thought ridiculous, how to attack other positions without leaving one's own. If in *The Thin Seam* Christopher Jack could have learned to kid more and worry less, his position between scholarship and pitmanship might have been more tenable.

Everyone in authority came under the egalitarian lash of Jack Common's kidding. Was he serious? Hard to tell. What about religion? Well, it's good to get the kiddars to Sunday School so the parents can enjoy a nice lie down. If the working class, unlike their betters, are good humoured and unenvious, then let us all praise the Church because 'a great lot of them [have been] conceived on the day of grace'.[71] Or, what about professional chaps? Well, they are just like Will, out for what they could get. So the doctor becomes 'the lad with the flowing beard', the vicar is a cake scoffer, and teachers are to be pitied because they claim to know 'what culture is appropriate to the worker' when in fact they do not. As Common drily remarks: 'They hold revolutions about that question, in some places.'[72] Do artists fare any better? Not really. Thoreau's ascetic purity, stylish in some quarters, is almost *de rigeur* in Heaton, as in the case of Mrs McGrewin. Personally advised by her pawnbroker, she had designed her home to a bare and stylish perfection 'which even Thoreau himself had never contemplated'.[73] As for Mr Holman Hunt, as witnessed on granny's wall, he was obviously a sly creeping Jesus with doorstep techniques in salesmanship. And as for socialists! Why man everybody knows that 'A good political conscience is an excellent foundation for adultery'.[74] Common's heaviest blows however are kept for the end and are all the more venomous because they are more innocent. Here is The Kiddar's Manifesto of August 1917: 'Willing Employer Wanted' –

I beg to apply for the post. I am fourteen years of age, strong, healthy, bright, punctual, clean and willing. My parents are working-class, my environment is working-class, the school I have just left is working-class, and with your kind assistance I feel qualified to become working-class myself . . .

As a member from birth of the community of the streets I am aware that individual success for one of our sort, if contrived and not accidental, incurs a personal severance from the rest. That makes a man ridiculous, you know. The self-promoted working-man is as much a living anomaly as the wealthy

both are set against established authorities: 'There is no joking then, unless there is an order which can be overturned or at least challenged by the establishment of new communities and relationships'. Roger D. Abrahams, 'Joking: The Training of the Man of Words in Talking Broad', in Thomas Kochman (ed.), *'Rappin' and Stylin' Out* (Urbana, 1972), p. 237.
[71] Common, *Kiddar's Luck*, p. 97.   [72] *Ibid.*, p. 114.   [73] *Ibid.*, p. 166.   [74] *Ibid.*, p. 135.

priest, the socially approved poet, the knighted scientist or the bearded lady. Hedged-off, therefore, as I am from a conventional or an infamous success by these parallel electric fences, it is probable I shall tread the daily round for a regular pittance all my life . . .

It is this uncertain and qualified endurance I now place at your disposal. No doubt you'd prefer something better. Believe me, what I offer so frankly is what you are increasingly likely to get from any one of that host who might sign themselves as I do. Yours truly, W KIDDAR. (*Kiddar's Luck*, pp. 197–98)

There is great humour and pleasure in all this but the sly hatred of Common's novel appears to have been lost on its reviewers. Thought in the 1930s to have been one of the men most likely to write The Great Proletarian Novel, by 1951 Common wasn't going to do it because no one was. The very idea of such a thing had gone off.[75] The Cold War wrung its retractions and, undetected in its politics, *Kiddar's Luck* was given up to another discourse, that of the 'into unknown England' tradition of good-natured appeals from the wrong side of the tracks. In these terms, reviewers generally liked the book. In it they found what they couldn't find elsewhere, and that was a plebby Geordie naturalism. Carrying a sort of calculated spontaneity, this was life imitating art. Swiped from the scullery table, this 'back street realism' was a rich piece of composite northern industrial truth, 'Real life just banged down on the page, slice by slice . . . a very simple story, hardly a story at all' – 'there is nothing studied here', having 'no more plot than any social report' but nevertheless rendering other accounts 'faked and overstrained'. With its 'good talking style' and naive grammar, it was a 'literature which defeats the literary'.[76] Perhaps this was what proletarian

---

[75] Andy Croft, *Red Letter Days: British Fiction in the 1930s* (London, 1990), pp. 337–40. Common was not the only 'proletarian writer' to suffer from a Cold War climate. The former South Shields miner Harold Heslop had five novels published in English and Russian between 1926 and 1935 and his best, *The Earth Beneath*, in 1946. This was his last published work until the posthumous publication of his autobiography eleven years after his death: Harold Heslop, *Out of the Old Earth*, edited, with an introduction, by Andy Croft and Graeme Rigby (Newcastle, 1994).

[76] Norman Shrapnel in *The Guardian*, 30 November 1951; Wilson Midgeley, on North of England Home Service, BBC, 19 December 1951; *Manchester Evening News*, 27 December 1951; V. S. Pritchett, in *The Bookman*, n.d., *Common Papers 141*; John Redfern in *The Daily Express*, 24 November 1951; Midgeley, *Ibid*. The regional reviews laid a charge of coarseness and crudity: *Evening Chronicle*, 23 November 1951; *Gateshead Post*, 23 November 1951; *Northern Star*, 9 December 1951 – but the *Newcastle Journal*, 28 December 1951, thought that its grim tale would 'rank of consequence in our local social history'. Common had to wait until his literary obituary before receiving his best and most accurate review, by Sid Chaplin, in *The Sunday Times*, 12 May 1968. There is evidence that Cookson's publishers understood his greatness: see letter of Hodson to Common, 9 February 1951. Two of Turnstile's four directors were J. B. Priestley and Raymond Mortimer. Walter Allen understood it too: broadcasting on the Home Service, 30 December 1951, he drew attention to the self-consciousness of Common's 'art' and the authenticity of his voice.

writing was? – 'no nicely brought-up little writer out slumming' but a man, a plumber maybe, 'without a tie, gate crashing a bridge party in Purley'[77] yet winning them over in the end. And not just Purley. Joe Archer wrote to Common from an oil-tanker in the Red Sea:

It is very popular aboard here and is quickly 'snatched up' as soon as some-one finishes it. I guess that's because we're nearly all Geordies . . . Thanks again for a swell book.[78]

But Jack Common could never readily conform to anyone's expecta-tions. In the 1930s he had had trouble finding his own voice because he was stranded amidst so many others. Writing as one of the decent working folk who was also a wry intellectual commentator brought its stylistic difficulties.[79] Trying to be clever *and* proletarian, literary *and* casual, found him stumbling into occasional brilliance but with some odd juxtaposing. Caught between at least two regions, two dialects, two classes, and Marxisms old and new, Common learned how to deftly retain his freedom to criticize one, as a writer, without appear-ing to have deserted the other, as a working man. In his use of written language, for example, we can appreciate the difficulties in trying to maintain such a fine balance. To write in standard English might appear disloyal to his own regional dialect. To write phonetically, on the other hand, might appear worse than disloyal – it might appear that he had gone over to the other side lock, stock and vowel: 'As a dialect speaker myself it would be an odd snobbery to apply the courtier-clown convention and put my characters into semi-phonetics'.[80] So Common had to control the distance, as it were, between what he was and what he had been, between what he said and how he said it. He found his clearest voice in *Kiddar's Luck*.

Truth of the documentary sort *Kiddar* was praised for required un-derstatement and a straight face. So did kidding. And here, Common realized, were possibilities for a caustic political style which could be both playful and serious together. Some of this style can be spotted

---

[77] 'He introduces you to the purpose of a poss tub. It turns out to be for rinsing clothes'. Redfern, *Express*.

[78] Joe Archer, S. S. Red Bank, to Jack Common, 9 January 1953, *Common Papers 58*.

[79] Writing and reviewing for *The Eleventh Hour, New Statesman and Nation, New Britain, The Aryan Path* and *Tribune* ('Commoner'), Common addressed such diverse issues as Anti-Semitism, Adver-tising, India, Planning, Sport, Doctors, Rurality, Spengler and Adler, Headgear, Marxism, Fascism and Organic Communities. He tended to write as a Marxist of the cultural substruc-ture, a position which brought him into conflict with his editors – as in May and June 1935 with the editors of *Eleventh Hour: Common Papers 157*.

[80] But do not suppose 'that the cast is high-class. Nobody in this novel is that': Jack Common, 'Reading Directions', *The Ampersand* (London, 1954), pp. v, vi.

early, as in his 1934 *Cure for Bourgeoiserie*[81] where it is hard to tell the difference between bourgeois sufferers and marxist healers, a state of affairs best left to speak for itself and fighting talk from a man whose brow was used to model Karl Marx's bust in Highgate Cemetery. In a 1952 letter to his publishers promising eight more books – 'and the sooner they are done the better' – Common kids them by making it hard to tell ambition from intention, a characteristic publishers' gambit.[82] In *Kiddar's Luck*, the man who called himself a Revolutionary Material-ist with One Leg Free had his wayward way. He does not allow the North East to slump into its own clammy world on the inside any more than he allows Socialism to document all the answers from the outside. True to his place and to his self, the novel stays regional by thrusting from the edge to the centre and it stays proletarian by refusing to move one inch from where it is. He declares the knowing irony of his people. Unlike *Kate Hannigan*, *Kiddar's Luck* is not open to everyone, but it is a regional novel more generous in its fit than *The Thin Seam*. Common's region was not so much a place as an idiom, not so much a script as a performance, not so much a look as an eyeful. Jack Common succeeded in showing the North East not its 'character', but its own broad gesture – '*Hallo, Kiddars! How's yor luck?*'

In the nation, all places are equal but some places are more equal than others. The less equal places with the less equal experiences are denoted, in England at least, as 'regions'. Certainly, when a company wishes to publicize itself as having branches in London-Paris-New York, it is not alluding to its regionality. It is declaring instead that the experience (and resource, and reputation) of being in these places is richer and more universal than the experience of being in other places. In England, to be called a region from some metaphorical 'centre' is an act of

---

[81] 'How? If you have any reason to suspect yourself of being bourgeois in some way, if your bowels are sluggish, if you have a tendency to sell things or save money, if you find yourself attached to your possessions or interested in credit schemes, if you think you would like to lead the workers, then you cannot do better than take a good stiff dose of antibourgeois cathartic. This is the invention of Karl Marx, a man himself considerably afflicted . . .' (*New Britain*, 11 April 1934). In 1951 it appears there were some old scores to settle. *Kiddar's Luck's* worst review, damning with a little faint praise, came from *The Daily Worker*, 13 December 1951. The review got everything wrong: it claimed that the book was not a proletarian novel while, in fact, it was the best of that unlikely breed; it claimed that the book was not political while, in fact, it was political from the first word to the last, though not perhaps in the *Worker*'s sense; it claimed that the book was about accepting your lot while, in fact, it was about surviving your lot and, finally, it claimed that *Kiddar's Luck* was cynical while in fact it gleamed with hope because, contrary to all expectation, Will was still the undefeated champ.

[82] Jack Common to Michael Hodson, 9 December 1952, *Common Papers 29*.

patronage: the history of a mining village was local; the history of a coalfield was regional; but the history of Hobart House, headquarters of British Coal, was 'national'. Understood in this way, regions are category errors used to fix a place's relationship to power rather than geography. There are no regions, only ways of looking at people in their place.

From the late nineteenth century the essential meaning of 'Englishness' moved south and found its home somewhere in the English countryside.[83] Other English places had to adjust, particularly those which were seen to be opposite in meaning, such as 'the industrial North'. One adjustment involved making a regional identity and shaping it as complementary to, or in opposition to, or in some relationship with, an essential national identity. Whichever way, acts of enclosure occurred which sought to reveal differences and seek out the kinds of distinctive experience not usually represented in a southern-centred Englishness.[84] Thus, Phyllis Bentley's *The English Regional Novel* (1941) celebrated the genre for its down-to-earth realism, its native landscape and its concrete setting, for its folksy-democratic characters, and their pithiness. Not surprisingly for 1941, Bentley saw these solid characteristics as adornments to the national glory of reading, writing and being English. As David Storey's northern (ex-) working-class protagonist, Pasmore, says to his southern middle-class colleague, Coles, 'For you morality is a function of the sensibility, whereas for me, brought up in a world of working-class aphorisms, it is a thing of fetishes and customs'.[85] Bentley lived in times which sought out the regions, and their most prominent class, in order to prosecute a people's war. Later, the regional-northern genre found a new role, of which Storey was a part, but the southern heartlands of English sensibility continued to award the honours and titles as they saw fit. Yorkshire and Lancashire were just about northern enough to have honorary English status. The North East was not. Catherine Cookson may be one of the most read authors in the English language, but she is not in the *Oxford Companion to English Literature*. Nor, for that matter, is Sid Chaplin or Jack Common.[86]

[83] Alun Howkins, 'The Discovery of Rural England', in Robert Colls and Philip Dodd (eds.), *Englishness. Politics and Culture, 1880–1920* (London, 1986).

[84] Robert Colls, 'Born-Again Geordies', in Robert Colls and Bill Lancaster (eds.), *Geordies. Roots of Regionalism* (Edinburgh, 1992).

[85] Phyllis Bentley, *The English Regional Novel* (London, 1941), pp. 43–46; David Storey, *Pasmore* (Harmondsworth, 1976), p. 16.

[86] Though she is mentioned in the *Oxford Guide to British Women Writers*, Joanne Shattock (ed.) (Oxford, 1993).

So this North East 'region' is someone else's category error which, nevertheless, has lived to find real meaning. In our consideration of Kate, and Jack and Sid, their contribution to that meaning was made in a three-way relationship which began in the year of publication, and goes on. First, historically; in the relationship of the region in 1950–51 to the identities it had had, and was hoping to have. Second, personally; in the relationship of the region at this time to the authors' feelings about themselves, and others. And third, nationally; in the relationship of the region to the power-brokers of politics and culture in the south. After 1950–51, the reception and a large part of the reputation of the three novels hung on the interaction of these three relationships. In 1955 F. R. Leavis praised D. H. Lawrence as 'the greatest writer of our own phase of civilization', as the one responsible for rendering in *The Rainbow*, 'the transmission of the spiritual heritage in an actual society'.[87] In Leavis's Lawrence there is nothing much of the regional epitaph, but in his notion of a biography of the spirit lies another way of understanding what writers do within the relationships which condition their writing. Sid Chaplin, Catherine Cookson and Jack Common each left something 'of the spiritual heritage' of 'an actual society'. They transmitted meanings of what it was to be drawn to the North East in 1950–1 and, more than that, they contributed massively to how the North East was represented thereafter. After the humiliations of the 1930s, Chaplin, Cookson and Common each established in their own way the North East region as a people's democracy; alive and kicking and no one's province but its own.

How will their transmissions endure? Will their writings continue to be a part of our own valued history? Will they join new regional narratives, within a devolved United Kingdom or perhaps within a European federal union? We can hazard some guesses, although it has to be admitted that of late some big players have joined the identity game. The ubiquity and expertise of image-making, for instance, is now an important part of mass communications. Selling places has become business. Indeed, in terms of regional development and regeneration, it is the first business. But publishing is itself a part of the identity game and Cookson for one has enjoyed unparallelled success in playing it. Should a market remain, it is unlikely that these writers will be lost. Can a market remain?

---

[87] F. R. Leavis, *D. H. Lawrence. Novelist* (London, 1955), pp. 9, 145.

Of the three, Chaplin's was the novel most related to the post-war world. The North East was moving into a new and younger phase and Christopher Jack was part of that phase. What could be brought from the old to the new? Could it endure, and on what terms? Well, in terms of class struggle and a labour movement which exposed that struggle – the answer has been that it could not endure. Sid lived to see its prospects fade and die. In 1994 Mark Hudson's *Coming Back Brockens*[88] marked the death and won prizes for it. In Sid's time mining villages were known for their turbulence and life; now they were known for desolation. Hudson waits on windy street corners waiting for men who used to be miners who will show him where the pit used to be. Pit closures in County Durham began to gather pace from the late 1950s. As the pits closed and the miners shrank in number, then Christopher Jack's *realisation* of Durham was bound to shrink with them. As this happened, Chaplin substituted regional issues in place of class issues. He deployed the cultural strength of his region to compensate for the shrinking presence of its miners. If the North East can be seen as a great property, once upon a time Chaplin and his men built its foundations. But the site was ready for re-developing. The demolishers were at hand, with planning permission. Chaplin's response was an impulsively egalitarian People's Northumbria. Now that the last pit has been closed, Chaplin's change of stance from class to region may lend his work longer life. In a new century's Europe-of-the-Regions, it is to be hoped that his writing will endure, maybe to feed the identity which all little peoples will need and the sympathetic coherence which all Europe must find. It is not unlikely that the heritage and culture people will find Kimberley Gardens and leave a blue plate there.

Cookson's was the novel most related to the pre-war world. Her North East is forever 1929. Stuck fast in her self-absorption, and enjoying a dazzling commercial success which continues, Cookson traversed a mental landscape of women. There is still considerable power in her evocation, even if that imagined landscape of hers has narrowed and dried into ever more bizarre and surreal encounters. So long as the region is represented as a man's world where women have to find the emotional strength to fight for truth and valour and their own selfhood,

---

[88] Mark Hudson, *Coming Back Brockens. A Year in a Mining Village* (London, 1994). Hudson's book is not unlike *The Thin Seam* in other respects: both are autobiographical, both are realist, and both concern questions of family, region, loyalty and going back. In *The Thin Seam*, Christopher Jack decides to stay and fight; in *Brockens*, as its title implies, there is nothing to stay and fight for.

it appears the formula will continue to sell.[89] However, as class and gender relations shift, it is less possible to see a long future for this writing. Again, if the North East can be seen as a great property, Cookson made her way as the little skivvy maid who scrubbed the fender with dreams so big that not even the big house was big enough. Now upstairs-downstairs attitudes have changed and the strategies of the masters, and especially the maids, is utterly different. For a generation of girls who could revel in the provocative sexuality of a Madonna with rosary beads, and where the shame of 'illegitimacy' has all but disappeared, it is difficult indeed to see Cookson's obsessions as continuing to attract, except as an emotional period piece. Her writing seems destined to become a blue plate memory of grandmothers.

Kiddar's Luck was for the epoch. Jack Common's North was located across the divide of capital and labour and, although these clusters of potential have changed their names, the divide has not diminished. The most basic questions surrounding the unfair allocation of life chances, the tyranny of money and the global compression of time and space show no sign of resolution. Common was too knowing to trust theoreticians, too ironic to back the state and too wilful to believe what he was told. Chaplin's was the insider's view of the inside. So too was Cookson's. In both these writers there was always a measure of security stemming from ignorance of worlds they could not know or had only passed through. By contrast Common's was a view both from the inside and the outside and there he found freedom, as he put it, as from the end of a gang plank. Not many people have heard of Jack Common. If the North East can be seen as a great property, Common was its disinherited son. A ragged trousered ironist, he might end up as the one who most knew the score, but was least willing to tell. Newcastle's only literary plaque hangs on his wall.

Catherine Cookson died on 11 June 1998, just before this book was published. Tom Cookson died shortly thereafter.

---

[89] It is not long since even liberal-feminist intellectual newspapers continued to peddle an all-male North East cast. See pieces by Dougan, Mapplebeck, Whittaker and Kelly, in a regional feature, 'Waiting for a new boat to come in', *The Guardian*, 1 September 1980. Among the names ... Stephenson G, Stephenson R, Palmer, Armstrong, Parsons, Swan, Hawthorn, Ridley, Wilson, Common, Bunting, Bede, Rae, Jobling, Reed, Learmouth, Grainger, Dobson, Clayton, Erskine, Collingwood, Hawks' men, Cowen, Hadrian. All these men, not counting footballers!

I would like to thank Mrs Rene Chaplin, Mrs Rosie Colls, Mrs Catherine Cookson, Mr Tom Cookson, Mr Nick Everett and Mrs Jean Shaw for their help in the making of this chapter. It is dedicated to my mother, Margaret Archer, who was born during the lock-out of 1926 in a Harton Colliery pit row.

CHAPTER 8

Emyr Humphreys: regional novelist?

M. Wynn Thomas

'Where were you when you were fifteen?'
The question puzzled me. Why should he ask and damn it why
should he ask. Fifteen, where was I? . . .
'In a school', I said, 'In North-East Wales.'
Lars laughed but I didn't mean it as a joke.
'That's funny the way you divide up Wales. Does anybody else do
it but you?'[1]

Emyr Humphreys' lifelong work as a novelist has largely consisted of a
resolute expansion of this unintentional geopolitical 'joke', at the ex-
pense of those of his readers who, like Lars, grow increasingly incredu-
lous. How, they object, can an area of Britain that is itself routinely
described and treated as a 'region' possibly claim to have regions of its
own? Isn't the term 'region' (generously upgraded on sensitive occasions to 'principality') good enough for it? Doesn't Wales realise that to
be recognised as a region is in itself a considerable achievement, a
significant concession granted by a notoriously centralist British state?
The splitting of the political atom, the supposedly irreducible unit of
the British nation-state, has caused trouble enough in itself. It really is
preposterous to hear that Wales, the new irreducible unit, the veritable
quark of the British political system, now regards itself as internally
divided, and diverse.

There are some who will no doubt feel that such remarks are
perfectly reasonable, and prominent among them will presumably be
those who indignantly regard the word 'region' as being an innocent geographical expression, totally above political suspicion. ' "Provincial" is
a term which is often used slightingly', wrote R. P. Draper recently,
'but "regional" seems to attract no such derogatory usage. This is

[1] Emyr Humphreys, *The Gift* (London, 1963), p. 19.

perhaps because it carries with it none of the hierarchically subordinate implications of "provincial". "Regional" suggests a division of a larger unit, but without the larger being necessarily dominant.[2] However much truth, as distinct from wishful thinking, there may be in these words – and clearly there is some – they will not help us to understand Emyr Humphreys' refusal to treat or regard Wales as a cultural region of Britain; though they will greatly help us understand his attachment to the idea of Wales as a region of Europe. To the regionalism of Britain, as Humphreys sees it, the best guide is his late friend and fellow Welshman Raymond Williams:

a further effect of the dominant modern political meaning of 'nation' is the specification of subordinate units of a 'nation' as 'regions'. This term carries a linguistic irony, in that its root meaning relates to an 'area of rule,' (from Latin *regere* = to rule).[3]

The best of Emyr Humphreys's fiction relates to the 'politics' of regionalism, as defined here by Williams, in three different but inter-connected ways. It consciously departs from the various methods devised for treating Wales in literature as a constituent region of the Anglo-British nation; it explores the major regions of Wales with a view to preparing the ground and establishing the conditions for constructing a separate modern Welsh nation; and it (much more tentatively) reflects on Wales's position in Europe.

Emyr Humphreys's native region is the north-eastern corner of Wales, the existence of which Lars, in *The Gift*, found so funny. The novelist was born in Prestatyn in 1918 and raised in nearby Trelawnyd (then called Newmarket), and his best-known novel *A Toy Epic*, which won the Hawthornden Prize in 1958, is a fictional account of boyhood and adolescence in an area that had, a few years earlier, been home to the young Emlyn Williams. This coincidence is an interesting one from the point of view of the 'regional' debate, because the work of these two writers clearly shows how the same locale can be 'regionalised' by literature in strikingly different ways.[4]

Williams established his great popular reputation as an actor-

[2] R. P. Draper (ed.), *The Literature of Region and Nation* (London, 1989), p. 4.
[3] Raymond Williams, 'Review and Further Questions', in *Language in Use* (Milton Keynes, 1981), p. 10.
[4] For a fuller treatment of this subject see M. Wynn Thomas, 'Flintshire and the Regional Forecast', *The New Welsh Review*, vol. 3, no. 1 (Summer, 1990), pp. 10–5.

playwright with the staging in London, in 1937, of *The Corn is Green*, a semi-autobiographical play that shows the transformation of Morgan Evans, a young, semi-literate, Welsh-speaking miner, from awkward pit-pony into awe-struck Oxford scholar. The play was, in fact, rooted in Williams's own experience of growing up in a relatively poor, Welsh-speaking family and gradually finding, thanks to the encouragement of an inspirational teacher, that he could use his exceptional scholastic talent to fulfil his youthful fantasies of escape to a distant world of glamour and romance. Late in life, he returned to this early transformative experience in the first volume of his autobiography, *George*, and dealt with it in a way that did justice to its density and complexity, bringing out the losses as well as the gains involved in the momentous changes he underwent as a youngster.[5] The subtle psycho-social specificity of *George* contrasts with the marketable simplicities in which the play trades. In order to discover the market whose forces are at work here one need look no further than the opening stage-directions of *The Corn is Green*: the play is set, we are told, 'In the living-room of a house in Glansarno, a small village in a remote Welsh countryside'.[6] This, then, is Lars country; a made-to-measure image of Wales designed to fit exactly into the limited space available for it in the Great British mentality. 'Somewhere in Wales' is, by definition, like everywhere else in Wales. This is quark-talk, and the play ingeniously exploits its grammar and vocabulary. Its all-purpose Welshness predictably includes a troupe of singing, coal-black miners, a virtually monoglot and moronic Welsh ancient who speaks a comically sibilant English, and a mildly hypocritical, hymn-singing, sexually frustrated Nonconformist. Whilst the play goes out of its way to put in the occasional good, if patronising, word for the Welsh language, its main thrust is the need for talent and intelligence to escape from Wales as soon as possible. At the climactic moment, Morgan Evans' mentor and teacher, Miss Moffat, foresees a glorious future for her protegé as 'a great statesman of our country'. Needless to say, 'our country' here means a Britain that is virtually synonymous with English values. The picture of (north-east) Wales offered in *The Corn is Green* is painted in the red, white and blue colours of what Ned Thomas has called 'Contributionism':[7] this is the

---

[5] Emlyn Williams, *George: An Early Autobiography* (London, 1961).
[6] References are to Emlyn Williams, *The Corn is Green* (London, 1981).
[7] Ned Thomas, 'Images of Ourselves', in John Osmond (ed.) *The National Question Again* (Llandysul, 1985), pp. 306–19.

belief (most notoriously well expressed by Arnold and Eliot) that Wales will best fulfil itself by contributing to the great stream of English life (and literature).

'I was brought up in a broad valley in one of the four corners of Wales.' These, the opening words of *A Toy Epic*, are spoken by a boy called Michael, but they also speak for Emyr Humphreys.[8] Throughout his long career he has stood four-square on the ground of Welsh sociocultural separateness, using his novels to show how Wales, like any other society, paradoxically holds together as a distinctive system of differences, which is signified geographically here by the 'placing' mention of 'the four corners of Wales'. Elsewhere, as we shall see, he uses the regional diversity of Wales to map out the divisions produced by recent history in Welsh society, but in *A Toy Epic* he gives these divisions a local habitation and a name – grounding them in a single region centered on Rhyl, a town which is textualised as 'Llanelw'.

This is, of course, Emyr Humphreys' own native region, and his first published novel, *The Little Kingdom* (1946), begins with a view from a vantage-point near Rhyl, also telling us a great deal about Humphreys' mature view of his home territory. A farmer, Richard Bloyd, gazes 'across the water', where he sees 'the Wirral emerge from the early morning mist; [and] become once more a solid and substantial rich-green sea-girt land, speckled with red-roofed houses'.[9] The scene suggests an England that is a sight for sore Welsh eyes; a realm of magic, enticingly prosperous and magnetically, majestically strong. Ever since Tudor times (as Humphreys would put it), this England has been a powerful kingdom of the Welsh mind, a myth controlling consciousness.[10] Emyr Humphreys grew up in a region where this myth was palpable – where the physical proximity of England meant that the power and attraction of Englishness was a fact of life as solid and substantial as the Wirral is to Bloyd. The novelist can usefully be thought of as a product of the border-county of Flintshire, and like other writers raised in border-country he has an ingrained sensitivity to cultural contrasts. In Raymond Williams' case this kind of background perhaps helped make him a dispassionate inquisitor of social structures, as well as a lifelong searcher after community. In the young Emyr Humphreys' case it meant that his Welshness was never simply and unproblematically given; rather, it was a potential for the identity that he first painfully

[8] All references are to Emyr Humphreys, *A Toy Epic*, M. Wynn Thomas (ed.), (Bridgend, 1989).
[9] Emyr Humphreys, *The Little Kingdom* (London, 1946), p. 5.
[10] See Emyr Humphreys, *The Taliesin Tradition* (Bridgend, 1990), *passim*.

discovered and then deliberately chose to realise. This awareness of Welshness as a cultural condition constantly needing to be won, or redeemed, from Englishness has been at the heart of virtually everything that Humphreys has ever written. In this respect his native region could be said to have made him a novelist ideally equipped to portray a Wales that has come to resemble one large border-country throughout this century. The Welsh poet Bryan Martin Davies wrote 'Ynom mae y clawdd' ('The border is *within* us') recently after settling near to Offa's Dyke, close to Emyr Humphreys's childhood haunts.[11]

The appearance of the Wirral, in the opening lines of Humphreys' very first novel, is particularly appropriate since it was in Wallasey that Saunders Lewis was born in 1893 and it was through the writings and the political activities of this charismatic if controversial figure that the young Humphreys discovered the secret key to the social geography of his region. In addition to being a Welsh-language poet and dramatist of European stature, Lewis was first a founder-member and then long-time President of Plaid Cymru, the Welsh Nationalist party established in 1925.[12] In 1936 he galvanized Wales, and polarised Welsh opinion, when together with two highly regarded and respectable friends he set fire to the buildings of a bombing-school under construction in the Llŷn peninsula. It was intended as a symbolic gesture of protest against an act of cultural vandalism perpetrated by an English government apparently indifferent to outraged public opinion throughout Wales. Penyberth, the farmhouse demolished to make room for the 'school', was a medieval building that occupied a significant place in the history of Welsh literary culture. The arson attack was only the first act in a powerful political drama that kindled the imagination of Emyr Humphreys, who was then in the sixth form of Rhyl County School. When the arsonists were brought to trial in Caernarfon, Saunders Lewis made a speech from the dock which remains a classic statement of a culture's right to safeguard its existence. After the jury had failed to agree on its verdict, the case was moved to London where the three were, unsurprisingly, found guilty and sentenced to prison terms. The whole affair changed Emyr Humphreys's bearings decisively. He began

[11] Bryan Martin Davies, 'Ynom mae y clawdd', *Deuoliaethau* (Llandysul, 1976), p. 47.
[12] For a brief survey of Saunders Lewis' life and work, see Meic Stephens (ed.), *The Oxford Companion to the Literature of Wales* (Oxford, 1986). Translations from his work, along with introductory essays, are collected in Alun R. Jones and Gwyn Thomas (eds.), *Presenting Saunders Lewis* (Cardiff, 1973). See also *Saunders Lewis*, the monograph by Bruce Griffiths in the Writers of Wales Series. Twelve of Lewis' plays have been published in a translation by Joseph Clancy (Llandybie, 1985).

thereafter to see his part of Flintshire in relation to Penyberth and to understand that he had been raised not next to the Wirral but in 'one of the four corners of Wales'.

Emyr Humphreys became a regional writer, therefore, when, after leaving home, in imagination, for Penyberth he then returned to Newmarket and nearby Rhyl. From then on his native place was to be, for him, intimately and inseparably connected to his new mental geography, because Saunders Lewis had finally enabled him to understand the silences, inconsistencies and incongruities that he had looked on uncomprehendingly in his early social background. His parents had occasionally spoken Welsh to each other, but never to him; he had been taken to church, although most of his mother's family, who lived nearby, were staunch chapel people; the village in which he'd grown up bore the English name 'Newmarket', and yet the majority of its inhabitants were Welsh-speaking: in these odd features of his upbringing he could now see the subtle and complex signs of English social hegemony and the gradual subordination of indigenous Welsh culture. One could perhaps then say that Emyr Humphreys was able to reconstruct his native place as textual region only after he had been taught how to read his locality like a book by Saunders Lewis.

As Geoffrey Hartman has reminded us, in the work of any artist topography is also inevitably tropography,[13] and so the very lie of the land in A Toy Epic is the physical geography of the Rhyl area, not altered yet transfigured so that it outwardly signifies the inner social and cultural structures of the locality, as they are perceived by Emyr Humphreys in the light of Penyberth. Iorwerth, the timid Welsh-speaker and earnest chapel-goer, is brought up on a secluded inland farm where life sometimes seems so innocently stable and idyllic that his father and mother sit on each side of the fire 'like two figures on a Christmas card' on a winter evening (p. 32). The brash seaside resort of Llanelw is where Albie lives. Having migrated there from the neighbouring countryside, his parents have graduated to the urban working-class and their native language of Welsh is a source of embarrassment to them, a social stigma with which they do not wish to disadvantage their son. Albie is disadvantaged, however, by the loving expectations his parents have of him: he grows up precociously sensible, studious and responsible, contrasting with the engagingly casual third boy, Michael,

---

[13] See 'Words, Inscriptions and Romantic Nature Poetry', in F. W. Hilles and H. Bloom (eds.), From Sensibility to Romanticism (Oxford, 1965), pp. 389–413.

a vicar's son. His home is almost literally a half-way house between
farm and town, a staging post between traditional Welsh Nonconformist
culture and the modern Wales that Llanelw, visible from the hill that
dominates the village, represents in many ways. Eager to go wherever
this vista leads, the growing Michael, with the active encouragement of
his mother and the passive consent of his father, discards the remnants
of the Welsh-language culture that encumber his family.

Here, then, in the barest of outlines, is Emyr Humphreys's region,
but of course what makes it a credible place is the elaborately intricate
narrative cross-hatching that adds depth to the social portrait. Iorwerth
is not only sustained but psychologically maimed by his conservative
background, which both retards his emotional development and ill
equips him to deal with the many modern solvents that attack the firm
set of traditional values he has inherited. The impressive nineteenth-
century religious culture that produced him is exhausted. As for Albie,
he has been brought up in a cul-de-sac in more senses than one. As
he grows older, he finds himself to be hemmed in and turned back
on himself by aspects of his upbringing. His schooling has cut him off
from the working-class with which he increasingly wants to identify,
yet his home environment makes him uncomfortable in the bourgeois
world that his doting parents would have him enter, and their Welsh-
language society has been deliberately closed to him. Michael's is the
unexpected success story of the novel, since in late adolescence he
discovers a way forward into adulthood when he rediscovers Welsh
Wales – experienced not on Iorwerth's dishearteningly passive terms,
but as the inspiration for a militant cultural crusade.

A Toy Epic is constructed as a series of interior monologues, with
each of the three boys 'speaking' in turn. It takes this form partly
because the text was first broadcast as a serialised radio play in Welsh,
under the title *Y Tri Llais* – the three voices. It was first heard in early
1958, and must have invited comparison at the time with another very
recent 'play for voices', *Under Milk Wood*, broadcast in 1953. Dylan
Thomas's piece is, of course, much the more dazzling of the two, and
it is justifiably therefore the more famous by far, but in other important respects it is an inferior work. Its Welshness is brilliantly bogus, its
characters are as cosily cute as the creatures in a Walt Disney cartoon,
and the play is full of verbal kitsch. *Under Milk Wood* seems ripe for the
kind of comment that Seamus Heaney passed on Dylan Thomas in an
outstanding recent essay on regional literature. Thomas, he said, now
seems to have been marginalised: 'a case of somebody who accepted

the regional weather forecast [authoritatively broadcast from distant London] even as he seemed to be totally involved with his own weather . . . *Under Milk Wood* [is] symptomatic of a not irreprehensible collusion with the stereotype of the voluble Taffy.'[14]

Heaney further remarks of Thomas that 'his was a clear case of a provincial imagination as defined by Patrick Kavanagh: always looking over its shoulder to see if the metropolis was in favour of its subjects and procedures'. In his best prose work, *Portrait of the Artist as a Young Dog*, Thomas could, however, be said to have turned this very aspect of his imagination to advantage by making the comic-pathetic plight of a provincial youth the subtext of several of the atmospheric period pieces that comprise this generally under-rated collection of stories. Dylan Thomas was deliberately brought up by his father to know little about Wales, and as a result he himself cared even less. For him the country north and west of Swansea was only Cwmdonkin Park writ large: it existed simply as an adventure playground for the imagination that his Welsh-speaking father had so lovingly anglicised, and as the stuff of which hyperbole was made. This is not the place to consider the genuine success that he undoubtedly made of his ignorance, but rather to ponder the implications for Emyr Humphreys of Roland Mathias's observation that Dylan Thomas was not 'a product of a Welsh community, [but] had much more in common with boys of the sixties and seventies in not being a product of a community at all.'[15]

This want of a sense of belonging to a Wales-wide community is what most of Emyr Humphreys' novels are intended to supply. This in turn helps to explain why – in spite of the modernist techniques the novelist sometimes uses and the effects of indeterminacy that he achieves – the novels are still somehow nineteenth-century in their scope and ambition. They are so, I think, not only by virtue of their social realism but because of the uses to which that is put, and so it is no coincidence that Raymond Williams's study of *The English Novel from Dickens to Lawrence* can provide us with useful insights. 'The problem of the knowable community,' says Williams, 'with its deep implications for the novelist, is then clearly a part of the social history of early nineteenth-century England and of the imaginative penetration and recoil which was the creative response . . . Indeed it is to just this problem of knowing a

[14] Seamus Heaney, 'The Regional Forecast', in Draper, *Literature of Region and Nation*, pp. 10–23.
[15] Roland Mathias, 'Lord Cutglass, Twenty Years After', in *A Ride Through the Wood* (Bridgend, 1985), pp. 57–78. See also James A. Davies, 'A Picnic in the Orchard: Dylan Thomas' Wales', in Tony Curtis (ed.), *Wales: The Imagined Nation* (Bridgend, 1986), pp. 42–65.

community – of finding a position, a position convincingly experienced, from which community can begin to be known – that one of the major phases in the development of the novel must be related.'[16] Williams relates the form that the English novel took during the last century to the extensive social changes to which the fiction was responding. As Emyr Humphreys sees it, Wales has been shaken with peculiar violence by history for a century, with the result that most of the social connectives that tied the country together have been seriously weakened or fractured.

The core bourgeois society which late nineteenth-century Welsh Nonconformity had created and served was discredited after the First World War (which it publicly supported), not least because its religious, cultural and political beliefs were anathema to the new, cosmopolitan and increasingly radical inhabitants of the industrial valleys of the south, where the population of the country was overwhelmingly concentrated by 1900. There the reigning ideology soon came to be socialism in a variety of forms, and the realities of economic life as experienced by a proletariat partly comprised of immigrants meant that in the south there was little sense of connection, let alone of solidarity, with the Welsh-language culture that remained in the largely rural north and west. The contraction of Welsh-language culture coincided with an extraordinary renaissance of its literature, largely under the auspices of the first generation of university-educated scholars, artists and intellectuals, and as the plight of the culture became plainer this intelligentsia began to be politicised.[17] This is the background that produced Saunders Lewis, and it is also the milieu that Emyr Humphreys entered a generation later, after being 'converted' by Lewis and having commenced learning Welsh. The best of his novels deal directly or indirectly with the version of modern Welsh history summarised above, and they do so in an attempt to create what might be called a common front of the imagination – a front broad enough to include deep differences of social experience and yet strong enough in imagination to see how these differences relate to each other as elements in the historical composition of a single, knowable Welsh community.

It is not surprising, then, that Humphreys' best novel is the one in which he discovered the best formal means of constructing a cat's cradle of relationships – between different periods of twentieth-century

---

[16] Raymond Williams, *The English Novel from Dickens to Lawrence* (London, 1970), pp. 15–6.

[17] Emyr Humphreys' own account of this important chapter in modern Welsh culture can be found in *The Triple Net* (London, 1988).

Welsh history, between the several regions of the country, between its
two languages and its social classes. *Outside the House of Baal* (1965) plays
one day in the life of two ageing people off against their entire past,
stretching back to the turn of the century.[18] Kate, an irascible but
indomitable widow, has devoted her declining years to keeping house
for her brother-in-law, J. T. Miles, a mild-mannered Calvinistic Methodist minister for whom she feels a blend of exasperated affection and
contempt. They live together on a nondescript estate, built on land that
used to belong to the farm on which Kate was raised. In everything
but name, the North Wales seaside town where they live is Llanelw,
from *A Toy Epic*, and behind the candyfloss entertainments of the garish
sea-front lie genteel suburbs full of geriatrics. And just as Iorwerth's
farm contrasted with Llanelw's pleasureland, so 'Argoed', Kate's old
home, is the spectre at the feast of modern consumerism. But life on
that farm, half a century earlier, is shown to have been far from idyllic.
Kate's father used to dominate the family like an Old Testament patri-
arch, severe, dignified, petulant and ceaselessly demanding. His were
the qualities of Nonconformity at its worst.

What makes this novel almost unique, among the work of modern
Welsh writers in English, however, is its refusal to write Nonconformity
off, its insistence on taking it at its full, if finally indeterminate, moral
weight. Through the character of J. T., Emyr Humphreys has succeeded
in making the character of Welsh Nonconformity itself problematic.
From the very beginning – when the aged minister's venerable head
rolls on the pillow as he struggles to break wind – J. T.'s nobility is
constantly compromised without ever being completely subverted. He
is in fact a moral enigma, innocently selfless on one reading of his
history, inherently selfish on another; a kind of holy fool, puzzling
as Dostoevsky's Prince Mishkin or Greene's Monsignor Quixote. His
actions only compound the mystery, as is apparent when his morally
admirable yet self-regarding attempt to reach a fatally wounded soldier,
whilst serving as a stretcher-bearer in the First World War, results in
the predictable death of his protesting young partner. Years later this
pattern is repeated, when he unconsciously neglects his wife and children
as he puts his all into helping the unemployed. To try and resolve this
enigma would be a mistake, because the whole novel is constructed
to maximise the difficulties of passing final judgement on J. T. and
the tradition that he represents. Indeed it is deliberately designed to

---

[18] First published by Eyre and Spottiswoode in 1965 this novel was recently reissued as an
Everyman Paperback (London: Dent, 1988). References are to the original edition.

frustrate the impulse to judge, so that the reader is driven instead to examine the grounds of judgement: the values brought to the novel by the reader and the social influences behind them.

As a young minister, J. T. is drawn to serve in the mining valleys of South Wales, and quickly finds that the people there are as ignorant of his native region as he is of theirs:

– Where you from then?
The young collier tapped his teeth with the match.
– I'm from North Wales, J. T. said.
– Down 'ere on a visit?
J. T. cleared his throat and clasped his hands together tightly. He pressed his
    back into the upholstery behind him.
– Preaching, J. T. said.
The collier nodded sympathetically.
– Lot of preachers in North Wales, aren't there?
He smiled encouragingly. J. T. smiled back.
– Makes you think sometimes who does the work. (p. 127)

Emyr Humphreys uses the boundless good-will of the pacifist J. T. as he organizes seaside camps for the unemployed, to bring out the very different temper of the valleys people, seasoned political fighters all, convinced of the need to destroy an exploitative economic system. His Welshness seems to them to be of a piece with the rest of his anachronistic philosophy. Humphreys allows each of these two regional cultures to reflect on the other, setting up the kind of dialectic first patented by Scott in *Waverley* and since used by scores of writers from Pushkin to Ishiguro. There is no authorial comment, let alone judgement, on the respective merits and deficiencies of Welsh-language chapel society and the industrial community, yet a sense emerges of a lost historical opportunity, of a failure to connect the two to their mutual benefit. This impression arises primarily from the disheartening picture given in the novel of forgetful Welsh society since the Second World War, where the virtues (however imperfect) of *both* pre-war communities have been seemingly obliterated, engulfed by a tide of consumerism and hedonistic individualism.

To some South Walians, however, Emyr Humphreys himself seems as foreign a cultural figure as J. T. was to the collier, and like J. T. he is sometimes regarded as a preacher of a lost cause who knows nothing of the real work which fashioned life in the mining valleys. In his recent lively survey of the Anglo-Welsh novel, Dai Smith relegated Emyr Humphreys to a footnote, acknowledging his 'outstanding' quality, but describing his work as part of 'a sectional intelligentsia's attempt to understand their role in twentieth-century Wales.'[19] Since Dai Smith's account is as lively as it has been influential, and as it leads to a view of Welsh regionalism very different to that gained from Emyr Humphreys's novels, it deserves to be summarised here. As Professor Smith sees it, the growth of south Wales by the late nineteenth-century into one of the world's greatest industrial regions made it ' "a problem" for the continuity of other Welsh traditions'. Coalfield society stood for the 'overthrowing of a cultural overlordship (Welsh, nonconformist, sanctified by rurality) and the embracing of alien gods (non-Welsh, socialist-syndicalist, rootless)'. Furthermore, since two-thirds of the country's population was concentrated there, the area seemed set to export these iconoclastic attitudes to the rest of Wales, until, that is, this 'work-society' went into a steep decline from the twenties onwards.[20]

The regional novelists in which Dai Smith is interested are those who attempted, with varying degrees of success, to develop new kinds of imaginative fictions suitable for the new social realities they'd experienced in the coalfield.[21] This meant gradually learning to reject the conventional forms – like melodrama, historical romance and documentary realism – which could only falsify the industrial experience. It also meant rejecting the temptation to treat South Wales life as the destruction of a semi-rural-cum-early-industrial Welsh Eden (the romantic fantasy brilliantly exploited by Richard Llewellyn in *How Green Was My Valley* in 1939). Above all, perhaps, the writers had 'to break the fetters of that provincialism which labelled their concerns as parochial as they were geographically limited'. This change of *mentalité* did not come until the thirties, when a whole new seam of English-language writing seemed suddenly to have been discovered in Wales. During that decade of the Depression, fiction of real quality was produced by Jack Jones, Rhys Davies, Glyn Jones, Gwyn Jones and Lewis Jones, and after the war the valleys' reputation as the talent-belt of Anglo-Welsh literature was confirmed by the appearance first of Gwyn Thomas, and later of writers such as Alun Richards and Ron Berry.[22]

---

[19] Dai Smith, 'A Novel History', in Curtis, *Wales: The Imagined Nation*, pp. 131–58. The quotations that follow come from this essay.

[20] This version of recent Welsh history is more fully worked out in Dai Smith, *Wales! Wales?* (London, 1984).

[21] The best account of this socially inspired fictional experimentation is that by Raymond Williams, 'The Welsh Industrial Novel', in *Problems in Materialism and Culture* (London, 1984), pp. 213–29.

[22] The best survey of this literature is still Glyn Jones, *The Dragon Has Two Tongues* (London, 1968). There are also monographs on each of these writers in the *Writers of Wales* series, Meic Stephens and Brinley Jones (eds.) (Cardiff: University of Wales Press).

Committed as he is to this version of Welsh regionalism in which South Wales exists as a largely self-made region that worships its creator and is unassimilable to a 'Greater Wales', Dai Smith is understandably chary of an Emyr Humphreys who has, in his view, 'used South Wales history since the 1930s as a "control factor" in novels principally about other matters'. He and the novelist are, however, agreed that contemporary Wales is '[an] emptiness from which a new beginning must be made', and that 'to imagine now is, at one and the same time, to admit the dreadful sense of completion, of an historical process ended, and yet affirm the refusal to lose the common memories which make human beings transmitters as well as receivers'. South Wales in particular is, on Professor Smith's reckoning, a sociocultural 'vacuum', which is precisely where Emyr Humphreys would like to come in, since he believes England, like Nature, abhors a vacuum, and will quickly fill it. It is imperative, therefore, that present-day Wales takes steps to fill this space itself, by developing the capacity to see the two linguistic cultures of Wales, and their related regions, as aspects of a single, if complex, historical situation. His novels are in part his chosen instrument for re-introducing all the inhabitants of modern Wales to the fullness of their own, largely neglected, past as a people. They are his attempt to explain the Welsh to themselves and thus to supply them with at least the raw materials of an holistic national identity. This intention was inscribed in *Outside the House of Baal*, and it is the same sense of mission that has sustained him throughout the twenty years spent working on *Bonds of Attachment*, a series of seven novels that encompass the history of Wales from Investiture (1911) to Investiture (1969); from the period when Lloyd George knew everybody's father to the time when everybody knew George Thomas' Mam.[23]

In a note addressed to himself when he embarked on the series, Emyr Humphreys described it as meant 'to be a companion to *Outside the House of Baal*, working laterally in space instead of linearly in time'.[24] In the event, he managed to have it both ways, creating a sequence that covers a large area both of time and country. When joined together, the novels map out the fractured social and political terrain of

---

[23] The series consists of the following novels, listed in chronological sequence: *Flesh and Blood* (London, 1974); *The Best of Friends* (London, 1978); *Salt of the Earth* (London, 1985); *An Absolute Hero* (London, 1986); *Open Secrets* (London, 1988); *National Winner* (London, 1971); *Bonds of Attachment* (London, 1991). All the novels have been reissued in Sphere Paperback.

[24] The quotation comes from a private letter (8 September 1982), reproduced here by kind permission of the author.

twentieth-century Wales by following the erratic progress through this
landscape of a single imaginary character, Amy Parry – 'the compuls-
ory heir of the historical process', as Emyr Humphreys has called her.
She is first introduced, in *Flesh and Blood*, as a spirited young girl who is
enabled, by education, to free herself from the pinched circumstances
of her early upbringing on the North Wales coast, near the town of
Llanelw. In the novels that follow she moves hopefully out into a
Wales-wide world, only to blunder into its cultural divides before falling
victim to the verbose ideological disputes by which the Wales of the
thirties, like the Wales of the nineties, is hopelessly riven.

During her time at college she and a few kindred spirits become *The
Best of Friends*, as the title of the second novel somewhat ironically puts
it, but the avid cultural nationalism of this group of confused young
Welsh-speaking idealists struggles to find adequate political expression.
Amy becomes increasingly aware of the counter-claims upon her, raised
as she has been in poverty, of the international socialist gospel being
preached in the remote, and in certain respects foreign, valleys of the
industrial south. Intelligent though she is, Amy is not given to dissect-
ing her situation with intellectual composure. Instead she becomes
thoroughly entangled in her emotional attachments – the result of
her divided social and political loyalties – to fundamentally dissimilar
people. *Salt of the Earth* explores the consequent turmoil of her life, and
concludes with the death of Enid Prydderch More, the young friend
whose natural goodness and firmness of purpose had at least provided
Amy with some light by which to steer her turbulent course. The next
novel, *An Absolute Hero*, shows her adrift, trying still to take her bearings
from her memories of Enid, but unable to find, in the increasingly
harsh political climate of the thirties, any new relationship which will
really sustain her. Her marriage of complicated convenience to John
Cilydd More, a Welsh poet and nationalist, is put under intolerable
strain when war breaks out and Amy enthusiastically identifies with the
'British' war effort. In *Open Secrets* she is seen spending more and more
of her time in London, braving the blitz in order to do the remedial
social work which, she hopes, will pave the way for a post-war Labour
government.

Amy's gradual pilgrimage, or defection, from nationalism to socialism is completed only when, in *National Winner*, she is comfortably
ensconced in affluence having married Lord Brangor, by which time
she retains only a purely sentimental attachment to Wales and her
political beliefs have been toned down to a very tasteful pink. In the

meantime her three sons, each the child of a different father, have grown into manhood and Emyr Humphreys uses them, both in *National Winner* and in the concluding novel *Bonds of Attachment*, to explore contrasting aspects of post-war culture in Wales. Gwydion is an international media-person, a born hustler and fixer; Bedwyr is a devoted family man who finds further refuge from an incomprehensible society in his conscientious work as an architect. The third son, Peredur, is the odd one out, being gawky, neurotic, and unbiddable. To Amy's discomfiture he becomes increasingly obsessed with finding out what exactly became of her first husband, his father, and his blundering search for the truth occupies most of the final novel. His relationship to a deliberately amnesiac Amy is illustrative of modern Wales' relationship to its past, as Emyr Humphreys has elsewhere described it:

[Any people who have lost touch with their past] are ideally conditioned for manipulation by mechanised superstructures operating for either profit or power or a judicious mixture of both. Such a people can be sufficiently sustained on synthetic substitutes for their own history; a nice balance of sedative and convenience food that can be controlled and adjusted to keep the masses in a state of complaisant lassitude. Too abrupt a change to the mother's milk of unadulterated history always entails the risk of a rash and a fever of activity.[25]

Complaisant Amy, content to forget her misguided young passions for nationalism and socialism, is aghast to find her erratic son intent on disinterring the past.

However inadequate a summary of the seven novels the foregoing may have been, it was necessary to attempt it if only in order to convey the ambitious scale of the series. In order to cover such a large and highly diversified area of historical experience, Emyr Humphreys needed to provide himself with an organising structure that would allow maximum freedom to manoeuvre. The key device he adopted was that of composition by short, free-standing scenes, deliberately leaving to the reader the work of producing a larger sequential narrative by self-assembly. In addition, Humphreys refrained from establishing a clear point-of-view within each scene, preferring instead to alter focus and perspective frequently, rather in the way that camera angles change in a television or film production.[26] In fact Humphreys has acknowledged

---

[25] Humphreys, *The Taliesin Tradition*, p. 229.
[26] These aspects of Emyr Humphreys's technique are discussed by Ioan Williams, 'The Land of the Living', *Planet*, 52 (1985), pp. 97–105.

that his experience of working as a television producer (and scriptwriter) did influence his novel-writing during the construction of the sequence. The outcome of all this is a series of novels that return a much more open verdict on the history of Wales this century than my tendentious summary would suggest. Indeed, Emyr Humphreys seems less interested in passing final judgement on his characters and their actions than in getting readers to reflect on their own motives for judgement – the values and ideologies that determine assessment. To put it differently, he makes the readers aware that they are not observers of, but participants in, the great historical debates that shape his characters' lives. He writes historical novels with a difference – novels that historicise the reader. It is not surprising that one of the writers he greatly admires is Bertolt Brecht.

Another prominent feature of the series *Bonds of Attachment* is that the writing is lean enough to have made some complain that it is anorexically thin. But to say this is to fail to understand the cultural politics of Emyr Humphreys's style. One approach to this subject is suggested by a remark Emyr Humphreys once laughingly made in a radio interview:

'I thank God that I was born a North-Walian and don't have the golden endless eloquence of the South Walians, so that being economical comes natural! In my writing I try to use as few words as possible, because this is one way of partially reflecting the great glories of the epigrammatically terse Welsh poetic tradition, as opposed to the oral tradition which lies behind the South Wales style, where the flourishing of many words is considered to be the acme of "the bard".'[27]

Implicit in Emyr Humphreys' restrained use of language, then, is a refusal to play 'the voluble Taffy', as Heaney put it when discussing Dylan Thomas.

The matter is, though, worth exploring further and can usefully be considered with reference to a couple of lines from one of the first and greatest examples of 'regional literature' in English. Wordsworth's 'Michael' opens with a recommendation to leave the London road and strike into what seems at first to be inhospitably local territory. 'If from the public way you turn your steps/ Up the tumultuous brook of Green-head Gill . . .'. 'Green-head Gill': the name is uncompromisingly local, uncouth and yokel to the ears of the genteel. It is a challenging

---

[27] The remark was made during the course of a discussion between Emyr Humphreys and R. S. Thomas, chaired by the present author, broadcast in the programme *Mother's Tongue, Not Mother Tongue* (BBC Radio 4, August 1987).

sign – or warning – that Wordsworth means to go native and speak the very language of the region. Of course he does not literally do so – it was left to Scott to do that nervously in *Waverley*, when he ventured to use a modified form of the Scottish vernacular that he thought was guaranteed to make his book a commercial disaster and himself a laughing-stock. Hence Scott's choice of protective anonymity. But Wordsworth *is* true to Green-head Gill in a different way, since he develops a style of writing that does magnificent justice to the character and quality of life of the vanishing 'statesmen' of the Lake district.

The problem Wordsworth solved, in his own way, was how to mediate the life of a region to a wider world without distortion and without condescension. That this is, at bottom, a problem of language is something that writers in Wales do not need to be told, since modern Welsh writing in English began with passages like the following: 'There's sayings for you! What for you laugh, boys bach! Is not the Judge of the Earth right? Would you laugh at Daniel? At Elijah? Why for you laugh? You will have, dear me, to change your thinks if you will wear the White Shirts'. This is an excerpt from *My People*, a collection of stories that was called 'the literature of the sewer' in Wales when it was published in 1915, with an outraged Lloyd George scheming to have it banned. The collection is the most outrageous example of regionalist literature to have been produced in Wales, and it continues to this day to influence the way Welsh English-language writers from Wales write. Though its regionalism is beyond doubt, its precise character remains open to question. Recent scholars and critics have tended to treat *My People* as primarily a product of regional conflict *within* Wales. Evans is seen to be participating in a feud between the traditional, rural, Welsh-speaking west – strongly Nonconformist and staunchly Liberal – and the increasingly socialist, English-speaking, industrialised and secular south-east – the coalfield society discussed by Dai Smith. Evans himself came from the west, but moved to the edge of the coalfield as a young man, and thereafter viewed his native region with different eyes, seeing it as backward, feudal and full of religious hypocrisy. The 'clotted idiocies' of his style, as one of his innumerable enemies put it, can therefore be relished as an example of satiric licence. Evans is, by this reckoning, a writer of genius who devised a baroque language to convey the inscape of *his* people's character.[28]

---

[28] See the excellent introduction by the editor, John Harris, to Caradoc Evans, *My People* (Bridgend, 1987). See also M. Wynn Thomas, '*My People* and the Revenge of the Novel', *The New Welsh Review*, vol. 1, no. 1 (Summer 1988), pp. 17–22.

Others, however, have always regarded Evans' work in an altogether harsher, not to say an unforgiving, light, seeing in it a regionalism of a base and cringing kind. They see him as the creator of what one mocking commentator has recently called 'a mean and peasant land', and they believe him to have been in very truth the 'Welsh renegade' that Lloyd George immediately dubbed him. His crime is to have traduced Wales in order to titillate the English, and viewed in this context his language does indeed appear to be simply that of the stage-Welshman gone mad.[29] Welsh speakers have, understandably, inclined to this view, angered in particular at Evans' literal translation of Welsh syntax and idiomatic expression into English for cheap comic effect. They point out, very properly, that English sounds equally ridiculous when reproduced word for word in Welsh. Evans seems to them to be a sorry example of the colonial mentality.

It is this Caradoc Evans, in both his incarnations, who was the patron saint or satyr of the first full generation of Welsh writers to write in English. He is the imp of the perverse whose enlivening presence can be detected in the work of Dylan Thomas and his contemporaries, and he is also the (fallen) angel with whom Emyr Humphreys has, in a way, silently wrestled throughout his career. The plain, spare style of Humphreys' mature novels is a reaction both against Evans and against 'the sons of Caradoc',[30] as the Anglo-Welsh writers of the thirties have been called, in two respects. First it is a deliberate avoidance of the picturesque, as part of the process of normalising Welsh life as depicted in English-language fiction. Secondly, it is used by Emyr Humphreys to render Welsh-language speech into ordinary English, so that Welsh is treated not as antiquated, limited and quaint but as a modern sophisticated language which comes as naturally to those who speak it as English does to the English. 'We were as Danes in Denmark all day long', wrote Wallace Stevens in one poem, meaning that what it is now fashionable to call the 'arbitrariness' or artificiality of their language and culture is for the most part concealed from the indigenous population.[31] By the same token Emyr Humphreys has endeavoured in his novels to show his characters living 'as the Welsh in Wales all day long'.

[29] See D. Tecwyn Lloyd, 'The Romantic Parody', in *Planet*, 31, 1976, 29–36 and 'Wales – See England', by the same author, *Planet*, 34, 1976, 36–47.
[30] The phrase was used by the writer and scholar Gwyn Jones. See his essay, *The First Forty Years: Notes on Anglo-Welsh Literature* (Cardiff, 1957).
[31] Wallace Stevens, 'The Auroras of Autumn', section 9, *Collected Poems* (London, 1965), p. 419.

Emyr Humphreys's victory over Caradoc and his sons has, inevitably been won at a price. In eschewing regional dialects he has also deprived himself, as a writer, of a rich linguistic resource. One thinks of what Tony Harrison has been able to achieve, for example, by wittily acting the literary Luddite, out to smash 'the looms of owned language'.[32] Geoffrey Hill's extraordinary achievements as an archaeologist of the regional mind is also beyond Humphreys' self-appointed limits, as is (to take two examples from the novel at random) Chinua Achebe's movingly dignified rendering of Obi tribal speech in *Things Fall Apart* and Ruth Prawer Jhabvala's subtle reproduction of the demotic English of the sub-continent in *Esmond in India*.

In writing about his 'region' of Wales and *its* regions as intently as he has, Emyr Humphreys has always been acutely aware of Wales not only as a special instance, but as an exemplary case. He has always felt that its efforts to resist the homogenising effects of modern western civilisation parallel and prefigure the efforts of other countries, both small and large. Indeed Seamus Heaney has noted – in an essay that is already deservedly well-known – how Ted Hughes, Geoffrey Hill and Philip Larkin have become

> hoarders and shorers of what they take to be the real England. All three treat England as a region – or rather treat their region as England – in different and complementary ways. I believe they are afflicted with a sense of history that was once the peculiar affliction of the poets of the other nations who were not themselves natives of England but who spoke the English language. The poets of the mother culture, I feel, are now possessed of that defensive love of their territory which was once shared only by those poets whom we might call colonial – Yeats, MacDiarmid, Carlos Williams. They are aware of their Englishness as deposits in the descending storeys of the literary and historical past. Their very terrain is becoming consciously precious. A desire to preserve indigenous traditions, to keep open the imagination's supply lines to the past . . . to perceive . . . a continuity of communal ways, and a confirmation of an identity which is threatened – all this is signified by their language.[33]

There are, of course, very evident historical reasons for this change of cultural attitude. In an interesting essay, written between 1975 and 1978 but published rather later, Raymond Williams noted how 'a particular dominant version of this island, its people and its society was spread throughout the world at the time of the domination of a particular ideology and a particular class'. The anglocentric British ideology

[32] Tony Harrison, *Selected Poems* (London, 1987), p. 112.
[33] Seamus Heaney, 'Englands of the Mind' in *Preoccupations* (London, 1980), pp. 150–1.

has decayed as the historical circumstances that produced it and were confirmed by it have changed. Now, therefore, the different regions and nations of Britain are left to search both their past and their present for satisfactory new identities. And Williams's thoughtful, cautious description of the form this search is taking in Wales is also an excellent apologia for Emyr Humphreys's fiction:

In Wales . . . we have always been aware of the deep differences between industrial South Wales, rural North and West Wales, and the very specific border country from which I myself come. We don't get past that by inventing a pseudo-historical or romantic Welshness: indeed that would only divide us further. We get past it by looking and working for unity in the definition and the development of a modern Wales, in which the really powerful impulses – to discover an effective community and to take control of our own energies and resources – can be practically worked through.[34]

Emyr Humphreys' work as a novelist is an important part of this continuing process of working through. Time alone will tell how these 'impulses', and his novels, will work out in the end.

[34] 'Are we becoming more divided?', *Radical Wales*, 23 (Autumn 1989), pp. 8–9.

CHAPTER 9

Scotland and the regional novel

Cairns Craig

Regionalism is an almost all-embracing category in relation to the Scottish novel: simply by virtue of *being* Scottish, almost all Scottish novels will be identified as regional within the traditions of the *English* novel, rather than representing an alternative national tradition. And because 'Scottishness' has been identified primarily with lower-class or working-class Scots (middle-class Scots being those who have been 'anglified'), Scottish novels will almost inevitably fulfil the key features of the regional novel as identified by Keith Snell in his Introduction to this volume – locale, dialect and a primarily lower class community. There is, however, an equally insistent regionalism within the borders of Scotland itself. Scottish novelists may construct their narratives as paradigms of a national consciousness, but they generally do so by locating their narrative within strictly demarcated regional boundaries, and as a consequence almost all the major Scottish novelists are identified with specific areas of Scotland – whether it is John Galt and George Douglas Brown with Ayrshire, Lewis Grassic Gibbon and Nan Shepherd with the Mearns, Neil Gunn with Sutherland and Caithness, George Mackay Brown with Orkney, or James Kelman with Glasgow.

The division between Highland and Lowland, the existence of three languages (Gaelic, Scots and English), the huge population migrations into and out of the country in the eighteenth and nineteenth centuries[1] – these, together with a political commitment to the processes of the British Empire rather than a resistance to it, made it impossible for Scotland to achieve the kind of unified culture demanded by, and constructed

[1] A fifth of the Scottish population now comprises of people who are the descendants of immigrants from Ireland; there were large movements of middle Europeans and particularly middle-European Jews into Scotland in the period around the First World War, and many people from the Scottish Highlands moved to Lowland Scotland in the nineteenth century. As a result, Lowland Scotland has been a melting-pot of immigrants, while at the same time exporting its skilled working class in large numbers to join Highland emigrants in North America, South Africa and Australasia.

by, nineteenth-century nationalism:[2] without statehood and a national 'centre', the regions of Scotland represented semi-autonomous domains which could be presented either as microcosms of a Scottishness trying to re-assert itself, or as substitutes for a Scottishness which had failed to maintain an independent national tradition.

Given the pervasiveness of regionalism in Scottish writing, what I want to do here is not to map the Scottish regional novel in detail, but to explore the ways in which its origins created paradigmatic narrative structures that were to shape the novel in Scotland and to influence the development of regional writing beyond Scotland – for regionalism is not simply foundational to the Scottish novel, regionalism in Scotland is foundational to the regional novel itself.

I UNION AND REGION

The importance of Scottish novelists in the development of regional writing in the early nineteenth century – not only Scott and Galt, but many of those associated with *Blackwood's Magazine*[3] – is not simply the product of a particularly fertile period in Scottish writing which coincides with the development of the form of the regional novel. Nor is it simply that Scotland was ideal territory for the regional novel, since its cultural conditions – distance from the centres of cultural and political power, unique forms of landscape, and distinctive local modes of speech and manners – matched those which have come to characterise the general requirements of the genre. Rather, regionalism was a direct outcome of the Union of 1707, and Scotland's incorporation into the new political entity of the United Kingdom. Regionalism was the means by which Scotland negotiated the complex relationship between its distinctive cultural past, its present incorporation into a greater whole and its possible future submersion in English culture. The value attributed to local identity developed precisely as the counterbalance to the powerful sense that Scotland was disappearing into a homogeneous and 'universal' English culture. It is only in this dialectic between local distinction and universal homogeneity that the regional gains its

---

[2] For analyses of Scotland's relationship to the traditions of nationalism, see Tom Nairn, *The Break-Up of Britain: Crisis and Neo-Nationalism* (London, 1977); David McCrone, Stephen Kendrick and Pat Straw (eds.), *The Making of Scotland: Nation, Culture and Social Change* (Edinburgh, 1989); Craig Beveridge and Ronald Turnbull, *The Eclipse of Scottish Culture* (Edinburgh 1989), and my own *Out of History: Narrative Paradigms in Scottish and English Culture* (Edinburgh, 1996).

[3] For the role of *Blackwood's Magazine* in the development of the Scottish novel, see Francis Russell Hart, *The Scottish Novel* (London, 1978).

significance and becomes an object worthy of attention and articulation. Equally, it is only where there is an audience who share a common language, but without sharing a common past or a common local culture, that the regional can be articulated and understood as something other than outright difference.

The Union demanded integration, but the very process of integration required first the identification of significant differences, differences which had to be explained and accommodated in the construction of a new relationship between the known and the unknown. Dr Johnson notes the tension in *A Journey to the Western Islands of Scotland*:[4]

To write of the cities of our own island with the solemnity of geographical description, as if we had been cast upon a newly discovered coast, has the appearance of a very frivolous observation; yet as Scotland is little known to the greater part of those who may read these observations, it is not superfluous to relate . . .

The 'known' is governed by English codes and English norms but the unknown in Scotland ought not to be the alien or the foreign: it is from the disjunction between familiarity ('our own island') and strangeness that description of the regional begins:[5]

The Lowlands of Scotland had once undoubtedly an equal portion of woods with other countries. Forests are every where gradually diminished, as architecture and cultivation prevail by the increase of people and the introduction of arts. But I believe few regions have been denuded like this, where many centuries must have passed in waste without the least thought of future supply. Davies observes in his account of Ireland, that no Irishman had ever planted an orchard. For that negligence some excuse might be drawn from an unsettled state of life, and the instability of property; but in Scotland possession has long been secure, and inheritance regular, yet it may be doubted whether before the Union any lowlander between Edinburgh and England had ever set a tree.

Johnson moves from the general ('other countries') through comparisons within the British Isles ('Davies . . . account of Ireland') to the ultimate validation of English values in the influence of the Union. The integration of Scotland and England will eventually bring the Scots into an acceptance of the values of English (agri)culture, but for a time difference will need to be explained to those who read as an alternative to making Johnson's journey for themselves.

[4] Samuel Johnson, *A Journey to the Western Islands of Scotland* (1775; London, 1984), p. 42.
[5] *Ibid.*, p. 40.

Travel of this kind performs exactly the duality of the regional novel
in relation to its audience: the tracks of the travellers begin to bind the
landscapes and territories, as well as the languages, of 'our own island'
into a new unity. The post-roads and the military roads are the integrat-
ing filaments from which it becomes possible to perceive and appreciate
diversity, precisely because diversity has been subdued within unity and
is no longer threatening to it.[6] It is the context of this initial formation
of the regional that is dramatised by Smollett's *Humphry Clinker* (1771):
Smollett's characters journey towards Scotland through the new multi-
national world of the United Kingdom, in which literature plays a key
role in the absorption of local distinctiveness into cultural unity:

Curious to know upon what the several talents of my fellow-guests were
employed, I applied to my communicative friend Dick Ivy, who gave me to
understand, that most of them were, or had been, understrappers, or journeymen, to more creditable authors, for whom they translated, collated, and com-
piled, in the business of bookmaking; and that all of them had, at different
times, laboured in the service of our landlord, though they now set up for themselves in various departments of literature. Not only their talents, but also their
nations and dialects were so various, that our conversation resembled the
confusion of tongues of Babel. We had the Irish brogue, the Scotch accent,
and foreign idiom, twanged off by the most discordant vociferation ... The
Scotchman gives lectures on the pronunciation of the English language, which
he is now publishing by subscription.[7]

The multiplicity of accents seeking integration into the English language is matched by the multiplicity of environments through which
Smollett's travellers pass. His central figure, Matthew Bramble, travels
for the benefit of his health, and assumes that 'at this time of day, I
ought to know something of my own constitution',[8] but the constitution that needs to be understood is that of the Union, and it is only
when he arrives in Scotland, and learns to appreciate it, that his own
'constitution' will improve:

we are both unjust and ungrateful to the Scots; for, as far as I am able
to judge, they have a real esteem for the natives of Southern Britain; and
never mention our country, but with expressions of regard – Nevertheless,
they are far from being servile imitators of our modes and fashionable vices.
All their customs and regulations of public and private oeconomy, of business
and diversion, are in their own stile. This remarkably predominates in their

---

[6] See Eric Pawson, *Transport and Economy: the Turnpike Roads of Eighteenth-Century Britain* (London, 1977).
[7] Tobias Smollett, *Humphry Clinker* (1771; London, 1967), p. 158.   [8] *Ibid.*, p. 1.

looks, their dress and manner, their music, and even their cookery. Our 'squire declares, that he knows not another people upon earth, so strongly marked with a national character.[9]

Travel discovers this specifically national character, but the epistolary form of the novel emphasises the communicability of all parts of the Kingdom with every other: the content of the characters' letters trace their steps through the differences of the country, while by their form the letters enmesh the diversity of nations and classes in a single communicative system.[10] The potential divisiveness of the multivocal text is thus dissolved by the uncovering of an inherent but concealed unity – just as Humphry, the accidentally acquired servant, turns out to be Bramble's natural son – and that unity is celebrated in the symbolic weddings which bring the discordant representatives of the various countries into 'union'. The island will be established as 'our own'[11] precisely to the extent that its local differences are acknowledged and yet recognised as inter-related.

In *Humphry Clinker* Smollett enacts the discovery of regional diversity as the counterpoint to political integration, and thereby prefigures the explicitly stated purpose of Maria Edgeworth's *Castle Rackrent*:

The Editor hopes his readers will observe, that these are 'tales of other times': that the manners depicted in the following pages are not those of the present age: the race of the Rackrents has long since been extinct in Ireland . . . There is a time when individuals can bear to be rallied for their past follies and absurdities, after they have acquired new habits and a new consciousness. Nations as well as individuals gradually lose attachment to their identity, and the present generation is amused rather than offended by the ridicule that is thrown upon their ancestors . . .

When Ireland loses her identity by an union with Great Britain, she will look back with a smile of good-humoured complacency on the Sir Kits and Sir Condys of her former existence.[12]

---

[9] *Ibid.*, p. 259.

[10] If the novel, as Benedict Anderson has argued – in *Imagined Communities: Reflections on the Origin and Spread of Nationalism* (London, 1983) – is fundamental to the construction of the 'imagined community' of the nation, the post must be no less significant in the establishment of a standard language that defines a particular national grouping.

[11] See Linda Colley, *Britons: Forging the Nation* (New Haven and London, 1992), p. 13 ff, for a discussion of the importance of the idea of the 'island' in the construction of a British identity to which the Scots could be admitted. Colley quotes a letter from the Duke of Newcastle in which he says that the Scots have to be accepted because 'we must consider that they are within our island'.

[12] Maria Edgworth, *Castle Rackrent* (1800; Oxford, 1995).

Castle Rackrent may be the first regional *novel*, but the issues from which it starts are precisely those with which Scottish writers had been struggling throughout the eighteenth century: the mode of *Castle Rackrent* is a prose version of Burns's satires upon Ayrshire manners, whether in dramatic monologues like 'Holy Willie's Prayer' or in narratives like 'The Holy Fair' or 'Tam O'Shanter'. Both in their structure and their language, Burns's poems, like Edgeworth's novel, point in two directions: inwards and backwards to a local dialect-speaking community, and outwards and forwards to a general audience in English. The piquancy of local forms of speech and local morality is enclosed within shared and trans-regional linguistic and cultural values. Edgeworth's ironic vernacular narrator, like Burns's characters, asserts the value of regionalism only by being, at the same time, open to evaluation by a more enlightened, more 'universal' value-system that author and reader are assumed to share through the language of English.

If the regional novel, as Keith Snell implies in the Introduction to this volume, is a genre which has been assigned a very low status in English writing, that may account for the low status in which many Scottish works have been held, both within the traditions of literature in English and within Scotland itself. The point was made powerfully by Edwin Muir, in *Scott and Scotland* (1936), in his comparison of the development of modern Scottish literature with that of modern Irish literature:

Irish nationality cannot be said to be any less intense than ours; but Ireland produced a national literature not by clinging to Irish dialect, but by adopting English and making it into a language fit for all purposes. The poetry of Mr Yeats belongs to English literature, but no one would deny that it belongs to Irish literature pre-eminently and essentially. The difference between contemporary Irish and contemporary Scottish literature is that the first is central and homogenous, and that the second is parochial and conglomerate; and this is because it does not possess an organ for the expression of a whole and unambiguous nationality. Scots dialect poetry represents Scotland in bits and patches, and in doing that it is in no doubt a faithful enough image of the present divided state of Scotland. But while we cling to it we shall never be able to express the central reality of Scotland . . . The real issue in contemporary Scottish literature is between centrality and provincialism; dialect poetry is one of the chief supports of the second of these two forces; the first can hardly be said to exist at all.[13]

---

[13] Edwin Muir, *Scott and Scotland* (London, 1936), pp. 179–80.

For Muir, the fragmentation of Scots into regional dialects is at the heart of Scottish provincialism; and Scottish provincialism is at the heart of the failure of Scottish culture. If the Scottish novel is essentially regional, that can only be, for Muir, because the 'regional' is a symptom of the failure of culture, and the regionalism of Scotland's novelists a symptom of their inability to escape that failure. The continued existence of 'Scots' as a dialect prevented the acceptance of English as the medium of literature in Scotland and is, for Muir, the ultimate blockage to Scotland's self-expression, its ensnarement in provincialism. Walter Scott, probably the most significant single influence on the development of the regional novel, is, in Muir's eyes, a failure precisely because of his regional commitment, for those regional commitments are nothing but symptoms of a failed culture:

> His Scots, it is true, was far better than his English, and he produced in his dialogue the best Scots prose that has ever been written. But as the Scots vernacular did not come out of a unity, he felt that it could not express a unity; so for the structural, the unifying part of his work he relied upon English . . . he lived in a country which could not give an organic form to his genius.[14]

In this view the division in Scott's language, the very basis of his presentation of the regional, is the reason for his failure: it is, therefore, to the traditions of dialect writing that we need to turn to understand the structure of regionalism in Scotland.

II DIALECT AND DIALOGUE

David Hume's major competitor in Scottish philosophy in the eighteenth century was Thomas Reid, but the competition between them was most intent in their scrupulous effort to avoid Scotticisms.[15] This obsession points to what has been seen as the fundamental division in eighteenth-century Scottish culture, between those (Thomson, Hume, Adam Smith) committed to the purification of Scottish speech into a 'universally' acceptable standard by the removal of its regional imperfections, and those committed to the maintenance of the traditions

---

[14] *Ibid.*, pp. 175–6.
[15] Hume described his own speech as a 'corrupt Dialect', *The Letters of David Hume*, J. Y. T. Greg (ed.) (Oxford, 1961), pp. i, 255; Thomas Sheridan commented that 'Reid's book was the most correct of any that North Britain had produced, for that he had not found one Scotticism in it', quoted Gordon Turnbull, 'James Boswell: Biography and the Union', *The History of Scottish Literature 2, 1660–1800*, Andrew Hook (ed.), p. 160. See Robert Crawford's, *Devolving English Literature* (Oxford, 1992), pp. 23 ff.

of the Scottish vernacular (Ramsay, Fergusson, Burns). Over the past twenty years, however, a succession of critics have shown how false is this divide. After the Union, Scottish writers cannot help but be involved in the 'universal' culture of English, either as a result of its direct pressure upon their local situation or because they want to play a part on the Imperial stage; the more effectively English is acquired, however, and the more rigorously the cultural traditions of English are studied, the more sensitive both speakers and writers become to what remains of the local forms of language – whether it is the sensitivity of those who are trying to extirpate the Scotticisms from their speech or the sensitivity of those who are trying to prevent the death of the local dialect.

In eighteenth-century Scotland the search for the rules of correct English, and the establishment of the discipline of 'Rhetoric and Belles Lettres' to study it,[16] go hand in hand with the development of dialect and regional literature, and those who are most engaged in the establishment of the new rhetorical discipline are often those who are most engaged in the exploring or in responding to the regional – and vice versa. Dugald Stewart comments after meeting Burns that, 'Nothing perhaps was more remarkable among his various attainments, than the fluency, and precision, and originality of his language, when he spoke in company; more particularly as he aimed at purity in his turn of expression, and avoided more successfully than most Scotchmen, the peculiarities of Scottish phraseology'.[17] The element in Burns which Edwin Muir considered to be his greatest weakness – 'where poetry is written in a variety of dialects with no central language as a point of reference, it is impossible to evolve a criterion of style (there is no standard of Scots poetic style)'[18] – has come to be considered his greatest strength, the outstanding poems demonstrating an ability to modulate *between* Scots and English, between 'high' and 'low', between 'local' and 'universal'. As Tom Crawford points out, the Ayrshire peasantry 'were hardly strangers to abstract English diction ... For generations, farmers and labourers had been familiar with the Authorised Version of the Bible, English theological works, and interminable sermons full of words like "effectual calling"',[19] so that the interaction *between* Scots and English in Burns's poetry is neither evasive nor the symptom of some cultural

---

[16] For the origins of the Scottish discipline of English Literature, see Crawford, *Devolving English Literature*, chs. 1 and 2.
[17] Quoted by Thomas Crawford, *Burns: A Study of the Poems and Songs* (Edinburgh, 1965), p. 103.
[18] Muir, *Scott and Scotland*, p. 29.   [19] Crawford, *Burns*, p. 3.

flaw: it is the appopriate way, in this specific time and place, in which experience is articulated.

Whatever Muir's distrust of Burns in 1936, the influence of Burns on the development of the regional novel in Scotland was immense. Burns's use of local dialect, and the acceptance of that dialect as a literary language by a broad audience in the whole of the English-speaking world, meant that Scots was both valued and understood by readers in English. The dialect speech of Scottish characters was not simply the phonetic rendition of the voices of the uneducated: it was the speech of those who had behind them a powerful poetic tradition, and a tradition, moreover, that gave special status to the poor and the outcast. In Burns's poetry the toils or joys of the working family (as in 'The Cotter's Saturday Night') are the model of a true humanity – one which speaks in dialect and yet is the local repetition of a universal Christian tradition rendered in English:

> The Sire turns o'er, with patriarchal grace,
>   The big *ha'-Bible*, ance his *Father's* pride;
> His bonnet rev'rently is laid aside,
>   His *lyart haffets* wearing thin and bare;
> Those strains that once did sweet in ZION glide,
>   He wales a portion with judicious care;
> '*And let us worship GOD!*' he says with solomn air.[20]

Burns's poetry validates the social and the spiritual meaning of lower-class regional life, justifying their speech as both eloquent and honest – a speech that can utter itself in due humility, but also in due pride, alongside the word of God. 'The honest man, though e'er sae poor, /Is king o' men, for a' that.'[21]

Scott's *The Antiquary* has a moment which is typical of many similar encounters in the Scottish novel: Jonathan Oldbuck is expatiating ('On the left hand you may see some slight vestiges of the *porta sinistra*, and on the right one side of the *porta dextra* wellnigh entire') to his young friend Lovel on the antiquity of an earth-bank in his locale:

'Yes, my dear friend, from this stance it is probably, – nay, it is nearly certain, that Julius Agricola beheld what our Beaumont has so admirably described! – From this very Prætorium –'

---

[20] 'The Cotter's Saturday Night', 12, *Burns: Poems and Songs*, James Kinsley (ed.), (Oxford, 1968), p. 119.
[21] 'Song – For a' that and a' that', *ibid.*, p. 602.

A voice from behind interrupted his ecstatic description –
'Prætorian, here, Prætorian there, I mind the bigging o't.'
Both at once turned round, Lovel with surprise, and Oldbuck with mingled
surprise and indignation, at so uncivil an interruption. An auditor had stolen
upon them, unseen and unheard, amid the energy of the Antiquary's enthusiastic declamation, and the attentive civility of Lovel. He had the exterior
appearance of a mendicant . . .
'What is that you say, Edie?' said Oldbuck, hoping, perhaps, that his ears
had betrayed their duty. 'What were you speaking about?'
'About this bit bourock, your honour,' answered the undaunted Edie, 'I
mind the bigging o't.'[22]

Edie, the ancient beggar who cannot be encouraged to live under a
roof, is, through the vernacular, able to identify accurately – 'bit bourock'
– what Oldbuck has inflated with latinate rhetoric into a fantasy genea-
logy for his environment: certain kinds of truth are local, and it takes
local speech to voice them accurately.

Such moments deliberately invert eighteenth- and nineteenth-century
middle-class Scottish society's effort to integrate itself into English speech.
That drive gave rise to a huge number of 'pronouncing dictionaries',
aimed at explaining to Scots how to avoid speaking 'vulgarly' in English. The intent of these books was to provide techniques for identifying the specifics of 'provincial' pronunciation in order to overcome them;
their effect, however, was to provide an armoury of techniques by which
novelists could notate regional accent. In Walker's *Rules to be Observed by
the Native of Scotland for attaining a just Pronunciation of English*, for instance,
the following is recorded:

With respect to quantity, it may be observed, that the Scotch pronounce
almost all their accented vowels long. Thus, if I am not mistaken, they
would pronounce *habit, hay-bit; tepid, tee-pid; sinner, see-ner; conscious, cone-shus*;
and *subject, soobject*; it is not pretended, however, that every accented vowel is
so pronounced, but that such pronunciation is very general, and particularly
the *i*. This vowel is short in English pronunciation where the other vowels are
long; thus *evasion, adhesion, emotion, confusion*, have the *a, e, o*, and *u*, long; and
in these instances the Scotch would pronounce them like the English; but in
vision, decision &c. where the English pronounce the *i* short, the Scotch lengthen
this letter by pronouncing it like *ee*, as if the words were written *vee-ision, decee-
sion*, &c. and this peculiarity is universal.[23]

[22] Walter Scott, *The Antiquary* (1816; London, 1907), p. 41.
[23] J. A. Walker, *A Critical Pronouncing Dictionary* (1791), p. xi; quoted in Charles Jones, *Sylvester
Douglas: A Treatise on the Provincial Dialect of Scotland* (Edinburgh, 1991), p. 29.

In such primers the quality of attention to the phonetic characteristics of regional speech provides not only the mechanisms by which regional accent can be transcribed, but also ensures an audience well-versed in written versions of the oral. Those who, like Scott and Hogg, had been involved in the transcription of ballad literature had to acquire a subtle sense of how to present the oral in the written, and, as William Donaldson has pointed out,[24] that oral awareness was intensified by the development of the newspaper reporter's shorthand, with its emphasis on capturing the sounds rather than dictionary spellings of words. The greatest of the nineteenth-century novelist-journalists, William Alexander, provides an intensely detailed representation of local speech in the North-East of Scotland:

'Nae doot o' that; but leuk at this,' and the souter took up a newspaper containing a report of the General Assembly, which he had carefully conned. 'Here's the debate on pawtronage – "Mr Cunningham moved that the Assembly resolve and declare that patronage is a grievance, has been attended with much injury to the cause of true religion in the Church and kingdom, is the main cause of the difficulties in which the Church is at present involved, and that it ought to be abolished;" and that was sec-ondit by an Mr Buchan o' Berwickshire, Mr Macrory taul' me. Foo cud ony richt-thinkin' man back-speak a motion like that noo?'

'I daursay Gushets winna dee't, but aw b'lieve him an' Maister Sleekaboot raither differs aboot the benefits o' pawtronage,' said the Smith, with a sly twinkle in his eye.[25]

Here, the written narrative voice of the novel, in English, contains the Scots-speaking voices, in conversation, which contain English writing that they vocalise from the newspaper. The oral and the written, the local and the standardised, are not antitheses but incorporate one another in a continual dialogue – in this case, one in which a proposition in standard English is validated by being in conformity with vernacular 'richt-thinking'.

Such detailed representation of the phonetic variety of speech becomes, in Scott and his successors, a key element in the dramatisation of character, not simply in terms of distinctive voices but as beings whose essential nature is related to their regional origins and to the truths which can only be known by the close interaction with a specific

---

[24] William Donaldson, Introduction to William Alexander, *Johnny Gibb of Gushetneuk* (East Linton, 1995), p. ix.
[25] *Ibid.*, p. 141.

environment. Clearly, this opened up the potential for comic disjunction between the standard language of reader and author, and the dialect speech of characters, a disjunction which could have operated within
the conventions typical of the eighteenth-century novel (and thereafter
of much of the English tradition), in which the hierarchy of intellect
and morality accompanies the hierarchy of speech patterns. But in Scott
(as in the case of Edie above), and in much of the Scottish tradition,
that relationship between language and moral stance is inverted: instead
of the narrative voice of the author representing the apex of a linguistic
system which is graded downwards from its all-encompassing universality, Scott establishes an ironic, disjunctive relationship between the
voices in his novels, one in which the narrative voice – self-consciously
rhetorical and therefore potentially self-deluding – is mocked by the
voices of his most perceptive characters, whose speech is regional,
vernacular and therefore close to reality.

Indeed, if the protagonists of Scott's novels are usually middle class
and English-speaking, the heroic figures are lower class and regionally
accented. Thus, when the Antiquary goes to the house of the Muckle-
backits after the death of their son Steenie, and

> came in front of the fisherman's hut, he observed a man working intently, as
> if to repair a shattered boat which lay upon the beach, and going, up to him,
> was surprised to find it was Mucklebackit himself. 'I am glad,' he said, in a
> tone of sympathy – 'I am glad, Saunders, that you feel yourself able to make
> this exertion.'
>
> 'And what would ye have me to do,' answered the fisher gruffly, 'unless I
> wanted to see four children starve, because ane is drowned? It's weel wi' you
> gentles, that can sit in the house wi' handkerchers at your een when ye lose a
> friend; but the like o' us maun to our wark again, if our hearts were beating
> as hard as my hammer.'[26]

It is the vernacular speaker who, over and again in the novels of Scott,
represents a trustworthy moral centre, just as in Hogg's *Confessions of a
Justified Sinner* it is the Scots speakers who are able to discern the truth
about a world to which both Robert Wringhim (and the Editor who
reconstructs his narrative) are blind.[27] The vernacular tradition – sometimes in defiance of the writer's own politics – aligns him or her with
the 'folk', with their interests and their values: the demotic is the root of
the democratic. And if, as George Davie has argued, the 'democratic

---

[26] Scott, *The Antiquary*, p. 307.
[27] See Douglas Gifford, *James Hogg* (Edinburgh, 1976) for a discussion of the use of Scots in *The Confessions of a Justified Sinner*.

intellect' is at the centre of Scottish cultural tradition,[28] that democracy
has manifested itself in the novel in a commitment to the linguistic and
cultural traditions of the lower classes.

It is in this context that the novel of 'education', whether from the
pupil's or the teacher's point of view, has played a central role within
the regional novel in Scotland, because it is within the educational
system that the conflict between local forms of language and standard
English is at its most intense, and the commitments of the characters
are tested. The most famous instance of this is Chris Guthrie in Lewis
Grassic Gibbon's *A Scots Quair*, and the fact that,

two Chrisses there were that fought for her heart and tormented her. You
hated the land and the coarse speak of the folk and learning was brave and
fine one day and the next you'd waken with the peewits crying across the
hills, deep and deep, crying in the heart of you and the smell of the earth in
your face, almost you'd cry for that, the beauty of it and the sweetness of the
Scottish land and skies.[29]

It is a conflict that is to be repeated in many Scottish regions, where
the standardised language of the educational system comes into conflict with a language that is expressive of place. In Fionn MacColla's
The Albannach, for instance, phonetic transcription of Gaelic speakers'
English is used to mock the inferiorism of their desire for integration
into the imperium of the English language:

He had gone to a meeting of that society which the Gaelic-speaking students
have, for practising the English. Donald MacAskill, M.A., B.Sc., read a paper
on 'The Contribution of the Gael to the Making of the Empire'. . . . For
three-quarters of an hour it was that a Lewis-man had explored a corner of
Canada, a Skyeman had found a river in Australia, a Lochaber man had
given his name to a hill in New Zealand . . . Donald MacAskill, M.A., B.Sc.,
to his peroration: The '45 and the efictions were the Providence of God. But
for them the Highlanders would neffer haff entered into their heritage, the
map would not pee cuffered with Highland names . . .

Murdo said he wished to disagree. They were orgies of rape and theft, of
destruction and bloody murder. Any Highlander who gloried in them was a
slave. Their 'heritage' was a farce and a delusion. It was to clean pots for the
English. Their language was to die in two generations. They deserved it.[30]

In a technique used by many Scottish writers the oral is made to generate a double meaning when transcribed for the eye, as the evictions

[28] George Davie, *The Democratic Intellect* (Edinburgh, 1961).
[29] Lewis Grassic Gibbon, *A Scots Quair* (London, 1946), p. 37.
[30] Fionn MacColla, *The Albannach* (1932; Edinburgh, 1971), pp. 146–8.

in the Highlands become '*efictions*' in the mouths of those who would justify them. A similar dialectic between oral and written is presented in this passage from William McIlvanney's *Docherty*:

'. . . What's wrong with your face, Docherty?'
'Skint ma nose, sur.'
'How?'
'Ah fell an' bumped ma heid in the sheuch, sur.'
'I beg your pardon?'
'Ah fell an' bumped ma heid in the sheuch, sur.'
'I beg your pardon?'
In the pause Conn understands the nature of the choice, tremblingly, compulsively, makes it.
'Ah fell an' bumped ma heid in the sheuch, sur.'
The blow is instant. His ear seems to enlarge, is muffed in numbness . . .
'That, Docherty, is impertinence. You will translate, please, into the mother-tongue.'[31]

The numbed 'ear' signifies the suppression of the oral by the written, the local by a 'mother-tongue' unvoiced by any mother in the novel.

The division between the standard English of novelistic narration and the dialect speech of the characters is often seen as an impediment to successful construction of a novel, a division leading to a necessary incoherence or to the writer's inadequacy in one language or the other. But this is to turn into a binary opposition what, in fact, in the texture of the novels, is not a simple opposition between dialect and standard English, but a series of gradations and distinctions that links the two together and challenges the very exclusivity on which the division between dialect and standard English is based. The necessity of rendering dialect creates a dialectic between the written and spoken, a dialectic which undermines the centrality and certainty of the narrative voice that is aligned with standard English, and therefore with the value systems of integration into the 'higher', the 'educated' culture of that standard English voice.

In this respect, Nan Shepherd's novels of the 1920s and '30s – *The Quarry Wood* and *The Weatherhouse* – represent one of the great achievements of the Scottish regional novel. Shepherd creates a narrative voice which is equally at home in standard (literary) English and in the vernacular, a narrator for whom the use of the vernacular is not a declension into a vulgar form of speech, but a bilingualism necessary to accurately express the world she is describing:

[31] William McIlvanney, *Docherty* (Edinburgh, 1975), p. 109.

Later a powdery sunlight filled the room, irradiating the feathery caddis from the blankets that had drifted into corners. The steer of life floated in from the road. Hens cackled, dogs barked, women scolded, crying on their bairns in sharp resonant voices that carried far through the empty winter air. Peter Mennie stamped along the road with the post-bag, his greeting still in the air when already his voice clanged up from Drocherty. The littlins bickered past from school, chasing cats and hens, flinging stones, calling names after an occasional stranger or carrying on for his benefit a loud and important conversation mainly fictitious. And the bigger the loons, with stolen spunks that had all but burned holes in their pooches through the day, fired the whins along the roadside. Prometheus with a vulture indeed! – They tortured the wrong side of his body, those undiscriminating gods. A good old-fashioned skelping would have served the nickum better. What had he to do with anything as sophisticated as a liver?[32]

The apparently effortless transition from the vernacular, because it is the *mot juste* (caddis, steer), to vernacular usages that are appropriate to her characters (pooches, nickum), to literary usages (Prometheus, undiscriminating gods) allows her to create an ironic juxtaposition between the values of the community she is describing (skelping as retribution) and the values which are brought to it from outside. The narrative voice does not seek to separate itself from the colloquialism of the characters' speech, but allows their vocabulary and speech patterns to become an essential and integral element in its own – just as her central characters will be equally at home in vernacular speech or 'standard' English.

However, her use of language is only a specific instance of a much larger experiment which Shepherd is engaged in, an experiment which is crucial to the development of the regional novel in Scotland. If dialect-speech is the index of a higher rather than a lower form of knowledge and morality, and dialect is the expression of a communal identity set against the demands of individual self-fulfilment defined by integration into the world of English-speakers, then the focus of the novel has to be the community rather than the individual. In Shepherd's novels the role of protagonist is constantly displaced from the individual to the community, and the story of the characters whom we take to be 'central' to the plot are suspended to allow the stories of other characters to intrude, and thereby to emphasise that it is only in relation to the many narratives of the whole community that an individual's story makes any sense. Just as, in his late writing, Burns submerged

[32] Nan Shepherd, *The Quarry Wood* (1928; Edinburgh, 1987), p. 203.

himself into the folk culture of his region and disappeared as an individual artist, so in Shepherd's novels the stories of the central characters
(Martha and *The Quarry Wood*, Garry Forbes in *The Weatherhouse*) are
told through a complex weaving of other narratives in which they seem
to become simply the background characters of some other narrative.
This is not simply an extravagant use of a sub-plot; for Shepherd's
narrator sets out to discomfit our expectations by constantly gesturing
to other stories which the very requirements of the novel would thrust
to the margins of the narrative:

'I suppose it's impossible that you'd ever come across her,' Martha said
when she had told Madge's story.
'Just about it,' said Sally cheerfully. 'Still, there's no knowing. There's
queerer things happen than we've the right to expect.' And she began to tell
her niece the queer things that happen.
'I've had a venturesome life,' said Sally.
A footnote to her life might have run: For venturesome read betrayed,
persecuted, forsaken, hampered and undaunted: but the general public finds
footnotes uncomfortable reading and leaves them alone.[33]

Shepherd's novels are built out of a whole series of footnotes, footnotes
which are a constant revelation of the stories which may seem insignificant and yet without which the supposedly 'central' narrative would
be given an entirely false valuation. Her characters always have to find
their way back to community, to an acceptance of a complex inter-
weaving of multiple voices and narratives as the context of individual
action, and the community is distinguished morally from the bottom
up rather than the top down.
    The irony which pervades Shepherd's narratives is the outcome of a
century of exploration by Scottish novelists of the disjunction between
the educated voice of the narrator and the dialect voice of the characters:
sometimes this takes the form of a central character who, in *writing* his
or her own story, aspires to a position of authority in relation to the
community around him which is mocked by the story itself (Galt,
Annals of the Parish; Stevenson, *The Master of Ballantrae*; Jenkins, *Fergus
Lamont*); sometimes it takes the form of a third-person narrative voice
whose authority is undermined by its distance from dialect voices (as in
George Friel's Glasgow novels); what it produces is an inner dialectic in
which the centrality of the value system that goes with educated speech

[33] *Ibid.*, pp. 181–2.

and writing is counteracted by the voices of the common people who are the true foundation of Scottish culture.

The most powerful versions of this displacement occur when the dialect voice actually takes over the narrative, performing a linguistic equivalent of a revolution in which the voices of power are ousted by the voices of the powerless. The prototype of this is in Scott's *Redgauntlet*, when 'Wandering Willie's Tale' suddenly disrupts the exchange of letters between the educated gentlemen who are the novels' apparent protagonists:

Far and wide was Sir Robert hated and feared. Men thought he had a direct compact with Satan – that he was proof against steel – and that bullets happed aff his buff-coat like hailstanes from a hearth – that he had a mear that would turn a hare on the side of Carrifra-gawns – and muckle to the same purpose, of whilk anon. The best blessing they wared on him was, 'Deil scowp wi' Redgauntlet!' He wasna a bad maister to his ain folk though, and was weel aneugh liked by his tenants.[34]

In *Redgauntlet* the dialect voice is only allowed a brief dominance; its intrusion prefiguring the threat of revolution that is the novel's theme, but it is a technique that was to be used on a grander scale by Lewis Grassic Gibbon in *A Scots Quair*. Gibbon's explicit theme may be the destruction of the peasantry and the development of an industrial society, but it is dramatised as the loss and recovery of a communal voice. The first volume of the trilogy – *Sunset Song* – ends with Chris Guthrie observed in the gossiping communal voice from which she has emerged:

Well, well it might be so and it mightn't; but one night Dave Brown climbed up the hill from the Knapp, to see old Brigson about buying a horse, and heard folk speaking inside the kitchen and he took a bit keek round the door. And there near the fire stood Chris herself, and the Reverend Colquhoun was before her, she was looking up into the minister's face, and he'd both her hands in his. And *Oh my dear, maybe a second Chris, maybe a third, but Ewan has the first for ever!* she was saying.[35]

Chris's marriage to the minister takes her into the educated classes at the very moment when, in the aftermath of the First World War, the peasantry from which she was sprung is being destroyed, and with them the oral traditions through which the novel is narrated. In *Grey Granite*, however, the final part of the trilogy, the communal voice of the folk is recreated among the urban masses, as the voice of Chris's

---

[34] Walter Scott, *Redgauntlet* (1824; London, 1906), p. 113.
[35] Lewis Grassic Gibbon, *A Scots Quair*, p. 190.

son Ewan, educated, English-speaking, merges into a new communal
voice as the workers come under attack from the police during a strike:

Chaps cried *Get on with, Jim, what's wrong?* Syne the news came down, childes
passing it on, their faces twisted with rage or laughing, they hardly bothered
to curse about it, the police were turning the procession back down into Paldy
by way of the wynds. It wasn't to be let near the Town Hall at all, the Provost
had refused to see them or Trease.

   And then you heard something rising in you that hadn't words, the queerest-
like sound, you stared at your mates, a thing like a growl, low and savage, the
same in your throat. And then you were thrusting forward like others – *Never
mind the Bulgars, they can't stop our march!*[36]

The new voice may sound like a 'growl, low and savage' to the ears of
the educated, but it is the voice of a renewed communality, an urban
dialect in the process of formation that will match the old dialect of the
countryside – a prediction, almost, of the estranged and monologuing
voices of James Kelman's protagonists, seeking after community in the
residue of the industrial city, in an urban environment where the isolated individual becomes the site of a multiplicity of competing voices,
a dialogue of dialects no longer distributed between different characters
in the narrative but interiorised in an inner dialectic:

The man frowned as he packed the cans into the bag. He sniffed, pushed the
bag through the space in the grille; then he passed out the bottle of Grouse
and the packets of chocolate and sweeties which Pat stuffed into his pockets.
It was ridiculous. The idea of charging for carrier bags was just so absolutely
fucking ridiculous. And obviously the auld bastard pocketed the five pences
for himself. What chance could there ever be for the world when dirty skunks
like the latter were in positions of power! Durty skinks like the latter, having
arrived via the flagstones of Vulcan, armed with a bunch of fish suppers á la
the good Rossi, whose pathway through the hordes of hysterical flagellants
   Goya. Goya said that. O did he. Yes, he fucking did.[37]

In Kelman's prose the structures, vocabulary and pronunciation of the
oral ('dirty skunks . . . Durty skinks') is interwoven with the organisation and tonality of the literate and the literary ('having arrived via the
flagstones of Vulcan'), but the dialogue between the two has been
internalised into the consciousness of a character whose very identity
is the tormented unresolvability of that opposition. The failure of the
character, however, is the image-in-reverse of the success of the novel,
for in the novel the opposition between the local and the universal,

---

[36] *Ibid.*, p. 395.   [37] James Kelman, *A Disaffection* (1989; London, 1990), p. 258.

between the regional and central has been dissolved in the union of standard and dialect forms of speech, in the destruction of the barriers by which local dialect is excluded from the narrative voice that represents the common language of author and reader.

In the Scottish tradition, the regional novel is not a subset of some more central version of the novel, and the dialect novel not a local version of the metropolitan novel of manners; regionality is part of the insistence that the fundamental truths of Scottish culture are to be found among the folk, rather than among those who have acquired, through careful training of their voices and their writing, an English raised to apparent universality by extirpating all signs of localism. The 'regional' is part of a radical populism that connects the folk collectors of the eighteenth century through the radicals of the nineteenth century and the socialists of the early twentieth to the 'anarchist' opponents of established culture in the late twentieth, a radical populism that raids high culture only to bring it back to earth, back to the housing estate, back to the liberation of the voice of the folk.

III ASSOCIATION AND MEMORY

If Burns is the source of the power and status of the vernacular in Scottish regionalism, it is from the work of his much-derided eighteenth-century competitor for the mantle of most influential Scottish poet – James MacPherson, translator-author of the *Ossian* poems – that other key elements in the Scottish regional novel stem. We can see the impact of *Ossian* in the response of Smollett's travellers in *Humphry Clinker*, when they are in the Highlands.

We have had princely sport in hunting the stag on these mountains – These are the lonely hills of Morven, where Fingal and his heroes enjoyed the same pastime; I feel an enthusiastic pleasure when I survey the brown heath that Ossian was wont to tread; and hear the wind whistle through the grass – When I enter our landlord's hall, I look for the suspended harp of that divine bard, and listen in hopes of hearing the aerial sound of his respected spirit – The poems of Ossian are in every mouth.[38]

The poems of Ossian are in every mouth, of course, in English, but they transform their 'region' from a barren heath to a place imbued with special significance because of its literary connotations. The Highlands was perhaps the first 'region' to be transformed in its significance

---

[38] Smollett, *Humphry Clinker*, p. 277.

by this fusion of landscape and literature, but the transformation which
the *Ossian* poems wrought made them a focus for Scottish Enlightenment theories of art, theories which in turn were to have a profound
influence on the structure of regionalism. At the core of those theories
was the conception of 'association' as the fundamental principle of the
human mind, a conception which was both to justify the local and to
provide the mechanism for its dramatisation.

Although the principle of association as one of the modes of operation of the human mind derived from Locke, and had been imple-
mented in mechanistic fashion by Hartley in his *Observations on Man*,[39] it
was in Hume's work that it was elevated to a metaphysic, constituting
the very basis of reality rather than simply an explanation of a portion
of it. For Hume, the principles by which ideas are associated in the
mind explained not only the operations of the psyche but the very
nature of reality. Following Hume, or his challenger Reid, from whom
derived the 'Common Sense' school of philosophy, several generations
of Scottish theorists worked out a complex psychologism based on the
principle of association, designed both to explain eighteenth century neo-
classicism and the newer emphasis on the sublime. Archibald Alison's
Essays on the Principles of Taste (1790)[40] represent a summation of many of
the theories developed in the previous forty years, and they begin from
the fact that aesthetic experience is not *of* objects of a specific kind but
in a certain operation of the mind:

When any object, either of sublimity or beauty, is presented to the mind, I
believe every man is conscious of a train of thought being immediately
awakened in his imagination, analogous to the character and expression of
the original object. The simple perception of the object, we frequently find, is
insufficient to excite these emotions, unless it is accompanied with this operation of the mind, unless, according to common expression, our imagination is
seized, and our fancy busied in pursuit of all those trains of thought, which
are allied to this character or expression.[41]

Alison unifies the Burkean division between the beautiful and sublime
by making them both versions of the operation of associations: the

[39] For the origins of association theory, see Walter Jackson Bate, *From Classic to Romantic* (Harvard,
    1949), and, in particular, Ernest Lee Tuveson, *The Imagination as a Means of Grace* (Berkeley,
    1960).
[40] Archibald Alison, *Essays on the Nature and Principles of Taste* (Edinburgh, 1790). Alison's essay was
    to become the basis of much nineteenth-century thinking on aesthetic principles through
    Francis Jeffrey's adoption of it in the entry on 'Taste' in the *Encyclopaedia Britannica* (1812).
[41] Alison, *Essays on the Nature and Principles of Taste*, p. 2.

objects themselves are significant only insofar as they have the capacity to stimulate the mind into a train of associative connections, a train which *is* itself the aesthetic experience.

The unity which this creates, however, also poses a problem, the problem which obsessed Scottish aesthetic theory: if the power of art lies in its capacity to stimulate associations, how is there to be any standard of good taste, how are we to distinguish between appropriate and inappropriate associations? The initial answer to this question is posed in terms of neo-classical universalism – that which has survived longest and is most universally appreciated is best; this view is quickly recognised, however, to be a function of education and class, so that 'good taste' itself ceases to be universal and comes to be agreement between those of a certain background who are inducted into taste by having their minds filled, at an early age, with associations appropriate to classical culture:

the time when nature began to appear . . . in another view than as something useful to human life, was, when [we] were engaged in the study of classical literature . . . The beautiful forms of ancient mythology with which the fancy of the poets peopled every element, are now ready to appear in [our] minds upon the prospect of every scene. In most men, at least, the first appearance of poetical imagination is at school, when their imaginations begin to be warmed by the descriptions of ancient poetry, and when they have acquired a sense, as it were, with which they can behold the face of nature.[42]

Training in classical poetry produces the appropriate store of associative connections which allow the natural world to be experienced aesthetically rather than in terms of utility. Differences in background, differences in the kinds of associative patterns which their memory makes possible, will thus distinguish different categories of people, with the consequence that only those with suitable means to stock their memories with appropriate associations and able to avoid corrupting that stock with utilitarian associations, can achieve full aesthetic appreciation:

the diversity of tastes corresponds to the diversity of occupations . . . It is only in the higher stations accordingly or liberal professions of life, that we expect to find men either of delicate or comprehensive taste. The inferior stations of life, by contracting the knowledge and affections of men, within very narrow limits, produces insensibly a similar contraction in their notions of the beautiful and sublime.[43]

[42] *Ibid.*, p. 45.   [43] *Ibid.*, p. 62.

Association theory thus explained current standards of taste. Contained within it, however, was a radical alternative to the social and cultural uniformity of neo-classicism: if aesthetic experience is indeed founded on the quantity and differentiation of memories available to enter into the associative experience, perhaps the minds of those in inferior social situations were just as well-stocked as the minds of the 'higher stations'; perhaps those minds simply responded to different kinds of stimuli; perhaps, indeed, they were stocked with associations more appropriate to the natural world and did not depend on the artifices of past culture for their associative pleasures.

Association theory opened up the possibility that a common mechanism of the mind produced a diversity of aesthetic experiences between which there could be no evaluative distinction: the only basis of discrimination was the number and intensity of the associations which the object produced or a particular mind experienced. Thus any object was capable of being the focus of aesthetic experience, and any mind might have a store of memories which could generate the kind of sustained train of associative connections that constitute the very essence of aesthetic experience. By this means, neo-classic universalism is reversed into the most detailed particularism:

There is no man, who has not some interesting associations with particular scene, or airs, or books, and who does not feel their beauty or sublimity enhanced to him, by such connections. The view of the house where one was born, of the school where one was educated, and where the gay years of infancy were passed, is indifferent to no man. They recall so many images of past happiness and past affections, they are connected with so many strong or valued emotions, and lead altogether to so long a train of feelings and recollections, that there is hardly any scene which one ever beholds with so much rapture.[44]

The purely local becomes the most powerful of associative influences: this may mean that the most powerful associations are always uniquely personal and incommunicable, but that simply switches focus from the object of attention to the operation of the mind in the process of association. What is interesting is not the particular place but the interaction of the place with a mind fitted to experience it in a particular way:

I approached my native north, for such I esteemed it, with that enthusiasm which romantic and wild scenery inspires in the lovers of nature. . . . The Cheviots rose before me in frowning majesty; not, indeed, with the sublime

44 *Ibid.*, p. 15.

variety of rock and cliff which characterizes mountains of the primary class, but huge, round-headed, and clothed with a dark robe of russet, gaining, by their extent and desolate appearance, an influence upon the imagination, as a desert district possessing a character of its own.[45]

In Scott's *Rob Roy*, Frank Osbaldistone approaches a landscape which is 'native', a landscape uniquely different from general categories, such as the sublime, and yet 'possessing a character of its own'. The latter phrase points in two directions: the landscape has its own unique characteristics which make it interesting, but it also 'possesses the character' of those who have grown up in it by being the foundation of their associational processes. They are in its possession: to understand the landscape is to be aware of it in their minds; to understand their minds one has to know the landscape. Landscape is knowable only through the return of the 'native'.[46]

It is on the basis of this fusion of a particular environment with the particularity of the mind 'possessed' by it that regionalism came to be founded: the territory of a particular region is a blank until infused with a memory which brings it to life by being stimulated to the recollection of its past. The universalism of classical culture is displaced by a particularism that requires the reader to read works of literature by learning to understand the environment in which they are set. As Hugh Blair insists in his discussion of *Ossian*:

Every country has a scenery peculiar to itself: and the imagery of a good poet will exhibit it. For as he copies after nature, his allusions will of course be taken from those objects which he sees around him, and which have struck his fancy. For this reason, in order to judge of the propriety of poetical imagery, we ought to be, in some measure, acquainted with the natural history of the country where the scene of the poem is laid.[47]

A double process is involved in the reading of these particularist works of literature: on the one hand, the reader has to acquire 'the natural history' of the environment that will make it meaningful; on the other, the work of literature peoples the landscape with precisely the stock of

---

[45] Walter Scott, *Rob Roy* (1817; London, 1906), p. 37.

[46] The title of Hardy's novel is appropriate here, since Hardy was deeply influenced by associationist theories of art: see Tom Paulin, *Thomas Hardy and the Poetry of Perception* (London, 1975).

[47] Hugh Blair, *The Works of Ossian, the Son of Fingal, Translated from the Galic Language by James MacPherson*, 2 vols. (London, 1765), 2, p. 408. I am indebted for the background to the publication of *Ossian* and for the development of Blair's theories to Steve Rizza, 'A Bulky and Foolish Treatise? Hugh Blair's *Critical Dissertation* Reconsidered', in Howard Gaskill (ed.), *Ossian Revisited* (Edinburgh, 1991).

associations which make it aesthetically interesting. Literature and environment feed into each other in a mutually enriching fashion: nature becomes more associatively interesting because of the literature which has been set in it and the literature becomes more associatively charged because of the significance of its environment.

Out of associationist theory there develops what might be described as psychological regionalism: each region creates a certain kind of psyche because of the associations with which it stocks the mind; each psyche is regional because of the ways its associative processes work; the interconnection of mind and region is stimulating to the reader's associative processes precisely because they are so different from his or her own. It is from this necessary fusion of present place with past associations that the regional novel takes its reminiscent character: the power of the place can only be experienced by seeing it in the perspective of an accumulation of past associations; it is not the immediately present landscape or environment which constitutes regionality, but a landscape in time, suffused with memories. John Buchan's *Witchwood* (1927), begins with a paradigmatic associative structure:

The old folk are gone, too, and their very names are passing from the countryside . . . The farmers are mostly new men, and even the peasant, who should be the enduring stock, has shifted his slow bones. I learned from the postman that in Woodilee today there was no Monfries, no Sprot, but one Pennecuik, and only two bearers of the names of Ritchie and Shillinglaw, which had once been as plentiful as ragwort. In such a renovated world it was idle to hope to find surviving the tales which had perplexed my childhood.[48]

The 'renovated world' is a world which has lost its memory, but to the eyes of Buchan's narrator there comes a moment when the landscape suddenly inspires in him, or attracts out of him, a buried memory 'and I knew that I saw Woodilee as no eye had seen it for three centuries':

I realised that all memory of the encircling forest had not gone from Woodilee in my childhood, though the name of Melanudrigill had been forgotten. I could hear old Jock Dodds, who had been keeper on Calidon for fifty years, telling tales for my delectation, as he sat and smoked on the bog stone by the smithy. He would speak of his father, and his father's father . . .[49]

Present is connected back to past by a series of linked associative memories which are the foundation of the region's identity in time, as opposed to its simple appearance in contemporary space.

[48] John Buchan, *Witchwood* (1927; Edinburgh 1988), p. 2.   [49] *Ibid.*, p. 4.

The tradition of associationist aesthetics is very different from the high Romantic conception of the imagination: association theory does not validate the imagination's ability to offer transcendence of the terms of human life and does not make the human mind a replica of God's original act of creation. Association is a humanist basis for aesthetic experience, linking the perceiving subject with the world by looping through the past as created and constructed by other human beings. Coleridge himself commented on this difference when he compared his own imagination with Walter Scott's:

Dear Sir Walter Scott and myself were exact but harmonious opposites in this; – that every old ruin, hill, river or tree called up in his mind a host of historical or biographical associations . . . whereas for myself, notwithstanding Dr Johnson, I believe I should walk over the plain of Marathon without taking more interest in it than in any other plain of similar features.[50]

Landscape is for Scott, as James Reed has argued, defined by the relationship between humanity and history, rather than between humanity and God, and its significance, therefore, is precisely *regional*: perception of the meaning of a landscape requires 'seeing' the past in it, and adducing from the remnants of the past the customs and manners of the human beings who were shaped by their environment:

What [Scott] does is see man, and the works of man, in a total landscape: land, buildings, people, manners, history, fused by time. . . . Scott's man leaves in his wake ruined towers, decaying abbeys, flints, spearheads, broken helmets, bones; legacies of feudal faith and a romantic chivalry. Every walk or ride with Scott was a History Trail imbued, like his writing, with the anecdotal, reminiscent richness of the experienced and informed observer.[51]

The observer's memory, with its stock of associations, connects with the landscape's remnants of human action to produce a train of associations that can reconstruct a particular way of life. A landscape does not become truly 'regional' until it is both the origin – in terms of the influence of environment on manners – and the stimulus – in terms of prompting recollection of the past by virtue of associations – of a reconstructed identity, looping from present into past and back to present again through the memories of an appropriately mindful observer.

The low status generally accorded to the regional novel may well be a function of the low status given to associative memory when

[50] Coleridge, *Table Talk*, 4 August 1833; quoted by James Reed, *Sir Walter Scott: Landscape and Locality* (London, 1980), p. 10.
[51] Reed, *Sir Walter Scott: Landscape and Locality*, p. 9.

compared to the powers of the imagination in our primarily romantic aesthetics. But as Reed emphasises, this mode of observation has a very different intentionality from romantic modes of perception with their emphasis on memory as preserving those 'spots of time' which give us access to a transcendent truth. Associative memory takes us back into the world as the formative environment of human character and also as the recollection, in its scattered debris and in its names, of human actions in time. It is memory in service of the secular world of a humanity under continual threat from time's erasure of their actions, rather than memory in service of the imagination's return to its origin in the oneness of the Godhead: it is memory in service of difference rather than oneness.

The two typical elements of associative art – the encounter with a new object which stimulates association by its strangeness, and the return to an almost forgotten personal past through the re-establishment of links of memory – form the archetypal plot structures of psychological regionalism. The first is the novel of travel and encounter in a strange environment such as Scott regularly uses when he sets his heroes to travel into alien territories. It is a plot which mimics the experience of the reader as s/he travels into a world whose manners and customs are unknown and without established and governing associative principles. The second is the novel of reminiscence, in which the region operates as stimulus to the re-collection of a personal past associated with a specific environment. In the first we travel in space in order to add to our stock of memories, in the second we travel in time to re-encounter lost memories. In the first we make sense of the strange by trying to relate it to the familiar, as Scott has Waverley do when he first enters a Scottish village and tries to relate the scene to memories of certain kinds of art:

Three or four village girls, returning from the well or brook with pitchers and pails upon their heads, formed more pleasing objects; and, with their thin, short gowns and single petticoats, bare arms, legs, and feet, uncovered heads, and braided hair, somewhat resembled Italian forms of landscape. Nor could the lover of picturesque have challenged either the elegance of their costume, or the symmetry of their shape . . .[52]

In the second we try to make sense of the past by re-ordering it in the context of a familiar landscape, as in Stuart Hood's *A Storm from Paradise*:

⁵² Walter Scott, *Waverley* (1814; Harmondsworth, 1972), p. 75.

Each time I return I make my way to the fort and look out over the countryside in which, before these peripeties, I was formed, where so many things were
seen, heard, felt to which I had no answers: mysteries spun by my parents, by
visitors to the house, by the men and women I met in the streets of the village,
to all of which I have still in some cases no solution and so can allow my
fantasies to expand over that landscape in a game of recall and mystification
that is at once a pain and a pleasure.[53]

The final sentence points towards what is typical of both of these forms
– the disjunction between reality and recollection, between personal
memory and a real history; it is in the ironies of that disjunction that
the most significant novelistic developments were to be made. At one
end of the spectrum there is Scott's Waverley, who travels in a world
that is in large part the creation of his own mind in defiance of the
actual – 'so much pleased with the placid ideas of rest and seclusion
excited by this confined and quiet scene, that he forgot the misery and
dirt of the hamlet he had left behind him';[54] delighted by his own associations, Waverley continually fails to see the reality behind the picturesque. At the other end of the spectrum is the Reverend Balwhidder in
Galt's *Annals of the Parish*, a narrator whose memories of each year of
his time in the parish of Dalmailing (1760–1810) forms an associative
chain which defines the nature of his psyche, while at the same time
being played off against the associations that the reader will have of
the same years: indeed, in Balwhidder's case it is often the fact that he
has so few associations with some of the most remarkable years of
European history that is striking:

Whether it was owing to the malady of my imagination, throughout the greatest part of this year, or that really nothing particular did happen to interest
me, I cannot say, but it is very remarkable that I have nothing remarkable to
record.[55]

Waverley and Balwhidder are the opposite ends of the same process,
but the outcome is remarkably similar: Waverley encounters the strangeness of a new region as a stimulus to associations so rich and fertile
that he cannot see what is actually in front of him, while poverty of
recollection makes Balwhidder blind to the world around him by the
pressure of endless triviality. They represent the two limits of the associative process: one entirely drawn from literature and disconnected
from reality, the other trapped entirely in the daily – and forgettable

---

[53] Stuart Hood, *A Storm from Paradise* (1985; London, 1988), pp. 17–18.   [54] Scott, *Waverley*, p. 77.
[55] John Galt, *The Annals of the Parish* (1821; Oxford, 1967), p. 141.

– realities of mundane life. The structural pattern they establish has its modern equivalents in the protagonists of novels like Robin Jenkins's *Fergus Lamont* and Janice Galloway's *The Trick is to Keep Breathing.*[56]

The ironies of the associative novel of regional experience go back to the debate over the Ossianic poems: are they the real recollection of primitive epics still in the mouths of the people of the Highlands, real associations with this landscape, or are they fakes, an associative process imposed on the world? The danger of the associative process is that the reader/traveller will experience the associations with no less intensity because they are false; indeed, after a time it may become impossible to discriminate between the real and the false, so imbued is the landscape with associations garnered from art. The truth or falsehood of the associations has to be justified from some other source, by some other process of deduction, which is why the debate about the Ossianic poems turned not only on their power or their effectiveness, but on their relationship to history, a relationship which was to provide one of the fundamental and enduring narrative paradigms of the regional novel in Scotland.

IV FICTION AND HISTORY

Association theory was to have profound consequences in Scottish culture: as Adam Smith, following Hume, was to note, scientific experiment did not provide us with truth, but better associative processes, and nowhere was this more evident than in the understanding of the past, for the mind,

endeavors to find out something which may fill up the gap, which, like a bridge, may so far at least unite those seemingly distant objects, as to render the passage of the thought betwixt them smooth, and natural, and easy. The supposition of a chain of intermediate, though invisible, events, which succeed each other in a train similar to that in which the imagination has been accustomed to move, and which link together those two disjointed appearances, is the only means by which the imagination can fill up this interval, is the only bridge which, if one may say so, can smooth its passage from one object to another.[57]

[56] Robin Jenkins, *Fergus Lamont* (Edinburgh, 1978); Janice Galloway, *The Trick is to Keep Breathing* (Edinburgh, 1989).
[57] Adam Smith, *Astronomy*, 2, pp. 7–8, quoted in W. P. D. Wightman and J. C. Bryce (eds.), *Adam Smith, Essays on Philosophical Subjects, with Dugald Stewart's Account of Adam Smith*, Ian Ross (ed.), (Oxford, 1980), p. 19.

The demands of associative linkage were to provide one of the justi-
fications for what came to be known as 'conjectural history', which
Dugald Stewart, in his account of the life of Adam Smith, presents in
the following terms:[58]

Whence the origin of the different sciences and of the different arts; and by
what chain has the mind been led from the first rudiments to their last and
most refined improvements? Whence the astonishing fabric of the political
union; the fundamental principles of which are common to all governments;
and the different forms which civilized society has assumed in different ages of
the world? On most of these subjects very little information is to be expected
from history; . . . In want of this direct evidence, we are under a necessity
of supplying the place of fact by conjecture; and when we are unable to
ascertain how men have actually conducted themselves upon particular
occasions, of considering in what manner they are likely to have proceeded,
from the principles of their nature, and the circumstances of their external
situation.

'Conjectural history' provides a hypothesis about the total structure
of human development, one which cannot be proven but which will
account for such evidence as we have about the human past: from it
derives the conception of human society developing through fixed stages,
each with a social structure appropriate to the economic underpinnings
of the society. MacPherson's 'translations' were not constructed simply
to show off the quality of a past literature: they were part of the project
of justifying 'conjectural history' by illustrating with further evidence
the relationship between the stages of history and specific kinds of culture.
For MacPherson and Blair, the Ossian poems provided exemplary evidence that the underlying development of human society corresponded
to the narrative of 'conjectural history', and that a Homeric style of
literature would therefore exist in each society at an appropriate stage
in its development. Homeric epic was not a unique event but simply
the expression of a stage of human development; the art of the earliest
stages of human society will be

Irregular and unpolished [as] we may expect the productions of uncultivated
ages to be; but abounding, at the same time, with that enthusiasm, that vehe-
mence and fire, which are the soul of poetry. For many circumstances of
those times which we call barbarous, are favourable to the poetic spirit. That
state in which human nature shoots wild and free, though unfit for other
improvements, certainly encourages the high exertions of fancy and passion.[59]

---

[58] *Ibid.*, p. 292.   [59] Blair, *The Works of Ossian*, 2, p. 314.

Equally, modern societies will show a severe decline in the power of the poetic imagination because modern societies are, through their development of complex organisations and civilised manners, essentially prosaic.

What was most striking about the application of the theories of conjectural history, however, was not its stadialist conception of the past (which was common to all the Scottish Enlightenment theorists and was to be taken over by Marx) but that it turned history into geography: to travel into the Highlands is not simply to travel into a backward, unimproved world, nor is it simply to travel into a particular kind of daunting landscape – it is to travel in time, it is to experience the most distant past as a living reality on one's own doorstep. Even more, however, geography becomes psychology, for travel in space becomes an encounter with the state of mind of humanity at an earlier stage in its development. It is not a *different* society that the traveller encounters by journeying into the landscape of an earlier society: it is the original version of one's own, a literal return to origins.

The triptych of history = geography = psychology as the outcome of conjectural history, was to be incorporated into Scottish regionalism and made the bases on which the local could be seen as a paradigm of the universal. Far from being marginal or eccentric, the local represents the embodiment of a particular stage of history and becomes the essential medium for exploring the trajectory of history: the distinction of the different stages of history can only be seen in and through the contrast between different locales.

We see this at work in Scott when Waverley travels to the Highlands, because his journey in space becomes a journey in time (back into a primitive world) and that journey in time becomes a psychological journey in which imagination displaces reason – precisely because imagination is the dominant faculty among primitive peoples. Waverley submits to his own imagination because that imagination has now found an environment that liberates it from the constraints of the rational order of a developed society. The revolt of the Jacobite rebels may thus be bound to fail because it is a revolt of an earlier stage of historical development against a later one, an earlier form of the operation of the human mind against one that has supplanted it, but the mind in the process of aesthetic reflection moves counter to the world of progress and returns us to our historical origins. Conjectural history's enfolding of the totality of historical development within a specific regional environment becomes one of the key narrative principles of the Scottish regional novel. It is in this sense that Galt saw his Ayrshire novels as 'theoretical histories',[60] allowing us to discover the universal agencies of historical change within a specific regional context. The region becomes, as it were, the channel through which history must pass as it moves from stage to stage, and it is only in the regional environment that the real structure of that history can be discerned.

What is crucial, however, is that conjectural history shifted the locus of historical development from the political to the social: the centres of political power (and therefore the geographical centres of power) are not where you need to look for the processes of history. They will be observable most clearly where the political is submerged in the social, rather than the other way round – in the novel of provincial or regional life rather than the novel of metropolitan life. If the broad scope of conjectural history can best be isolated in the analysis of the remnants of Gaelic culture in the Highlands (as in *Rob Roy*), then the specific transitions of history can best be discovered in the apparently provincial world of places like Galt's small-town Ayrshire. In Galt's novels we do not find the reminiscent regionalism of *Castle Rackrent*, with its gesture towards a past that has been made redundant by progress; rather we are presented with the conflict between the dynamics of two kinds of narrative – the long, slow but sustained narrative of social change and the brief and episodic narrative of ordinary life. It is the disjunction between these two narratives which – in novels like *Annals of the Parish* and *The Ayrshire Legatees* – Galt exploits, and if his technique has often been mocked because it ended in the sentimentalism of late nineteenth-century Scottish 'Kailyard' writing, it is among the earliest explorations of what came to be one of the most powerful traditions in nineteenth-century English writing; the novel of provincial life as the index of historical change.

Conjectural history, however, is not only used in this microscopic fashion by Scottish writers. In the twentieth century particularly, it has provided the narrative structure by which the totality of the historical process can be dramatised in a single narrative by focusing on a specific region. It is this that Grassic Gibbon makes the structural principle of *A Scots Quair*, taking us from the Druids, those 'coarse devils of men in the times long syne, they'd climb up and sing their foul heathen songs around the stones; and if they met a Christian missionary they'd

---

[60] John Galt, *Literary Life* (1834), pp. i, 226. For a discussion of the way in which Galt uses this conception see James Kinsley, 'Introduction', *Annals of the Parish* (Oxford, 1986), pp. vi–x.

gut him as soon as look at him',[61] to the Depression of the 1930s and the communist activism that foretells the next stage of history. That total narrative, however, is symbolically re-enacted in the lives of the principal characters, for each volume of the trilogy represents not just a particular slice of the period between 1908 and the 1930s, but the stages of the development of history in its entirety as we move from the peasant community to the small industrial town to the modern city, and the alienating effects of each of those stages is represented in the dominant psychological traits of the characters.

Such use of conjectural history does not derive simply from the fact that it was a key part of the Scottish intellectual tradition: in a society deprived of a political history, with no significant political events around which to structure the sense of its own development, conjectural history provides both a narrative foundation and, in its emphasis on the *social*, a sense of the significance of local action. The narrative of such novels – as, for instance, in Naomi Mitchison's *The Bull Calves* (1948) – allows characters to re-enact or re-present the defining stages of historical development within their own local cultural environment. Conjectural history thus instantiates the large-scale movement of human development at the local level, enabling apparently provincial history to acquire significance by becoming the microcosmic model through which universal developments can be conjecturally discerned.

The equivalence of psychology and geography, however, have provided an alternative model for the application of conjectural history, one in which the geographically distinct becomes the location of a past whose psychological values have been lost to more progressive societies. Adam Ferguson recognised in his *Essay on Civil Society*[62] that progress was not always gain, and that there were, in primitive societies, virtues other than the power of the imagination which had been lost to more progressive peoples – a point that Scott dramatises in *Waverley*, when Evan offers himself and five others to die instead of his clan chief.[63] Rather than the region being the environment in which history's totality can be dramatised, the region becomes the repository of a past which the progress of history may *seem* to have made redundant, but a past which, through regionalism, can be re-encountered and its values – if only at a psychological level – re-incorporated into the modern world.

---

[61] Grassic Gibbon, *A Scots Quair*, p. 23.
[62] See Fania Oz-Salzberger, 'Introduction', *Adam Ferguson: An Essay on the History of Civil Society* (Cambridge, 1995), pp. xix–xx.
[63] Scott, *Waverley*, ch. 68.

From *Ossian* and Scott stems a tradition of this regionalism of time, in which the rural environments of Scotland – and particularly the Highlands and Islands – come to represent earlier stages of human history, waiting to be encountered as a psychological predecessor of or, indeed, an alternative to modernity. This may offer itself as the escapism of the Celtic Twilight in the novels and stories of Fiona MacLeod, but it also provides a fundamental moral and structuring principle in the novels of Neil Gunn and George Mackay Brown, as they wrestle with the destructive consequences of modernity. In Gunn's *The Silver Darlings* (1941), for instance, the clearance of people from the land and the establishment of new communities on the shore, is enacted as a series of journeys by young Finn – journeys that move progressively further out into the new environment of the ocean but which, at the same time, enact a passage back to earlier times, with an accompanying psychological recuperation of the culture which the Clearances are in the process of destroying. The region – those fishing communities of the Moray Firth in which Gunn set so many of his novels – gains its identity by being the recollection of an earlier Celtic culture which seems to be on the edge of extinction. Rather than the tragic destruction of an earlier stage of history by a later that we see in *Waverley*, Gunn achieves a reversal of the necessity of historical destruction by having the new community discover its identity in and through the older one. Similarly in Mackay Brown's *Greenvoe* (1972), an Orkney island succumbs to the forces of progress in the form of a defence establishment that requires the clearing of the people from the island; though this generation may have been defeated, their island continues to exist not simply as a territory, but as a psychological environment which continues in memories and rituals that will, in the end, reclaim it. The region may represent a past in relation to the eyes of modernity, one already enlarged by progress, but through landscape and the memories that haunt it, the region retains the power to resist incorporation into the unidirectional development of history and so continues to offer an alternative to it.

Indeed, it is arguable that these two models of conjectural history are typical of Lowland and Highland Scotland. In Lowland Scotland the tradition exploits the region as microcosmic model of the trajectory of history. In the Highlands and Islands, however, regionalism offers itself as an alternative to historical progress – or, at any rate, as a dramatisation of values that are lost in the process of modernisation. The division between the meaning and significance of these two forms of regionality has become part of the discourse of the Scottish novel, a counterpoint through which alternative figurations of the value of historical progress can be dramatised. Thus the movement between different kinds of regionality – with accompanying shifts in historical perspective and psychology – is dramatised in novels such as Gunn's *The Serpent* (1943), which moves between Highlands and Lowlands and re-enacts the whole process of Enlightenment, industrialisation and the destruction of Gaelic-speaking communities in the life of one man, or Robin Jenkins's *The Changeling* (1958), with its shifts between Glasgow slums and the landscape of Argyle, and *Fergus Lamont* (1979), which, like *The Serpent*, tries to encompass all the dimensions of Scotland's past through its geographical shifts from urban slums to Western Isles. This structure also forms the underpinning of Alasdair Gray's *Lanark*, a conjectural history of the future as well as the past, and one in which the Highland landscape provides a double perspective to match the double narrative of realistic Glasgow urbanism and fantasy science fiction:[64]

From grey rooftops on the left rose the mock Gothic spire of the university, the Kilpatrick hills, patched with woodlands and with the clear distant top of Ben Lomond behind the eastward slope. Thaw thought it queer that a man on that summit, surrounded by the highlands and overlooking deep lochs, might see with a telescope this kitchen window, a speck of light in the low haze to the south.

To be able to look from both directions, from the region of urban Glasgow, representative of modernity, and from the region of the Highlands, representative of ancient memory, has been the burden of much Scottish writing over the past two centuries, turning the stages of conjectural history into visible geographical territory in the multiplicity of Scotland's landscapes and the histories inscribed in them. In the abutment of Lowland and Highland it as though the beginning and the end of the whole historical process sit side by side with one another, and regionality has become emblematic, as it were, of a double directionality, in which the insistent forward progress of history is countermanded by the insistent recollective force of associative memory.

It is this double directionality of the regional that Neil Gunn dramatises in *Highland River* (1937): as the central character moves back against the direction of the river, against the direction of history, re-encountering both his own early life and the life of his people through an associative memory that 'evokes immense perspective in human time; tribes hunting

[64] Alasdair Gray, *Lanark* (Edinburgh, 1981), p. 275.

and trekking through lands beyond the horizons of history';[65] and it is the accruals of such memory that make resistance to modernity possible:[66]

Man would not endure for ever the horror of that girl trapped in the slums. If not openly, then by secret violent ways he will destroy the black cage. Kenn, who has never belonged to revolutionary political societies, knows what moves them. Old as the rocks, nameless as the old woman, warm as sunshine, insinuating as the wind, is this river that flows down the straths of time.

The mind flows back against the river flowing forward; they are emblematic of the region as associative recollection and model of historical progress, each requiring and renovating the other, a unique environment in which the intertwining of geography and history and psychology is both an acceptance of the processes of time and a recuperation of the past, is both a lingering sense of loss and the sense of a past still lingering in the environment if only the memory can reach out and connect with it. At the core of the regional novel are magical, haunted places, dynamoes of memory, places – 'as though the spots had absorbed in some mysterious way not only the thought but the very being of the dark men of pre-history.'[67]

v

There are important Scottish writers who are not subscribers to the traditions of Scottish regionalism – one thinks, for instance, of Muriel Spark, Alan Massie, Ian Banks and A. L. Kennedy among contemporary writers – and there are writers who exploit regionalism occasionally and variously – Robert Louis Stevenson and Margaret Oliphant in the nineteenth century – but much contemporary Scottish novel-writing continues to be rooted in the vitality of the local. Such a dominance of regionalism has often led to the perception that the Scottish novel in the earlier part of the twentieth century is 'traditional' and 'anti-experimental' (MacDiarmid, after all, described Neil Gunn's novels as taking place in 'Scottshire'). But in its commitment to the culture of the 'folk' – whether the 'folk' of traditional rural communities or the 'folk' of the industrial city – the Scottish novel, almost uniquely, places the local and the regional as the main strand of its traditions, and that requires a very different kind of experimentalism from the experiments

---

[65] Neil Gunn, *Highland River* (1937; London, 1974), p. 121.   [66] *Ibid.*, p. 197.   [67] *Ibid.*, p. 61.

of high modernism: not escape from the 'nightmare of history' but reconnection with the conjecture of a history; not assumption of the totality of the English language as one's own, but the creation of an environment in which there are no boundaries between standard and dialect forms of speech. It is from within the apparently restrictive boundaries of regionality that the imposed boundaries of history and of language can be breached.

CHAPTER 10

Mapping the modern city: Alan Sillitoe's Nottingham novels

Stephen Daniels and Simon Rycroft

As a literary form, the novel is inherently geographical. The world of the novel is made up of locations and settings, arenas and boundaries, perspectives and horizons. Various places and spaces are occupied or envisaged by the novel's characters, by the narrator and by audiences as they read. Any one novel may present a field of different, sometimes competing, forms of geographical knowledge and experience, from a sensuous awareness of place to an educated idea of region and nation. These various geographies are coordinated by various kinds of temporal knowledge and experience, from circumscribed routines to linear notions of progress or transformation.[1]

From its formulation in the eighteenth century, the novel has been a speculative instrument for exploring and articulating those material, social and mental transformations we call modernisation. The novel was first associated with the transformation of London into a world metropolis, representing the capitalist city to its bourgeois citizens as 'accessible, comprehensible and controllable'.[2] Its scope was not confined to the city; early novelists charted transformations in the countryside and colonies too. The refinement of the novel as a genre was commensurate with the refinement of a number of geographical discourses, such as town planning, estate improvement, cartography and topographical painting, which surveyed and re-ordered the spaces of the modernising

We wish to thank Alan Sillitoe for his co-operation. Robert Bartram, Zena Forster, John Giggs, John Lucas and David Matless offered helpful comments on earlier drafts of this chapter.

[1] J. A. Kestner, *The Spatiality of the Novel* (Detroit, 1978); Yi Fu Tuan, 'Literature and Geography' in David Ley and Marwyn Samuels (eds.), *Humanistic Geography: Prospects and Problems* (1978), pp. 194–206; John Barrell, 'Geographies of Hardy's Wessex', *Journal of Historical Geography*, vol. 8 (1982), pp. 347–61 (reprinted in the present volume); Edward Said, 'Jane Austen and Empire', in Terry Eagleton (ed.), *Raymond Williams: Critical Perspectives* (Cambridge), pp. 150–64.

[2] J. Bender, *Imagining the Penitentiary: Fiction and Architecture of Mind in Eighteenth Century England* (Chicago, 1987), p. 65.

world.[3] From the time of Defoe, the novel has been fashioned and refashioned as an instrument for representing various geographies in different phases, forms and sites of modernisation.[4]

In this chapter we examine the geographies of novels by Alan Sillitoe set in and around Nottingham. We consider how the novels explore conflicts in the modernisation of working-class areas of the city from the 1920s to the 1950s, in particular the clearance of slums, the building of new housing estates and the emergence of a consumer culture. It was a time when the city corporation, proud of its progressive social and economic planning, promoted Nottingham as 'the modern city'. We focus on the geographies of the novels' Nottingham born male protagonists, local rebel Arthur Seaton in *Saturday Night and Sunday Morning* (1958), RAF conscript Brian Seaton in *Key to the Door* (1961) and *The Open Door* (1989) and internationalist guerilla Frank Dawley in *The Death of William Posters* (1965). These novels take us beyond transformations of mid-century Nottingham to transformations overseas, to the violent ending of colonial rule in Malaya and Algeria.

We situate these novels in terms of a number of Sillitoe's other writings: autobiography, travel writing, literary criticism, poetry, political journalism.[5] We also consider a range of other cultural discourses which bear upon the novels, including aerial photography, urban sociology, and classical mythology. Above all we wish to show the importance of maps, map reading and map-making to the geographies of the novels. This was the subject of an interview that we conducted with Alan Sillitoe in 1991 which provides a main source for this chapter.[6]

---

[3] Simon Varey, *Space and the Eighteenth-century English Novel* (Cambridge, 1990); Nicholas Alfrey and Stephen Daniels (eds.), *Mapping the Landscape: Essays on Art and Cartography* (Nottingham, 1990); Stephen Daniels, 'Re-visioning Britain: Mapping and Landscape Painting, 1750–1830', in Katherine Baetjer, *Glorious Nature: British Landscape Painting, 1750–1850* (New York, 1993), pp. 61–72.

[4] Ian Watt, *The Rise of the Novel* (Harmondsworth, 1957); Raymond Williams, *The Country and the City* (London, 1973); Malcolm Bradbury, 'The Cities of Modernism', in Malcolm Bradbury and James Mcfarlane (eds.), *Modernism* (Harmondsworth, 1976), pp. 96–104; Michael Seidel, *Epic Geography: James Joyce's Ulysses* (Princeton, 1976); Marshall Berman, *All That is Solid Melts Into Air: The Experience of Modernity* (London, 1983); Edward Said, *Culture and Imperialism* (New York, 1993).

[5] Sillitoe's many works are catalogued in David E. Gerard, *Alan Sillitoe: A Bibliography* (London, 1988) along with many works of criticism and commentary. This has proved a valuable resource for this chapter. Also valuable is the Sillitoe collection at the Central Library, Nottingham, especially the file of newspaper cuttings on his early career. The most comprehensive work of criticism on Sillitoe is Stanley S. Atherton, *Alan Sillitoe: A Critical Assessment* (London, 1979). A study of Sillitoe with points of connection with this article is H. M. Daleski, 'The Novelist as Map Maker' in Hedwig Bock and Albert Werthein (eds.), *Essays on the Contemporary British Novel* (Frankfurt, 1986).

[6] An edited transcript of this interview is provided in Simon Rycroft, *Ordinance and Order in Alan Sillitoe's Fictional Topography*, Working Paper, no. 13, Department of Geography, University of Nottingham, 1991.

Firstly we will examine the issue of mapping in relation to Sillitoe's life and work, his literary influences and the modernisation of Nottingham. Secondly we will consider the connections between mapping, modernism and masculinity. The third and largest part of the chapter analyses the texts and contexts of the novels. Finally we compare the geographies of Nottingham in these novels with geographies of the city in official and academic publications of the time.

In this chapter we try to re-vision the relationship between 'geography and literature'[7] in a way which takes account of some recent developments in cultural geography and literary criticism.[8] We consider geography and literature not as the conjunction of two essentially distinct, coherent disciplines, or orders of knowledge – objective and subjective, real and imaginative, and so – but as a field of textual genres – the novel, the poem, the travel guide, the map, the regional monograph – with complex overlaps and interconnections. We have brought out both the worldliness of literary texts and the imaginativeness of geographical texts. The imaginativeness of texts consists in the images they express, in the way they construct, through modes of writing or composition, and however empirically, particular and partial views of the world. The worldliness of texts consists in the various contexts – biographical, economic, institutional, geographical – which are entailed by texts and make them intelligible.

MAPS AND THE MAN

Home is like a fortress of an army which prides itself on its mobility . . . Departing from the base, feet define geography, the eyes observe and systematize it . . . As the base line in surveying is essential for the formation of a map and all points on it, so the connected points of birth, place, and upbringing are – for any person, and even more so for a writer – factors never to be relinquished.[9]

---

[7] Douglas C. D. Pocock (ed.), *Humanistic Geography and Literature* (London, 1981); William E. Mallory and Paul Simpron-Housely (eds.), *Geography and Literature: A Meeting of the Disciplines* (Syracuse, 1987).

[8] Trevor J. Barnes and James S. Duncan (eds.), *Writing Worlds: Discourse, Text and Metaphor in the Representation of Landscape* (London, 1992); Felix Driver, 'Geography's Empire: Histories of Geographical Knowledge', *Society and Space*, vol. 10 (1992), pp. 23–40; Stephen Daniels, *Fields of Vision: Landscape Imagery and National Identity in England and the United States* (Cambridge and Princeton, 1993); Edward Said, *The World, the Text and the Critic* (London, 1983); John Barrell (ed.), *Painting and the Politics of Culture: New Essays on British Art* (Oxford, 1992).

[9] Alan Sillitoe, 'We all start from home', *Bulletin de la Société des Anglicistes de l'Enseignment Supérieur*, September 1987, pp. 6–16.

Alan Sillitoe was born and raised in the Radford area of Nottingham, a nineteenth-century working-class suburb to the west of the city centre. Sillitoe recalled the Radford of his childhood as a labyrinthine world:

Even when you knew every junction, twitchell and double entry (a concealed trackway which, connecting two streets, figured high in tactics of escape and manoeuvre) you never could tell when a gas lamp glowed that someone in the nearby dark was not using its light as an ambush pen. Neither did you know what waited behind the corner it stood on . . . You invented perils, exaggerated pitfalls, occasionally felt that you even called them up. Potholes became foxholes, and foxholes as often or not turned into underground caverns full of guns and ammunition, food, and later, more gold than Monte Cristo ever dreamed of. In such streets you could outdream everybody.[10]

As a child Sillitoe envisaged his neighbourhood in terms of the underground worlds of the novels which then dominated his reading: *The Count of Monte Cristo* and, more strongly still, *Les Misérables*.

Les Misérables took me through the prolonged crisis of childhood . . . I read the book again and again . . . till most of it was fixed firmly in . . . From an early age I was more familiar with the street names of Paris than those of London . . . Exotic though it was in many ways, *Les Misérables* seemed relevant to me and life roundabout . . . Gavroche, the street urchin who reminded me vividly of one of my cousins . . . the revolutionary fighting in the streets of Paris . . . when Jean Valjean rescues one of the wounded fighters from one of the about-to-be overrun barricades by carrying him through the sewers.[11]

The physiography of Nottingham, and its attendant folklore, gave credence to the Parisian connection. Under the city, carved out of a cave system, is a complicated network of chambers dating back to medieval times. These were used for storage, dwelling, gambling and, during the Second World War, as air raid shelters. Their occasional occupation throughout Nottingham's history by outlaws and rebels sustained a local mythology of a clandestine underworld, much like that of Paris as set out in *Les Misérables*.[12]

In *Les Misérables* the counterpoint of the underworld is the spacious, systematic new city planned by Baron Haussmann for Napoleon III.[13] Haussman's plan was a city-wide vision which directly opposed the Parisian underworld, clearing poor districts to make way for a system

[10] Alan Sillitoe, *Alan Sillitoe's Nottinghamshire* (London, 1987), p. 3.
[11] Alan Sillitoe, 'Mountains and Caverns', in *Mountains and Caverns*, pp. 152–60 (p. 156); Sillitoe, 'We All Start from Home', p. 12; Alan Sillitoe, 'The Long Piece' in *Mountains and Caverns*, p. 12.
[12] David Kempe, *Living Underground: A History of Cave and Cliff Dwelling* (London, 1988).
[13] Victor Hugo, *Les Misérables* (Harmondsworth, 1982), esp. pp. 399–410.

of broad boulevards, public buildings, parks, parades and classical perspectives. It was a spectacular vision, planned from a height, in a new survey of the city from especially constructed towers, and best seen in panoramic views.[14] Haussman's Paris is in many ways the vantage point of Hugo's novel. The narrator looks back to events of 1815–32 from the perspective of the 1860s, reconstructing, with the help of old maps, the social geography which Haussman erased. Hugo's 'aerial observer' does not always have a clear view, peering down into the 'silent, ominous labyrinth' of the insurrectionary districts (as the reader 'peered into the depths' of another 'labyrinth of illusion', the conscience of the fugitive Valjean).[15] While sympathetic to the plight of *les misérables*, the novel tracks them with a consciously cartographic eye.

In Sillitoe's Nottingham novels, the urban underworld is similarly counterpointed by a newly planned, systematic, self-consciously modern city. From the 1920s, the City Corporation promoted Nottingham as 'the modern city' with 'wide thoroughfares, well-proportioned buildings, and an entire absence of the smoke and grime usually associated with industry . . . creating a broad spaciousness that other cities envy and seek to emulate'. In official guides and publications, the structure of this modern city was displayed in aerial photographs: the new city hall (the Council House) and civic square, bright new factories, broad boulevards and spacious suburban estates. The Corporation was particularly keen on the new aerodrome built outside the city, in 1928, the second in Britain to be licensed: 'the city of Nottingham has always been in the forefront in the matter of aviation'.[16]

During Sillitoe's youth the country beyond Radford – estate land developed with a mixture of parkland, plantations, collieries, allotments and cottages – was comprehensively modernised. The Corporation purchased a large swathe of this land and built a spacious zone of boulevards, public parks and housing estates (fig. 1). The 2,800 houses of the Aspley estate (1930–2) (fig. 2) were intended for newly married couples from Sillitoe's Radford or to rehouse families from cleared slum areas. There was a school at the centre of the estate, a showpiece of the city's enlightened educational policy, but few other social facilities

---

[14] David Pinkney, *Napoleon III and the Rebuilding of Paris* (Princeton, 1958); T. J. Clark, *The Painting of Modern Life: Paris in the Art of Manet and his Followers* (London, 1984).

[15] Hugo, *Les Misérables*, pp. 945–7, 208.

[16] Nottingham Corporation, *Nottingham: Queen City of the Midlands. The Official Guide* (Cheltenham, 1927), pp. 25, 35–7, 62–5; British Association for the Advancement of Science, *A Scientific Survey of Nottingham* (London, 1937), pp. 9–18; J. D. Chambers, *Modern Nottingham in the Making* (Nottingham, 1945).

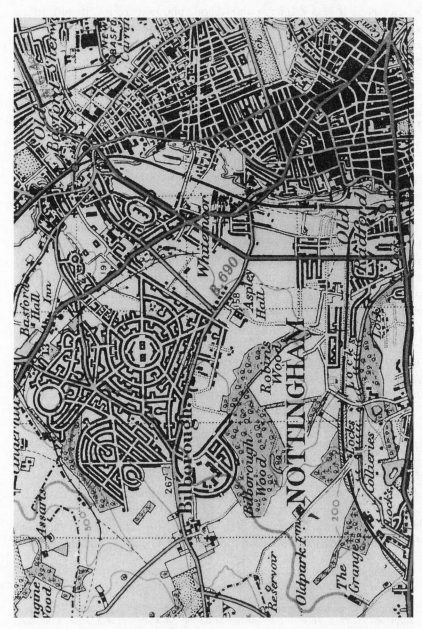

1 Enlarged detail of north-west Nottingham. Reproduced from the 1946 1:63,360 Ordnance Survey map.

2 'The attractively laid-out Aspley Housing estate, with the William Crane schools in the centre, viewed from an aeroplane'. From *Nottingham Official Handbook* (10th edn, 1939).

or places of work. The new working-class suburb contrasted pointedly with the old; its elegant curves, crescents and concentric circles served to emphasise the town's intricate network of terraces, back-streets and alleys.[17] Sillitoe's autobiographical story of childhood gang-fights is set on this modern frontier: 'Our street was a straggling line of ancient back-to-backs on the city's edge, while the enemy district was a new housing estate of three long streets which had outflanked us and left us a mere pocket of country in which to run wild.'[18]

Despite, or perhaps because of, the fact that his family remained in Radford, Sillitoe sought a heightened consciousness of Nottingham in a passion for maps as well as books. He taught himself to read maps as

[17] Robert Mellors, *Old Nottingham Suburbs: Then and Now* (Nottingham, 1914), pp. 25–60; Chambers, *Modern Nottingham*, pp. 47–8; C. J. Thomas, 'Some Geographical Aspects of Council Housing in Nottingham', *East Midland Geographer*, vol. 4 (1966), pp. 88–98; C. J. Thomas, 'The Growth of Nottingham Since 1919', *East Midland Geographer*, vol. 5 (1971), pp. 119–132; R. Silburn, 'People in their Places' in *One Hundred Years of Nottingham* (Nottingham, 1981), pp. 16–35.
[18] Alan Sillitoe, 'The Death of Frankie Butler' in *The Loneliness of the Long Distance Runner* (London, 1985), pp. 154–74 (p. 156).

he learnt to read novels, and made maps as he learned to write. Born into a poor family, suffering the insecurities of chronic unemployment, Sillitoe 'latched onto maps in order to pull myself into the more rarefied and satisfying air of education and expansion of spirit'. Maps helped make sense of Nottingham, clarified its character and development. And they connected the city to a wider world. 'The first time I saw a map I wanted to leave home'.[19] Sillitoe collected maps of all kinds. A large scale estate map from his grandfather's cottage on the fringe countryside beyond Radford became a 'dream landscape' as this land began 'to be covered by houses and new roads'. An inch-to-the mile Ordnance Survey map of the Aldershot area marked with tactical exercises, a gift from a retired guardsman next door, 'gave a picture I could relate to the land in my own district. Every cottage and copse was marked, every lane and footpath'. At school he watched 'with wonder and fascination' as the teacher took a wheeled metal cylinder and rolled gleaming outlines of Europe or North America on the page, 'it was the action of a magic wand'.[20]

The magic of maps was not just conceptual but technical, maps as artefacts not just images. As a child Sillitoe made maps of all kinds, of both real and imaginary places, drawn on wallpaper, in the flyleaves of books, drawn 'with the same attention to detail as my lace-designer uncle put into his intricate patterns before they were set up on Nottingham machines'. Sillitoe esteemed maps as agents of modern, material transformation, 'a highway built where one had not existed before . . . a new town settled on the edge of sandy or forest wastes'.[21] Wartime conditions heightened Sillitoe's map consciousness. With signposts removed, and street maps torn out of city guides, the war 'turned everyone into a spy and me into my own surveyor'. With the aid of a War Office manual Sillitoe taught himself triangulation and 'with a simple compass and the expedient of pacing' made a detailed map of his neighbourhood.[22]

Failing a scholarship exam, Sillitoe left school at fourteen, to take a variety of factory jobs, including a spell as a lathe operator in the Raleigh bicycle factory at the end of his street, then turned over to war

---

[19] Alan Sillitoe, *Raw Material* (London, 1972), p. 98.
[20] Rycroft, *Ordinance and Order*, pp. 11–12; Alan Sillitoe, 'Maps' in Sillitoe, *Mountains and Caverns*, pp. 62–3.
[21] Sillitoe, *Raw Material*, pp. 98–9.
[22] Rycroft, *Ordinance and Order*, pp. 11–12; Sillitoe, 'Maps', p. 68; Sillitoe, 'We All Start from Home', p. 9.

production, making components for aircraft engines. Here, especially through his membership of the Transport and General Workers Union, he acquired a political education. 'I found it impossible to work in a factory without believing that socialism was the ultimate solution for all life on this planet'.[23] Sillitoe also enlarged his local geographical knowledge. With his first wages he purchased a bicycle and explored as far as the Peak District and the Lincolnshire coast. In the absence of signposts a map was a necessity. In a Foreword to a history of the Raleigh company Sillitoe spelled out the benefits of the cyclist's vantage point, 'that it is often possible to see over the hedge at the horizon beyond. One can also stop and admire the view, or pause to consult a map with no trouble at all'.[24] It is the revelatory vantage point of regional survey recommended to young urban excursionists of the time, one enshrined in Ellis Martin's illustration (fig. 3) of the cyclist on the cover of the Popular Edition One Inch Ordnance Survey Maps.[25]

During the war, Sillitoe joined the Air Training Corps based at the local aerodrome. Here he acquired a military-geographical education, learning radio-telegraphy, flight theory, meteorology and photogrammetry. The vertical viewpoint offered on training flights over Nottingham from a de-Haviland bi-plane was a revelation. The oblique panorama of the topographical observer gave way to a broader, more penetrating vision:

This bird's eye snapshot appeared to be just as valuable as the dense intricacies that came with lesser visibility on the ground . . . It was easy to pick out factories and their smoking chimneys, churches and park spaces, the Castle and the Council House, as well as the hide-outs and well-trodden streets that had seemed so far apart but that now in one glance made as small and close a pattern as that on a piece of lace . . . From nearly two thousand feet the hills appeared flat, and lost their significance, but the secrets of the streets that covered them were shown in such a way that no map could have done the job better.[26]

During and immediately after the war, progressive experts, including professional geographers, hoped that increased flying experience and

[23] Alan Sillitoe, 'The Long Piece' in *Mountains and Caverns*, pp. 9–49 (p. 17).
[24] Alan Sillitoe, Foreward to G. H. Bowden, *The Story of the Raleigh Cycle* (London, 1975), p. 9.
[25] David Matless, 'The English Outlook' in Alfrey and Daniels, *Mapping the Landscape*, pp. 28–30; David Matless, 'Regional Surveys and Local Knowledges: The Geographical Imagination in Britain, 1918–39', *Transactions of the Institute of British Geographers*, vol. 17 (1992), pp. 464–80 (p. 469).
[26] Sillitoe, 'Maps', p. 70; Sillitoe, 'We All Start from Home', p. 10. For more details of his air training, Alan Sillitoe, 'A Cadet Remembers', *Air Cadet News*, March 1981, p. 5.

familiarity with aerial photography would re-order ordinary people's perceptions of the world and their place in it. In 1946 David Linton told the Geographical Association that

the air view of the ground . . . has become a familiar thing to us all . . . Direct flying experience . . . has been extended to a great body of service personnel, ATC cadets and others, and war films and war photographs have brought some appreciation of the airman's point of view to virtually the whole adult population.[27]

The advantages of the airman's point of view were cumulative:

As we leave the ground our visual and mental horizon expands, and we have direct perception of space-relations over an ever widening-field, so that we may see successively the village, the town, the region, in their respective settings. The mobility of the aircraft makes our range of vision universal . . . We may fly to the ends of the earth.[28]

This expanding field of vision was seen to be potentially one of inter-national citizenship, connecting the local with the global in a new post-war world order.[29]

Sillitoe's internationalism maintained its leftward bearing. He saw his air-training as preparation for 'the fight against fascism', but the war ended too soon for Sillitoe to participate and he was posted to Malaya by the RAF, to take part in the fight against communist insurgents in 1948. Here as a wireless operator he was required 'against my political beliefs' to give bearings to bombers trying to 'hunt out the communist guerillas in the jungle' and maintained his 'accustomed accuracy' with 'lessening enthusiasm'.[30]

In Malaya Sillitoe took up writing in a desultory way, 'odd poems and scraps of prose – generally concerned with the beauties of scenery – to pass away the fourteen-hour shifts in my radio hut at the end of the runway'.[31] Upon demobilisation, back in England, Sillitoe was diagnosed as having tuberculosis and, in response, wrote voraciously. During eighteen months convalescence in an army camp Sillitoe began a 'feverish bout of urgent writing', filling empty wireless logbooks with dozens of poems, sketches and bits of description, some of which were used in later published works. The most sustained of these pieces was

---

[27] D. L. Linton, *The Interpretation of Air Photographs* (London, 1947), p. 3.   [28] *Ibid.*, p. 5.

[29] E. G. R. Taylor, *Geography of an Air Age* (London, 1945).

[30] Alan Sillitoe, 'National service' in *Mountains and Caverns*, pp. 50–8 (p. 56).

[31] Sillitoe, 'The Long Piece', p. 24.

a thirty-page narrative of a six-day jungle-rescue exercise he had navigated three months before in Malaya, based on a diary and maps of the area he had drawn up before embarking.[32] Sillitoe also read the canon of western literature, modern works like the novels of D. H. Lawrence and Dostoevsky as well as Latin and Greek classics newly available in Penguin paperback translations. At the same time, through a correspondence course, Sillitoe 'really got to grips with the proper science of surveying', with a view to a career in 'the mundane occupation of making maps'. But 'as my writing took over my whole existence [so] I left off the studies in surveying' and set about the task 'of getting into the map of my own consciousness'.[33]

Returning to Nottingham in 1950, Sillitoe wrote a few short stories, some published in a local magazine, and a long novel, 'a vainglorious mish-mash of Dostoevsky, D. H. Lawrence and Aldous Huxley', promptly rejected by a London publisher.[34] In a second-hand bookshop he met Ruth Fainlight, an American writer and poet and the woman he was to marry. Because of Sillitoe's illness, they decided to move to the sunnier climate of southern Europe, subsisting on Sillitoe's Air-Force pension. Expecting to be away for six months, they stayed six years, by which time Sillitoe had established his vocation as a writer.

In southern Europe Sillitoe and Fainlight 'were culturally severed from England'. 'The magazines we read, the people we met, the books we got hold of, came from Paris, or New York or San Francisco'.[35] Sillitoe was part of a great post-war migration to the Mediterranean of English writers and artists.[36] Robert Graves, then working on *The Greek Myths*, lived nearby in Majorca and gave Sillitoe and Fainlight access to his library. Sillitoe wrote some poems on classical heroes and a fantasy novel but Graves suggested he 'write a book set in Nottingham, which is something you know about'. From a series of unpublished short stories and sketches centring on the character of Arthur Seaton, 'a young anarchic roughneck', Sillitoe completed the first draft of *Saturday Night and Sunday Morning* in 1956–7.[37] 'The factory and its surrounding area ascended with a clarity that might not have been so intense had I not looked out over olive groves, lemons and orange

[32] *Ibid.*, pp. 21, 24.   [33] Sillitoe, 'Maps', pp. 71–2.   [34] Sillitoe, 'The Long Piece', p. 26.
[35] Sillitoe, 'The Long Piece', p. 10.
[36] David Mellor, *A Paradise Lost: The Neo-Romantic Imagination in Britain, 1935–55* (London, 1987), pp. 69–70.
[37] Sillitoe, 'The Long Piece', pp. 19–33.

orchards ... under a clear Mediterranean sky'.[38] Writing the novel, Sillitoe was reminded of the clear view of his first training flight over Nottingham, but felt, at the dawn of the space-age, launched further into orbit: 'I re-drew my maps and made my survey as if from a satellite stationed above that part of the earth in which I had been born'.[39]

Sillitoe's cultural exile, and the sense of homeplace it sharpened, invites comparison with the local collier's son who, writing in southern Europe, defined Nottingham and its region as a literary landscape, D. H. Lawrence. In an essay on Lawrence Sillitoe regards his forbear's exile as a condition of his realistic grasp of the people and places of his upbringing, but notes that the longer Lawrence sojourned in sunny, southern landscapes, the more he 'began to lose his grip on local topography'. In *Lady Chatterley's Lover* Nottinghamshire was reduced to 'a sort of black-dream country that did not seem human or real'. Sustained exile incorporated Lawrence in that pastoral literary tradition which bewails the 'ruination of sweet and rural England' and nourishes an 'unreasonable hatred of the urban and industrial landscape'. Sillitoe also suggests something Oedipal in this 'unreasonable hatred', the rejection of the masculine world of the mining country: 'he had to go to those places where the female spirit of the Virgin Mary was in the ascendant, where mother-worship of the Latins was the norm'. In contrast, Sillitoe maintained his grip on local topography, not just by returning to England, and occasionally to Nottingham, but by sustaining a documentary vision, not sliding from a strictly cartographic to a softly scenic idea of landscape. Mapping offered Sillitoe both a pre-literary definition of Lawrence's country and a way of keeping his forbear in his sights. Reading Lawrence, Sillitoe reaches for the one-inch maps which remind him of the cycle trips to the country he made as a boy, years before he realised that Lawrence had portrayed it in his novels. And the essay on Lawrence ends with an imaginative journey, viewing key places in his novels from various hilltops in and around Nottingham: 'such roaming is a constant wonder of triangulation, surveys that fix themselves in the heart and stay there'.[40]

Writing, Sillitoe is surrounded by maps, 'a street plan of Nottingham, a large-scale trench-map of the Gommecourt salient in 1916, marked

[38] Alan Sillitoe, 'Alan Sillitoe', *Author* (Autumn 1983), pp. 28–30 (p. 30).
[39] Rycroft, *Ordinance and Order*, pp. 16–17; Sillitoe, 'Maps', p. 70; Sillitoe, 'We All Start from Home', p. 13.
[40] Alan Sillitoe, 'Lawrence and District', in *Mountains and Caverns*, pp. 128–144 (quotations on pp. 133, 131, 141).

by the advancing death-lines of the Sherwood Foresters, a relief chart of Deception Island, and a topographical map of Israel flanked by the Mediterranean and the Jordan River – different regions I cannot shut my eyes to'.[41] Sillitoe's study resembles an operations room. 'Just as a general needs maps upon which to plan his campaign', Sillitoe declares, 'so an author requires them for his novels and stories'.[42]

For Sillitoe maps are not just a framework for writing, but a medium of citizenship.[43] On a visit to Leningrad in 1964 he admired the 'colourful, complex' map of the city hanging in Lenin's headquarters, 'a campaign street plan of the October rising', a map that 'is sure to be looked at and studied on many a South American or Asian wall'. 'I could have followed its intricacies for many an hour. Every self-respecting man should, with a plan of the city he lives in, practice schemes for an insurrection in times of war or trouble, or for its defence should an insurrection ever come about'.[44]

On the same trip to the Soviet Union, Stalingrad is envisaged as a New Jerusalem in a modernist *mappa mundi*:

I felt that Stalingrad was in the middle of the world, a place where the final battle between good and evil was fought out. It was also the last battle of the Bolshevik Revolution, and may be the final decisive contest of the world, the turning point of humanity in its struggle between science and magic, science and barbarity.[45]

In a poem of 1964, Stalingrad is transposed onto Nottingham:

A map of Stalingrad pinned on
A plan of Nottingham
For easy reference from crossbred stories:
Coloured elbows of the Don and Volga
Chase the tape worm artery of the Trent
To merge in Stalinham and Nottingrad,
Spartak and Calverton . . .

Trent, the Volga and the Don run quiet
Consistent river drawn to widening seas
While men and women talk in the

[41] Sillitoe, *Raw Material*, pp. 174–5.
[42] Sillitoe, 'Maps', p. 68; Rycroft, *Ordinance and Order*, pp. 13–15.
[43] Sillitoe's political sympathies shifted in the 1970s from the Soviet Union to Israel, although his sense of citizenship remained fairly constant. See Alan Sillitoe, 'Iron in the sand', *Geographical Magazine*, November 1978, pp. 137–42; Alan Sillitoe, 'My Israel', *New Statesman*, 20 December 1974, pp. 890–2.
[44] Alan Sillitoe, *Road to Volgograd* (London, 1964), p. 81.   [45] *Ibid.*, p. 41.

Canteens of Raleigh and the Red October,
At evening by the lights of Netherfield-Dubovka
Walk similar embankments and announce their love
To rivers snaking over peacetime faces.[46]

MAPPING AND MODERNITY

To emphasise the mapping impulse in Sillitoe's work and life and its pre-war roots is to revise the conventional interpretation of his writing. Sillitoe is concerned to accurately document local characters and their environment but he cannot simply be grouped with consciously English, realist contemporaries like Larkin, Amis and Osborne.[47] In its continental allusions, cosmopolitan vantage point, and mythological register, Sillitoe's writing may be situated in an earlier modernist tradition, one which includes authors he esteems: Hugo, Lawrence, Conrad and Joyce.

The very conventions of mapping which help to fix Nottingham's geography also release the author and his subject from purely local, vernacular associations, and they co-ordinate Nottingham to other cities and their cultural traditions. Sillitoe exploits both the documentary aspect of mapping and its metaphorical aspect, the transposition of cultural meanings and associations from one place to another. Mapped onto the modernisation of Nottingham, the upheaval and reconstruction of its urban fabric, are epic geographies of insurgent Paris and Stalingrad.

In Sillitoe's Nottingham novels, as in *Les Misérables*, the process of surveying proceeds vertically as well as horizontally in excavations or transections of the urban underworld. Sillitoe quotes from Hugo's novel in characterising the authorial view as stratigraphic, both documenting, as if from a mountain top, the 'external facts' of culture and, as if in the depths of a cavern, its 'hearts and souls'.[48] This vertical axis has long been a central trope in European literature. In Ovid's *Metamorphoses* it is the separation of the world of the labyrinth occupied by the Minatour, the beast-man, and that of the air occupied by Dedalus, the bird-man. The development of ballooning, the building of skyscapers and the invention of the aeroplane activated this vertical axis as a defining trope of modernism. As authors upheld a civilised superstructure of spirit and vision, populated by figures like Joyce's Stephen Dedalus or

[46] Alan Sillitoe, *A Falling Out of Love and Other Poems* (London, 1964).
[47] David Lodge, *The Modes of Modern Writing: Metaphor, Metonymy and the Typology of Modern Literature* (Ithaca, New York, 1977), p. 213.
[48] Sillitoe, 'Mountains and Caverns', p. 152.

Geddes' heroic aviator, so they also excavated a primitive substructure of unreason and bodiliness, populated by figures like Hugo's *les misérables* or D. H. Lawrence's coal miners.[49]

Sillitoe's main characters in his Nottingham novels are variously positioned on this vertical axis. While Brian Seaton transcends Nottingham to achieve a cerebral, cosmopolitan vision, one vested like Sillitoe's in maps and air-mindedness, his brother Arthur remains local and visceral, prowling the warren of streets. Dedalus and Minatour. The third character Frank Dawley never achieves a fully aerial view. After speculating on 'what Nottingham looked like from the air, he fell like a stoned and frozen bird back near the middle of it'.[50] But Dawley does escape the city on an internationalist underground quest, as a guerilla fighter in North Africa.

As Alison Light has pointed out, there is a distinctly masculine positioning and scope to this radical mode of literary modernism, in its heroic, worldly visions of free movement, political liberation, sexual autonomy and economic independence.[51] Such visions were occasionally awarded to women, in the airmindedness of some of Virginia Woolf's free-spirited female characters[52] and in the educated, panoramic visions of some of D. H. Lawrence's. The opening of Lawrence's *The Rainbow* (1915) finds men archaic and earthbound, women modern and outward looking:

The women looked out from the heated, blind intercourse of farm life, to the spoken world beyond . . . She (*sic*) stood to see the far-off world of cities and governments and the active scope of men, the magic land to her, where secrets were made known and desires fulfilled . . . to discover what was beyond, to enlarge their own scope and freedom.[53]

Sillitoe's Nottingham novels are, by contrast, comprehensively masculine, and are structured almost entirely on the expression or repression of male desire, whether in its more visceral or more educated forms.

---

[49] Michael Grant, *Myths of the Greeks and Romans* (London, 1989), pp. 385–6; Merrill Schleier, *The Skyscraper in American Art, 1890–1930* (New York, 1986), pp. 5–68; Stephen Kern, *The Culture of Space and Time, 1880–1914* (Cambridge Mass., 1983), pp. 242–7; Valentine Cunningham, *British Writers of the Thirties* (Oxford, 1988), pp. 168–73, 241–65; David Matless, 'Preservation, Modernism and the Nature of the Nation', *Built Environment*, vol. 16 (1990), pp. 179–91; Wendy B. Faris, 'The Labyrinth as Sign' in Mary Ann Caws, *City Images: Perspectives from Literature, Philosophy and Film* (New York, 1991), pp. 33–41; Rosalind Williams, *Notes on the Underground: An Essay on Technology, Society and the Imagination* (Cambridge MA, 1990), pp. 51–81.

[50] Alan Sillitoe, *The Death of William Posters* (London, 1965), p. 73.

[51] Alison Light, *Forever England: Femininity, Literature and Conservatism between the Wars* (London, 1991), p. 24.

[52] Gillian Beer, 'The Island and the Aeroplane' in Homi Bhaba (ed.), *Nation and Narration* (London, 1990).

[53] D. H. Lawrence, *The Rainbow* (Harmondsworth, 1989), pp. 42–3.

3 Cover, *Nottingham*, sheet 54, Ordnance Survey popular
edition one-inch map of England and Wales (1921).

4 Cover, *Nottingham, 'The Queen City of the Midlands' Guide* (6th edn, 1921).

Indeed what aligns Sillitoe's novels with the gritty realism of his English contemporaries is the hardness of their male positioning and address, their aggressive, misogynistic heroes, individuated largely by running battles with women.

The very belligerence of Sillitoe's heroes, and the portrayal of Nottingham as a sexual battleground, does at least make his women characters a force to be reckoned with. There is a local context for this. The prevailing mythology of modern Nottingham is feminine. The industrialisation in the city of the lace, hosiery and clothing industries, with a conspicuous increase of female workers, was accompanied by a new urban folklore of formidable, independent women, economically, politically and sexually.[54] This was famously mobilised by D. H. Lawrence in *Sons and Lovers* (1913) in the figure of the hero's lover, lace worker Clara Dawes, a ten year veteran of the women's movement. Moreover the myth was incorporated in the regal figure which imaged the 'City Beautiful' modernism in official civic publicity, 'Queen of the Midlands'. Guidebooks used this feminine image to promote Nottingham as progressively pure and healthy, free from the grime and drabness usually associated with coalfield areas (fig. 4).[55] All

[54] Emrys Bryson, *Portrait of Nottingham* (London, 1983), pp. 150–61.
[55] Nottingham Corporation, *Nottingham 'The Queen City of the Midlands'*.

local manufacturing industries employed a large proportion of women, and promotional literature was keen to show them working in bright, spacious surroundings. In contrast, Sillitoe's novels evoke a harsher, grimier, more masculine world, the carboniferous industrialisation which shadows both Lawrence's novels and city guides. The factory floor, and work generally, is represented almost entirely as a male preserve, as are most public spaces in the novels. It is not just that Sillitoe's male characters rebel against the authority of women. The texts of his Nottingham novels rebel against authoritative texts of the city.

ANGRY YOUNG MAN

Saturday Night and Sunday Morning charts a year in the life of Arthur Seaton, machinist in a Nottingham bicycle factory, and young urban rebel. The longer part of the novel, 'Saturday Night', describes Arthur's work and, more extensively, his escapes from work, his drinking bouts, sexual conquests, street fights, fishing trips and belligerent fantasies. The brief and more reflective 'Sunday Morning' finds Arthur recovering from one Saturday night's excess and contemplating, reluctantly, the 'safe and rosy path' to marriage, family and suburban life.

Saturday night was 'one of the fifty-two holidays in the slow-turning Big Wheel of the year'.[56] The Big Wheel is the driving structure of the novel. It figures as a carnivalesque Big Wheel which eventually appears in the episode at the huge Goose Fair in central Nottingham, at the giddy climax of the novel's and the city's recreational calendar. The novel is also geared to an industrial Big-Wheel, the imperative of factory work driving men and machines. The cycle of the seasons is subordinate to the urban Big-Wheel: 'As spring merged into summer or autumn became winter Arthur glimpsed the transitional mechanisms of each season only at the weekend, on Saturday or Sunday, when he straddled his bike and rode along the canal bank into the country to fish'.[57] Correspondingly, there is little organic development in the novel's narrative. Each chapter (and most were originally drafted as separate pieces) is a largely discrete component in the circular structure. In both its industrial and recreational expressions the Big-Wheel of *Saturday Night and Sunday Morning* is fixed, offering little escape from the city and

---

[56] Alan Sillitoe, *Saturday Night and Sunday Morning* (London, 1976), p. 9.   [57] *Ibid.*, p. 133.

its culture, even in the form of the bicycles that Arthur Seaton's factory produces. Movement in the novel is circumscribed, largely vertical. Reading the novel is like riding the Big-Wheel. At some points readers and, on occasion, characters achieve a panoramic view of the city and its surroundings, before being plunged into its lower depths.

First published in 1958, *Saturday Night and Sunday Morning* helped to frame its cultural moment. It appeared at the time of a spate of accounts of urban working-class life by academics, playwrights, novelists and documentary film makers. Many were concerned with the effect of a burgeoning consumer culture on working-class life. The very idea of 'community' was counterpointed by the emergence of a new working-class affluence and individualism.[58] The most notable ethnography of the time is Richard Hoggart's *The Uses of Literacy*, an account, largely a reminiscence, of working-class life in Hunslet first published in 1957 and issued by Penguin the following year. Like Sillitoe, Hoggart was an exile from his working-class upbringing, but a more academically educated scholarship boy, with a greater sense of Englishness and a frankly sentimental sense of the homeliness and neighbourliness of his upbringing. He charts the traditions of working-class culture and their corruption by the 'admass' world of 'chain-store modernisimus', pin-ups, pop music and pulp fiction. Hoggart reserves particular scorn for the 'juke-box boys', with 'drape suits, picture ties and an American slouch'.[59]

Saturday Night and Sunday Morning was aligned to a male-centred genre of plays and novels, including John Osborne's *Look Back in Anger* (1956) and John Braine's *Room at the Top* (1957), authored by and largely featuring so-called 'Angry Young Men'.[60] In contrast to politely accented literature set in the Oxbridge-London belt and its overseas outliers, the Angries' work was rivetted in lower-class quarters of provincial towns and cities and largely articulated by aggressive, straight talking, often foul-mouthed, male heroes. The Angries' world seemed at the time shockingly visceral, short on wit and irony, and long on sex and violence and general bodiliness. *Saturday Night and Sunday Morning* opens with Arthur Seaton in a drinking match, knocking-back seven gins and ten

[58] Robert Hewison, *In Anger: Culture in the Cold War* (London, 1981), pp. 163–80; Tim Price, 'The Politics of Culture: *Saturday Night and Sunday Morning*', unpublished Ph.D thesis, University of Nottingham, 1987.
[59] Richard Hoggart, *The Uses of Literacy* (Harmondsworth, 1958), pp. 24, 40–1, 46–7, 50.
[60] Atherton, *Alan Sillitoe*, pp. 15–21; Peter Hitchcock, *Working-Class Fiction in Theory and Practice: A Reading of Alan Sillitoe* (London, 1989), pp. 22–49.

5 Arthur Seaton cycles home. From *Saturday Night and Sunday Morning* (1960).
BFI Stills Archive.

pints of beer in quick succession, falling down the pub stairs and vomiting over a nicely dressed middle-aged man and his wife. *Saturday Night and Sunday Morning* made John Braine's *Room at the Top* 'look like a vicarage tea-party' announced the *Daily Telegraph*; it was, claimed the *New Statesman*, 'very much the real thing'.[61]

The popular reputation of *Saturday Night and Sunday Morning* was established with the release in 1960 of a film of the novel.[62] Scripted by Alan Sillitoe and directed by Karel Reisz, it starred Albert Finney as Arthur Seaton and featured the Nottingham streets, factories, pubs, canals and housing estates described in the novel (fig. 5). Switching

---

[61] Arthur Marwick, '*Room at the Top, Saturday Night and Sunday Morning* and the "Cultural Revolution" in Britain', *Journal of Contemporary History*, vol. 19 (1984), pp. 127–52; Lynne Segal, 'Look Back in Anger: Men in the Fifties', in Rowena Chapman and Jonathan Rutherford (eds.), *Male Order: Unwrapping Masculinity* (London, 1988), pp. 68–96.
[62] Alan Sillitoe, 'Saturday Night and Sunday Morning' screenplay, in *Masterworks of the British Cinema* (London, 1974), pp. 267–328.

between high-angled long-shots and darker, short-focused scenes, some-times accompanied by Arthur's thoughts, the film opened up the gap between the panoramic and labyrinthine worlds of the text. This was, as Terry Lovell notes, 'a point of enunciation' in a number of British films and television programmes of working-class life of the time, one especially suited to the position of the adult working-class male looking back on the world he had left. 'Within the familiar landscape, such a viewer is offered a potent figure of identification in the young, sexually active male worker, because he may identify in him a fantasy projec-tion of the self he might have become had he remained'.[63]

Tied into the film's release was a million selling paperback edition of the novel. This was issued by Pan (regarded, in contrast to Penguin, as a distinctly low-brow publisher), marketed in the lurid 'sex-and viol-ence' style associated with American pulp fiction, and largely sold from the racks of newsagents. The front cover (fig. 6) features an illustration of a tough looking Arthur Seaton against the mean streets of Notting-ham. The back cover shows a still from the film of Arthur seducing a workmate's wife and, in the wake of the controversial publication of *Lady Chatterley's Lover*, the announcement of a new author 'from Law-rence country . . . who might well have startled Lawrence himself'. Readers were promised 'a raw and uninhibited story of a working-class district of Nottingham and the people who live, love, laugh and fight there'. In giving a trans-atlantic gloss to the novel, Pan made connections with American works with rebellious male heroes, like Jack Kerouac's *On the Road* which they issued in 1958 – although there was no disguising that Arthur Seaton was a very English rebel, a rebel without a car.[64]

Saturday Night and Sunday Morning does not dwell on material depriva-tion, moral improvement or community spirit. In a world of acceler-ated industrial production, full employment and rising wages, the novel traces the pursuit of pleasure and a new consumer passion among the working-class. The bicycle factory is booming, with the introduction of piece-work and streamlined production. The thousands who work there take home good wages.

No more short-time like before the war, or getting the sack if you stood ten minutes in the lavatory reading your *Football Post* – if the gaffer got on to you

---

[63] Terry Lovell, 'Landscapes and Stories in 1960s British Realism', *Screen*, vol. 31 (1990), pp. 357–76.
[64] Price, 'The Politics of Culture', pp. 162–5; Hitchcock, *Working-Class Fiction*, pp. 75–8.

6 Cover of the paperback edition of *Saturday Night and Sunday Morning* (Pan Books, 1960).

now you could always tell him where to put the job and go somewhere else
... With the wages you got you could save up for a motor-bike or even an old
car, or you could go for a ten-day binge and get rid of all you'd saved.[65]

Television aerials are 'hooked on to almost every chimney, like a string
of radar stations, each installed on the never-never'. Seaton's father
has sufficient money to chain-smoke Woodbines in front of the television all evening, his mother to hold her head high in the Co-op and
nonchalantly demand 'a pound of this and a pound of that', now 'she
had access to week after week of solid wages that stopped worry at
the source'. The new affluence has not subdued the 'empty-bellied
pre-war battles'; it has aggravated and enlarged them: 'feuds merged,
suppressed ones became public'.[66]

Arthur Seaton spends much of his wage-packet on himself. For a
weekend night out he chooses from 'a row of suits, trousers, sports
jackets, shirts, all suspended in colourful drapes and designs, good-
quality tailor-mades, a couple of hundred quid's worth, a fabulous
wardrobe'.[67] Described as a Teddy boy, Arthur seems to fit the newly
affluent image of working-class youth which alarmed commentators of
both Right and Left.[68] He comes close to Raymond Williams' contemporary definition of a 'consumer', a word with imagery drawn from
'the furnace or the stomach' which 'materializes as an individual figure
(perhaps monstrous in size but individual in behaviour)'.[69] Yet in many
ways Arthur is a traditional, even anti-modern urban delinquent, the
bloody-minded freeborn-Englishman which left-wing writers recruited
as makers of the English working-class.[70] Arthur's leisure pivots on the
pub: 'I'm a six foot pit prop that wants a pint of ale'. He is contemptuous of many modern commodities, notably television with its implications of passive, domesticated manhood,[71] and cars, with their associations
of suburban living. Indeed, he physically attacks the only car to appear
in the novel. The consumer good that Arthur values most is the one he
helps to produce, the bicycle.[72]

---

[65] Sillitoe, *Saturday Night and Sunday Morning*, p. 27.   [66] *Ibid.*, pp. 26–8, 48, 130.   [67] *Ibid.*, p. 174.
[68] Geoffrey Pearson, *Hooligan: A History of Respectable Fears* (London, 1983), pp. 12–24.
[69] Raymond Williams, *The Long Revolution* (Harmondsworth, 1965), p. 322.
[70] E. P. Thompson, *The Making of the English Working Class* (New York, 1963), pp. 77–101.
[71] Cf. Lynn Spigel, 'The Suburban Home Companion: Television and Neighbourhood in Post-
war America', in Beatriz Colomina (ed.), *Sexuality and Space* (Princeton, 1992), pp. 185–217.
[72] Sillitoe has said that because he was out of the country for most of the Fifties, 'what I was
doing, I think, was really bringing my experience from the Forties up into the Fifties'. 'An
Interview with Alan Sillitoe', *Modern Fiction Studies*, vol. 21 (1975–6), p. 176. Sillitoe's Nottingham
seems in some respects more like 1960 'Worktown' (Bolton), about which Mass Observation
commented:

Arthur Seaton is confident, 'cocksure'.[73] He has a mind to take on all figures of authority, 'fighting every day until I die . . . fighting with mothers and wives, landlords and gaffers, coppers, army, government',[74] and all monuments of authority, the factory in which he works, the city hall, the castle which broods over the city. Arthur is against all authority, except the authority of men over women.[75] In this he has a local ancestry in D. H. Lawrence's working class heroes, notably the men in *Nottingham and the Mining Country* (1930), figures whose roving 'physical, instinctive' masculinity, cultivated at work underground, is trapped and tamed by women no less than by schools, cinemas or machines.[76] But Arthur also has a more contemporary connection in the comic-strip culture of the time, in the war comics of rugged individualists taking on the enemy single-handed and in the tough, street-wise boy-heroes of the *Beano* and *Dandy*, forever in scrapes with authority figures: teachers, policemen, and strong-armed mothers.[77]

Arthur Seaton's world is a labyrinthine zone, recurrently described as a 'jungle' or 'maze'. Arthur prowls the back-streets of the city, or the footpaths of the adjacent country, part guerilla, part predatory beast 'caught in a game of fang-and-claw'.[78] At the fairground, Arthur passes up the aerial thrill of the Big-Wheel for the subterranean thrill of the Ghost Train. 'Assailed by black darkness and horrible screams from Hell', Arthur tangles with Death in the form of 'the luminous bones of a hanging skeleton', 'kicking and pummelling until his arms emerged from the heavy black cover, glistening skeleton bones looking like tiger-streaks over his back, head, and shoulders'.[79] Each outing was 'an expedition in which every corner had to be turned with care, every pub considered for the ease of tactical retreat in terms of ambush'.[80] Known and successfully navigated, the streets offer warm security.

> Despite the telly, despite increased working class car ownership, despite the whole complex of commodity fetishism which *looks* as if it is changing the way ordinary people in England live . . . the pub still persists as a social institution. Qualitatively and quantitatively. Never having had it so good doesn't mean only washing machines and holidays abroad; it is also more beer. (Tom Harrisson, *Britain Revisited*. (London, 1961), p. 194).

[73] Sillitoe, *Saturday Night and Sunday Morning*, p. 45.   [74] *Ibid.*, p. 224

[75] Nigel Gray, *The Silent Majority: A Study of the Working-class in Post-war British Fiction* (London, 1973), pp. 123–7; Jonathan Dollimore, 'The Challenge of Sexuality', in Alan Sinfield (ed.), *Society and Literature, 1945–70* (London, 1983), pp. 51–85; Segal, 'Look Back in Anger', pp. 80–1.

[76] D. H. Lawrence, 'Nottingham and the Mining Country', in *Selected Essays* (Harmondsworth, 1981), p. 117.

[77] Segal, 'Look Back in Anger', p. 87; George Perry and Alan Aldridge, *The Penguin Book of Comics: A Slight History* (Harmondsworth, 1975), p. 5.

[78] Rycroft, *Ordinance and Order*, pp. 21–2; J. R. Ogersby, 'Alan Sillitoe's *Saturday Night and Sunday Morning*', in G. R. Hibbard (ed.), *Renaissance and Modern Essays* (London, 1966), p. 217.

[79] Sillitoe, *Saturday Night*, pp. 167–8.   [80] *Ibid.*, p. 209.

Walking the streets on winter nights kept him warm . . . stars hid like snipers, taking aim now and again when clouds gave them a loophole. Winter was an easy time for him to hide his secrets, for each dark street patted his shoulder and became a friend, and the gaseous eye of each lamp glowed unwinking as he passed. Houses lay in rows and ranks, a measure of safety in such numbers, and those within were snug and grateful fugitives from the broad track of bleak winds that brought rain from the Derbyshire mountains and snow from the Lincolnshire Wolds.[81]

On the way home from a night's skirmishing with his brother:

The maze of streets sleeping between tobacco factory and bicycle factory drew them into the enormous spread of its suburban bosom and embraced them in sympathetic darkness. Beyond the empires of new red-bricked houses lay fields and woods that rolled on to the Erewash valley and the hills of Derbyshire.[82]

In charting the moral order of the city, Sillitoe is careful to distinguish the warmth of the old industrial suburb where Arthur lives from both the bleakness of the new residential suburbs on the outer heights of the city and the dankness of a low-lying slum area called The Meadows by the river near the city centre. The Meadows is presented as a dark, decayed, chaotic district, inhabited by drunks and prostitutes and Arthur's Aunt Ada. After a life of 'dole, boozing, bailiffs' Aunt Ada had 'the personality of a promiscuous barmaid'. Her 'horde of children' are, in contrast to Arthur's rebellious posturing, ferocious, almost feral figures, 'always escaping, on the run, in hiding, living with whores, thieving for food and money because they had neither ration books nor employment cards', fending for themselves 'in such a wild free manner that Borstal had been their education and a congenial jungle their only hope'.[83]

If Arthur haunts the streets of *Saturday Night and Sunday Morning*, it is because domestic interiors are a woman's realm, inhabited by his mother, aunt, mistresses and fiancé, in which men are either absent or marginalised. A formidable female challenge to Arthur's authority, and a main target of his abuse, is a more public figure who surveys the streets. Stationed at the end of his yard, *en route* to the factory, is the gossip Mrs Bull, 'ready to level with foresight and backsight at those that crossed her path in the wrong direction':

---

[81] *Ibid.*, p. 171   [82] *Ibid.*, p. 120.
[83] *Ibid.*, pp. 78, 134, 78. Arthur's cousins are the prototype for the hero of Sillitoe's 1961 short story 'The Loneliness of the Long-distance Runner', in Sillitoe, *The Loneliness of the Long Distance Runner*, pp. 9–54.

Deep-set beady eyes traversed the yard's length from streets to factory, were then swivelled back from the factory wall to where she was standing, ranging along upstairs and downstairs windows, no point of architecture or human movement escaping her. It was rumoured that the government had her name down for a reconnaissance unit in the next war.[84]

Mrs Bull controls networks of knowledge which Arthur can barely discern. Her 'malicious gossip travelled like electricity through a circuit, from one power-point to another, and the surprising thing was that a fuse was so rarely blown'.[85] Arthur attempts to sabotage the system. Playing the role of sniper, he shoots Mrs Bull with an air rifle, bruising her cheek, stinging her into wild gesticulation, confirming her as the slapstick figure of boy's comics.

'Once a rebel, always a rebel', Arthur Seaton pleads at the end of the novel before he dons 'suit, collar, and tie' to meet his fiancé Doreen one cold spring Sunday morning 'on the outskirts of the housing estate' where they are destined to live.[86] If Arthur's industrial neighbourhood offered him a measure of snug security, the new modern estates on the edge of the city are bleak, aerial landscapes. '[Up] Broxtowe, on the estate, I like living in them nice new houses,' announces Doreen. 'It's a long way from the shops, but there's plenty of fresh air'. 'My sister married a man in the air force . . . and they've got a house up Wollaton. She's expecting a baby next week'.[87] Arthur and Doreen 'take a long walk back to her house, by the boulevard that bordered the estate', the 'safe and rosy path' to domesticity.[88] To a disinterested observer they 'seemed like a loving and long-engaged couple only kept back from marriage by the housing shortage'. But to Arthur the 'new pink-walled houses gave an even gloomier appearance than the black dwellings of Radford'. The very image of 'the modern city' in official publicity, the spacious new housing estate, is, for Arthur, a trap:

Arthur remembered seeing an aerial photo of it: a giant web of roads, avenues and crescents, with a school like a black spider lurking in the middle.[89]

NEW MAN

In a 1965 sequel to *Saturday Night and Sunday Morning*, *The Death of William Posters*, Frank Dawley, a political extension of Arthur Seaton, rebel turned revolutionary, strives to break out of Arthur's world and

[84] Sillitoe, *Saturday Night*, p. 121.   [85] *Ibid.*, p. 121.   [86] *Ibid.*, pp. 207, 209.
[87] *Ibid.*, p. 154.   [88] *Ibid.*, p. 160.   [89] *Ibid.*, p. 161.

his view of it.[90] Through twelve years of factory work and marriage Dawley 'had brooded and built up the Bill Posters legend',[91] the legend of a local social bandit:

There's been a long line of William Posters, a family of mellow lineage always hoved up in some cellar of Nottingham Streets. His existence explains many puzzles. Who was General Ludd? None other than the shadowy William Posters, stockinger, leading on his gallant companies of Nottingham lads to smash all that machinery . . . Who set fire to Nottingham Castle during the Chartist riots? Later, who spat in Lord Roberts' face when he led the victory parade in Nottingham after the Boer War. Who looted those shops in the General Strike?[92]

Frank 'wondered what Nottingham looked like from the air, but fell like a stoned and frozen bird back near the middle of it'.[93] He eventually breaks out of the labyrinth of Nottingham, or rather, through its demolition during re-development, has it broken for him:

One street funnelled him into space, a view across rubble that a few months ago had been a populous ghetto of back-to-backs and narrow streets. He lit a fag, to absorb the sight of all these acres cleared of people, smashed down and dragged to bits. It wasn't unpleasant, this stalingrad of peace.[94]

As the labyrinth had been cleared, so William Posters had been unearthed, exposed and destroyed. 'Bill Posters, thank God, had died at last in the ruins of Radford-Stalingrad . . . crushed to death under the slabs and bricks, beams and fireplaces'.[95]

[Dawley] walked into space, few paces taking him across a clearly marked street plan on which as a kid each moss-dewed corner and double entry had seemed miles from each other . . . Streets in all directions had been clawed and grabbed and hammered down, scooped up, bucketed, piled, sorted and carted off. Where had all the people gone? Moved onto new estates, all decisions made for them, whereas he also wanted to uproot himself but must make his own moves.[96]

'Exploding out of life so far', Dawley leaves 'wife, home, job, kids' and the place 'where he had been born, bred and spiritually nullified'.[97] First he heads east for the Lincolnshire wolds. 'His mind had changed with the landscape since leaving Nottingham; surprising him at times by its breadth'.[98] Dawley's broadmindedness is framed by the copy of *Dr Zhivago* he carries, its evocation of the 'big country' and 'wide open

[90] Rycroft, *Ordinance and Order*, pp. 20–1. [91] Sillitoe, *The Death of William Posters*, p. 16.
[92] *Ibid.*, p. 18. [93] *Ibid.*, p. 73. [94] *Ibid.*, pp. 73–4. [95] *Ibid.*, p. 309. [96] *Ibid.*, p. 74.
[97] *Ibid.*, p. 16. [98] *Ibid.*, p. 11.

spaces' of Russia[99] and enlarged by his affair with a middle-class woman and his introduction to her library.

Criss-crossing the country like a fugitive, Dawley heads south, for north London, and another conquest of another middle-class wife, Myra Bassingfield. As Dawley's horizons expand, those of the jilted husband, George, close in. George Bassingfield is a professional geographer, lecturer at the London School of Economics, author of *New Aspects of Geography*. 'Few people knew the land of England as well as George, or had a deeper feeling for it . . . the subtleties of land and people were profoundly fascinating, and George was lord of all he surveyed when their composite reactions to land and air tied in with his knowledge and sympathy'. But in middle-age 'his visionary eyes did not seek harmony any more, but fixity into which people and the three elements slotted with neatness and safety'.[100] Indeed, Frank and Myra

left him standing, looking into the tall drawn curtains that opened onto the back garden . . . Life had always seemed a straight road, and he hadn't even been foxed by a simple dead-end or caught in a false cul-de-sac. Instead he was now trapped in an unsurveyable maze of footpaths darkened by tall hedges. Such a labyrinth was extreme torment for a mind that could exist only on order and calm, which wanted everything measured and shaped, reduced to a beautiful design and set down on paper. The last few days had drawn him into the labyrinth, like a doomed fly fixed in helplessness until the spider-god came out for him.[101]

Frank and Myra leave the cramped world of England, heading south for France, Spain, Morocco, eventually Algeria. Here Dawley enlists as a guerilla fighter with the FLN during the War of Independence.

This novel and its sequel, *A Tree on Fire* (1967), appear to be shaped by Sillitoe's reading of the theory and practice of guerilla warfare, some in preparation for his script for a projected film on Che Guevara.[102] The spatiality of guerilla warfare, 'drifting and subtle . . . arabesques', 'the spider's web of revolution'[103] characterise Frank Dawley's tactics throughout his journeying. His quest evokes Che Guevara's notion of the socialist 'new man', evolving from the 'wolfman' of capitalist competition,[104] and also the high-tech ideology of Khruschev's Soviet Union. Dawley envisages a modernist, machine-tooled utopia:

[99] *Ibid.*, pp. 38, 55.   [100] *Ibid.*, pp. 199–200.   [101] *Ibid.*, pp. 243–4.
[102] Alan Sillitoe, '"Che" Guevara', in *Mountains and Caverns*, pp. 121–7.
[103] Sillitoe, *The Death of William Posters*, p. 308; Alan Sillitoe, *A Tree on Fire* (London, 1967), p. 427.
[104] Michael Lowy, *The Marxism of Che Guevara: Philosophy, Economics and Revolutionary Warfare* (London, 1973), pp. 25–8.

All I believe in is houses and factories, food and power stations, bridges and coalmines and death, turning millions of things out on a machine that people can use. It's no use harping back to poaching rights and cottage industries. We've got to forget all that and come to terms with cities and machines and moon landings. We're going to become new men, whether we like it or not, and I know I am going to like it.[105]

AIRMAN

It is Brian Seaton, Arthur's eldest brother, who acquires an airborne cartographic view of the world in *Key to the Door* (1961) and its sequel *The Open Door* (1989). The course of Brian Seaton's life parallels Alan Sillitoe's own, from factory work in Nottingham, to National Service in Malaya to embarking, as a writer, for the south of France. It is these novels which challenge the prevailing stereotype of Sillitoe's Nottingham as a 'northern' province of a London-centred nationalist culture. For Brian Seaton 'London didn't exist';[106] it was a place you passed over in a more global vision. South of the river Trent is not southern England but southern Europe, the Trent is a 'magic band of water' separating 'oak from olive, mildew from hot pines and baking rock'.[107]

Key to the Door begins in 1930s Nottingham with the destitute Seaton family on the run from the bailiffs and the slum clearance programme of 'a demolishing council'. While some slum dwellers take 'the benefit of new housing estates', father Harold Seaton 'clung to the town centre because its burrow was familiar'.[108] Eventually they are forced out by the bulldozers, and bombardment from the air. One area of 'broken and derelict maze' is set aside 'to be the target of bombs from buzzing two-winged aeroplanes, the sideshow of a military tattoo whose full glory lay on the city's outskirts'.[109] The Seaton family take refuge in a cottage in a still-rough, semi-rural, warren-like area at the edge of the city. It is a frontier zone about to feel the turbulent force of modernisation, to be turned into a 'tipscape', filled with rubble from the old slums, levelled and developed. 'Then they'll make an aerodrome', Brian speculates, 'to bomb old houses like ourn was on Albion Yard'.[110]

What they actually make is a bright new estate, lit by electricity, 'magically blessed' with a mains water-supply, marked out with broad boulevards, and the first new houses:

---

[105] Sillitoe, *The Death of William Posters*, p. 259.   [106] Rycroft, *Ordinance and order*, p. 9.
[107] Alan Sillitoe, *The Open Door* (London, 1989), p. 335.
[108] Alan Sillitoe, *Key to the Door* (London, 1989), p. 17.   [109] *Ibid.*, p. 17.   [110] *Ibid.*, p. 78.

Pink houses of new estates were spilling into the countryside. Men with black and white poles and notebooks came across the new boulevards into lanes and fields; they set theodolites and dumpy levels pointing in sly angles at distant woods . . . invading Brian's hideouts, obliterating his short-cuts and concealed tracks.[111]

Brian is enthralled with the men and machines.

Instead of woods and fields, houses would appear along new roads, would transform the map in his mind. The idea of it caught at him like fire.[112]

Brian Seaton grows up with Alan Sillitoe's passion for books and maps. 'Moulded by an addiction to *Les Misérables*' he envisages war in the streets of Nottingham with barricades and sandbag parapets. On a huge war-map of Europe he follows the progress of the Red Army on the eastern front. Brian Seaton works in a claustrophobic factory world, in the 'underground burrow' of the boiler room, having to dig out soot from flues.

Having to work in the dark set him thinking of coalmines and pit ponies, and the fact that he would go crackers if he didn't get out and prove he wasn't buried a thousand feet underground. Jean Valjean traipsing through the sewers was better than this, though I expect Edmond Dantes in *his* tunnels didn't feel too good either . . . This is how you get TB he thought, by breathing black dust like this for hour after hour.[113]

Brian pulls himself out of this subterranean world, to join the airforce as a wireless operator in Malaya, and a life of 'morse and mapmaking', doing guard duty in a 'worn out part of the British empire'.[114]

The Open Door (1989) finds Brian Seaton negotiating the labyrinth of the Malayan jungle. It was 'a place where you could be as much at home as in any maze of streets' but for Seaton, the imperial outsider, it remains intractable, a heart of darkness. 'The jungle had inflicted a deadly bite by drawing him through the valley of the shadow'.[115] With map and compass, he struggles unsuccessfully through this predatory world towards the summit of a 4,000 foot peak, Gunong Barat. And writing it up, from his diary notes, he remains gripped by the experience. 'Unable to sleep, he dreamed of creepers and decomposing trees, and blades of water waving down cliff-faces enlarged my memory's infallible magnifying glass'.[116]

[111] *Ibid.*, p. 191.   [112] *Ibid.*, p. 192.   [113] *Ibid.*, p. 243.   [114] *Ibid.*, pp. 301, 433.
[115] Sillitoe, *The Open Door*, p. 75.   [116] *Ibid.*, p. 74.

Returning to Nottingham, Seaton deploys his cartographic intelligence on a more pliant subject, the woman he seduces by tracing 'a map
upon her back'. He also embarks on an exotic travelogue, 'looking at
the Beautiful Horizon, plodding through Bangkok, eating the Sandwich
Islands, swimming off Madagascar, trekking the five-fingered forests of
Gunong Barat . . .'.[117] He tries it on his younger brother Arthur too, in
offering the lad the kind of educated, reflective prospect of Nottinghamshire that Arthur will, as the rebellious youth in *Saturday Night and
Sunday Morning*, never achieve. Brian takes Arthur on a bus-ride beyond
the city for a spot of fraternal bonding on Misk Hill.

'Who showed yer where it was?'
'I found it on a map. The top's over five hundred feet above sea level.'
'Will I be able to breathe? He ran on to the plateau of a large field, arms in
front like pistons . . .
Suburbs started three miles away, houses and factories under mountainous
cloud. Faint haze emphasised the rich squalor of memorable dreams, his past
in a semicircle from north to south . . .
'It's smashin' up 'ere.' Arthur hurled a stick . . .
A shunting train was pinpointed by feathers of smoke. Brian held him tight.
'Don't ever leave it. It's your hill'.
'Eh, fuck off!' Arthur broke away. 'Are yo' trying to fuck me, or summat?'
Brian laughed. 'Come on loony, let's get down.'[118]

EAST MIDLAND GEOGRAPHIES

In this chapter we have presented Sillitoe's novels as a field of different, sometimes conflicting forms of geographical knowledge and experience. To do this we have shown how the narratives of the novels are
interleaved with a variety of discourses on Nottingham and its region,
on other modernising cities, on an internationalist politics of citizenship,
and, pre-eminently, on geography, specifically maps and map-reading.
In this exercise we hope to further the recent broadening of the history
of geography beyond the usual internal, linear, professional histories,
to take account of 'lateral associations and social relations of geographical knowledge'.[119]

Sillitoe's novels chart the modernisation of Nottingham in a way
which combines and competes with official, commercial and academic
geographies of the city and its region.

---

[117] *Ibid.*, pp. 167, 174. [118] *Ibid.*, p. 291. [119] Driver, 'Geography's Empire', p. 35.

In the period covered by the novels, the city corporation's publications represent Nottingham as a model 'modern city'. Through careful planning, economic and social development was orderly and integrated, creating the framework for a prosperous, enlightened city and citizenry. From 1954 this progressive view was endorsed, and extended to the city's hinterland by the regional journal, *The East Midland Geographer*. Under the founding editorship of K. C. Edwards, himself active in local regional planning and policy making, the journal charted infrastructural developments in the city and its region: the modernisation of the mining industry, the rationalisation of the railways, the building of municipal estates, the construction of motorways.[120] The region's representativeness in landscape and human activity made it 'an epitome of the English scene'. 'Its importance in the economic development of the country moreover is continually growing and is likely to increase vastly in the future'.[121] This was not just a forward-looking view; developments in the past were narrated as part of the same progressive story. In a series of public lectures on the development of Nottingham, from the mid-1930s to mid-1960s, Edwards charted the expansion and consolidation of the city into 'a coherent, closely-knit economic and social entity'.[122]

1958, the year that K. C. Edwards told this story of Nottingham in his address at Nottingham University to the conference of the Institute of British Geographers, the first instalment of Alan Sillitoe's *Saturday Night and Sunday Morning* was published. Like professional planners and geographers, Sillitoe framed land and life in terms of maps, but he charted a different, darker story. Sillitoe's image of the city and its citizenry is not one of coherence and continuity, of community building, but of conflict and upheaval, explosive physical and social change. As on a military map, the city is envisaged as a field of battle. There are, as we have shown, many mediations in this vision, including representations of insurgent Stalingrad, Petrograd, Paris and Nottingham itself during the Luddite and Reform riots. If official and academic versions of Nottingham's geography were written in that progressive, optimistic,

[120] T. W. Freeman, 'Twenty-Five Years of "The East Midland Geographer"', *East Midland Geographer*, vol. 7 (1979), pp. 95–9.

[121] K. C. Edwards, editorial introduction, *East Midland Geographer*, vol. 1 (1954), p. 2.

[122] K. C. Edwards, 'Nottingham and its Region', in British Association for the Advancement of Science, *A Scientific Survey of Nottingham* (London, 1937), pp. 25–38; K. C. Edwards, 'The Geographical Development of Nottingham', in K. C. Edwards (ed.), *Nottingham and Its Region* (London, 1966), pp. 363–404; K. C. Edwards, 'Nottingham: Queen of the Midlands', *Geographical Magazine*, September 1965, p. 347.

enlightened discourse of modernism, Sillitoe's version was written in modernism's counter-discourse of violence, oppression and exclusion.[123]

It is not surprising that City officials responded cooly to the international success of *Saturday Night and Sunday Morning*, and accused Sillitoe moreover of stirring up the sort of trouble that the novel described.[124] Now both parties stand condemned. The City Corporation is accused of pulling down 'Victorian and Edwardian treasures' to make way for 'modern monstrosities', and Sillitoe is condemned for tarnishing the world that remained standing. The renovation of Nottingham's derelict textile district, the Lace Market, as a heritage spectacle promised a more stylish future. 'Ten years ago the Queen of the Midlands had a slightly dowdy look [now] it is no longer the dirty city of Alan Sillitoe's *Saturday Night and Sunday Morning*'.[125] It is too soon to say if post-industrial planning will erase the memory of Arthur Seaton, or the mythology which sustained him. As recently as the summer of 1993, Albert Finney's scowling portrait of Arthur Seaton was spotted, printed on the T-shirts of protestors against the closure of local collieries.

[123] Stuart Hall and Bram Gieben, *Formations of Modernity* (Cambridge, 1993), p. 14. A collection of writings on Nottingham written in terms of this counter-discourse, to which Sillitoe contributed an article on 'Poor People', is the theme issue of *Anarchy 38: A Journal of Anarchist Ideas*, April 1964.

[124] Young, 'The Politics of Culture', pp. 195–6; Rycroft, *Ordinance and Order*, p. 18.

[125] *Nottingham Evening Post*, Supplement, 1988.

Index

Index